MICROECONOMICS
SIXTH EDITION
PARKIN

STUDY GUIDE

MARK RUSH
University of Florida

Addison
Wesley

Boston San Francisco New York
London Toronto Sydney Tokyo Singapore Madrid
Mexico City Munich Paris Cape Town Hong Kong Montreal

Study Guide to Accompany Parkin, *Microeconomics*, 6/e

ISBN: 0-201-95976-3
2 3 4 5 6 7 8 9 10 CRS 06 05 04 03

HOW TO EARN AN A!

■ Introduction

My experience has taught me that what students want most from a study guide is help in mastering course material in order to do well on examinations. I have developed this *Study Guide* to respond specifically to that demand. Using this *Study Guide* alone, however, is not enough to guarantee that you will do well in your course. In order to help you overcome the problems and difficulties that most students encounter, I have some general advice on how to study, as well as some specific advice on how best to use this *Study Guide*.

Economics requires a different style of thinking than what you may encounter in other courses. Economists make extensive use of assumptions to break down complex problems into simple, analytically manageable parts. This analytical style, while ultimately not more demanding than the styles of thinking in other disciplines, feels unfamiliar to most students and requires practice. As a result, it is not as easy to do well in economics on the basis of your raw intelligence and high-school knowledge as it is in many other courses. Many students who come to my office are frustrated and puzzled by the fact that they are getting A's and B's in their other courses but only a C or worse in economics. They have not recognized that economics is different and requires practice. In order to avoid a frustrating visit to your instructor after your first test, I suggest you do the following.

♦ *Don't rely solely on your high-school economics.* If you took high-school economics, you have seen the material on supply and demand which your instructor will lecture on in the first few weeks. Don't be lulled into feeling that the course will be easy. Your high-school knowledge of economic concepts will be very useful, but it will not be enough to guarantee high scores on exams. Your college or university instructors will demand much more detailed knowledge of concepts and ask you to apply them in new circumstances.

♦ *Keep up with the course material on a weekly basis.* Skim the appropriate chapter in the textbook *before* your instructor lectures on it. In this initial reading, don't worry about details or arguments you can't quite follow — just try to get a general understanding of the basic concepts and issues. You may be amazed at how your instructor's ability to teach improves when you come to class prepared. As soon as your instructor has finished covering a chapter, complete the corresponding *Study Guide* chapter. Avoid cramming the day before or even just the week before an exam. Because economics requires practice, cramming is an almost certain recipe for failure.

♦ *Keep a good set of lecture notes.* Good lecture notes are vital for focusing your studying. Your instructor will lecture on a subset of topics from the textbook. The topics your instructor covers in a lecture should usually be given priority when studying. Also give priority to studying the figures and graphs covered in the lecture.

Instructors do differ in their emphasis on lecture notes and the textbook, so ask early on in the course which is *more* important in reviewing for exams — lecture notes or the textbook. If your instructor answers that both are important, then ask the following, typical economic question: which will be more beneficial — spending an extra hour re-reading your lecture notes or an extra hour re-reading the textbook? This question assumes that you have read each textbook chapter twice (once before lecture for a general understanding, and then later for a thorough understanding); that you have prepared a good set of lecture notes; and that you have worked through all of the problems in the appropriate *Study Guide* chapters. By applying this style of analysis to the problem of efficiently allocating your study time, you are already beginning to think like an economist!

♦ *Use your instructor and/or teaching assistants for help.* When you have questions or problems with course material, come to the office to ask questions. Remember, you are paying for your education and instructors are there to help you learn. I am often amazed at how few students come to see me during office hours. Don't be shy. The personal contact that comes from one-on-one tutoring is professionally gratifying for instructors as well as (hopefully) beneficial for you.

♦ *Form a study group.* A very useful way to motivate your studying and to learn economics is to discuss the course material and problems with other students. Explaining the answer to a question *out loud* is a very effective way of discovering how well you understand the question. When you answer a question only in your head, you often skip steps in the chain of reasoning without realizing it. When you are forced to explain your reasoning aloud, gaps and mistakes quickly appear, and you (with your fellow group members) can quickly correct your reasoning. The "You're the Teacher" questions in the *Study Guide* and the Review questions at the end of each textbook chapter are extremely good study group material. You might also get together *after* having worked the *Study Guide* problems, but *before* looking at the answers, and help each other solve unsolved problems.

♦ *Work old exams.* One of the most effective ways of studying is to work through exams your instructor has given in previous years. Old exams give you a feel for the style of question your instructor may ask, and give you the opportunity to get used to time pressure if you force yourself to do the exam in the allotted time. Studying from old exams is not cheating, as long as you have obtained a copy of the exam legally. Some institutions keep old exams in the library, others in the department. Students who have previously taken the course are usually a good source as well. Remember, though, that old exams are a useful study aid only if you use them to *understand* the reasoning behind each question. If you simply memorize answers in the hopes that your instructor will repeat the identical question, you are likely to fail. From year to year, instructors routinely change the questions or change the numerical values for similar questions.

♦ *Use the Economic Place web site.* One of the most exciting features of the textbook is the opportunity it offers to use The Economics Place web site. Michael Parkin, the author of the textbook, has been a leader in developing for the web site new, *useful* features that help students learn. You definitely should check out the web site because of all the help it offers. The textbook has complete details about the web site.

■ Using Your *Study Guide*

You should only attempt to complete a chapter in the *Study Guide* after you have read the corresponding textbook chapter and listened to your instructor lecture on the material. Each *Study Guide* chapter contains the following sections.

Key Concepts. This first section is a short summary, in point form, of all key definitions, concepts and material from the textbook chapter. Key terms from the textbook appear in bold. Each term in bold is in the glossary of the textbook. This first section is designed to focus you quickly and precisely on the core material that you *must* master. It is an excellent study aid for the night before an exam. Think of it as crib notes that will serve as a final check of the key concepts you have studied.

Helpful Hints. When you encounter difficulty in mastering concepts or techniques, you will not be alone. Many students find certain concepts difficult and often make the same kinds of mistakes. I have taught over 30,000 students the principles of economics and I have seen these common mistakes often enough to have learned how to help students avoid them. The hints point out these mistakes and offer tips to avoid them. The hints focus on the most important concepts, equations, and techniques for problem solving. They also review crucial graphs that appear on every instructor's exams. I hope that this section will be very useful, because instructors always ask exam questions designed to test these possible mistakes in your understanding.

Self-Test. This will be one of the most useful sections of the *Study Guide.* The questions are designed to give you practice and to test skills and techniques you must master to do well on exams.

There are plenty of multiple-choice type of questions and other types of questions in the Self-Test, each with a specific pedagogical purpose. Indeed, this book contains over 825 multiple choice questions in total! Before I describe the four parts of the Self-Test section, here are some general tips that apply to all parts.

Use a pencil to write your answers in the *Study Guide* so you have neat, complete pages from which to study. Draw graphs wherever they are applicable. Some questions will ask explicitly for graphs; many others will not but will require a chain of reasoning that involves shifts of curves on a graph. *Always draw the graph.* Don't try to work through the reasoning in your head — you are much more likely to make mistakes that way. Whenever you draw a graph, even in the margins of the *Study Guide,* label the axes. You may think that you can keep the labels in your head, but you will be confronting many different graphs with many different variables on the axes. Avoid confusion and label. As an added incentive, remember that on exams where graphs are required, instructors will deduct points for unlabelled axes.

Do the Self-Test questions as if they were real exam questions, which means do them *without looking at the answers.* This is the single most important tip I can give you about effectively using the *Study Guide* to improve your exam performance. Struggling for the answers to questions that you find difficult is one of the most effective ways to learn. The adage "no pain, no gain" applies well to studying. You will learn the most from right answers you had to struggle for and from your wrong answers and mistakes. Only after you have attempted all the questions should you look at the answers. When you finally do check the answers, be sure to understand where you went wrong and why the right answer is correct.

There are many questions in each chapter, and it will take you somewhere between two and six hours to answer all of them. If you get tired (or bored), don't burn yourself out by trying to work through all of the questions in one sitting. Consider breaking up your Self-Test over two (or more) study sessions.

The four parts of the Self-Test section are:

True/False and Explain. These questions test basic knowledge of concepts and your ability to apply the concepts. Some of the questions challenge your understanding, to see if you can identify mistakes in statements using basic concepts. These questions will identify gaps in your knowledge and are useful to answer out loud in a study group.

When answering, identify each statement as *true,* or *false.* Explain your answer in *your words* in one sentence in the space underneath each question.

Multiple-Choice. These more difficult questions test your analytical abilities by asking you to apply concepts to new situations, manipulate information and solve numerical and graphical problems.

This is a most frequently used type of exam question, and the Self-Test contains many of them.

Read each question and all four choices carefully before you answer. Many of the choices will be plausible and will differ only slightly. You must choose the one *best* answer. A useful strategy in working these questions is first to eliminate any obviously wrong choices and then to focus on the remaining alternatives. Don't get frustrated or think that you are dim if you can't immediately see the correct answer. These questions are designed to make you work to find the correct choice.

Short Answer. Each chapter contains several Short Answer questions. Some are straightforward questions about basic concepts. They can generally be answered in a few sentences or, at most, in one paragraph. Others are problems. The best way to learn to do economics is to do problems. Problems are also the second-most popular type of exam question — practice them as much as possible!

You're the Teacher. Each chapter contains from one to three questions that either cover very broad issues or errors that are all too common among students. These questions may be the most valuable you will encounter for use in your study group. Take turns by pretending that you are the teacher and answer the questions for the rest of your group. Who knows, you may like this process so much that you actually do become a professor at a university teaching economics!

Answers. The Self-Test is followed by answers to all questions. Unlike other study guides on the market, I have included complete answers because I believe that reading complete answers will help you master the material ... and that's what this *Study Guide* is all about! But do *not* look at an answer until you have attempted a question. When you do finally look, use the answers to understand where you went wrong and why the right answer is correct.

As you work through the material, you'll find that the true/false and multiple choice questions, as well as their answers, are identified by a heading from the textbook. If you find that you are missing a lot of questions from one particular section, it is time to head back to the textbook and bone up on this material! In other words, *use* the textbook and this study guide to pull the A you want to earn!

Chapter Quiz. The last page in each chapter contains another 10 multiple questions covering the material in the chapter. These are questions that I and other instructors have included on our exams. Because these questions have been written by several instructors, they differ in style from the others in the chapter and so are a very good tool to be sure that you grasp the material. You can use the questions immediately after you finish each chapter, or else you can hoard them to help you prepare when exam time rolls around. In either case, the answers are given at the back of the book.

Part Overview Problem. Every few chapters, at the end of each of the parts of the textbook, you will find a special problem (and answer). These multi-part problems draw on material from the part you have just concluded and are similar to the "Reading Between the Lines" sections in your textbook. There is also a self-test that contains four multiple choice questions drawn from each chapter in the section. The questions are in order, with the first four from the first chapter in the section, the second four from the second chapter, and so forth. If you miss several questions from one chapter, you'll know to spend more time on that chapter when preparing for your exam. These multiple choice questions are written in a different style than those in the chapter because instructors have different ways of writing questions. By encountering different styles, you will be better prepared for *your* test.

Final Exams. At the end of the *Study Guide* are two multiple choice final exams and answers. These are final exams that I have used in my class at the University of Florida. You should use them to help you study for the final exam in your class.

If you effectively combine the use of the textbook, the *Study Guide, Economics in Action,* and all other course resources, you will be well prepared for exams. You will also have developed analytical skills and powers of reasoning that will benefit you throughout your life and in whatever career you choose.

■ Your Future and Economics

After your class is concluded, you may well wonder about economics as a major. The last essay in this *Study Guide*, written by Robert Whaples, helps examine your future by discussing whether economics is the major for you. I invite you to read this chapter and consider the information in it. Economics is a major with a bright future so I think you'll be interested in this important chapter.

■ Final Comments

I have tried to make the *Study Guide* as helpful and useful as possible. Undoubtedly I have made some mistakes; mistakes that you may see. If you find any, I, and succeeding generations of students, would be grateful if you could point them out to me. At the end

of my class at the University of Florida, when I ask my students for their advice, I point out to them that this advice won't help them at all because they have just completed the class. But, comments they make will influence how future students are taught. Thus, just as they owe a debt of gratitude for the comments and suggestions that I received from students before them, so too will students after them owe them an (unpaid and unpayable) debt. You are in the same situation. If you have questions, suggestions, or simply comments, let me know. My address is on the next page, or you can E-mail me at RUSH@DALE.CBA.UFL.EDU. Your input probably won't benefit you directly, but it will benefit following generations. And, if you give me permission, I will note your name and school in following editions so that any younger siblings (or, years down the road, maybe even your children!) will see your name and offer up thanks.

To date, students who have uncovered errors and to whom we all owe a debt of gratitude include:

♦ Jeanie Callen at the University of Minnesota-Twin Cities.

♦ Brian Mulligan at the University of Florida

♦ Patrick Lusby at the University of Florida

♦ Jonathan Baskind at the University of Florida

♦ Breina Polk at Cook College at Rutgers University

♦ Ethan Schulman at the University of Iowa

♦ Adrian Garza at the University of Iowa

♦ Curtis Hazel at the University of North Florida

♦ Zhang Zili at American University

♦ Valerie Stewart at the University of Georgia

♦ Rob Bleeker at The Ohio State University

♦ Katherine Hamilton at the University of Florida

♦ Dennis Spinks at The Ohio State University

♦ Debbie McGuffie at the University of Florida

♦ Daniel Glassman at the University of Florida

♦ Thomas Cowan at the University of Florida

♦ Christopher Bland at the University of Florida

♦ Richard Caitung at the University of Florida

♦ Kristin L. Thistle at the University of Florida

I owe Avi J. Cohen, of York University, and Harvey B. King, of University of Regina. Their superb study guide for the Canadian edition of Michael Parkin's book was a basis for this study guide. Much of what is good about this book is a direct reflection of their work.

Robert Whaples of Wake Forest University wrote the section of the *Study Guide* dealing with majoring in economics. He also checked an earlier edition of the manuscript for errors and provided questions that I use in this edition. Robert is a superb economist and this book is by far the better for this fact! Another brilliant teacher, Carol Dole of the State University of West Georgia, also supplied questions that I use with this edition. I think it fair to say that the clever questions are the work of Carol and Robert. For this edition, Ms. Cynthia Westermann-Clark proofread the entire manuscript. I wish I could report that she found no errors... but such reporting would be dishonest. She found many errors and I think I adopted each suggestion she made.

I need to thank Michael Parkin and Robin Bade. Michael has written such a superior book that it was easy to be enthusiastic about writing the *Study Guide* to accompany it. Moreover, both Michael and Robin have played a hands on role in creating this *Study Guide* and have made suggestions that vastly improved the *Study Guide*.

I want to thank my family: Susan, Tommy, Bobby, and Katie, who, respectively: allowed me to work all hours on this book; helped me master the intricacies of FTPing computer files; let me postpone riding bicycles with him until after the book was concluded; and would run into my typing room to share her new discoveries. Thanks a lot!

Finally, I want to thank Lucky, Pearl, and Butterscotch who sat at my feet and next to the computer in a box (and occasionally meowed) while I typed.

Mark Rush
Economics Department
University of Florida
Gainesville, Florida 32611
May, 2002.

Table of Contents

WHAT IS ECONOMICS?

Key Concepts

■ Definition of Economics

The fundamental economic problem is **scarcity**, which is the inability to satisfy all our wants. Because the available resources are never enough to satisfy everyone's wants, choices are necessary.

Economics is the social science that studies the choices people, businesses, governments, and societies make as they cope with scarcity.

♦ **Microeconomics** is the study of choices that individuals and businesses make, the way these choices interact, and the influences that governments exert on these choices.

♦ **Macroeconomics** is the study of the effects on the national economy and the global economy of the choices that individuals, businesses, and governments make.

■ Three Big Microeconomic Questions

Microeconomics explores three big questions.

The first question is "What goods and services are produced and in what quantities?" **Goods and services** are the objects that people value and produce to satisfy wants. The United States produces more services than goods.

The second question is "How are goods and services produced?" The resources that businesses use to produce goods and services are called **factors of production.** There are four categories:

♦ **Land:** the "gifts of nature" such as land, minerals, and water.

♦ **Labor:** the work time and work effort people devote to producing goods and services.

♦ **Capital:** the tools, instruments, machines, buildings, and other constructions that businesses now use to produce goods and services.

♦ **Entrepreneurship:** the human resource that organizes land, labor, and capital.

The third question is "For whom are goods and services produced?" To earn an income, people sell the services of the factors of production they own. Land earns **rent;** labor earns **wages;** capital earns **interest;** and entrepreneurship earns **profit.**

■ Three Big Macroeconomic Questions

Macroeconomics explores three big questions.

The first question is "What determines the standard of living?"

♦ The **standard of living** is the level of consumption that people enjoy, on the average, and is measured by average income per person.

The second question is "What determines the cost of living?"

♦ The **cost of living** is the amount of money it takes to buy the goods and services that a typical family consumes. A rising cost of living is called **inflation** and a falling cost of living is called **deflation.**

The third question is "Why does our economy fluctuate?"

♦ The periodic but irregular up-and-down movement in production and jobs is called the **business cycle.**

■ The Economic Way of Thinking

A choice involves a **tradeoff**, that is, something is given up to get something else. Microeconomic tradeoffs include the "what" tradeoffs, the "how" tradeoffs, and the "who" tradeoffs.

♦ The **big tradeoff** is the tradeoff between equality and efficiency that occurs as a result of government programs redistributing income.

Macroeconomic tradeoffs include the standard of living tradeoff.

♦ The **output-inflation tradeoff** occurs because government policy actions to lower inflation also lower output and policy actions that boost output increase inflation.

The **opportunity cost** of a choice is the highest-valued alternative foregone. Opportunity cost is not all the alternatives foregone, only the highest-valued alternative foregone. All tradeoffs involve an opportunity cost.

Choices are made in small steps, which means choices are made at the **margin**.

♦ The benefit that arises from an increase in an activity is called **marginal benefit.**

♦ The cost of an increase in an activity is called **marginal cost.**

When making choices, people compare the marginal cost of an action to the marginal benefit of the action. Changes in marginal cost and/or marginal benefit affect the decisions made. So choices respond to **incentives**, which are inducements to take a particular action.

■ Economics: A Social Science

Economists distinguish between:

♦ Positive statements — statements about what is. These can be shown to be true or false through observation and measurement.

♦ Normative statements — statements about what ought to be. These are matters of opinion.

Economic science is a collection of positive statements that are consistent with the real world. Economic science uses three steps to progress:

♦ Observation and measurement — economists observe and record economic data.

♦ Model building — an **economic model** is a description of some aspect of the economic world that includes only those features of the world that are needed for the purpose at hand.

♦ Testing — a model is tested to determine how well its predictions correspond with the real world. An **economic theory** is a generalization that summarizes what we think we understand about economic choices that people make and the performance of industries and entire economies.

When developing models and theories, economists use the idea of **ceteris paribus,** which is Latin for "other things being equal", to focus on the effect of one particular factor.

In the development of theories and models, two fallacies are possible:

♦ Fallacy of composition — the assertion that what is true for a part must be true for the whole, or what is true for the whole must be true for each of the parts.

♦ *Post hoc* fallacy — the assertion that one event caused another because the first occurred before the second.

Helpful Hints

1. **CHOICES AND INCENTIVES :** The basic assumption made by economists about human behavior is that people try to make themselves as well off as possible. As a result, people respond to changed incentives by changing their decisions. The key idea is that an individual compares the additional (or "marginal") benefit from taking an action to the additional (or "marginal") cost of the action. If the marginal benefit from the action exceeds the marginal cost, taking the action makes the person better off, so the person takes the action. Conversely, if the marginal benefit falls short of the marginal cost, the action is not taken. Only the *additional* benefit and *additional* cost are relevant because they are the benefits and costs that the person will enjoy and incur if the action is undertaken. Keeping straight the distinction between additional benefits and costs versus total benefits and costs is a vital part of economics, particularly of microeconomics.

2. **MODELS AND SIMPLIFICATION :** In attempting to understand how and why something works (for example, an airplane or an economy), we can use description or we can use theory. A description is a list of facts about something. But it does not tell us which facts are essential for understanding how an airplane works (the shape of the wings) and which facts are less important (the color of the paint). Scientists use theory to abstract from the complex descriptive facts of the real world and focus only on those elements essential for understanding. These essential elements are fashioned into models — highly simplified representations of the real world.

In a real sense, models are like maps, which are useful precisely because they abstract from real world detail. A map that reproduced all the details of the real world (street lights, traffic signs, electric wires) would be useless. A useful map offers a simplified view, which is carefully selected according to the purpose of the map. A useful theory is similar: It gives guidance and insight into how the immensely complicated real world functions and reacts to changes.

Questions

■ True/False and Explain

Definition of Economics

1. Scarcity is a problem only for the poor.

2. Macroeconomics studies the factors that change national employment and income.

Three Big Microeconomic Questions

3. Answering the question "What goods and services are produced?" automatically answers the question, "How are goods and services produced?"

4. An example of the "how" question is: "How does the nation decide who gets the goods and services that are produced?"

Three Big Macroeconomic Questions

5. "For whom are goods and services produced?" is one of the big macroeconomic questions.

6. A rising cost of living is called inflation.

7. In a business cycle, an expansion follows the peak.

The Economic Way of Thinking

8. Tradeoffs mean that you give up one thing to get something else.

9. There is no such thing as a "how" tradeoff because a business uses only way to produce its products.

10. The output-inflation tradeoff refers to the point that lowering inflation increases output.

11. The opportunity cost of buying a slice of pizza for $3 rather than a burrito for $3 is the burrito.

12. By comparing the cost and benefit of a small change you are making your choice at the margin.

Economics: A Social Science

13. A positive statement is about what is; a normative statement is about what will be.

14. The idea of *ceteris paribus* is used whenever a *post hoc* fallacy is being examined.

■ Multiple Choice

Definition of Economics

1. The fact that wants cannot be fully satisfied with available resources reflects the definition of
   a. the standard of living.
   b. scarcity.
   c. the output-inflation tradeoff.
   d. for whom to produce.

2. Studying the effects choices have on the national economy is part of
   a. scarcity.
   b. microeconomics.
   c. macroeconomics.
   d. global science.

Three Big Microeconomic Questions

3. Which of the following is <u>NOT</u> one of the three big microeconomic questions?
   a. What goods and services are produced?
   b. How are goods and services produced?
   c. For whom are goods and services produced?
   d. Why are goods and services produced?

4. The question, "Should personal computers or mainframe computers be produced?" is an example of the
   a. "what" question.
   b. "how" question.
   c. "where" question.
   d. "for whom" question.

5. People have different amounts of income. This observation is most directly related to which of the big microeconomic questions?
   a. The "what" question.
   b. The "how" question.
   c. The "why" question.
   d. The "for whom" question.

Three Big Macroeconomic Questions

6. Of the following, which country or region has the highest standard of living?
   a. Japan
   b. Central and Eastern Europe
   c. The United States
   d. Africa

7. During an inflation, the cost of living is _____ and the value of the dollar is _____.
   a. rising; rising
   b. rising; falling
   c. falling; rising
   d. falling; falling

8. Which of the following is the correct order for the parts of a business cycle?
   a. expansion, trough, recession, peak
   b. expansion, recession, trough, peak
   c. expansion, recession, peak, trough
   d. expansion, peak, recession, trough

The Economic Way of Thinking

9. The fact that Intel decides to produce CPU chips rather than memory chips best reflects a _____ trade-off.
   a. what
   b. how
   c. for whom
   d. standard of living

10. The standard of living tradeoff reflects trading off
    a. consumption in the United States for consumption in Africa.
    b. higher inflation for higher consumption.
    c. current consumption for economic growth.
    d. consumption and equality.

11. From 9 to 10 A.M., Fred can sleep in, go to his economics lecture, or play tennis. Suppose that Fred decides to go to the lecture but thinks that, if he hadn't, he would otherwise have slept in. The opportunity cost of attending the lecture is
    a. sleeping in *and* playing tennis.
    b. playing tennis.
    c. sleeping in.
    d. one hour of time.

12. When the government chooses to use resources to build a dam, these resources are no longer available to build a highway. This choice illustrates the concept of
    a. a market.
    b. macroeconomics.
    c. opportunity cost.
    d. marginal benefit.

13. To make a choice on the margin, an individual
    a. ignores any opportunity cost if the marginal benefit from the action is high enough.
    b. will choose to use his or her scarce resources only if there is a very large total benefit from so doing.
    c. compares the marginal cost of the choice to the marginal benefit.
    d. makes the choice with the smallest opportunity cost.

Economics: A Social Science

14. A positive statement is
    a. about what ought to be.
    b. about what is.
    c. always true.
    d. one that does not use the *ceteris paribus* clause.

15. Which of the following is a positive statement?
    a. The government must lower the price of a pizza so that more students can afford to buy it.
    b. The best level of taxation is zero percent because then people get to keep everything they earn.
    c. My economics class should last for two terms because it is my favorite class.
    d. An increase in college tuition will lead fewer students to apply to college.

16. An economic model includes
    a. only normative statements.
    b. no use of *ceteris paribus*.
    c. all known facts about a situation.
    d. only details considered essential.

17. The Latin term *ceteris paribus* means
    a. "false unless proven true."
    b. "other things the same."
    c. "after this, then because of this."
    d. "not correct, even though it is logical."

18. One student from a class of 30 can walk easily through a door. Assuming that all 30 students simultaneously therefore can walk easily through the same door is an example of the
    a. opportunity cost fallacy.
    b. fallacy of composition
    c. fallacy of substitution.
    d. *post hoc* fallacy.

19. The *post hoc* fallacy is the
    a. assertion that what is true for a part of the whole must be true for the whole.
    b. claim that one event caused another because the one event came first.
    c. use of *ceteris paribus* in order to study the impact of one factor.
    d. claim that the timing of two events has nothing to do with which event caused the other.

■ Short Answer Problems

1. "In the future, as our technology advances even further, eventually we will whip scarcity. In the high-tech future, scarcity will be gone." Do you agree or disagree with this claim? Explain your answer and what scarcity is. Why does the existence of scarcity require choices?

2. What are the factors of production? Focusing on the factors of production, describe the relationship between the big microeconomic question "How are goods and services produced?" and the question "For whom are goods and services produced?".

3. How do you think the standard of living changes in the different parts of the business cycle?

4. Why does your decision to buy a taco from Taco Bell reflect a tradeoff? Be sure to discuss the role played by opportunity cost in your answer.

5. "Education is a basic right. Just as kindergarten through 12th grade education is free, so, too, should a college education be free and guaranteed to every American." This statement can be analyzed by using the economic concepts discussed in this chapter to answer the following questions.
    a. What would be the opportunity cost of providing a free college education for everyone?
    b. Is providing this education free from the perspective of society as a whole?

6. Indicate whether each of the following statements is positive or normative. If it is normative, rewrite it so that it becomes positive. If it is positive, rewrite it so that it becomes normative.
    a. Policymakers ought to lower the inflation rate even if it lowers output.
    b. An imposition of a tax on tobacco products will decrease their consumption.
    c. Health care costs should be lower so that poorer people can afford quality health care.

7. In sciences such as chemistry, controlled experiments play a key role. How does that relate to economists' use of *ceteris paribus*?

■ You're the Teacher

1. Your friend asks, "Does everything have an opportunity cost?" Your friend has hit upon a very good question; provide an equally good answer!

2. "Economic theories are useless because the models on which they are based are totally unrealistic. They leave out so many descriptive details about the real world, they can't possibly be useful for understanding how the economy works." So says your skeptical friend. You'd like to keep your friend in your economics class so that you two can study together. Defend the fact that economic theories are much simpler than reality and help your friend realize that time spent studying economic theories is time well spent!

Answers

■ True/False Answers

Definition of Economics

1. **F** Scarcity exists because people's wants exceed their ability to meet those wants, and this fact of life is true for *any* person, rich or poor.

2. **T** Macroeconomics studies the entire economy; microeconomics studies separate parts of the economy.

Three Big Microeconomic Questions

3. **F** Almost always, goods and services can be produced many different ways, so the "how" question must be answered separately from the "what" question.

4. **F** The "how" question asks, "How are goods and services produced?"

Three Big Macroeconomic Questions

5. **F** The "for whom" question is one of the three microeconomic questions.

6. **T** A rising cost of living is the definition of inflation.

7. **F** A recession follows the peak. An expansion follows the trough.

The Economic Way of Thinking

8. **T** The question gives the definition of a tradeoff.

9. **F** Businesses almost always can produce their products many different ways, so they face a "how" tradeoff when they choose which method they will use.

10. **F** The output-inflation tradeoff refers to the point that lowering inflation *decreases* output.

11. **T** The opportunity cost is the burrito that was foregone in order to buy the pizza.

12. **T** The definition of making a choice at the margin means that choice revolves around a small change.

Economics: A Social Science

13. **F** Although a positive statement is, indeed, about what is, a normative statement tells what policies should be followed.

14. **F** *Ceteris paribus*, Latin for "other things being equal," is used in order to focus on the effect from a change in one factor alone.

■ Multiple Choice Answers

Definition of Economics

1. **b** Scarcity refers to the observation that wants are unlimited but that the resources available to satisfy these wants are limited.

2. **c** Macroeconomics studies the national economy as well as the global economy.

Three Big Microeconomic Questions

3. **d** "Why" is not one of the three big microeconomic questions.

4. **a** The "what" question asks in part, "What goods and services are produced?"

5. **d** People with high incomes will get more goods and services than those with low incomes.

Three Big Macroeconomic Questions

6. **c** Of the areas listed, the United States has the highest standard of living.

7. **b** Inflation is defined as a rising cost of living and when the cost of living is rising, dollars are falling in value because each dollar buys fewer goods and services.

8. **d** Answer d is the correct ordering of the business cycle.

The Economic Way of Thinking

9. **a** The "what" tradeoff reflects Intel's decisions about "what" to produce.

10. **c** Economic growth will increase if people save more, but saving more means cutting current consumption of goods and services.

11. **c** The opportunity cost of an action is the (single) highest-valued alternative foregone by taking the action.

12. **c** Because the resources are used to build a dam, the opportunity of using them to build a highway is given up.

13. **c** Comparing marginal cost and marginal benefit is an important technique, especially in microeconomics.

Economics: A Social Science

14. **b** Positive statements describe how the world operates.

15. **d** This statement is the only one that tries to describe how the world actually works; all the others are normative statements that describe a policy that should be pursued.

16. **d** By including only essential details, economic models are vastly simpler than reality.

17. **b** *Ceteris paribus* is the economic equivalent of a controlled experiment: Its use allows us to determine the effect from each factor alone even though many factors might play a role in affecting a variable.

18. **b** In this case, the fallacy of composition is arguing that what is true for a part must necessarily be true for the whole.

19. **b** The usual *post hoc* fallacy is to claim that one event caused another because the first event occurred before the second.

■ Answers to Short Answer Problems

1. This claim is incorrect. Scarcity will always exist. Scarcity occurs because people's wants are basically unlimited, but the resources available to satisfy these wants are finite. As a result, not all of everyone's wants can be satisfied. For instance, think about the number of people who want to spend all winter skiing on uncrowded slopes. Regardless of the level of technology, there simply are not enough ski slopes available to allow everyone who wants to spend all winter skiing in near isolation to do so. Uncrowded ski slopes are scarce and will remain so.

   Because not all the goods and services wanted can be produced, choices must be made about which wants will be satisfied and which wants will be disappointed.

2. The four factors of production are land, labor, capital, and entrepreneurship. These are the resources used to produce goods and services, so the question asking how goods and services are produced asks which factors will be used. People earn their incomes by offering factors of production for use. Land earns rent, labor earns wages, capital earns interest, and entrepreneurship earns profit. The answer to the question asking for whom the goods and services are produced depends on people's incomes. So, for example, if more land is used to produce goods and services, then landowners' incomes will be higher so they will be able to acquire more of the goods and services that have been produced.

3. The standard of living is the level of consumption that people enjoy, on the average. The level of consumption depends on the amount of goods and services produced. During a business cycle, the standard of living will be lowest at the trough, because production is lowest. It will rise during an expansion and reach its maximum at the peak. During a recession the standard of living will fall.

4. The decision to buy a taco reflects a tradeoff because you have given up your funds in exchange for the taco. The opportunity cost of buying the taco is the highest-valued alternative given up. For instance, suppose that if you had not decided to buy the taco, you would then have used the funds to buy a burger from Burger King. In this case, the opportunity cost of buying the taco is the forgone burger because that is the highest-valued alternative given up.

5. a. Even though a college education may be offered without charge ("free"), opportunity costs still exist. The opportunity cost of providing such education is the highest valued alternative use of the resources used to construct the necessary universities and the highest valued alternative use of the resources (including human resources) used in the operation of the schools.

   b. Providing a "free" college education is hardly free from the perspective of society. The resources used in this endeavor would no longer be available for other activities. For instance, the resources used to construct a new college cannot be used to construct a hospital to provide better health care. Additionally, the time and effort spent by the faculty, staff, and students operating and attending colleges has a substantial opportunity cost, namely, that these individuals cannot participate fully in other sectors of the economy. Providing a "free" college education to everyone is not free to society!

6. a. This statement is normative. A positive statement is: "If policymakers lowered the inflation rate by 1 percentage point, then output would fall by 1 percent."

   b. This statement is positive. A normative statement is: "We should impose a tax on tobacco products in order to decrease their consumption."

   c. This statement is normative. A positive statement is: "If health care costs were lower, more poor people would receive health care."

7. Chemists can check the predictions of a model by conducting controlled experiments and observing the outcomes. For instance, when determining the effect of temperature on a particular reaction, chemists can ensure that, between different experiments, *only* the temperature changes. Everything else is held constant. Economists usually cannot perform such controlled experiments and instead must change one variable at a time in a model and compare the results. This approach involves the use of *ceteris paribus*, wherein only one factor is allowed to change. So, economists face more difficult and less precise model building and testing than is possible for the controlled experiments of chemists and other scientists.

■ You're the Teacher

1. "Virtually everything has an opportunity cost. People sometimes say that viewing a beautiful sunset or using sand from the middle of the Sahara Desert have no opportunity costs. But that isn't strictly true. Viewing the sunset has an opportunity cost in terms of the time spent watching it. The time could have been utilized in some other activity and, whatever the next highest-valued opportunity might have been, that is the opportunity cost of watching the sunset. Similarly, making use of sand from the Sahara also must have some opportunity cost, be it the time spent in gathering the sand or the resources spent in gathering it. So from the widest of perspectives, the answer is: Yes, everything does have an opportunity cost."

2. "Economic theories are like maps, which are useful precisely because they abstract from real world detail. A useful map offers a simplified view, which is carefully selected according to the purpose of the map. No map maker would claim that the world is as simple (or as flat) as the map, and economists do not claim that the real economy is as simple as their theories. What economists do claim is that their theories isolate the effects of real forces operating in the economy, yield predictions that can be tested against real-world data, and result in predictions that often are correct.

"I've got a book here that my parents gave to me by Milton Friedman, a Nobel Prize winner in Economics. Here's what he says on this topic: 'A theory or its 'assumptions' cannot possibly be thoroughly 'realistic' in the immediate descriptive sense.... A completely 'realistic' theory of the wheat market would have to include not only the conditions directly underlying the supply and demand for wheat but also the kind of coins or credit instruments used to make exchanges; the personal characteristics of wheat-traders such as the color of each trader's hair and eyes, ... the number of members of his family, their characteristics, ... the kind of soil on which the wheat was grown, ... the weather prevailing during the growing season; ... and so on indefinitely. Any attempt to move very far in achieving this kind of 'realism' is certain to render a theory utterly useless.'

"I think Friedman makes a lot of sense in what he says. It seems to me that theories have to be simple in order to be powerful and so I don't see anything wrong with the fact that economic theories leave out a bunch of trivial details."

From Milton Friedman, "The Methodology of Positive Economics," in *Essays in Positive Economics*. (Chicago: University of Chicago Press, 1953), 32.

Chapter Quiz

1. The most fundamental economic problem is
   a. reducing unemployment.
   b. health and health care.
   c. scarcity.
   d. decreasing the inflation rate.

2. Studying how an individual firm decides to set its price is primarily a concern of
   a. normative economics.
   b. macroeconomics.
   c. microeconomics.
   d. all economists.

3. Which of the following is a macroeconomic topic?
   a. Why has the price of a personal computer fallen over time?
   b. How does a rise in the price of cheese affect the pizza market?
   c. What factors determine the nation's inflation rate?
   d. How does a consumer decide how many tacos to consume?

4. When the economy produces fireworks for sale at the Fourth of July, it most directly is answering the _____ question.
   a. what goods and services are produced
   b. opportunity cost
   c. for whom are goods and services produced
   d. how are goods and services produced

5. When doctors have an average income that exceeds $250,000, the economy most directly is answering the _____ question.
   a. what goods and services are produced
   b. opportunity cost
   c. how are goods and services produced
   d. for whom are goods and services produced

6. Which of the following is NOT a big *macroeconomic* question?
   a. How are goods and services produced?
   b. What determines the cost of living?
   c. Why does our economy fluctuate?
   d. What determines the standard of living?

7. The big tradeoff between equality and efficiency reflects the point that
   a. policy actions to lower inflation also lower output.
   b. if more of one good is produced, less of another can be produced.
   c. taxing productive activities means producing fewer goods and services.
   d. None of the above answers is correct.

8. Opportunity cost is
   a. zero for services, because services do not last for very long, and positive for goods, because goods are long lasting.
   b. paid by society not by an individual.
   c. the highest-valued alternative given up by making a choice.
   d. all the alternatives given up by making a choice.

9. In economics, positive statements
   a. are only about facts that economists are certain (are "positive") are true.
   b. tell what policy the government ought to follow.
   c. depend on value judgments.
   d. in principle, can be tested to determine if they are true or false.

10. The fallacy of composition is the (false) statement
    a. that theory is necessary to better understand the real world.
    b. that models can be normative in nature without any positive conclusions.
    c. that people's free will makes predicting their behavior futile.
    d. that what is true for the whole must necessarily be true for the part.

The answers for this Chapter Quiz are on page 367

A p p e n d i x

GRAPHS IN ECONOMICS

■ Graphing Data

Graphs represent quantity as a distance on a line. On a graph, the horizontal scale line is the *x-axis*, the vertical scale line is the *y-axis*, and the intersection of the two scale lines is the *origin*.

The three main types of economic graphs are:

♦ **Time-series graphs** demonstrate the relationship between time, measured on the *x*-axis, and other variable(s), measured on the *y*-axis. Time-series graphs show the variable's level, direction of change, speed of change, and **trend**, which is its general tendency to rise or fall.

♦ **Cross-section graphs** show the values of a variable for different groups in a population at a point in time.

♦ **Scatter diagrams** plot the value of one variable against the value of another to show the relationship between two variables. Such a relationship indicates how the variables are *correlated*, not whether one variable *causes* the other.

■ Graphs Used in Economic Models

The four important relationships between variables are:

♦ **Positive relationship** or **direct relationship** — the variables move together in the same direction, as illustrated in Figure A1.1. The relationship is upward-sloping.

♦ **Negative relationship** or **inverse relationship** — the variables move in opposite directions, as shown in Figure A1.2. The relationship is downward-sloping.

FIGURE **A1.1**

A Positive Relationship

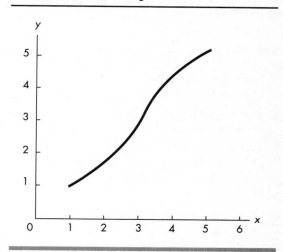

FIGURE **A1.2**

A Negative Relationship

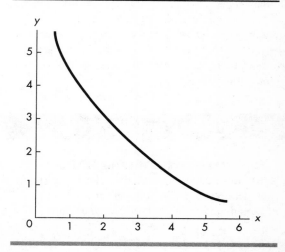

♦ **Maximum or minimum** — the relationship reaches a maximum or a minimum point, then changes direction. Figure A1.3 shows a minimum.

♦ **Unrelated** — the variables are not related so that, when one variable changes, the other is unaffected. The graph is either a vertical or horizontal straight line, as illustrated in Figure A1.4.

A relationship illustrated by a straight line is called a **linear relationship.**

■ The Slope of a Relationship

The **slope** of a relationship is the change in the value of the variable on the *y*-axis divided by the change in the value of the variable on the *x*-axis. The formula for slope is $\Delta y/\Delta x$, with Δ meaning "change in."

A straight line (or linear relationship) has a constant slope. A curved line has a varying slope, which can be calculated two ways:

♦ *Slope at a point* — by drawing the straight line tangent to the curve at that point and then calculating the slope of the line.

♦ *Slope across an arc* — by drawing a straight line across the two points on the curve and then calculating the slope of the line.

■ Graphing Relationships Among More Than Two Variables

Relationships between more than two variables can be graphed by holding constant the values of all the variables except two (the *ceteris paribus* assumption, that is, "other things remaining the same") and then graphing the relationship between the two with, *ceteris paribus*, only the variables being studied changing. When one of the variables not illustrated in the figure changes, the entire relationship between the two that have been graphed shifts.

Helpful Hints

1. **IMPORTANCE OF GRAPHS AND GRAPHICAL ANALYSIS :** Economists almost always use graphs to present relationships between variables. This fact should not "scare" you nor give you pause.

FIGURE **A1.3**
A Minimum

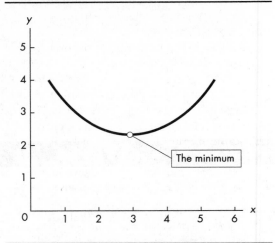

FIGURE **A1.4**
No Relationship

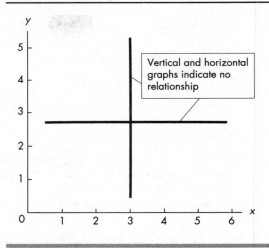

Economists do so because graphs *simplify* the analysis. All the key concepts you need to master are presented in this appendix. If your experience with graphical analysis is limited, this appendix is crucial to your ability to readily understand economic analysis. However, if you are experienced in constructing and using graphs, this appendix may be "old hat." Even so, you should skim the appendix and work through the questions in this *Study Guide.*

2. **CALCULATING THE SLOPE :** Often the slopes of various relationships are important. Usually what is key is the sign of the slope — whether the slope is positive or negative — rather than the actual value of the slope. An easy way to remember the formula for slope is to think of it as the "rise over the run," a saying used by carpenters and others. As illustrated in Figure A1.5, the *rise* is the change in the variable measured on the vertical axis, or in terms of symbols, Δy. The *run* is the change in the variable measured on the horizontal axis, or Δx. This "rise over the run" formula also makes it easy to remember whether the slope is positive or negative. If the rise is actually a drop, as shown in Figure A1.5, then the slope is negative because when the variable measured on the horizontal axis increases, the variable measured on the vertical axis decreases. However, if the rise actually is an increase, then the slope is positive. In this case, an increase in the variable measured on the x-axis is associated with an increase in the variable measured on the y-axis.

FIGURE **A1.5**
Rise Over The Run

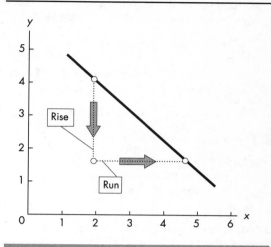

FIGURE **A1.6**
True/False Questions 3, 4, 5

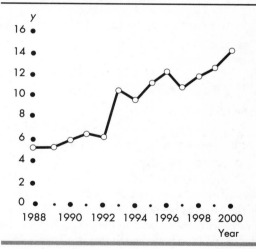

Questions

■ True/False and Explain

Graphing Data

1. The origin is the point where a graph starts.

2. A graph showing a positive relationship between stock prices and the nation's production means that an increase in stock prices causes an increase in production.

3. In Figure A1.6 the value of y decreased between 1996 and 1997.

4. In Figure A1.6 the value of y increased most rapidly between 1999 and 2000.

5. Figure A1.6 shows a trend with y increasing, generally speaking.

6. A cross-section graph compares the values of different groups of a variable at a single point in time.

Graphs Used in Economic Models

7. If the graph of the relationship between two variables slopes upward to the right, the relationship between the variables is positive.

8. If the relationship between y (measured on the vertical axis) and x (measured on the horizontal axis) is one in which y reaches a maximum, the slope of the relationship must be negative before and positive after the maximum.

9. To the left of a minimum point, the slope is negative; to the right, the slope is positive.

10. Graphing things that are unrelated on one diagram is <u>NOT</u> possible.

The Slope of a Relationship

11. It is possible for the graph of a positive relationship to have a slope that becomes smaller when moving rightward along the graph.

12. The slope of a straight line is calculated by dividing the change in the value of the variable measured on the horizontal axis by the change in the value of the variable measured on the vertical axis.

13. For a straight line, if a large change in y is associated with a small change in x, the line is steep.

14. The slope of a curved line is <u>NOT</u> constant.

15. The slope of a curved line at a point equals the slope of a line tangent to the curved line at the point.

Graphing Relationships Among More Than Two Variables

16. *Ceteris paribus* means "everything else changes."

17. The amount of corn a farmer grows depends on its price and the amount of rainfall. The curve showing the relationship between the price of a bushel of corn and the quantity grown is the same curve regardless of the amount of rainfall.

■ Multiple Choice

Graphing Data

1. Demonstrating how an economic variable changes from one year to the next is best illustrated by a
   a. one-variable graph.
   b. time-series graph.
   c. linear graph.
   d. cross-section graph.

2. You notice that, when the inflation rate increases, the interest rate also tends to increase. This fact indicates that
   a. there might be false causality between inflation and the interest rate.
   b. higher inflation rates must cause higher interest rates.
   c. a scatter diagram of the inflation rate and the interest rate will show a positive relationship.
   d. a cross-section graph of the inflation rate and the interest rate will show a positive relationship.

3. You believe that the total amount of goods produced in the United States has generally increased. In a time-series graph illustrating the total amount produced, you expect to find
   a. an upward trend.
   b. no relationship between time and the amount of goods produced.
   c. an inverse relationship between time and the amount of goods produced.
   d. a linear relationship.

4. You hypothesize that more natural gas is sold in the Northeast when winters are colder. Which of the following possibilities would best reveal if your belief is correct?
   a. A time-series diagram showing the amount of natural gas sold in the Northeast during the last 30 years.
   b. A time-series diagram showing the average temperature in the Northeast during the last 30 years.
   c. A scatter-diagram plotting the average temperature in the Northeast against the amount of natural gas sold.
   d. A trend diagram that plots the trend in natural gas sales over the last 30 years against the average temperature in the Northeast 30 years ago and this year.

5. Which type of graph can mislead?
   a. A time-series graph.
   b. A cross-section graph.
   c. A scatter diagram.
   d. *Any* type of graph might mislead.

Graphs Used in Economic Models

6. If variables x and y move up and down together, they are
   a. positively related.
   b. negative related.
   c. unrelated.
   d. trend related.

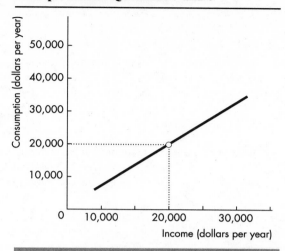

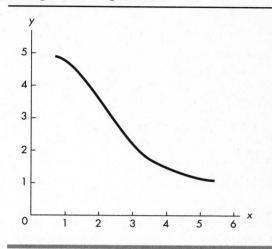

7. In Figure A1.7 when income equals $20,000, what does consumption equal?
   a. $0
   b. $10,000
   c. $20,000
   d. Impossible to tell

8. The relationship between income and consumption illustrated in Figure A1.7 is
   a. positive and linear.
   b. positive and nonlinear.
   c. negative and linear.
   d. negative and nonlinear

9. The term "direct relationship" means the same as
   a. correlation.
   b. trend.
   c. positive relationship.
   d. negative relationship.

10. Figure A1.8 shows
    a. a positive relationship.
    b. a time-series relationship.
    c. a negative relationship.
    d. no relationship between the variables.

11. The relationship between two variables, x and y, is a vertical line. Thus x and y are
    a. positively correlated.
    b. negatively correlated.
    c. not related.
    d. falsely related.

The Slope of a Relationship

12. The slope of a negative relationship is
    a. negative.
    b. undefined.
    c. positive to the right of the maximum point and negative to the left.
    d. constant as long as the relationship is nonlinear.

13. A linear relationship
    a. always has a maximum.
    b. always has a constant slope.
    c. always slopes up to the right.
    d. never has a constant slope.

FIGURE **A1.9**

Multiple Choice Questions 14 and 15

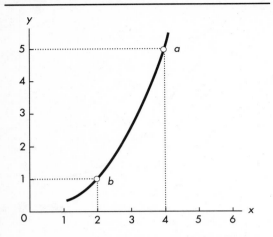

FIGURE **A1.10**

Multiple Choice Questions 16 and 17

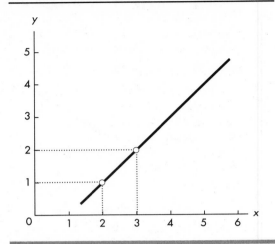

14. The relationship between x and y in Figure A1.9 is
    a. positive with an increasing slope.
    b. positive with a decreasing slope.
    c. negative with an increasing slope.
    d. negative with a decreasing slope.

15. In Figure A1.9 the slope across the arc between points a and b equals
    a. 5.
    b. 4.
    c. 2.
    d. 1.

16. In Figure A1.10, between $x = 2$ and $x = 3$, what is the slope of the line?
    a. 1
    b. −1
    c. 2
    d. 3

17. In Figure A1.10 how does the slope of the line between $x = 4$ and $x = 5$ compare with the slope between $x = 2$ and $x = 3$?
    a. The slope is greater between $x = 4$ and $x = 5$.
    b. The slope is greater between $x = 2$ and $x = 3$.
    c. The slope is the same.
    d. The slope is not comparable.

Graphing Relationships Among More Than Two Variables

FIGURE **A1.11**

Multiple Choice Questions 18, 19, 20

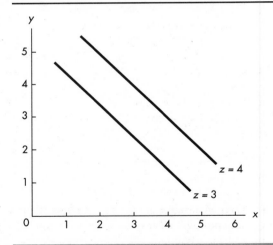

18. In Figure A1.11 x is
    a. positively related to y and negatively related to z.
    b. positively related to both y and z.
    c. negatively related to y and positively related to z.
    d. negatively related to both y and z.

19. In Figure A1.11, *ceteris paribus*, an increase in x is associated with

    a. an increase in y.
    b. a decrease in y.
    c. a decrease in z.
    d. None of the above answers is correct.

20. In Figure A1.11 an increase in z causes a

    a. movement up along one of the lines showing the relationship between x and y.
    b. movement down along one of the lines showing the relationship between x and y.
    c. shift rightward in the line showing the relationship between x and y.
    d. shift leftward in the line showing the relationship between x and y.

■ **Short Answer Problems**

1. a. The data in Table A1.1 show the U.S. unemployment rate between 1979 and 2001. Draw a time-series graph of these data.

   b. When was the unemployment rate the highest?

   TABLE **A1.2**

   Short Answer Problem 2

x	y
1	2
2	4
3	6
4	8
5	7
6	6

2. a. Use the data in Table A1.2 to graph the relationship between x and y.

   b. Over what range of values for x is this relationship positive? Over what range is it negative?

   c. Calculate the slope between $x = 1$ and $x = 2$.

   d. Calculate the slope between $x = 5$ and $x = 6$.

   e. What relationships do your answers to parts c and d have to your answer for part b?

3. a. In Figure A1.12, use the tangent line in the figure to calculate the slope at point b.

   b. Compute the slope across the arc between points b and a.

   c. Calculate the slope across the arc between points c and b.

TABLE **A1.1**

Short Answer Problem 1

Year	Unemployment rate
1979	5.8
1980	7.1
1981	7.6
1982	9.7
1983	9.6
1984	7.5
1985	7.2
1986	7.0
1987	6.2
1988	5.5
1989	5.3
1990	5.5
1991	6.7
1992	7.4
1993	6.8
1994	6.1
1995	5.6
1996	5.4
1997	5.6
1998	5.0
1999	4.2
2000	4.0
2001	4.8

FIGURE **A1.12**

Short Answer Problem 3

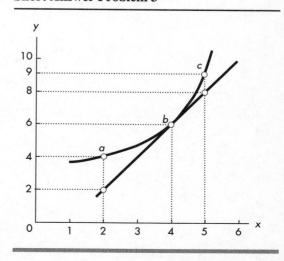

4. Can a curve have a positive but decreasing slope? If so, draw an example.

5. a. Bobby says that he buys fewer compact discs when the price of a compact disc is higher. Bobby also says that he will buy more compact discs after he graduates and his income is higher. Is the relationship between the number of compact discs Bobby buys and the price positive or negative? Is the relationship between Bobby's income and the number of compact discs positive or negative?

   b. Table A1.3 shows the number of compact discs Bobby buys in a month at different prices when his income is low and when his income is high. On a diagram with price on the vertical axis and the quantity purchased on the horizontal axis, plot the relationship between the number of discs purchased and the price when Bobby's income is low.

   c. On the same diagram, draw the relationship between the number of discs purchased and the price when Bobby's income is high.

   d. Does an increase in Bobby's income cause the relationship between the price of a compact disc and the number purchased to shift rightward or leftward?

TABLE **A1.3**

Short Answer Problem 5

Price (dollars per compact disc)	Quantity of compact discs purchased, low income	Quantity of compact discs purchased, high income
$11	5	6
12	4	5
13	3	4
14	1	3
15	0	2

■ **You're the Teacher**

1. "Hey, I thought this was an *economics* class, not a *math* class. Where's the economics? All I've seen so far is math!" Reassure your friend by explaining why the concentration in this chapter is on mathematics rather than economics.

2. "I don't understand why we need to learn all about graphs. Instead of this, why can't we just use numbers? If there is any sort of relationship we need to see, we can see it easier using numbers instead of all these complicated graphs!" Explain why graphs are useful when studying economics.

3. "There must be a relationship between the direction a curve is sloping, what its slope is, and whether the curve shows a positive or negative relationship between two variables. But I can't see the tie. Is there one? And what is it?" Help this student by answering the questions posed.

Answers

■ True/False Answers

Graphing Data

1. **F** The origin is where the horizontal and vertical axes start, *not* where the graph starts.

2. **F** The graph shows a correlation between stock prices and production, but that does not necessarily mean that an increase in stock prices causes the increase in production.

3. **T** According to the figure, *y* decreased from about 12 to about 10.

4. **F** Between 1992 and 1993, *y* rose the most.

5. **T** As the figure makes clear, there has been an upward trend in *y*. A time-series graph makes it more straightforward to identify a trend in a variable.

6. **T** This is the definition of a cross-section graph.

Graphs Used in Economic Models

7. **T** If the graph slopes upward to the right, then an increase in the variable measured along the horizontal axis is associated with an increase in the variable measured on the vertical axis.

FIGURE **A1.13**
True/False Question 8

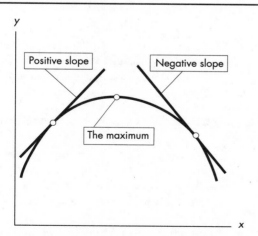

8. **F** As Figure A1.13 illustrates, before the maximum is reached, the relationship must be positive; af-

ter the maximum is attained, the relationship must be negative.

9. **T** To verify this answer, flip Figure A1.13 upside down. To the left of the minimum the line is falling, so its slope is negative; to the right the line is rising, so its slope is positive.

10. **F** If two unrelated variables are graphed on the same diagram, the "relationship" between the two is either a vertical or a horizontal straight line.

The Slope of a Relationship

FIGURE **A1.14**
True/False Question 11

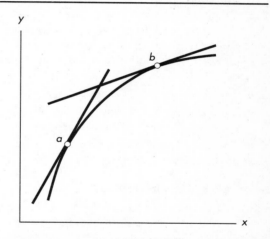

11. **T** Figure A1.14 shows a positive relationship whose slope decreases when moving rightward along it from point *a* to point *b*.

12. **F** Just the reverse is true: Divide the change in the variable on the *vertical* axis by the change in the variable on the *horizontal* axis.

13. **T** The definition of slope is $\Delta y/\Delta x$. So if a large change in *y* (the numerator) is associated with a small change in *x* (the denominator), the magnitude of the slope is relatively large. The large magnitude for the slope indicates that the line is relatively steep.

14. **T** Only the slope of a straight line is constant.

15. **T** This question tells precisely how to calculate the slope at a point on a curved line.

Graphing Relationships Among More Than Two Variables

16. **F** *Ceteris paribus* means that only the variables being studied change; all other variables do not change.

17. **F** For different amounts of rainfall, there are different curves showing the relationship between the price of a bushel of corn and the quantity that is grown.

■ Multiple Choice Answers

Graphing Data

1. **b** A time-series graph illustrates how the variable changes over time.

2. **c** A positive correlation between inflation rates and interest rates is reflected in a scatter diagram as a positive relationship; that is, the dots would tend to cluster along a line that slopes upward to the right.

3. **d** Any type of graph can be misleading.

4. **c** A scatter diagram will show the correlation between temperature and natural gas sales.

5. **a** The upward trend indicates a general increase in production over time.

Graphs Used in Economic Models

6. **a** In this case, an increase (or decrease) in x is associated with an increase (or decrease) in y, so the variables are positively related.

7. **c** Figure A1.7 shows that when income is $20,000 a year, then consumption is also $20,000 a year.

8. **a** The relationship is positive (higher income is related to higher consumption) and is linear.

9. **c** The term "positive relationship" means the same as "direct relationship."

10. **c** As x increases, y decreases; thus the relationship between x and y is negative.

11. **c** Figure A1.15 demonstrates that the change in y from 2 to 3 has no effect on x — it remains equal to 3.

The Slope of a Relationship

12. **a** A negative relationship has a negative slope; a positive relationship has a positive slope.

13. **b** A straight line — that is, a linear relationship — has a constant slope whereas nonlinear relation-

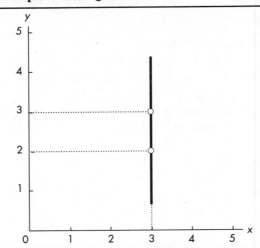

FIGURE **A1.15**
Multiple Choice Question 11

ships have slopes that vary. Thus the slope of a straight line is the same anywhere on the line.

14. **a** The slope is positive and, because the line is becoming steeper, the slope is increasing.

15. **c** The slope between the two points equals the change in the vertical distance (the "rise") divided by the change in the horizontal distance (the "run"), that is, $(5-1)/(4-2) = 2$.

16. **a** The slope equals the change in the variable measured along the vertical axis divided by the change in the variable measured along the horizontal axis, or $(2-1)/(3-2) = 1$.

17. **c** The figure shows a straight line. The slope of a straight line is constant, so the slope between $x = 4$ and $x = 5$ is the same as the slope between $x = 2$ and $x = 3$.

Graphing Relationships Among More Than Two Variables

18. **c** The curves showing the relationship between x and y demonstrate that x and y are negatively related. For any value of y, an increase in z is associated with a higher value for x, so x and z are positively related.

19. **b** Moving along one of the lines showing the relationship between x and y (say, the line with $z = 3$) shows that as x increases, y decreases.

20. **c** The higher value of z shifts the entire relationship between x and y rightward.

■ Answers to Short Answer Problems

FIGURE **A1.16**
Short Answer Problem 1

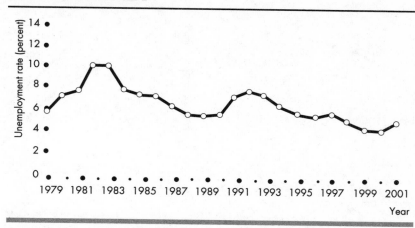

1. a. Figure A1.16 shows the time series of unemployment rates in the United States.

    b. The unemployment rate was the highest in 1982, when it equaled 9.7 percent.

FIGURE **A1.17**
Short Answer Problem 2

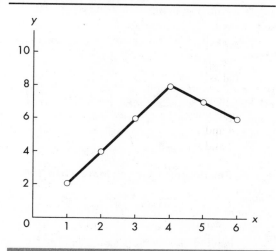

2. a. The relationship between x and y is illustrated in Figure A1.17.

    b. The relationship between x and y changes when x is 4. The relationship is positive between $x = 1$ and $x = 4$. Between $x = 4$ and $x = 6$, the relationship is negative.

    c. The slope equals $\Delta y/\Delta x$ or, in this case between $x = 1$ and $x = 2$, the slope is $(2 - 4)/(1 - 2) = 2$.

    d. Between $x = 5$ and $x = 6$, the slope is equal to $(7 - 6)/(5 - 6) = -1$.

    e. Over the range of values where the relationship between x and y is positive — from $x = 1$ to $x = 4$ — the slope is positive. Over the range where the relationship between x and y is negative — from $x = 4$ to $x = 6$ — the slope is negative. Thus positive relationships have positive slopes, and negative relationships have negative slopes.

3. a. The slope is $(8 - 2)/(5 - 2) = 2$.

    b. The slope is $(6 - 4)/(4 - 2) = 1$.

    c. The slope is $(9 - 6)/(5 - 4) = 3$.

4. Yes, a curve can have a positive, decreasing slope. Figure A1.18 (on the next page) illustrates such a relationship. In it, at relatively low values of x the slope is quite steep, indicating a high value for the slope. But as x increases, the curve becomes flatter, which means that the slope decreases. (To verify these statements, draw the tangent lines at points a and b and then compare their slopes.) This figure points out that there is a major difference between the value of a curve at some point, that is, what y equals, and what the curve's slope is at that point!

FIGURE **A1.18**
Short Answer Problem 4

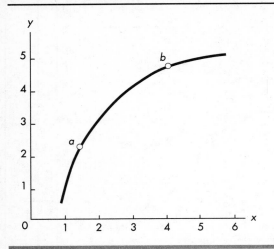

FIGURE **A1.19**
Short Answer Problem 5

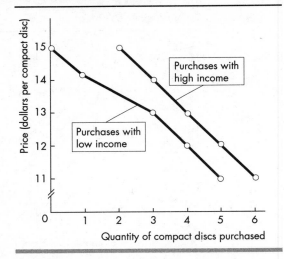

5. a. Because Bobby buys more compact discs when
       their price is lower, the relationship between the
       number of compact discs Bobby buys and the
       price is negative. Similarly, the relationship be-
       tween Bobby's income and the number of com-
       pact discs he buys is positive.

    b. Figure A1.19 illustrates the relationship between
       the price of a compact disc and the number
       Bobby buys when his income is low.

    c. Also illustrated in Figure A1.19 is the relation-
       ship between the number of compact discs
       Bobby buys and their price when Bobby's in-
       come
       is high.

    d. An increase in Bobby's income shifts the rela-
       tionship between the price of a compact disc and
       the number Bobby buys rightward.

■ You're the Teacher

1. "This *is* an economics class. But understanding
    some simple graphing ideas makes economics a lot
    easier to learn. Learning about graphing for its own
    sake is not important in this class; what is important
    is learning about graphing to help with the eco-
    nomics that we'll take up in the next chapter. So
    look at this chapter as a resource. Whether you al-
    ready knew everything in it before you looked at it
    or even if everything in it was brand new, anytime
    you get confused by something dealing with a tech-

nical point on a graph, you can look back at this
chapter for help. So, chill out; we'll get to the economics in the next chapter!"

2. "Graphs make understanding economics and the
    relationships between economic variables easier in
    three ways. First, graphs are extremely useful in
    showing the relationship between two economic
    variables. Imagine trying to determine the relation-
    ship between the interest rate and inflation rate if all
    we had was a bunch of numbers showing the inter-
    est rate and inflation rate each year for the past 30
    years. We'd have 60 numbers; good luck in trying
    to eyeball a relationship from them! Second, graphs
    can help us more easily understand what an eco-
    nomic theory is trying to explain because they allow
    us to see quickly how two variables are related. By
    showing us the general relationship, we can be as-
    sured that any conclusions we reach don't depend
    on the numbers that we decided to use. Finally,
    graphs sometimes show us a result we might not
    have otherwise noticed. If all we had were numbers,
    we could easily become lost trying to keep track of
    them. Graphs make our work easier, and for this
    reason we need to know how to use them!"

3. "The connection between the direction a line slopes,
    its slope, and whether the relationship is positive or
    negative is easy — once you see it! Take a look at
    Figure A1.20. In this figure, the line slopes upward
    to the right. The slope of this line is positive: An in-

FIGURE **A1.20**
You're the Teacher Question 3

FIGURE **A1.20**
You're the Teacher Question 3

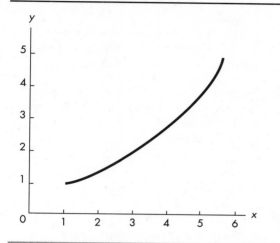

FIGURE **A1.21**
You're the Teacher Question 3

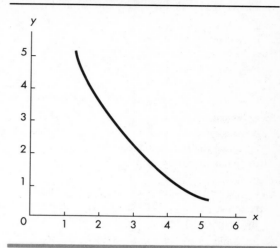

crease in x is associated with an increase in y. Because increases in x are related to increases in y, the graph shows a positive relationship between x and y.

Now look at Figure A1.21. Here the line slopes downward to the right. The slope of this line is negative: An increase in x is related to a decrease in y. Because x and y are inversely related, the relationship shown in Figure A1.21 is negative.

So, look: Positive relationships have positive slopes and negative relationships have negative slopes!

We can summarize these results for you so that you'll always be able to remember them by putting them all together:

Direction of line	Sign of slope	Type of relationship
Upward to the right ⇔	Positive ⇔	Positive
Downward to the right ⇔	Negative ⇔	Negative

This summary should help you keep everything straight. Things should be easier now."

Appendix Quiz

1. The vertical scale line of a graph is called the
   a. origin.
   b. scalar.
   c. *y*-axis.
   d. *x*-axis.

2. On a time-series graph, time is usually shown
   a. as a triangular area.
   b. as a rectangle.
   c. along the horizontal axis.
   d. at the origin.

3. A time-series diagram of the price of a purse between 1985 and 2001 has a downward trend. Hence the price of a purse
   a. is higher in 1985 than in 2001.
   b. is higher in 2001 than in 1985.
   c. definitely has fallen each year.
   d. None of the above.

4. A scatter diagram between two variables has a negative slope. Hence an increase in the variable measured on the vertical axis is associated with _____ the variable measured on the horizontal axis.
   a. an increase in
   b. no change in
   c. a decrease in
   d. no *consistent* change in

5. A graph shows the number of males and females majoring in economics in 2001. The kind of graph used to show this data would be
   a. a scatter diagram.
   b. a time-series graph.
   c. a cross-section graph.
   d. a Venn diagram.

6. Which of the following is true regarding a trend?
   a. Only a cross section graph shows trends.
   b. Both cross section and time-series graphs show trends.
   c. Only a time-series graph shows trends.
   d. Both time-series graphs and scatter plots show trends.

7. As a point on a graph moves upward and leftward, the value of its *x*-coordinate _____ and the value of its *y*-coordinate _____.
   a. rises; rises
   b. rises; falls
   c. falls; rises
   d. falls; falls

8. The slope of a line equals the
   a. change in *y* plus the change in *x*.
   b. change in *y* minus the change in *x*.
   c. change in *y* times the change in *x*.
   d. change in *y* divided by the change in *x*.

9. As a curve approaches a minimum, its slope will be
   a. positive before the minimum and negative after the minimum.
   b. negative before the minimum and positive after the minimum.
   c. remain constant on either side of the minimum.
   d. change, but in no consistent way from one curve to the next.

10. If the change in *y* equals 10 and the change in *x* equals −5,
    a. the slope of the curve is positive.
    b. the slope of the curve is negative.
    c. the curve must be a straight line.
    d. the slope cannot be calculated without more information.

The answers for this Appendix Quiz are on page 367

Chapter 2 THE ECONOMIC PROBLEM

Key Concepts

Production Possibilities and Opportunity Cost

The quantities of goods and services that can be produced are limited by the available amount of resources and by technology. The **production possibilities frontier** (*PPF*) is the boundary between those combinations of goods and services that can be produced and those that cannot.

FIGURE **2.1**
A *PPF* with Increasing Opportunity Costs

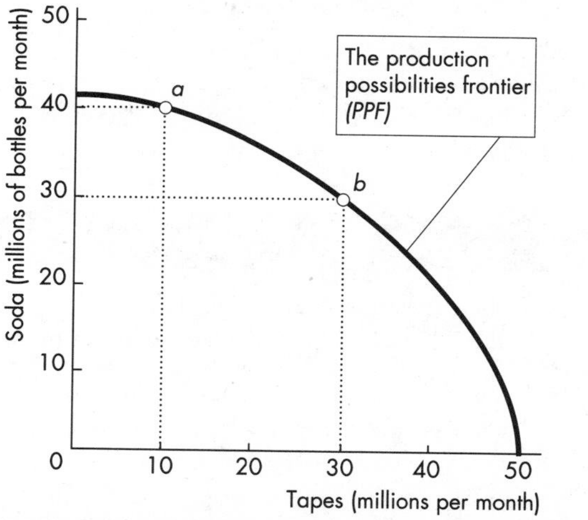

A *PPF* is illustrated in Figure 2.1. All production possibilities frontiers have two characteristics in common:

- Production points inside and on the *PPF* are attainable. Points beyond the *PPF* are not attainable.
- Production points on the *PPF* achieve **production efficiency** because more of one good can be obtained only by producing less of the other good. Production points inside the *PPF* are *inefficient*, with misallocated or unused resources.

Moving between points *on* the *PPF* involves a *tradeoff* because something must be given up to get more of something else. The opportunity cost of an action is the highest-valued alternative foregone. In Figure 2.1, the opportunity cost of obtaining 20 million more tapes by moving from point *a* to point *b* is the 10 million bottles of soda that are foregone. Opportunity cost is a ratio. It equals the decrease in the production of one good divided by the increase in the production of the other.

When resources are not equally productive in producing different goods and services, the *PPF* has increasing opportunity costs and bows outward, as illustrated in Figure 2.1. As more and more tapes are produced, the opportunity cost of a tape increases.

Using Resources Efficiently

- The **marginal cost** of a good is the opportunity cost of producing *one* more unit of it. Because of increasing opportunity cost, along a production possibilities frontier the marginal cost of an additional unit of a good increases as more is produced. So, the marginal cost curve, illustrated in Figure 2.2 on the next page, slopes upward.

  Preferences are a description of a person's likes and dislikes. Preferences can be described using the concept of marginal benefit. The **marginal benefit** from a good is the benefit a person obtains from consuming one more unit of it. The marginal benefit of a good is measured as the maximum amount someone is willing to pay for another unit of it. The marginal benefit from additional units of a good decreases as more is consumed. So the **marginal benefit curve**, which shows the relationship

FIGURE **2.2**
Efficient Use of Resources: *MB* and *MC*

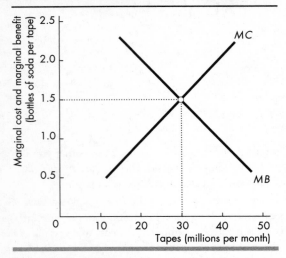

between the marginal benefit of a good and the quantity consumed, slopes downward as illustrated in Figure 2.2.

Allocative efficiency is reached when it is impossible to produce more of one good without giving up some other good that is valued more highly. Allocative efficiency occurs when the marginal benefit from another unit of a good equals its marginal cost. In Figure 2.2, producing 30 million tapes is the efficient allocation of resources between tapes and soda.

■ Economic Growth

Economic growth occurs when production expands. **Technological change,** the development of new goods and better ways of producing goods and services, and **capital accumulation,** the growth in capital resources, are two key factors that affect economic growth.

♦ Economic growth shifts the *PPF* outward. The faster it shifts, the more rapid is economic growth.

♦ The opportunity cost of economic growth is today's consumption.

♦ Nations that devote more resources to capital accumulation grow more rapidly.

■ Gains from Trade

♦ A person has a **comparative advantage** in producing a good if he or she can produce it at a lower opportunity cost than anyone else.

♦ Comparative advantage differs from absolute advantage. **Absolute advantage** occurs when a person can produce more goods in a given amount of time that another person.

Specialization according to comparative advantage and trading for other goods creates gains from trade because such specialization and exchange allows consumption (not production) at points outside the *PPF*.

♦ **Learning-by-doing** occurs when people become more productive in producing a good by repeatedly producing the good.

♦ **Dynamic comparative advantage** occurs when comparative advantage is the result of specializing in a good and becoming the lowest opportunity cost provider because of learning-by-doing.

■ The Market Economy

Property rights and markets have evolved to help reap the gains from specialization and trade.

♦ **Property rights** are social arrangements that set the terms of the ownership, use, and disposal of resources, goods, and services.

♦ A **market** is any arrangement that allows buyers and sellers to do business with each other. Markets pool information into a price, which signals buyers and sellers about the actions they should take.

Goods markets are where goods and services are bought and sold; factor markets are where factors of production are bought and sold. Markets coordinate decisions in the circular flow through price adjustments.

Helpful Hints

1. **ASSUMPTIONS OF THE *PPF*:** The *PPF* provides an example of the role played by simplifying assumptions in economic analysis. Clearly, no society in the world produces only two items but by assuming that there are such "two-good" nations, we can gain invaluable insights into the real world. For instance, we see that once a nation is producing on its production possibilities frontier, no matter how many goods it produces, to increase the production of one good necessarily has an opportunity cost in terms of some other good or goods that must be foregone. In addition, we also see that countries that devote a larger proportion of their resources to capital accumulation will have more rapid growth.

2. **INEFFICIENT PRODUCTION POINTS :** Points within the *PPF* curve are attainable but are inefficient. These production point occur whenever some inefficiency or misallocation emerges within the economy, such as excessive unemployment of any resource or an inefficient use of resources. Points beyond the *PPF* are unattainable. They are *not* classified as either efficient or inefficient because they are not production combinations that the society can reach.

FIGURE **2.3**

A *PPF* Between Corn and Cloth

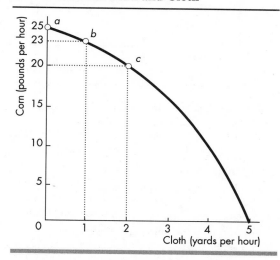

3. **CALCULATING OPPORTUNITY COST :** A helpful formula for opportunity cost results from the fact that opportunity cost is a ratio. Opportunity cost equals the quantity of goods you must give up divided by the quantity of goods you will get.

For instance, consider the nation whose *PPF* is in Figure 2.3. If we move along the *PPF* from *a* to *b*, what is the opportunity cost of an additional yard of cloth? The nation must give up 2 pounds of corn (25 – 23) to get 1 yard of cloth (1 – 0). So the opportunity cost of the first yard of cloth is 2 pounds of corn divided by 1 yard of cloth or 2 pounds of corn per yard of cloth. Next, if we move from *b* to *c*, the opportunity cost of the second yard of cloth is calculated the same way and is 3 pounds of corn per yard of cloth.

Questions

■ **True/False and Explain**

Production Possibilities and Opportunity Cost

FIGURE **2.4**

True/False Questions 1 and 2

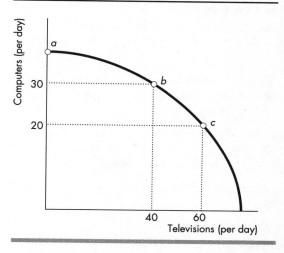

1. In Figure 2.4 point *a* is <u>NOT</u> attainable.

2. In Figure 2.4 the opportunity cost of moving from point *b* to point *c* is 10 computers.

3. From a point on the *PPF*, rearranging production and producing more of *all* goods is possible.

4. From a point within the *PPF*, rearranging production and producing more of *all* goods is possible.

5. Production efficiency requires producing at a point on the *PPF*.

6. Along a bowed-out *PPF*, as more of a good is produced, the opportunity cost of producing the good diminishes.

Using Resources Efficiently

7. The marginal cost of the 20th ton of cement equals the cost of producing all 20 tons of cement.

8. As people have more of a product, the product's marginal benefit decreases.

9. Efficiency is achieved by producing the amount of a good such that the marginal benefit of the last unit

produced exceeds its marginal cost by as much as possible.

Economic Growth

10. Economic growth is illustrated by outward shifts in the *PPF*.

11. Increasing a nation's economic growth rate has an opportunity cost.

Gains from Trade

12. Daphne definitely has a comparative advantage in producing sweaters if she can produce more than Lisa.

13. If two individuals have different opportunity costs of producing goods, both can gain from specialization and trade.

14. If the United States has an absolute advantage in growing corn and making computers, it must have a comparative advantage in growing corn.

15. Learning-by-doing can lead to dynamic comparative advantage.

The Market Economy

16. Buyers and sellers must meet face-to-face in a market.

17. Price adjustments coordinate decisions in goods markets, but not in factor markets.

■ Multiple Choice

Production Possibilities and Opportunity Cost

1. Production points on the *PPF* itself are
   a. efficient but not attainable.
   b. efficient and attainable
   c. inefficient but not attainable.
   d. inefficient and attainable.

2. If the United States can increase its production of automobiles without decreasing its production of any other good, the United States must have been producing at a point
   a. within its *PPF*.
   b. on its *PPF*.
   c. beyond its *PPF*.
   d. None of the above are correct because increasing the production of one good without decreasing the production of another good is impossible.

FIGURE 2.5
Multiple Choice Questions 3 and 4

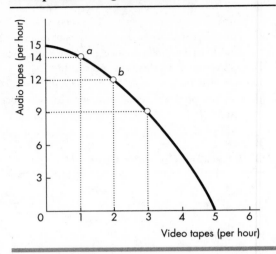

3. In Figure 2.5, at point *a* what is the opportunity cost of producing one more video tape?
   a. 14 audio tapes
   b. 3 audio tapes
   c. 2 audio tapes
   d. There is no opportunity cost.

4. In Figure 2.5, at point *b* what is the opportunity cost of producing one more video tape?
   a. 12 audio tapes
   b. 3 audio tapes
   c. 2 audio tapes
   d. There is no opportunity cost.

5. Production efficiency means that
   a. scarcity is no longer a problem.
   b. producing more of one good without producing less of some other good is not possible.
   c. as few resources as possible are being used in production.
   d. producing another unit of the good has no opportunity cost.

6. The existence of the tradeoff along the *PPF* means that the *PPF* is
   a. bowed outward.
   b. linear.
   c. negatively sloped.
   d. positively sloped.

7. The bowed-outward shape of a *PPF*
   a. is due to capital accumulation.
   b. reflects the unequal application of technology in production.
   c. illustrates the fact that no opportunity cost is incurred for increasing the production of the good measured on the horizontal axis but it is incurred to increase production of the good measured along the vertical axis.
   d. is due to the existence of increasing opportunity cost.

A nation produces only two goods — yak butter and rutabagas. Three alternative combinations of production that are on its *PPF* are given in Table 2.1. Use this information to answer the next three questions.

TABLE **2.1**

Production Possibilities

Possibility	Pounds of yak butter	Number of rutabagas
a	600	0
b	400	100
c	0	200

8. In moving from combination *a* to *b*, the opportunity cost of producing more rutabagas is
   a. 6 pounds of yak butter per rutabaga.
   b. 4 pounds of yak butter per rutabaga.
   c. 2 pounds of yak butter per rutabaga.
   d. 0 pounds of yak butter per rutabaga.

9. In moving from combination *b* to *a*, the opportunity cost of producing more pounds of yak butter is
   a. 0.10 rutabaga per pound of yak butter.
   b. 0.50 rutabaga per pound of yak butter.
   c. 1.00 rutabaga per pound of yak butter.
   d. 2.00 rutabagas per pound of yak butter.

10. Producing 400 pounds of yak butter and 50 rutabagas is
    a. not possible for this nation.
    b. possible and is an efficient production point.
    c. possible, but is an inefficient production point.
    d. an abhorrent thought.

Using Resources Efficiently

11. Moving along a bowed-out *PPF* between milk and cotton, as more milk is produced the marginal cost of an additional gallon of milk
    a. rises.
    b. does not change.
    c. falls.
    d. probably changes, but in an ambiguous direction.

12. The most anyone is willing to pay for another purse is $30. Currently the price of a purse is $40, and the cost of producing another purse is $50. The marginal benefit of a purse is
    a. $50.
    b. $40.
    c. $30.
    d. An amount not given in the answers above.

13. If the marginal benefit from another computer exceeds the marginal cost of the computer, then to use resources efficiently,
    a. more resources should be used to produce computers.
    b. fewer resources should be used to produce computers.
    c. if the marginal benefit exceeds the marginal cost by as much as possible, the efficient amount of resources are being used to produce computers.
    d. none of the above is correct because marginal benefit and marginal cost have nothing to do with using resources efficiently.

Economic Growth

14. Economic growth
    a. creates unemployment.
    b. has no opportunity cost.
    c. shifts the *PPF* outward.
    d. makes it more difficult for a nation to produce on its *PPF*.

15. The *PPF* shifts if
    a. the unemployment rate falls.
    b. people decide they want more of one good and less of another.
    c. the prices of the goods and services produced rise.
    d. the resources available to the nation change.

16. An increase in the nation's capital stock will
    a. shift the *PPF* outward.
    b. cause a movement along the *PPF* upward and leftward.
    c. cause a movement along the *PPF* downward and rightward.
    d. move the nation from producing within the *PPF* to producing at a point closer to the *PPF*.

17. One of the opportunity costs of economic growth is
    a. capital accumulation.
    b. technological change.
    c. reduced current consumption.
    d. the gain in future consumption.

18. In general, the more resources that are devoted to technological research, the
    a. greater is current consumption.
    b. higher is the unemployment rate.
    c. faster the *PPF* shifts outward.
    d. more the *PPF* will bow outward.

Gains from Trade

19. In order to achieve the maximum gains from trade, people should specialize according to
    a. property rights.
    b. *PPF*.
    c. absolute advantage.
    d. comparative advantage.

In one day Brandon can either plow 40 acres of land or plant 20 acres. In one day Christopher can either plow 28 acres of land or plant 7 acres. Use this information to answer the next four questions.

20. Which of the following statements about absolute advantage is correct?
    a. Brandon has an absolute advantage in both plowing and planting.
    b. Brandon has an absolute advantage only in plowing.
    c. Brandon has an absolute advantage only in planting.
    d. Christopher has an absolute advantage both in plowing and planting.

21. Brandon has
    a. a comparative advantage both in plowing and planting.
    b. a comparative advantage only in plowing.
    c. a comparative advantage only in planting.
    d. a comparative advantage in neither in plowing and planting.

22. Christopher has
    a. an absolute advantage only in planting.
    b. an absolute advantage only in plowing.
    c. a comparative advantage only in planting.
    d. a comparative advantage only in plowing.

23. Brandon and Christopher can
    a. both gain from exchange if Brandon specializes in planting and Christopher in plowing.
    b. both gain from exchange if Brandon specializes in plowing and Christopher in planting.
    c. exchange, but only Brandon will gain from the exchange.
    d. exchange, but only Christopher will gain from the exchange.

24. A nation can *produce* at a point outside its *PPF*
    a. when it trades with other nations.
    b. when it is producing products as efficiently as possible.
    c. when there is no unemployment.
    d. at no time ever.

25. A nation can *consume* at a point outside its *PPF*
    a. when it trades with other nations.
    b. when it is producing products as efficiently as possible.
    c. when there is no unemployment.
    d. at no time ever.

The Market Economy

26. Which of the following does <u>NOT</u> help organize trade?
    a. Property rights
    b. Markets
    c. The production possibilities frontier
    d. None of the above because all these answers given help organize trade.

27. In markets, people's decisions are coordinated by
    a. specialization according to absolute advantage.
    b. changes in property rights.
    c. learning-by-doing.
    d. adjustments in prices.

■ Short Answer Problems

1. What does the negative slope of the *PPF* mean?
   Why is a *PPF* bowed out?

2. In Figure 2.6 indicate which points are production
   efficient and which are inefficient. Also show which
   points are attainable and which are not attainable.

FIGURE **2.6**
Short Answer Problem 2

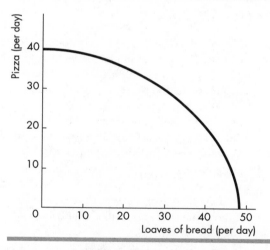

3. Sydna is stranded on a desert island and can either
   fish or harvest dates. Six points on her production
   possibilities frontier are given in Table 2.2.
   a. In Figure 2.7 plot these possibilities, label the
      points, and draw the *PPF*.
   b. If Sydna moves from possibility *c* to possibility
      d, what is the opportunity cost per fish?
   c. If Sydna moves from possibility *d* to possibility
      e, what is the opportunity cost per fish?
   d. In general, what happens to the opportunity
      cost of a fish as more fish are caught?
   e. In general, what happens to the opportunity
      cost of dates as more dates are harvested?
   f. Based on the original *PPF* you plotted, is a
      combination of 40 dates and 1 fish attainable?
      Is this combination an efficient one? Explain.

TABLE **2.2**
Sydna's Production Possibilities

Possibility	Dates gathered (per day)	Fish caught (per day)
a	54	0
b	50	1
c	42	2
d	32	3
e	20	4
f	0	5

FIGURE **2.7**
Short Answer Problem 3

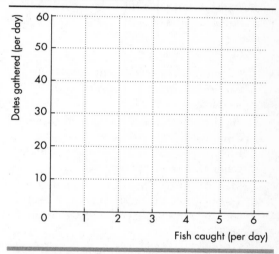

4. If the following events occurred (each is a separate
   event, unaccompanied by any other event), what
   would happen to the *PPF* in Problem 3?
   a. A new fishing pond is discovered.
   b. The output of dates is increased.
   c. Sydna finds a ladder that enables her to gather
      slightly more dates.
   d. A second person, with the same set of fishing
      and date-gathering skills as Sydna, is stranded
      on the island.

TABLE **2.3**

Marginal Benefit and Marginal Cost of Pizza

Slice of pizza	Marginal benefit of slice	Marginal cost of slice	Marginal benefit minus marginal cost
1	6.0	1.5	___
2	5.0	2.0	___
3	4.0	2.5	___
4	3.0	3.0	___
5	2.0	3.5	___
6	1.0	4.0	___

5. A nation produces only pizza and tacos. Table 2.3 shows the marginal benefit and marginal cost schedules for slices of pizza in terms of tacos per slice of pizza.

    a. Complete Table 2.3.

    b. For the first slice of pizza, after paying the marginal cost, how much marginal benefit — if any — is left?

    c. For the second slice, after paying the marginal cost, how much marginal benefit — if any — is left? How does your answer to this question compare to your answer to part (b)?

    d. Should the first slice of pizza be produced? Should the second one be produced? Explain you answers, especially your answer about the second slice.

    e. In a diagram, draw the marginal benefit and marginal benefit curves. Indicate the quantity of pizza slices that uses resources efficiently.

6. Bearing in mind the point that resources are limited, explain why is it important for a nation to use its resources efficiently.

7. Suppose that both the United States and France produce computers and wine. Table 2.4 shows what each country can produce in an hour.

    a. On graph paper, draw the *PPF* for the United States for one hour.

    b. On graph paper, draw the *PPF* for France for one hour.

    c. Complete Table 2.5.

    d. In what good(s) does the United States have a comparative advantage? France?

    e. Initially the United States uses half its resources to produce wine and half to produce computers.

TABLE **2.4**

Production in France and the United States

	Computers produced in an hour	Bottles of wine produced in an hour
United States	10,000	20,000
France	12,000	8,000

TABLE **2.5**

Short Answer Problem 7 (c)

	Opportunity cost of one computer	Opportunity cost of one bottle of wine
United States	___	___
France	___	___

How much wine and how many computers are produced in an hour in the United States? France also devotes half her resources to computers and half to wine. How many computers and bottles of wine does France produce in an hour? What is the total amount of wine produced by France and the United States in an hour? The total number of computers?

    f. Suppose that the United States specializes in wine and France in computers. What is the total amount of wine produced by France and the United States now? The total number of computers?

    g. What do your answers to parts (e) and (f) show?

8. How do property rights affect people's incentives to create new music?

■ **You're the Teacher**

1. "The idea of the production possibilities frontier is stupid. I mean, after all, who ever heard of a nation that produces only two goods. Come on, every nation produces millions, probably billions of goods. Why do I have to bother to learn about the production possibilities frontier when it is so unrealistic?" One reason for this student to learn about the production possibilities frontier is that it will probably be on the exams. But there are other reasons, too. Explain some of them to help motivate this student.

Answers

True/False Answers

Production Possibilities and Opportunity Cost

1. **F** *Any* point on the production possibilities frontier is attainable, even points where the *PPF* intersects the axes.

2. **T** The opportunity cost equals the number of computers foregone, in this case the fall from 30 computers at point *b* to 20 at point *c*.

3. **F** Points on the frontier are production efficient, so increasing the production of one good necessarily requires producing fewer of some other good.

FIGURE **2.8**
True/False Question 4

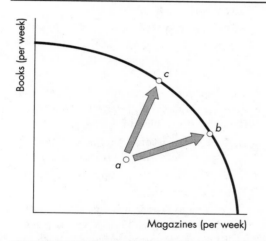

---

4. **T** Points within the frontier are inefficient, which means its possible to rearrange production and boost the production of all goods and services. This condition is illustrated in Figure 2.8, where from (the inefficient) point *a*, it is possible to move to points such as *b* or *c* where more of both books and magazines are produced.

5. **T** Production efficiency implies that the production of one good can be increased *only if* the production of another good is decreased, which is true only on the *PPF* itself.

6. **F** As more of a good is produced, the opportunity cost of additional units increases.

Using Resources Efficiently

7. **F** The marginal cost is the cost of the 20th ton itself, not the cost of producing all 20 tons.

8. **T** As people have more of a product, they are willing to pay less for additional units, which means that the marginal benefit of the product will decrease.

9. **F** For resources to be allocated efficiently, it is necessary for the marginal benefit of the last unit produced to equal the marginal cost of the unit.

Economic Growth

10. **T** As the *PPF* shifts outward, the nation is able to produce more of all goods.

11. **T** The opportunity cost is the loss of current consumption.

Gains from Trade

12. **F** Based on the information in the problem, Daphne has an absolute advantage, but without more information we cannot tell whether she has a comparative advantage.

13. **T** A key observation is that *both* individuals gain.

14. **F** Comparative advantage requires *comparing* the opportunity cost of producing corn in the United States with the opportunity cost of producing it elsewhere.

15. **T** Learning-by-doing means that the cost of producing a good falls as more is produced, so the nation (or person) ultimately acquires a comparative advantage in making the good.

The Market Economy

16. **F** Buyers and sellers communicate with each other in markets, but in most markets they do not meet face-to-face.

17. **F** Price adjustments coordinate decisions in all markets.

Multiple Choice Answers

Production Possibilities and Opportunity Cost

1. **b** *Only* points on the frontier are both attainable and efficient.

2. **a** Only from points within the frontier can the production of a good increase without decreasing the production of another good.

3. **c** By producing 1 more video tape, audio tape production falls by 2 (from 14 to 12), so the op-

portunity cost of the video tape is the ratio of 2
audio tapes to the 1 video tape, that is, 2 audio
tapes per video tape.

4. **b** As more video tapes are produced, the opportunity cost of an additional video tape gets larger.

5. **b** This answer is the definition of production
efficiency.

6. **c** When production is on the *PPF*, the tradeoff is
that if more of one good is produced, then some
other good must be foregone. This result means
that the *PPF* has a negative slope.

7. **d** Increasing opportunity cost means that, as more
of a good is produced, its opportunity cost increases. As a result, the *PPF* bows outward.

8. **c** Moving from *a* to *b* gains 100 rutabagas and
loses 200 pounds of yak butter, so the opportunity cost is (200 pounds of yak butter)/(100 rutabagas), or 2 pounds of yak butter per
rutabaga.

9. **b** 100 rutabagas are foregone, so the opportunity
cost is (100 rutabagas)/(200 pounds of yak butter), or 0.50 rutabagas per pound of yak butter.
Note how the opportunity cost of a rutabaga is
the inverse of the opportunity cost of a pound of
yak butter, as calculated in the answer to the
previous question.

10. **c** When 400 pounds of yak butter are produced, a
maximum of 100 rutabagas can be produced; if
only 50 rutabagas are produced, the combination is inefficient.

Using Resources Efficiently

11. **a** Along a bowed-out *PPF*, as more of a good is
produced, its marginal cost — the opportunity
cost of producing another unit — rises.

12. **c** The marginal benefit from a good is the maximum that a person is willing to pay for the good.

13. **a** The benefit from the computer exceeds the cost
of producing the computer, so society will gain
if resources are allocated so that the computer
is produced.

Economic Growth

14. **c** Economic growth makes attainable previously
unattainable production levels.

15. **d** An increase in resources shifts the *PPF* outward;
a decrease shifts it leftward. (A decrease in the
unemployment rate moves the nation from a

point in the interior of the *PPF* to a point closer
to the frontier.)

16. **a** Increases in a nation's resources create economic
growth and shift the nation's *PPF* outward.

17. **c** If a nation devotes more resources to capital
accumulation or technological development,
which are the main sources of growth, fewer resources can be used to produce goods for current
consumption.

18. **c** The more resources used for technological research, the more rapid is economic growth.

Gains from Trade

19. **d** Specializing according to comparative advantage
reduces the opportunity cost of producing goods
and services.

20. **a** Brandon can produce more of both goods than
Christopher, so Brandon has an absolute
advantage in both goods.

21. **c** Brandon's opportunity cost of planting an acre
of land is plowing 2 acres, whereas Christopher's
opportunity cost of planting an acre is plowing 4
acres.

22. **d** Christopher's opportunity cost of plowing an
acre is planting 1/4 an acre, while Brandon's opportunity cost is planting 1/2 an acre.

23. **a** By specializing according to their comparative
advantages, both can gain from exchange.

24. **d** The *PPF* shows the maximum amounts that can
be produced.

25. **a** When a nation specializes according to its comparative advantage and trades with another spe-
cialist nation, both can consume at levels beyond
their *PPFs*.

The Market Economy

26. **c** The production possibilities frontier shows the
limits to production and does not help organize
trade.

27. **d** Changes in prices create incentives for people to
change their actions.

■ Answers to Short Answer Problems

1. The negative slope of the *PPF* indicates that increasing the production of one good means that the
production of some other good decreases.

A *PPF* is bowed out because the existence of non-identical resources creates an increasing opportunity cost as the production of a good is increased. Because resources are not identical, some are better suited for producing one good than another. So when resources are switched from producing items for which they are well suited to producing goods for which they are ill suited, the opportunity cost of increasing the output of these goods rises.

FIGURE 2.9
Short Answer Problem 2

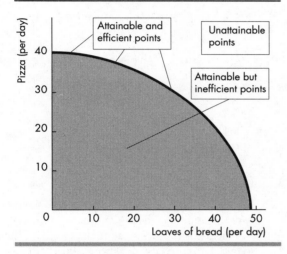

2. Figure 2.9 shows the efficient/inefficient points and attainable/not attainable points. The attainable but inefficient points are shaded; the attainable and efficient points lie on the *PPF* itself; and the unattainable points are located beyond the *PPF*.

3. a. Figure 2.10 shows the *PPF*.

   b. Moving from *c* to *d* means that the number of fish caught increases by 1 while the number of dates gathered falls from 42 to 32. Catching 1 fish costs 10 dates, so the opportunity cost of the fish is 10 dates. In terms of a formula, the opportunity cost of this fish is:

$$\frac{42 \text{ dates} - 32 \text{ dates}}{3 \text{ fish} - 2 \text{ fish}} = 10 \text{ dates per fish.}$$

   c. Moving from *d* to *e* indicates that the opportunity cost of the fish is 12 dates: The number of dates gathered falls from 32 to 20 while the number of fish caught increases by 1.

FIGURE 2.10
Short Answer Problem 3

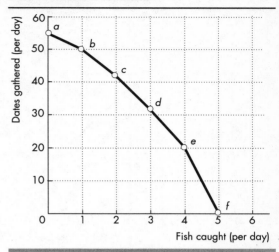

   d. As more fish are caught, the opportunity cost of an additional fish rises. In particular, the first fish has an opportunity cost of only 4 dates; the second, 8 dates; the third, 10 dates; the fourth, 12 dates; and the fifth, 20 dates.

   e. As more dates are gathered, the opportunity cost of a date rises. Moving from *f* to *e* shows that the first 20 dates cost only 1 fish so that the opportunity cost of a date here is 1/20 of a fish. Going from *e* to *d*, however, makes the opportunity cost of a date 1/12 of a fish. This pattern continues so that as more dates are gathered, their opportunity cost increases. Finally, moving from *b* to *a* has the largest opportunity cost for a date, 1/4 of a fish.

   As parts (d) and (e) demonstrate, there is increasing opportunity cost moving along the *PPF*. That is, as more fish are caught, their opportunity cost — in terms of foregone dates — increases and as more dates are gathered, their opportunity cost — in terms of foregone fish — also increases. It is these increasing opportunity costs that account for the bowed-outward shape of the *PPF*.

   f. This combination is within the *PPF* and is attainable. It is inefficient because Sydna could produce more of either or both goods. Therefore she is not organizing her activities as efficiently as possible.

FIGURE **2.11**

Short Answer Problem 4 (a)

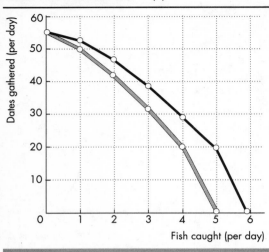

4. a. A new fishing pond increases the number of fish Sydna can catch, but it does not affect the maximum number of dates she can gather. Her *PPF* shifts generally as shown in Figure 2.11.

   b. Increasing her output of dates does not affect the *PPF*. Sydna might increase her gathering of dates either by moving from a point within the *PPF* to a point on (or closer to) the frontier or by moving along the frontier. Neither of these actions shifts the *PPF*.

FIGURE **2.12**

Short Answer Problem 4 (c)

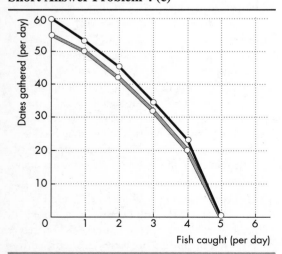

   c. The ladder increases the number of dates that Sydna can gather, but has no effect on the fish

that she can catch. As a result, the maximum number of dates increases, but the maximum number of fish does not change. The *PPF* shifts in the same general pattern as shown in Figure 2.12.

FIGURE **2.13**

Short Answer Problem 4 (d)

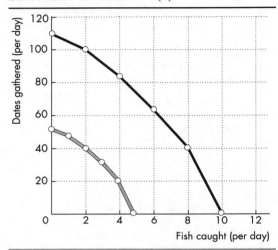

   d. Having a second worker on the island boosts both the number of dates that can be gathered *and* the number of fish that can be caught. If the second person has the same set of skills as Sydna, the *PPF* shifts out in a "parallel" manner, as illustrated in Figure 2.13. Be sure to note that the scales on the axes in Figure 2.13 are different from those on the axes in Figures 2.10–2.12.

TABLE **2.6**

Marginal Benefit and Marginal Cost of Pizza

Slice of pizza	Marginal benefit of slice	Marginal cost of slice	Marginal benefit minus marginal cost
1	6.0	1.5	4.5
2	5.0	2.0	3.0
3	4.0	2.5	1.5
4	3.0	3.0	0.0
5	2.0	3.5	−1.5
6	1.0	4.0	−3.0

5. a. Table 2.6 shows the answers.

   b. For the first slice of pizza, after paying the marginal cost, there is 4.5 of marginal benefit left.

c. For the second slice of pizza, after paying the marginal cost, there is 3.0 of marginal benefit left. After paying the marginal cost, there is less marginal benefit left for the second slice of pizza than for the first. There is less surplus because the marginal benefit of the second slice is less than that of the first slice and the marginal cost the second slice is more than that of the first one.

d. The first slice should be produced because the marginal benefit from the first slice exceeds its marginal cost. The second slice also should be produced for the same reason. As long as the marginal benefit from a slice of pizza exceeds its marginal cost, society benefits if the slice is produced. The "net benefit" from the first slice is more than that of the second slice, but as long as there is a positive net benefit, society benefits.

FIGURE **2.14**

Short Answer Problem 5 (e)

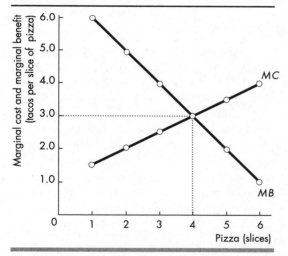

e. Figure 2.14 shows the marginal cost and marginal benefit curves. Four slices of pizza are the quantity that uses resources efficiently because the marginal benefit from the fourth slice equals its marginal cost. The marginal benefit for any greater quantity of pizza slices is less than the marginal cost of the slice, so producing these units would result in a net loss for society.

6. A nation should use its resources efficiently because it has only a limited quantity of them. If resources are used inefficiently, there is waste and fewer of people's wants can be satisfied. By producing effi-

ciently, society ensures that as many of the most important wants, measured by the marginal benefit from the goods that satisfy those wants, are satisfied.

FIGURE **2.15**

Short Answer Problem 7 (a)

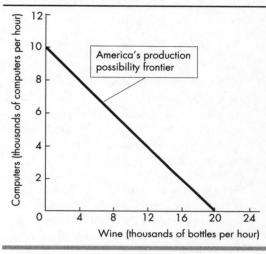

7. a. Figure 2.15 shows the *PPF* for the United States. The maximum amount of wine that can be produced is 20,000 bottles and the maximum number of computers that can be produced is 10,000.

FIGURE **2.16**

Short Answer Problem 7 (b)

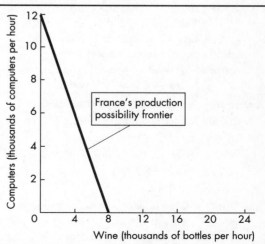

b. Figure 2.16 shows the French *PPF*.

TABLE 2.7

Short Answer Problem 7 (c)

	Opportunity cost of one computer	Opportunity cost of one bottle of wine
United States	2 bottles of wine	½ computer
France	2/3 bottles of wine	1½ computer

c. Table 2.7 shows the opportunity costs for the goods. To illustrate how this table was obtained, we can use the opportunity cost of a computer in the United States as an example. To produce one computer in the United States requires that resources work for 1/10,000 of an hour at manufacturing computers. So to produce an additional computer, resources must be switched from the wine industry to the computer industry for 1/10,000 of an hour. During this time, if left in the wine industry, the resources could otherwise have produced (1/10,000) (20,000 bottles of wine) or 2 bottles of wine. Hence to produce one additional computer in the United States, 2 bottles of wine are foregone. Two bottles of wine, then, are the opportunity cost of the computer. The rest of the opportunity costs are calculated similarly.

d. The United States has a comparative advantage in wine because the opportunity cost of a bottle of wine in the United States — ½ computer — is less than the opportunity cost of a bottle of wine in France —1½ computer. France has a comparative advantage in the production of computers, because its opportunity cost — 2/3 bottle of wine — is less than that in the United States — 2 bottles of wine.

e. In the United States, 5,000 computers and 10,000 bottles of wine are produced in an hour. In France, 6,000 computers and 4,000 bottles of wine are produced in an hour. Overall, 11,000 computers and 14,000 bottles of wine are produced in an hour.

f. With the United States specializing in wine, 20,000 bottles of wine are produced in an hour. Because France specializes in computers, 12,000 computers are produced in an hour.

g. With specialization, world computer production rises by 1,000 computers per hour and world production of wine rises by 6,000 bottles per hour. The fact that world production of wine and computers *both* increase demonstrates that specialization, according to comparative advantage, can boost world output of all goods.

8. Property rights play a key role in shaping the incentive to create new music or, more generally, to create *any* new computer program, book, pharmaceutical drug, and so forth. Creation is costly because resources, time, and effort must be devoted to this process. By securing the property right to new music, the musician stands to benefit greatly from the resources expended. But if the person cannot obtain a property right, anyone can copy the new music. In that case the musician's return will be dissipated when a lot of people copy the music and, indeed, someone else might reap the rewards. Property rights, by promising that the musician will personally benefit from the effort involved in creating the music, motivate significantly more new music than would occur in the absence of property rights.

■ **You're the Teacher**

1. "*All* economic models vastly simplify the complex reality. But that is no reason to throw them away. The lessons that can be learned from the simple two-good *PPF* carry over to the real world. For instance, the two-good *PPF* shows that there are limits to production. These limits are represented by the *PPF* curve, which divides attainable from unattainable production points. Now, just as you say, in the real world billions of goods are produced. But there are still limits. But no matter how many goods a nation produces, every nation faces a limit of how much it can produce, just as in the simple two-good *PPF* case.

"Plus, the simple *PPF* model demonstrates that production can be efficient or inefficient. This result is also true in the real world. "And, the two-good *PPF* shows that once production is efficient — a point on the *PPF* — increasing the output of one good has an opportunity cost because the production of the other good must be reduced. The same is true in our real world. If we are producing efficiently, if we want to produce more of one good, we have to give up other goods. So, based on the assumption that there are only two goods, the *PPF* teaches us stuff that we can apply everywhere, not just on the next test."

Chapter Quiz

1. Consider a constant slope *PPF* with a vertical intercept of 80 guns and a horizontal intercept of 120 tons of butter. The opportunity cost of increasing butter output from 30 to 31 tons is
   a. 1/2 gun.
   b. 2/3 gun.
   c. 1 gun.
   d. 1 1/2 guns.

2. A nation produces at a point outside its *PPF*
   a when it trades with other nations.
   b. when it produces inefficiently.
   c. when it produces efficiently.
   d. never.

3. Which of the following statements is true?
   a. All resources are made by people.
   b. Human resources are called labor.
   c. Capital is made only by labor.
   d. Human capital is a contradiction in terms.

4. A situation in which some resources are used inefficiently is represented in a *PPF* diagram by
   a. any point on either the vertical or horizontal axis.
   b. the midpoint of the *PPF*.
   c. a point outside the *PPF*.
   d. a point inside the *PPF*.

5. Robert has decided to write the essay that is due in his economics class rather than watch a movie. The movie he will miss is Robert's ____ of writing the essay.
   a. opportunity cost
   b. explicit cost
   c. implicit cost
   d. discretionary cost

6. The cost of textbooks ____ and the earnings foregone because of attending college ____ part of the opportunity cost of attending college.
   a. is; are
   b. is; are not
   c. is not; are
   d. is not; are not

7. The best alternative foregone from an action is called the action's
   a. "loss".
   b. "money cost".
   c. "direct cost".
   d. "opportunity cost".

8. The marginal benefit of a product is the
   a. benefit that the product gives to someone other than the buyer.
   b. maximum someone is willing to pay for that unit of the product.
   c. benefit of the product that exceeds the marginal cost of the product.
   d. benefit of the product divided by the total number of units purchased.

9. A marginal benefit curve has a ____ slope; a marginal cost curve has a ____ slope.
   a. positive; positive
   b. positive; negative
   c. negative; positive
   d. negative; negative

10. The production possibilities frontier will shift inward as a result of
    a. an increase in the production of consumption goods.
    b. an increase in R&D expenditure.
    c. an increase in population.
    d. destruction of part of the nation's capital stock.

The answers for this Chapter Quiz are on page 367

Reading Between the Lines

TWISTERS LEAVE AT LEAST 6 DEAD

On April 29 2002 the tragic effects of an outbreak of tornadoes were reported. These tornadoes swept through five states, Missouri, Illinois, Kentucky, Virginia, and Maryland. They killed at least six people and destroyed businesses, homes, and trains. The damage and deaths in the Midwest were thought to be the result of one F3 tornado (wind speeds of 180 mph) that touched down in a path that was over 100 miles long.

For details, go to The Economics Place web site, the Economics in the News archive, www.economicsplace.com/econ5e/einarchives.html

■ Analyze It

Tornadoes are one of nature's most destructive forces. They strike quickly and often without warning. They also create an economic impact because they affect the nation's production possibilities.

1. Presume a nation produces two goods, Good A and Good B. In a production possibilities diagram, show the effect of a major outbreak of destructive tornadoes.

Mid-Term Examination

■ Chapter I

1. Willy makes $25 an hour as a carpenter. He must take two hours off from work (unpaid) to go to the dentist to have a tooth pulled. The dentist charges $60. In terms of dollars, the opportunity cost of Willy's visit to the dentist is
   a. $25.
   b. $50.
   c. $60
   d. $110.

2. A company produces 100 units of a good at a cost of $400 or produces 101 units of the same good at a cost of $415 dollars. The $15 difference is
   a. the marginal benefit of producing 101 units.
   b. the marginal cost of producing the 101st unit.
   c. the marginal cost of producing the first unit.
   d. less than the average cost.

3. Positive statements are statements about
   a. prices.
   b. quantities.
   c. what is.
   d. what ought to be.

4. The branch of economics that studies individual markets within the economy is called
   a. macroeconomics.
   b. microeconomics.
   c. individual economics.
   d. market economy.

■ Chapter 2

5. Output combinations beyond the production possibility frontier
   a. result in more rapid growth.
   b. are associated with unused resources.
   c. are attainable only with the full utilization of all resources.
   d. are unattainable.

6. The *PPF* shifts inward as a result of
   a. a decrease in the production of consumption goods.
   b. an increase in R&D expenditure.
   c. an increase in population.
   d. the destruction of a portion of the capital stock.

7. Whenever a person can produce less of all goods than anyone else, that person
   a. should specialize in nothing.
   b. has a comparative advantage in something.
   c. should be self-sufficient.
   d. has a comparative advantage in nothing.

8. To obtain all the gains available from comparative advantage, individuals or countries must do more than trade, they must also
   a. specialize.
   b. save.
   c. invest.
   d. engage in research and development.

Answers

■ Reading Between the Lines

1. Tornadoes destroy part of the nation's ability to produce goods and services because they kill people and destroy capital. As a result, a severe outbreak of tornadoes decreases the nation's production possibilities and thereby shifts the nation's production possibilities frontier inward. Figure 1 shows the effect of an outbreak of tornadoes. In the figure, the initial production possibilities frontier is PPF_0. The tornadoes destroy resources and kill people, thereby shifting the production possibilities frontier inward to PPF_1.

Because the maximum amount of Good B that can be produced decreases more than the maximum amount of Good A, the figure shows a larger impact on Good B than on Good A. This difference might be because the tornadoes destroyed more capital equipment used to produce Good B or because the tornadoes killed more people who were especially skilled in producing Good B.

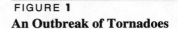

FIGURE 1
An Outbreak of Tornadoes

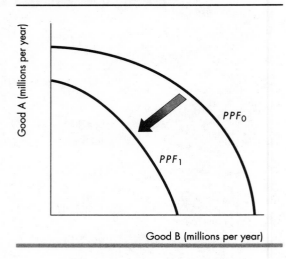

■ Mid-Term Exam Answers

1. d;   2. b;   3. c;   4. b;   5. d;   6. d;   7. b;   8. a.

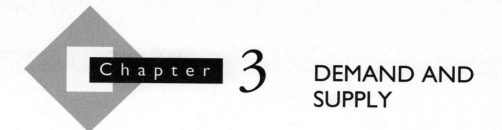

Chapter 3

DEMAND AND SUPPLY

Markets and Prices

A **competitive market** is one that has so many buyers and sellers so that no single buyer or seller can influence the price. The ratio of the money price of one good to the money price of another good is the **relative price**. The relative price of a product is the product's opportunity cost. The demand for and supply of a product depend, in part, on its relative price.

Demand

The **quantity demanded** of a good is the amount that consumers plan to buy during a time period at a particular price. The *law of demand* states that "other things remaining the same, the higher the price of a good, the smaller is the quantity demanded." Higher prices decrease the quantity demanded for two reasons:

♦ **Substitution effect** — a higher relative price raises the opportunity cost of buying a good and so people buy less of it.

♦ **Income effect** — a higher relative price reduces the amount of goods people can buy. Usually this effect decreases the amount people buy of the product that rose in price.

Demand is the entire relationship between the price of a good and the quantity demanded. A **demand curve** shows the inverse relationship between the quantity demanded and price, everything else remaining the same. For each quantity, a demand curve shows the highest price someone is willing to pay for that unit. This highest price is the *marginal benefit* a consumer receives for that unit of output.

FIGURE 3.1
Demand Curves

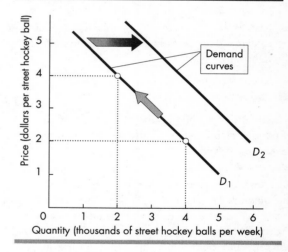

♦ Demand curves are negatively sloped, as illustrated in Figure 3.1.

♦ A change in the price of the product leads to a **change in the quantity demanded** and *a movement along the demand curve*. The higher the price of a good, the lower is the quantity demanded. This relationship is shown in Figure 3.1 with the movement along D_1 from 4,000 to 2,000 street hockey balls demanded per week in response to a rise in price from $2 to $4 for a street hockey ball.

A **change in demand** and *a shift in the demand curve*, occur when any factor that affects buying plans, other than the price of the product changes. An increase in demand means that the demand curve shifts rightward, such as the shift from D_1 to D_2 in Figure 3.1; a de-

45

crease in demand refers to a shift leftward. The demand curve shifts from changes in the following:

♦ *prices of related goods* — a rise in the price of a **substitute** increases demand and shifts the demand curve rightward; a rise in the price of a **complement** decreases demand and shifts the demand curve leftward.

♦ *expected future prices* — if a product's price is expected to rise in the future, the current demand for it increases and the demand curve shifts rightward.

♦ *income* — for a **normal good**, an increase in income increases demand and shifts the demand curve rightward; for an **inferior good** an increase in income decreases demand and shifts the demand curve leftward.

♦ *population* — an increase in population increases demand and shifts the demand curve rightward.

♦ *preferences* — if people decide they like a good more, its demand increases so the demand curve shifts rightward.

■ Supply

The **quantity supplied** is the amount of a good that producers plan to sell at a particular price during a given time period.

The *law of supply* states that "other things remaining the same, the higher the price of a good, the greater is the quantity supplied." **Supply** is the entire relationship between the price of a good and the quantity supplied. A **supply curve** shows the positive relationship between the price and the quantity supplied. For each quantity, the supply curve shows the minimum price a supplier must receive in order to produce that unit of output.

♦ Supply curves are positively sloped, as shown in Figure 3.2.

♦ A change in the price of the product leads to a **change in the quantity supplied** and a *movement along the supply curve*. It is illustrated in Figure 3.2 as the movement along S_1 from 2,000 street hockey balls supplied per week to 4,000 balls when the price rises from $2 for a ball to $4.

A **change in supply** is illustrated *as a shift in the supply curve*. An increase in supply is equivalent to a shift rightward in the supply curve, shown in Figure 3.2 as the shift from S_1 to S_2; a decrease in supply is a leftward shift in the supply curve. There is a change in

FIGURE 3.2
Supply Curves

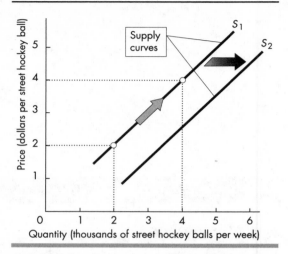

supply and a shift in the supply curve in response to changes in the following:

♦ *prices of productive resources* — a rise in the price (cost) of an input decreases supply and the supply curve shifts leftward.

♦ *prices of related goods produced* — a rise in the price of a *substitute in production* decreases supply and the supply curve shifts leftward; a rise in the price of a *complement in production* increases supply and the supply curve shifts rightward.

♦ *expected future prices* — if the price is expected to rise in the future, the current supply decreases and the supply curve shifts leftward.

♦ *number of suppliers* — an increase in the number of suppliers increases the supply and the supply curve shifts rightward.

♦ *technology* — an advance in technology increases supply and the supply curve shifts rightward.

■ Market Equilibrium

The **equilibrium price** is determined by the intersection of the demand and supply curves. It is the price at which the quantity demanded equals the quantity supplied. The **equilibrium quantity** is the quantity bought and sold at the equilibrium price. Figure 3.3 shows the equilibrium price, $3, and the equilibrium quantity, 3,000 street hockey balls per week. At a price below the equilibrium price, a shortage exists and the

FIGURE **3.3**
The Equilibrium Price and Quantity

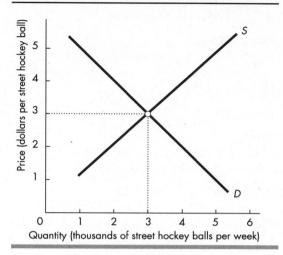

Quantity (thousands of street hockey balls per week)

price will rise. At a price above the equilibrium price, a surplus exists and the price will fall. Only at the equilibrium price does the price not change.

■ Predicting Changes in Price and Quantity

When either the demand *or* supply changes so that *one* of the demand or supply curves shifts, the effect on both the price (P) and quantity (Q) can be determined:

♦ An increase in demand (a rightward shift in the demand curve) raises P and increases Q.

♦ A decrease in demand (a leftward shift in the demand curve) lowers P and decreases Q.

♦ An increase in supply (a rightward shift in the supply curve) lowers P and increases Q.

♦ A decrease in supply (a leftward shift in the supply curve) raises P and decreases Q.

When both the demand and supply change so that both the demand and supply curves shift, the effect on the price *or* the quantity can be determined, but without information about the relative sizes of the shifts, the effect on the other variable is ambiguous.

♦ If both demand and supply increases (both curves shift rightward), the quantity increases but the price might rise, fall, or remain the same.

♦ If demand decreases (the demand curve shifts leftward) and supply increases (the supply curve shifts rightward), the price falls but the quantity might increase, decrease, or not change.

Helpful Hints

1. **DEVELOPING INTUITION ABOUT DEMAND :** When you are first learning about demand and supply, think in terms of concrete examples. Have some favorite examples in the back of your mind. For instance, when you hear "complementary goods" (goods used together), think about hot dogs and hot dog buns because few people eat hot dogs without using a hot dog bun. For "substitute goods" (things that take each other's place) think about hot dogs and hamburgers because they are obvious substitutes.

2. **DEVELOPING INTUITION ABOUT SUPPLY :** An easy and concrete way to identify with suppliers is to think of "profit": Anything that increases the profit from producing a product (except for the price of the good itself) increases the supply and shifts the supply curve rightward, whereas anything that decreases profit decreases the supply and shifts the supply curve leftward.

3. **SHIFT IN A CURVE VERSUS A MOVEMENT ALONG A CURVE :** Failing to distinguish correctly between a shift in a curve and a movement along a curve can lead to error and lost points on examinations. The difference applies equally to both demand and supply curves.

   The important point to remember is *that a change in the price of a good does not shift its demand curve; it leads to a movement along the demand curve.* If one of the other factors affecting demand changes, the demand curve itself shifts.

   Similarly, the supply curve shifts if some relevant factor that affects the supply, *other than the price of the good,* changes. A change in the price of the good leads to a movement along the supply curve.

4. **RULES FOR USING A SUPPLY/DEMAND DIAGRAM :** The safest way to solve any demand and supply problem is always to draw a graph. A few mechanical rules can make using supply and demand graphs easy. First, when you draw the graph, be sure to label the axes. As the course progresses, you will encounter many graphs with different variables on the axes. You can become confused if you do not develop the habit of labeling the axes. Second, draw the supply and demand curves as straight lines. Third, be sure to indicate and label the initial equilibrium price and quantity.

Now come two more difficult parts that you must practice. Suppose that you are dealing with a situation in which one influence changes. First, determine whether the influence shifts the demand or the supply curve. Aside from the effect of the expected future price, most factors generally shift only one curve and you must decide which one. Second, determine whether the curve that is affected shifts rightward (increases) or shifts leftward (decreases). From here on, it's more straightforward: Take the figure you have already drawn, shift the appropriate curve, and read off the answer!

FIGURE **3.4**
The Effect of an Increase in Demand

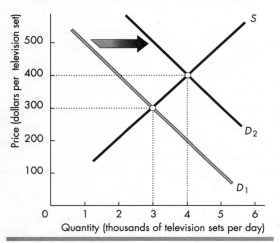

5. **CHANGES IN DEMAND DO NOT CAUSE CHANGES IN SUPPLY ; CHANGES IN SUPPLY DO NOT CAUSE CHANGES IN DEMAND :** Do not make the common error of believing that an increase in demand, that is, a rightward shift in the demand curve, causes an increase in supply, a rightward shift in the supply curve. Use Figure 3.4, which illustrates the market for television sets, as an example. An increase in demand shifts the demand curve rightward, as shown. This shift means the equilibrium price of a television rises (from $300 for a set to $400) and the equilibrium quantity increases (from 3,000 sets per day to 4,000). But the shift in the demand curve does not cause the supply curve to *shift*. Instead, there is a *movement along* the unchanging supply curve.

■ **True/False and Explain**

Markets and Prices

1. A good with a high relative price must have a low opportunity cost.

2. A product's relative price can fall even though its money price rises.

Demand

3. The law of demand states that, if nothing else changes, as the price of a good rises, the quantity demanded decreases.

4. A decrease in income decreases the demand for all products.

5. "An increase in demand" means a movement down and rightward along a demand curve.

6. New technology for manufacturing computer chips shifts the demand curve for computer chips.

Supply

7. A supply curve shows the maximum price required in order to have the last unit of output produced.

8. A rise in the price of chicken feed decreases the supply of chickens.

9. A rise in the price of orange juice shifts the supply curve of orange juice rightward.

Market Equilibrium

10. Once a market is at its equilibrium price, unless something changes, the price will not change.

11. If there is a surplus of a good, its price falls.

Predicting Changes in Price and Quantity

12. If the expected future price of a good rises, its current price rises.

13. A rise in the price of a product decreases the quantity demanded, so there can never be a situation with both the product's equilibrium price rising and equilibrium quantity increasing.

14. If both the demand and supply curves shift rightward, the equilibrium quantity definitely increases.

15. If both the demand and supply curves shift rightward, the equilibrium price definitely rises.

■ Multiple Choice

Markets and Prices

1. The opportunity cost of a product is the same as its
   a. money price.
   b. relative price.
   c. price index.
   d. None of the above.

2. The money price of a pizza is $12 per pizza and the money price of a taco is $2 per taco. The relative price of a pizza is
   a. $12 per pizza.
   b. $24 per pizza.
   c. 6 tacos per pizza.
   d. 1/6 pizza.

Demand

3. The law of demand concludes that a rise in the price of a golf ball _____ the quantity demanded and _____.
   a. increases; shifts the demand curve rightward.
   b. decreases; shifts the demand curve leftward.
   c. decreases; creates a movement upward along the demand curve.
   d. increases; creates a movement downward along the demand curve.

4. If a rise in the price of gasoline decreases the demand for large cars,
   a. gasoline and large cars are substitutes in consumption.
   b. gasoline and large cars are complements in consumption.
   c. gasoline is an inferior good.
   d. large cars are an inferior good.

5. A normal good is one
   a. with a downward sloping demand curve.
   b. for which demand increases when the price of a substitute rises.
   c. for which demand increases when income increases.
   d. None of the above.

6. Some sales managers are talking shop. Which of the following quotations refers to a movement along the demand curve?
   a. "Since our competitors raised their prices our sales have doubled."
   b. "It has been an unusually mild winter; our sales of wool scarves are down from last year."
   c. "We decided to cut our prices, and the increase in our sales has been remarkable."
   d. None of the above.

FIGURE **3.5**
Multiple Choice Question 7

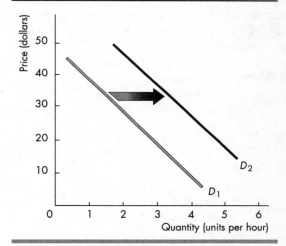

7. Which of the following could result in the shift in the demand curve illustrated in Figure 3.5?
   a. An increase in the quantity demanded
   b. A rise in the price of a substitute good
   c. A rise in the price of a complement
   d. A fall in the price of the product

Supply

8. A fall in the price of a good leads to producers decreasing the quantity of the good supplied. This result illustrates
   a. the law of supply.
   b. the law of demand.
   c. a change in supply.
   d. the nature of an inferior good.

9. Which of the following influences does <u>NOT</u> shift the supply curve?

a. A rise in the wages paid workers
b. Development of new technology
c. People deciding that they want to buy more of the product
d. A decrease in the number of suppliers

10. The price of jet fuel rises, causing the

a. demand for airplane trips to increase.
b. demand for airplane trips to decrease.
c. supply of airplane trips to increase.
d. supply of airplane trips to decrease.

11. In addition to showing the quantity that will be supplied at different prices, a supply curve can be viewed as the

a. willingness-and-ability-to-pay curve.
b. marginal benefit curve.
c. minimum-supply price curve.
d. maximum-supply price curve.

12. An increase in the number of producers of gruel _____ the supply of gruel and shifts the supply curve of gruel _____.

a. increases; rightward
b. increases; leftward
c. decreases; rightward
d. decreases; leftward

13. An increase in the cost of producing video tape shifts the supply curve of video tape _____ and shifts the demand curve for video tape _____.

a. rightward; leftward
b. leftward; leftward
c. leftward; not at all
d. not at all; leftward

14. To say that "supply increases" for any reason, means there is a

a. movement rightward along a supply curve.
b. movement leftward along a supply curve.
c. shift rightward in the supply curve.
d. shift leftward in the supply curve.

Market Equilibrium

15. If the market for Twinkies is in equilibrium, then

a. Twinkies must be a normal good.
b. producers would like to sell more at the current price.
c. consumers would like to buy more at the current price.
d. the quantity supplied equals the quantity demanded.

16. If there is a shortage of a good, the quantity demanded is _____ than the quantity supplied and the price will _____.

a. less; rise
b. less; fall
c. greater; rise
d. greater; fall

FIGURE **3.6**
Multiple Choice Question 17

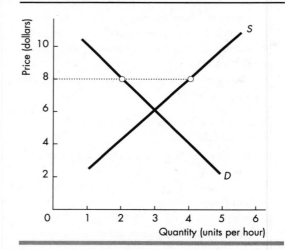

17. In Figure 3.6 at the price of $8 there is a

a. shortage and the price will rise.
b. shortage and the price will fall.
c. surplus and the price will rise.
d. surplus and the price will fall.

18. In a market, at the equilibrium price,
    a. neither buyers nor sellers can do business at a better price.
    b. buyers are willing to pay a higher price, but sellers do not ask for a higher price.
    c. buyers are paying the minimum price they are willing to pay for any amount of output and sellers are charging the maximum price they are willing to charge for any amount of production.
    d. None of the above is true.

Predicting Changes in Price and Quantity

19. For consumers, pizza and hamburgers are substitutes. A rise in the price of pizza _____ the price of a hamburger and _____ in the quantity of hamburgers.
    a. raises; increases
    b. raises; decreases
    c. lowers; increases
    d. lowers; decreases

20. How does an unusually cold winter affect the equilibrium price and quantity of anti-freeze?
    a. It raises the price and increases the quantity.
    b. It raises the price and decreases the quantity.
    c. It lowers the price and increases the quantity.
    d. It lowers the price and decreases the quantity.

21. You notice that the price of wheat rises and the quantity of wheat increases. This set of observations can be the result of the
    a. demand for wheat curve shifting rightward.
    b. demand for wheat curve shifting leftward.
    c. supply of wheat curve shifting rightward.
    d. supply of wheat curve shifting leftward.

22. A technological improvement lowers the cost of producing coffee. As a result, the price of a pound of coffee _____ and the quantity of coffee _____.
    a. rises; increases
    b. rises; decreases
    c. falls; increases
    d. falls; decreases

23. The number of firms producing computer memory chips decreases. As a result, the price of a memory chip _____ and the quantity of memory chips _____.
    a. rises; increases
    b. rises; decreases
    c. falls; increases
    d. falls; decreases

For the next five questions, suppose that the price of paper used in books rises and simultaneously (and independently) more people decide they want to read books.

24. The rise in the price of paper shifts the
    a. demand curve rightward.
    b. demand curve leftward.
    c. supply curve rightward.
    d. supply curve leftward.

25. The fact that more people want to read books shifts the
    a. demand curve rightward.
    b. demand curve leftward.
    c. supply curve rightward.
    d. supply curve leftward.

26. The equilibrium quantity of books
    a. definitely increases.
    b. definitely does not change.
    c. definitely decreases.
    d. might increase, not change, or decrease.

27. The equilibrium price of a book
    a. definitely rises.
    b. definitely does not change.
    c. definitely falls.
    d. might rise, not change, or fall.

28. Suppose that the effect from people deciding they want to read more books is larger than the effect from the increase in the price of paper. In this case, the equilibrium quantity of books
    a. definitely increases.
    b. definitely does not change.
    c. definitely decreases.
    d. might increase, not change, or decrease.

29. Which of the following definitely raises the equilibrium price?
    a. An increase in both demand and supply.
    b. A decrease in both demand and supply.
    c. An increase in demand combined with a decrease in supply.
    d. A decrease in demand combined with an increase in supply.

30. Is it possible for the price of a good to stay the same while the quantity increases?
    a. Yes, if both the demand and supply of the good increase by the same amount.
    b. Yes, if the demand increases by the same amount the supply decreases.
    c. Yes, if the supply increases and the demand does not change.
    d. No, it is not possible.

■ Short Answer Problems

1. a. This year the price of a hamburger is $2 and the price of a compact disc is $12. In terms of hamburgers, what is the relative price of a compact disc? In terms of hamburgers, what is the opportunity cost of buying a compact disc? How are the two answers related?
   b. Next year the (money) price of a compact disc doubles to $24 and the (money) price of a hamburger remains at $2. Now what is the relative price of a compact disc?
   c. The following year the (money) price of a compact disc stays at $24 and the (money) price of a hamburger doubles to $4. What is the relative price of a compact disc?
   d. In the next year, the (money) price of a compact disc doubles to $48 and the money price of a hamburger triples to $12. What is the relative price of a compact disc?
   e. Can a product's relative price fall even though its money price has risen? Why or why not?

2. a. When drawing a demand curve, what five influences are assumed not to change?
   b. If any of these influences change, what happens to the demand curve?
   c. When drawing a supply curve, what five influences are assumed not to change?
   d. If any of these influences change, what happens to the supply curve?

3. a. Table 3.1 presents the demand and supply schedules for comic books. Graph these demand and supply schedules in Figure 3.7. What is the equilibrium price? The equilibrium quantity?
   b. What is the marginal benefit received by the consumer of the 12,000,000th comic book? What is the minimum price for which a producer is willing to produce the 12,000,000th comic book?

TABLE **3.1**

Demand and Supply Schedules

Price (per comic book)	Quantity demanded (per month)	Quantity supplied (per month)
$2.50	14,000,000	8,000,000
3.00	13,000,000	10,000,000
3.50	12,000,000	12,000,000
4.00	11,000,000	13,000,000
4.50	10,000,000	14,000,000

FIGURE **3.7**

Short Answer Problem 3

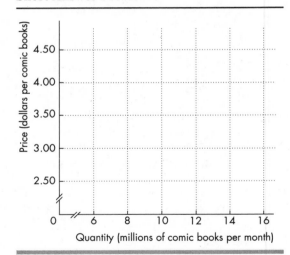

   c. Suppose that the price of a movie, a substitute for comic books, rises so that at every price of a comic book consumers now want to buy 2,000,000 more comic books than before. That is, at the price of $2.50, consumers now will buy 16,000,000 comics; and so on. Plot this new demand curve in Figure 3.7. What is the new equilibrium price? The new equilibrium quantity?

4. New cars are a normal good. Suppose that the economy enters a period of strong economic expansion so that people's incomes increase substantially. Use a supply and demand diagram to determine what happens to the equilibrium price and quantity of new cars.

5. Used records and used compact discs are substitutes. Use a supply and demand diagram to determine what happens to the equilibrium price and quantity of used records when the price of a used compact disc falls because of an increase in the supply of used discs.

6. Suppose we observe that the consumption of peanut butter increases at the same time its price rises. What must have happened in the market for peanut butter? Is the observation that the price rose and the quantity increased consistent with the law of demand? Why or why not?

7. Suppose that the wages paid oil workers fall. Use a supply and demand diagram to determine the effect this action has on the equilibrium price and quantity of gasoline.

8. Chemical companies discover a new, more efficient technology for producing benzene. Use a supply and demand model to determine the impact that this new method has on the equilibrium price and quantity of benzene.

9. The price of a personal computer has continued to fall in the face of increasing demand. Explain.

10. a. The market for chickens initially is in equilibrium. Suppose that eating buffalo wings (which, contrary to the name, are made from chicken wings) becomes so stylish that people eat them for breakfast, lunch, and dinner. Use a supply and demand diagram to determine how the equilibrium price and quantity of chicken change.

    b. Return to the initial equilibrium, before eating buffalo wings became stylish. Now suppose that a heat wave occurred and caused tens of thousands of chickens to die or commit suicide. Keeping in mind that dead chickens cannot be marketed, use a supply and demand diagram to determine what happens to the equilibrium price and quantity of chicken.

    c. Now assume that both the heat wave and fad strike at the same time. Use a supply and demand diagram to show what happens to the equilibrium price and quantity of chicken. (Hint: Can you tell for sure what happens to the price? The quantity?)

■ You're the Teacher

1. When you and a friend are studying Chapter 3, the friend says to you, "I really don't understand the difference between a 'shift in a curve' and a 'movement along' a curve. Can you help me? It's probably important to understand this, so what's the difference?" Explain the difference to your friend.

2. "This supply and demand model is nonsense. It says that if demand for some product decreases, the price of that good falls. But, come on — except for computers, how many times have you actually seen a price fall? Prices *always* rise, so don't try telling me that that they fall." The supply and demand model is sound; it is this statement that is nonsense. Show the speaker the error in that analysis.

Answers

■ True/False Answers

Markets and Prices

1. **F** A product's relative price is its opportunity cost.

2. **T** A good's relative price will fall if its money price rises less than the money prices of other goods.

Demand

3. **T** The law of demand points out the negative relationship between a product's price and the quantity demanded.

4. **F** Demand decreases for normal goods but increases for inferior goods.

5. **F** The term "increase in demand" refers to a rightward shift in the demand curve.

6. **F** Changes in technology are not a factor that shifts the demand curve. (Changes in technology will shift the supply curve.)

Supply

7. **F** The supply curve shows the *minimum* price that suppliers must receive in order to produce the last unit supplied.

8. **T** Chicken feed is a resource used to produce chickens, so a rise in its price shifts the supply curve of chickens leftward.

9. **F** The rise in the price of orange juice creates a movement along the supply curve to a larger quantity supplied (that is, upward and rightward), but it does not shift the supply curve.

Market Equilibrium

10. **T** Once at the equilibrium price, because the opposing forces of supply and demand are in balance, the situation can persist indefinitely until something changes.

11. **T** A surplus of a product results in its price falling until it reaches the equilibrium price.

Predicting Changes in Price and Quantity

12. **T** The rise in the future price shifts the demand curve rightward and the supply curve leftward, unambiguously raising the current price.

13. **F** The inverse relationship between the price and quantity demanded holds along a fixed demand curve. But if the demand curve shifts rightward,

the equilibrium price rises and the equilibrium quantity increases.

14. **T** The equilibrium quantity definitely increases when both the demand and supply increase.

15. **F** The price rises if the shift in the demand curve is larger than that in the supply curve; but if the shifts are the same size, the price does not change and if the supply shift is larger, the price falls.

■ Multiple Choice Answers

Markets and Prices

1. **b** A product's relative price tells how much of another good must be foregone to have another unit of the product, which is the opportunity cost of the product.

2. **c** The relative price of the pizza is its money price relative to the money price of a taco, which equals ($12 per pizza)/($2 per taco) or 6 tacos per pizza.

Demand

3. **c** The law of demand points out that a higher price decreases the quantity demanded and creates a movement upward along the demand curve.

4. **b** The definition of complementary goods is that a rise in the price of one decreases the demand for the other.

5. **c** This is the definition of a "normal good."

6. **c** A reduction in the price of the product leads to a movement along its demand curve.

7. **b** A rise in the price of a substitute shifts the demand curve rightward.

Supply

8. **a** The law of supply points out the positive relationship between the price of a product and the quantity supplied.

9. **c** A change in preferences shifts the demand curve, not the supply curve.

10. **d** Jet fuel is a resource used to produce airplane trips, so a rise in the price (cost) of this resource decreases the supply of airplane trips.

11. **c** For any unit of output, the supply curve shows the minimum price for which a producer is willing to produce and sell that unit of output.

12. **a** An increase in supply is reflected by a rightward shift of the supply curve.

13. **c** A change in the cost to produce a product shifts the supply curve but does not shift the demand curve.

14. **c** An "increase in supply" means that the supply curve shifts rightward; a "decrease in supply" means the supply curve shifts leftward.

Market Equilibrium

15. **d** At equilibrium, consumers and suppliers are simultaneously satisfied insofar as the quantity consumers are willing to buy matches the quantity producers are willing to sell.

16. **c** A shortage occurs when the price is below the equilibrium price. The quantity demanded exceeds the quantity supplied and the resulting shortage means the price rises until it reaches its equilibrium.

FIGURE **3.8**
Multiple Choice Question 17

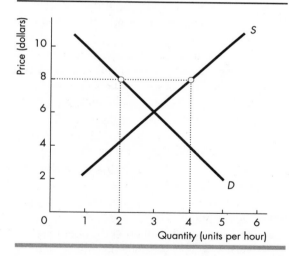

17. **d** There is surplus because, as illustrated in Figure 3.8, the quantity supplied at the price of $8 is 4. This quantity exceeds 2, the quantity demanded.

18. **a** Buyers cannot find anyone willing to sell to at a lower price and sellers cannot find anyone willing to buy at a higher price.

Predicting Changes in Price and Quantity

19. **a** The rise in the price of a pizza increases the demand for hamburgers, which results in a rise in

the price of a hamburger and an increase in the quantity of hamburgers.

20. **a** The cold winter shifts the demand curve rightward, as consumers increase their demand for antifreeze; the supply curve does not shift. As a result, the equilibrium price rises and the quantity increases.

FIGURE **3.9**
Multiple Choice Question 21

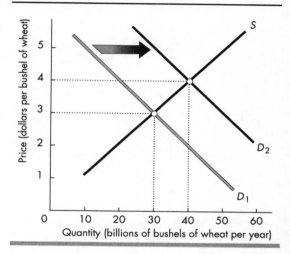

21. **a** Figure 3.9 shows that an increase in the demand for wheat, so that the demand curve shifts from D_1 to D_2, raises the price of wheat from $3 a bushel to $4 and increases its quantity from 30 billion bushels of wheat a year to 40 billion.

22. **c** The technological improvement increases the supply, that is, the supply curve shifts rightward. As a result, the quantity increases and the price falls.

23. **b** The decrease in the number of firms producing memory chips decreases the supply of memory chips, which raises the price and decreases the quantity of chips.

24. **d** Paper is a resource used in the manufacture of books, so a rise in the price of paper shifts the supply curve of books leftward.

25. **a** When people's preferences change so that they want to read more books, the demand curve for books shifts rightward.

26. **d** The equilibrium quantity increases if the increase in demand is larger than the decrease in

supply, decreases if the change in supply is larger, and does not change if the changes are the same size.

27. **a** Both the increase in demand and decrease in supply lead to a rise in the price, so the equilibrium price unambiguously rises.

FIGURE **3.10**
Multiple Choice Question 28

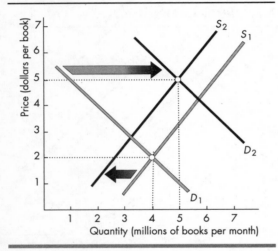

28. **a** If the shift in the demand curve exceeds the shift in the supply curve, the equilibrium quantity increases. This result is illustrated in Figure 3.10, where the quantity increases from 4 to 5 million.

29. **c** Separately, the increase in demand and decrease in supply both raise the price, so the two of them occurring together definitely raise the price.

30. **a** If both the demand and supply increase by the same amount, the price will not change and the quantity will increase.

■ **Answers to Short Answer Problems**

1.   a. The money price of a compact disc is $12 per compact disc; the money price of a hamburger is $2 per hamburger. The relative price of a compact disc is the ratio of the money prices, $12 per compact disc/$2 per hamburger, or 6 hamburgers per compact disc. For the opportunity cost, buying 1 compact disc means using the funds that otherwise could purchase 6 hamburgers. Hence the opportunity cost of buying 1 compact disc is 6 hamburgers. The relative price and the opportunity cost are identical.

b. The relative price of a compact disc is $24 per compact disc/$2 per hamburger or 12 hamburgers per compact disc.

c. The relative price of a compact disc is $24 per compact disc/$4 per hamburger, or 6 hamburgers per compact disc.

d. The relative price of a compact disc is $48 per compact disc/$12 per hamburger, or 4 hamburgers per compact disc.

e. Yes, a product's relative price can fall even though its money price rises. Part (d) gives an example of how that can occur: If a good's money price rises by a smaller percentage than the money price of other goods, then the product's relative price falls. Keep this result in mind when you use the supply and demand model because when the model predicts that the equilibrium price will fall, it means that the *relative* price, and not necessarily the money price, falls.

2.   a. The five influences that do not change along a demand curve are prices of related goods, income, the expected future price, population, and preferences.

b. If any of these factors change, the demand curve shifts.

c. The five influences that are held constant when you draw a supply curve are prices of productive resources, technology, number of suppliers, prices of related goods produced, and the expected future price.

d. If any of these influences change, the supply curve shifts. It is very important to remember what influences shift a supply curve and what shift a demand curve.

3.   a. Figure 3.11 (on the next page) shows the graph of the supply and demand schedules as S and D_1. The equilibrium price is $3.50 a comic book, and the equilibrium quantity is 12,000,000 comic books.

b. The person who buys the 12,000,000th comic book pays $3.50 for the comic book, and so $3.50 is the benefit this person receives from this comic book. The firm that produces the 12,000,000th comic book receives $3.50 for the book, and the supply curve shows that $3.50 is the minimum price for which this firm is willing to produce and sell the comic book.

FIGURE **3.11**
Short Answer Problem 3

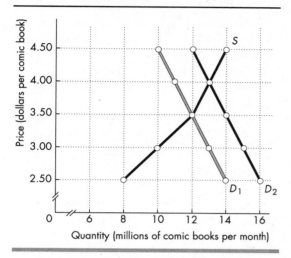

Quantity (millions of comic books per month)

c. The new demand curve is plotted in Figure 3.11 as D_2. The new equilibrium price is $4, and the new equilibrium quantity is 13 million.

FIGURE **3.12**
Short Answer Problem 4

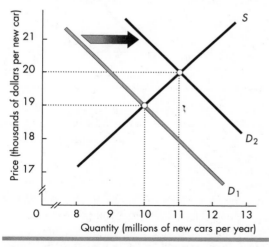

Quantity (millions of new cars per year)

4. Because new cars are a normal good, an increase in income increases the demand for them. Hence the demand curve shifts rightward, as shown in Figure 3.12. As a result, the equilibrium price rises (from $19,000 to $20,000 in the figure) and the equilibrium quantity also increases (from 10 million a year to 11 million in the figure).

FIGURE **3.13**
Short Answer Problem 5

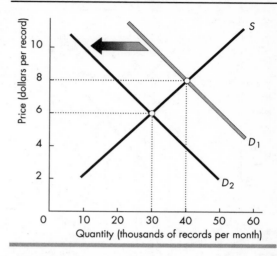

Quantity (thousands of records per month)

5. The fall in the price of a used compact disc, a substitute for used records, decreases the demand for used records. This change means the demand curve for used records shifts leftward, as shown in Figure 3.13. As a result, the price of a used record falls, (from $8 a record to $6 in the figure) and the quantity decreases (from 40,000 per month to 30,000 in the figure). Note that it is the shift in the demand curve that changed the price and that the shift in the demand curve did *not* shift the supply curve.

6. In order for both the equilibrium price and quantity of peanut butter to increase, the demand for peanut butter must have increased. The increase in demand leads to a rise in the price and an increase in the quantity of peanut butter.

The observation that both the price rose and the quantity increased is not at all inconsistent with the law of demand. The law of demand states that "other things remaining the same, the higher the price of a good, the smaller is the quantity demanded." A key part of this law is the "other things remaining the same" clause. When the demand curve for peanut butter shifts rightward, something else that increased the demand for peanut butter changed. Hence "other things" have not remained the same and by changing have resulted in a higher price and increased quantity of peanut butter.

FIGURE **3.14**

Short Answer Problem 7

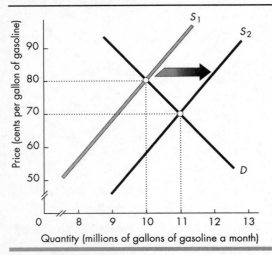

7. Lower wages reduce the price of a resource (labor) used to produce gasoline. As a result, the supply of gasoline increases. This change is illustrated in Figure 3.14, where the supply curve shifts rightward from S_1 to S_2. The increase in supply lowers the price of gasoline (from 80 cents a gallon to 70 cents in the figure) and increases the quantity (from 10 million gallons a month to 11 million).

FIGURE **3.15**

Short Answer Problem 8

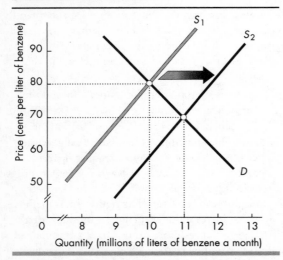

8. New technology increases the supply, so the supply curve shifts rightward. Then, as Figure 3.15 shows, the price falls (from 80 cents a liter to 70 cents in

the figure) and the equilibrium quantity increases from (10 million liters of benzene a month to 11 million).

This answer and the figure are virtually the same as those in problem 7. Even though a fall in wages and the development of new technology appear dissimilar, the demand and supply model reveals that both have the same effect on the price and quantity of the product. This model can easily accommodate these quite different changes. For this reason the demand and supply model is a very important economic tool.

FIGURE **3.16**

Short Answer Problem 9

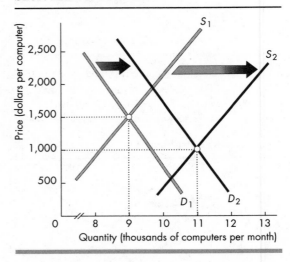

9. Personal computers have fallen in price although the demand for them has increased because the supply has increased even more rapidly. Figure 3.16 illustrates this situation. From one year to the next the demand curve shifted from D_1 to D_2. But over the year the supply curve shifted from S_1 to S_2. Because the supply has increased more than the demand, the price of a personal computer fell (in the figure, from $1,500 for a personal computer to $1,000). The quantity increased (from 9,000 personal computers a month to 11,000 in the figure).

10. a. With the change in people's preferences — so that they want more chicken wings and hence more chickens — the demand for chickens increases. The increase in the demand for chickens means that the demand curve for chickens shifts rightward. Figure 3.17 (on the next page) shows this change. As it demonstrates, the equilibrium

FIGURE **3.17**
Short Answer Problem 10 (a)

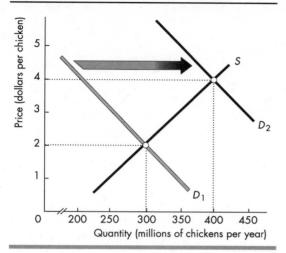

price rises (from $2 to $4 per chicken) and the equilibrium quantity of chickens increase (from 300 million to 400 million). Note that the change in people's preferences does not affect the supply of chicken, so the supply curve does *not* shift.

FIGURE **3.18**
Short Answer Problem 10 (b)

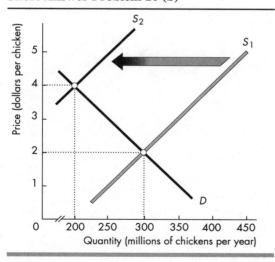

b. The heat wave decreases the number of chickens that can be supplied. This change shifts the supply curve for chickens leftward, as Figure 3.18 shows. As a result, the heat wave raises the price

FIGURE **3.19**
Short Answer Problem 10 (c)

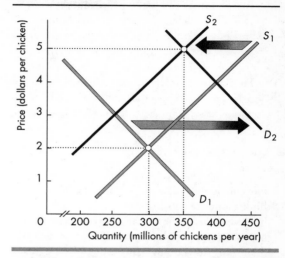

FIGURE **3.20**
Short Answer Problem 10 (c)

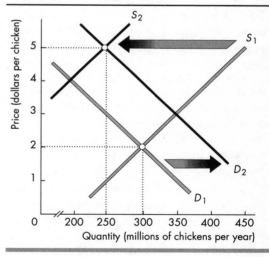

of a chicken (from $2 to $4) and decreases the quantity (from 300 million to 200 million).

c. If the demand increases *and* the supply decreases, the equilibrium price of a chicken rises. But the effect on the quantity is ambiguous. Figures 3.19 and 3.20 reveal the nature of this ambiguity. In Figure 3.19, the demand shift is larger than the supply shift, and the equilibrium quantity increases to 350 million chickens. But in Figure 3.20, the magnitude of the shifts is reversed, and the supply shift exceeds the demand shift. Because the supply shift is larger, the equilibrium quantity decreases to 250 million chickens. So unless you know which shift is larger, you cannot determine whether the quantity increases (when the demand shift is larger); decreases (when the supply shift is larger); or stays the same (when both shifts are the same size). However, regardless of the relative sizes, Figures 3.19 and 3.20 show that the price will unambiguously rise, coincidentally to $5 in both figures.

■ You're the Teacher

1. "The distinction between a 'shift in a curve' and a 'movement along a curve' is really crucial. Let's think about the demand curve; once you understand the difference for the demand curve, understanding it for the supply curve is easier. Take movies, OK? A lot of things affect how many movies we see in a month: the ticket price, our income, and so on. Start with the price. Obviously, if the price of a movie ticket rises, we'll buy fewer. The slope of a demand curve shows this effect. For the demand curve in Figure 3.21, when the price rises from $5 to $6 for a movie, the movement is from point *a* on the demand curve to point *b*. Our quantity demanded decreases from 5 movies a month to 4. So the rise in the price of the product has lead to a movement along the demand curve. The negative slope of the demand curve shows the negative effect that higher prices have on the quantity demanded.

"Now, let's suppose that our incomes fall and that as a result we're going to go to fewer movies. The demand curve's slope can't show us this effect because the slope indicates the relationship between the price and the quantity demanded. Instead, the whole demand curve is going to shift. That is, at any price we'll buy fewer tickets. Look at Figure 3.22 for instance. If the price stays at $6 a movie, the quantity we demand decreases from 4 movies a month to 2.

"But the same is true if the price is $5: If the price stays at $5 the quantity we demand decreases from 5 movies a month to only 3. Now, I don't mean to say that the price has to stay at $6 or at $5. All I'm saying is that at any possible price, the number of movies we'll see has decreased and I'm just using $6 and $5 as examples. So we're going to decrease the quantity demanded at $6 and at $5, *and* at every

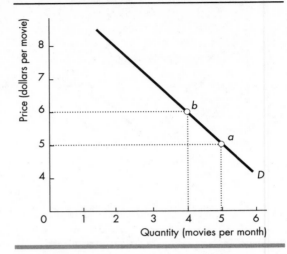

FIGURE **3.21**
You're the Teacher Question 1

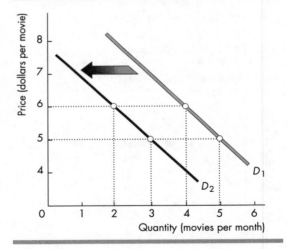

FIGURE **3.22**
You're the Teacher Question 1

other possible price. That means that we can draw a new demand curve (D_2) to show how much we demand at every price after our incomes fall. So, the drop in income has shifted the demand curve from D_1 to D_2. And, that's all there is to the difference between a 'movement along the demand curve' and a 'shift in the demand curve.' "

2. "You're missing a key point about the demand and supply model. This model predicts what happens to *relative* prices, not *money* prices. You're certainly right when you say that we don't often see a money

price fall. We live in inflationary times and most money prices usually rise. But when the demand and supply model says that the price falls, it means that the *relative* price falls. A good's relative price can fall even though its money price rises. For instance, if the money price of some product rises by 2 percent when the money prices of all other goods are rising by 4 percent, the first product's relative price has fallen. That is, its money price relative to every other money price is lower. If you think about it, relative prices change all the time, and at least half the time relative prices fall. Drops in relative prices aren't rare; they're common. So, don't be too hasty to throw away the demand and supply model. Not only are we going to see it on tests in this class, but it also works well to help us understand what happens to a product's (relative) price and quantity whenever there's a change in a relevant factor."

Chapter Quiz

1. When demand increases
   a. price falls and quantity decreases.
   b. price falls and quantity increases.
   c. price rises and quantity decreases.
   d. price rises and quantity increases.

2. Wants differ from demands insofar as
   a. wants are limited by income but demands are unlimited.
   b. wants require a plan to acquire a good, while demands require no such plan.
   c. wants imply a decision about which demands to satisfy, while demands require no such specific plans.
   d. wants are unlimited and involve no specific plan to acquire the good, while demands reflect a decision about which wants to satisfy and a plan to buy the good(s).

3. A complement is a good
   a. that can be used in place of another good.
   b. that is used with another good.
   c. of lower quality than another.
   d. of higher quality than another.

4. Suppose that people buy less of good 1 when the price of good 2 falls. These goods are
   a. complements.
   b. substitutes.
   c. normal.
   d. inferior.

5. A change in the price of a good _____ its supply curve and _____ a movement along its supply curve.
   a. shifts; results in
   b. shifts; does result in
   c. does not shift; results in
   d. does not shift; does not result in

6. Which of the following will shift the supply curve for good X leftward?
   a. A situation in which the quantity demanded of good X exceeds the quantity supplied.
   b. An increase in the price of machinery used to produce X.
   c. A technological improvement in the production of X.
   d. A decrease in the wages of workers employed to produce X.

7. A surplus results in the
   a. demand curve shifting rightward.
   b. supply curve shifting rightward.
   c. price falling.
   d. price rising.

8. If a product is a normal good and people's incomes rise, then the new equilibrium quantity is _____ the initial equilibrium quantity.
   a. greater than
   b. equal to
   c. less than
   d. perhaps greater than, less than, or equal to depending on how suppliers react to the change in demand.

9. In the market for oil, the development of a new deep sea drilling technology _____ the demand curve for oil and _____ the supply curve of oil.
   a. shifts rightward; shifts rightward
   b. does not shift; shifts rightward
   c. shifts leftward; shifts leftward
   d. does not shift; shifts leftward

10. Taken by itself, an increase in supply results in
    a. the price rising.
    b. the price falling.
    c. the demand curve shifting rightward.
    d. the demand curve shifting leftward.

The answers for this Chapter Quiz are on page 367

Chapter 4 ELASTICITY

Key Concepts

■ Price Elasticity of Demand

♦ The **price elasticity of demand** is a units-free measure of responsiveness of the quantity demanded of a good to a change in its price when all other influences on buyers' plans remain the same.

The price elasticity of demand equals the magnitude of:

$$\frac{\text{(percentage change in quantity demanded)}}{\text{(percentage change in price)}} = \frac{\Delta Q / Q_{ave}}{\Delta P / P_{ave}}$$

where "*ave*" stands for average.

♦ When the elasticity equals 0, the good has **perfectly inelastic demand** and the demand curve is vertical.

♦ When the elasticity is less than 1 and greater than 0, the good has **inelastic demand**.

♦ When the elasticity equals 1, the good has **unit elastic demand**.

♦ When the elasticity is greater than 1 and less than infinity, the good has **elastic demand**.

♦ When the elasticity equals infinity, the good has **perfectly elastic demand** and the demand curve is horizontal.

Elasticity is *not* equal to the slope of the demand curve. Along a linear demand curve the slope $(\Delta P/\Delta Q)$ is constant but the elasticity falls in magnitude when moving downward along the curve.

Price elasticity and total revenue $(P)(Q)$:

When demand is	A price cut results in
Inelastic (elasticity < 1)	a decrease in total revenue
Unit elastic (elasticity = 1)	no change in total revenue
Elastic (elasticity > 1)	an increase in total revenue

The **total revenue test** estimates the price elasticity of demand by noting how a change in price affects the total revenue spent on the product.

A person's expenditure on a good follows the same rules. If the good has an elastic demand, a price cut increases expenditure; if it has a unit elastic demand, a price cut does not change expenditure; and, if it has an inelastic demand, a price cut decreases expenditure.

The price elasticity of demand depends on three factors:

♦ *Substitutability* — the more close substitutes there are for the good, the larger is its price elasticity. Necessities generally have few substitutes and so have a small elasticity; luxuries generally have many substitutes and so have a large elasticity.

♦ *Proportion of income spent on the product* — the greater the proportion of income spent on a good, the larger is its price elasticity of demand.

♦ *Time elapsed since the price change* — the more time that has passed since the price changed, the greater is the price elasticity of demand.

■ More Elasticities of Demand

The **cross elasticity of demand** measures the responsiveness of demand for a good to a change in the price of a substitute or complement.

The cross elasticity of demand equals:

$$\frac{\text{(percentage change in the quantity demanded)}}{\text{(percentage change in the price of a related good)}}.$$

The sign of the cross elasticity of demand depends on whether the goods are substitutes or complements.

When	Then
the goods are substitutes	cross-elasticity > 0
the goods are complements	cross-elasticity < 0

The **income elasticity of demand** measures the responsiveness of the demand for a good to a change in income. The income elasticity of demand is defined as:

$$\frac{\text{(percentage change in the quantity demanded)}}{\text{(percentage change in income)}}$$

When	Demand is
income elasticity > 1	income elastic; normal good
0 < income elasticity < 1	income inelastic; normal good
income elasticity < 0	inferior good

■ Elasticity of Supply

The **elasticity of supply** measures the responsiveness of the quantity supplied to a change in its price when all other influences on selling plans remain the same.

The elasticity of supply equals:

$$\frac{\text{(percentage change in the quantity supplied)}}{\text{(percentage change in the price)}}$$

The size of the price elasticity of supply depends on:

- the ease with which additional resources can be substituted into the production process.
- the time since the price change.

The *momentary supply curve* shows the immediate response to a price change. The *short-run supply curve* shows how the quantity supplied responds to a change in price after some of the possible adjustments have been made. The *long-run supply curve* shows the response of the quantity supplied to a price change after all possible adjustments have been made.

Helpful Hints

1. **INTUITION BEHIND THE CONCEPT OF ELASTICITY :** Though there are many elasticity formulas in this chapter, *all* of the elasticity formulas measure how strongly a relationship responds to some change. The price elasticity of demand, for instance, indicates how strongly a change in a good's price affects the quantity demanded of the good, while the income elasticity of demand measures how strongly a change in income affects the demand for a good.

2. **WHY ELASTICITIES USE PERCENTAGES :** Percentages are a natural way to determine the importance of a change in price, income, or quantity. For example, which seems larger: a $1 hike in the price of a Big Mac served at the local McDonald's or a $1 increase in the price of the least expensive BMW sold at the nearest BMW dealer? The $1 rise in the price of the Big Mac is larger because it represents approximately a 50 percent boost. With the least expensive BMW selling for more than $20,000, a $1 rise in its price is minuscule, less than a 0.005 percent rise. Many consumers would respond to a $1 change in the price of a Big Mac; few would to a $1 change in the price of a BMW. Thus the best measure of the size of a price change is the percentage change.

3. **HOW TO RECALL THE ELASTICITY FORMULA :** Whether the percentage change in the quantity demanded or the percentage change in the price goes in the numerator for the price elasticity of demand is easy to forget. If you think of a kewpie doll, the sort of doll that is given away at carnivals for a display of an otherwise fairly useless talent, you should be able to keep the formula straight. The word kewpie is pronounced *q-p*, thereby telling us that "*q*" goes first (in the numerator) and that "*p*" goes second (in the denominator).

4. **PRICE ELASTICITY AND TOTAL REVENUE :** Total revenue equals price times quantity. To see why the price elasticity of demand tells us how a price change affects total revenue, think about a price rise. A price hike has two separate effects on total revenue. First, a higher price directly raises total revenue. Second, consumers respond to the higher price by decreasing the quantity they demand. The decrease in the quantity reduces total revenue. Which effect is larger? That depends on the price elasticity of demand. If demand is elastic, the percentage decrease in the quantity demanded exceeds the percentage rise in price and so the effect from the decreased quantity exceeds the impact from the higher price. Total revenue falls. But if demand is inelastic, the higher price dominates the decreased quantity and total revenue rises. Finally, if demand is unit elastic, the percentage decrease in the quantity demanded equals the percentage rise in price so the two effects offset each other, with no change in total revenue.

5. **WHY ONLY THE PRICE ELASTICITY OF DEMAND USES THE MAGNITUDE OF THE PERCENTAGE CHANGES :** The price elasticity of demand uses the absolute value of the percentage change in quantity demanded divided by the percentage change in price. However, neither the income elasticity nor the cross elasticity take the absolute value. Why the difference? Because the sign of the last two elasticities is important. The price elasticity of demand *always* is negative. The income elasticity, however, can be either negative or positive. A negative income elasticity indicates that the product is an inferior good and a positive income elasticity signifies that the product is a normal good. The sign of the cross elasticity also is important. A negative cross elasticity indicates that the two goods are complements and a positive cross elasticity means that the two goods are substitutes. Because the signs of the income elasticity and cross elasticity convey information, we retain the sign rather than discard.

Questions

■ True/False and Explain

Price Elasticity of Demand

1. The price elasticity of demand is the same as the slope of the demand curve.

2. The price elasticity of demand ranges from 0 to ∞.

3. The more demanders respond to a price change, the larger the price elasticity of demand.

4. If the price elasticity of demand is positive, the demand is elastic.

5. Exxon gasoline is likely to have an elastic demand.

6. Moving along a linear demand curve to lower prices and increased quantities, the price elasticity of demand does not change.

7. People spend more on rent than on soap, so the price elasticity of demand for housing is likely to be larger than the price elasticity of demand for soap.

8. The price elasticity of demand for food is largest in poor nations.

9. As more time passes after a price change, the price elasticity of demand becomes smaller.

10. Your local Domino's Pizza outlet estimates that the price elasticity of demand for its pizzas is 4.00, so if it raises the price it charges for its pizza, its total revenue will increase.

More Elasticities of Demand

11. The cross elasticity of demand between hot dogs and hot dog buns is negative.

12. A product that has an elastic demand if its income elasticity of demand exceeds 1.0.

13. An inferior good has an income elasticity that is negative; a normal good has an income elasticity that is positive.

Elasticity of Supply

14. The elasticity of supply equals the change in the quantity supplied divided by the change in price.

15. If a good has a vertical supply curve, its elasticity of supply equals 0.

■ Multiple Choice Questions

Price Elasticity of Demand

1. Suppose that a 10 percent hike in the price of a textbook decreases the quantity demanded by 2 percent. Then the price elasticity of demand for textbooks is
   a. 0.2.
   b. 2.0.
   c. 5.0.
   d. 10.0.

TABLE **4.1**

Multiple Choice Question 2

Price per volleyball (dollars)	Quantity demanded
19	55
21	45

2. Two points on the demand curve for volleyballs are shown in Table 4.1. What is the price elasticity of demand between these two points?
   a. 2.5.
   b. 2.0.
   c. 0.5.
   d. 0.4.

3. The quantity of new cars increases by 5 percent. If the price elasticity of demand for new cars is 1.25, the price of a new car will
   a. fall by 4 percent.
   b. fall by 5 percent.
   c. fall by 6.25 percent.
   d. fall by 1.25 percent.

4. Along a perfectly vertical demand curve, the price elasticity of demand
   a. equals 0.
   b. is greater than 0 but less than 1.0.
   c. equals 1.0.
   d. is negative.

5. Perfectly elastic demand is represented by a demand curve that
   a. is vertical.
   b. is horizontal.
   c. has a 45° slope.
   d. is a rectangular hyperbola.

6. The demand for a good is more price inelastic if
   a. its price is higher.
   b. the percentage of income spent on it is larger.
   c. it is a luxury good.
   d. it has no close substitutes.

7. Which of the following is likely to have the largest price elasticity of demand?
   a. An automobile
   b. A new automobile
   c. A new Ford automobile
   d. A new Ford Mustang

8. Business people often speak about price elasticity without actually using the term. Which statement describes a good with an elastic demand?
   a. "A price cut won't help me. It won't increase my sales, and I'll just get less money for each unit."
   b. "I don't think a price cut will help my bottom line any. Sure, I'll sell a bit more, but I'll more than lose because the price will be lower."
   c. "My customers are real shoppers. After I cut my prices just a few cents below those my competitors charge, customers have been flocking to my store and sales are booming."
   d. "The economic expansion has done wonders for my sales. With more people back at work, my sales are taking off!"

9. Moving upward along a linear demand curve, as the price rises and the quantity demanded decreases, the price elasticity of demand
   a. falls.
   b. does not change.
   c. rises.
   d. first rises and then falls.

10. If the price elasticity of demand equals 1.0, then as the price falls the
    a. quantity demanded decreases.
    b. total revenue falls.
    c. quantity demanded does not change.
    d. total revenue does not change.

11. A rise in the price of a product increases the total revenue from the product if the
    a. income elasticity of demand exceeds 1.
    b. good is an inferior product.
    c. product has an inelastic demand.
    d. product has an elastic demand.

12. By reviewing its sales records, IBM economists discover that when it lowers the price of its personal computers, the total revenue IBM obtains from the sale of its personal computers rises. Hence
    a. supply of IBM personal computers is elastic.
    b. demand for IBM personal computers is elastic.
    c. supply of IBM personal computers is inelastic.
    d. demand for IBM personal computers is inelastic.

13. If a 4 percent rise in the price of peanut butter causes total revenue from sales of peanut butter to fall by 8 percent, then peanut butter has a(n)
    a. elastic demand.
    b. inelastic demand.
    c. unit elastic demand.
    d. There is not enough information given to determine whether the demand for peanut butter is elastic, unit elastic, or inelastic.

14. When the price of a hot dog rises 10 percent, your expenditure on hot dogs increases. Hence, it is certain that
    a. hot dogs are a normal good for you.
    b. hot dogs are an inferior good for you.
    c. your demand for hot dogs is elastic.
    d. your demand for hot dogs is inelastic.

More Elasticities of Demand

15. For which of the following pairs of goods is the cross elasticity of demand positive?
    a. Tennis balls and tennis rackets
    b. Videotapes and laundry detergent
    c. Airline trips and textbooks
    d. Beef and chicken

16. A 10 percent increase in the price of a Pepsi increases the demand for a Coca Cola by 50 percent. Thus the cross elasticity of demand between Pepsi and Coca Cola is
    a. 50.0.
    b. 10.0.
    c. 5.0.
    d. 0.2.

17. A fall in the price of a paperback book from $6 to $4 causes a decrease in the quantity of magazines demanded from 1,100 to 900. What is the cross elasticity of demand between paperback books and magazines?
    a. 0.5
    b. −0.5
    c. 2.0
    d. Without information about what was the change in income, it is not possible to calculate the cross elasticity of demand.

18. Suppose that the *income* elasticity of demand for apartments is −0.2. This value indicates that
    a. the demand for apartments is price inelastic.
    b. the demand for apartments is unit elastic.
    c. a rise in the rent for apartments lowers the total revenue from renting apartments.
    d. apartments are an inferior good.

19. Beans are an inferior good; chicken is a normal good. When people's incomes rise, the demand for beans _____ and the demand for chicken _____.
    a. increases; increases
    b. increases; decreases
    c. decreases; increases
    d. decreases; decreases

20. A 10 percent hike in income increases the demand for coffee by 3 percent. Then the income elasticity of demand for coffee is
    a. −0.3.
    b. 3.3.
    c. 0.3.
    d. 10.0.

21. *All* normal goods have
    a. income elasticities of demand greater than 1.0.
    b. price elasticities of demand greater than 1.0.
    c. negative price elasticities of demand.
    d. positive income elasticities of demand.

Elasticity of Supply

22. Suppose that the price elasticity of supply for oil is 0.1. Then, if the price of oil rises by 20 percent, the quantity of oil supplied will increase
    a. by 200 percent.
    b. by 20 percent.
    c. by 2 percent.
    d. by 0.2 percent.

23. When the price of a CD is $13 per CD, 39,000,000 CDs per year are supplied. When the price is $15 per CD, 41,000,000 CDs per year are supplied. What is the elasticity of supply for CDs?
    a. 2.86
    b. 0.35
    c. 0.14
    d. 0.05

24. If the long-run supply of rice is perfectly elastic, then
    a. as people's incomes rise, the quantity of rice supplied decreases.
    b. as the price of *corn* falls, the quantity of *rice* demanded decreases.
    c. in the long run, a large rise in the price of rice causes no change in the quantity of rice supplied.
    d. in the long run, an increase in the demand for rice leaves the price of rice unchanged.

25. The elasticity of supply does <u>NOT</u> depend on
    a. resource substitution possibilities.
    b. the fraction of income spent on the product.
    c. the time elapsed since the price change.
    d. None of the above because all of the factors listed affect the elasticity of supply.

■ Short Answer Problems

1. Assume that the price elasticity of demand for oil is 0.2 in the short run and 0.8 in the long run. To raise the price of oil by 10 percent in the short run, what must be the decrease in the quantity of oil? In the long run, to have a 10 percent rise in the price of oil, what must be the decrease?

FIGURE **4.1**

Short Answer Problem 2

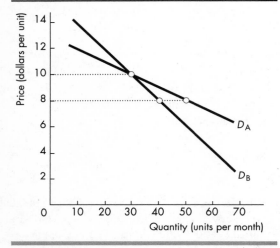

2. In Figure 4.1 which demand is more elastic between prices $10 and $8?

3. Why is the price elasticity of demand for food larger in poor nations than in rich nations?

4. Explain what perfectly elastic demand means. Sketch an example of a demand curve for a good with perfectly elastic demand. When will perfectly elastic demand occur? Be sure to use the notion of substitutes in your answer.

5. The supply curve for audio tapes is illustrated in Figure 4.2. Perhaps because of a rise in wages, the supply of tapes decreases so that for every possible quantity, the new supply curve lies above the old supply curve by $1.

   a. Suppose the demand for tapes is perfectly elastic and is such that the initial equilibrium price is $2 for a tape. After the decrease in supply, by how much does the price of a tape rise? Draw a figure to illustrate your answer.

   b. Suppose the demand for tapes is perfectly inelastic and is such that the initial equilibrium price of a tape is $2. In this case, by how much

FIGURE **4.2**

Short Answer Problem 5

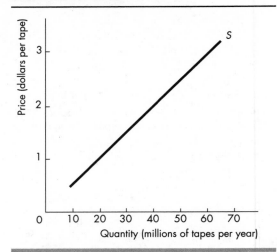

does the price of a tape rise? Draw a figure to illustrate this situation.

   c. Based on your answers to parts (a) and (b), when will an increase in costs raise the price of a product the most: When demand is elastic or when it is inelastic? When will it decrease the quantity the most? When demand is elastic or inelastic? Is there any situation under which the price does not change?

TABLE **4.2**

The Demand for Burritos

Price (dollars per burrito)	Quantity demanded (burritos per week)	Total revenue per week (dollars)
$8	30	_____
7	40	_____
6	50	_____
5	60	_____
4	70	_____
3	80	_____
2	90	_____
1	100	_____

6. Table 4.2 gives eight points on a demand curve for burritos.

   a. Graph this demand curve.

   b. Calculate the price elasticity of demand between $1 and $2; $2 and $3; $3 and $4; $4 and $5; $5 and $6; $6 and $7; and $7 and $8.

c. In Table 4.2, complete the last column.

d. Based on your answer to part (b), how does the price elasticity of demand change for a movement downward along this demand curve? How does this change relate to your answers in part (c) for total revenue at the different prices?

TABLE **4.3**

The Demand For Pizza

Price (dollars per slice of pizza)	Quantity demanded (slices of pizza per week)	Total revenue per week (dollars)
$8	12.5	_____
7	14.3	_____
6	16.7	_____
5	20	_____
4	25	_____
3	33.3	_____
2	50	_____
1	100	_____

---

7. Table 4.3 gives eight points on a demand curve for slices of pizza.

a. Graph the demand curve.

b. Calculate the price elasticity of demand between $1 and $2; $2 and $3; $3 and $4; $4 and $5; $5 and $6; $6 and $7; and $7 and $8.

c. Complete the last column in Table 4.3.

d. Based on your answers to parts (b) and (c), how does the total revenue per week relate to the price elasticity of demand at the different prices?

8. You are the manager of a local restaurant. You notice that when you lower the price of your meals, your total revenue rises. What conclusion can you draw about the demand for your restaurant's meals?

9. For automobiles, why does the elasticity of supply generally increase as more time passes after a price change?

10. The demand for a product permanently increases. Suppose that the long-run supply is more elastic than the short-run supply. When will the price of the product rise the most? Immediately after the demand change or in the long run? When will the quantity increase the most? Draw a graph to illustrate your answers.

■ You're the Teacher

1. "How can I use the price elasticity of demand formula to calculate the price elasticity of demand? Also how can I determine how much a decrease in quantity boosts the price or how much a price change affects the quantity demanded?" Your classmate is having trouble with some algebra. Once more, help out your friend by demonstrating how to use the formula for price elasticity to answer the questions.

2. "The whole idea of 'elasticity' is unnecessarily complicated! Take the price elasticity of demand; it tries to measure how strongly demanders respond to a price change. But the slope of the demand curve shows us that. The flatter the demand curve, the more consumers react to a price change. Clearly, economists should just use the slope of the demand curve as their measure of 'elasticity'. I don't know why they bother to use percentages except to make this idea hard!" Economists enjoy simple things as much as anyone, so they surely do not use percentages to make elasticity difficult to understand. Thus the speaker is making an error; correct the error in the analysis.

Answers

■ True/False Answers

Price Elasticity of Demand

1. **F** The slope of the demand curve equals $\Delta P/\Delta Q$, whereas the price elasticity of demand equals $(\Delta Q/Q_{ave})/(\Delta P/P_{ave})$.

2. **T** The smallest value for the price elasticity of demand, 0, reflects perfectly inelastic demand; the largest, ∞, indicates perfectly elastic demand.

3. **T** The stronger the response to a price change, the larger is the elasticity.

4. **F** Demand is elastic when the price elasticity of demand exceeds 1.0.

5. **T** Other brands of gasoline, such as Shell or Amoco, are close substitutes for Exxon, so the demand for Exxon gasoline is likely to be elastic.

6. **F** Moving downward along a linear demand curve, the price elasticity of demand falls.

7. **T** Generally, the larger the total budget share spent on a product, the greater is the price elasticity of demand.

8. **T** In poor nations food takes a larger portion of consumer spending, so the price elasticity of demand is larger.

9. **F** As more time passes, more changes in demand can occur, so demand becomes *more* elastic.

10. **F** The demand for Domino's Pizza is elastic, so rising the price decreases the quantity by so much that total revenue declines.

More Elasticities of Demand

11. **T** Hot dogs and hot dog buns are complements, so the cross elasticity of demand is negative.

12. **F** To be elastic, the *price* elasticity of demand must exceed 1.0.

13. **T** An increase in income decreases the demand for inferior goods and increases it for normal goods.

Elasticity of Supply

14. **F** The price elasticity of supply equals the *percentage* change in the quantity supplied divided by the *percentage* change in price.

15. **T** When the elasticity of supply equals zero, the supply is perfectly inelastic.

■ Multiple Choice Answers

Price Elasticity of Demand

1. **a** The price elasticity of demand is equal to (2 percent)/(10 percent) = 0.2.

2. **b** The price elasticity of demand between two points equals $(\Delta Q/Q_{ave})/(\Delta P/P_{ave})$. In this case we get (10/50)/($2/$20) = 2.

3. **a** Rearranging the formula for the price elasticity of demand gives (percentage change in price) = (percentage change in quantity demanded)/(elasticity of demand). So, the percentage change in price equals (5 percent)/(1.25) = 4 percent.

4. **a** When a product has a perfectly inelastic demand, the price elasticity of demand equals zero and the demand curve is vertical.

5. **b** "Perfectly elastic" means that a very small rise in the price means that the quantity demanded decreases to 0, which is the situation with a horizontal demand curve.

6. **d** If there are no close substitutes, demanders continue to buy the product even if its price is boosted substantially, which means that the demand is inelastic.

7. **d** There are many more substitutes for a new Ford Mustang than for the other goods. This answer is an example of the proposition that the more narrowly defined a good, the larger is its price elasticity of demand.

8. **c** This statement describes a situation whereby a small cut in price increased the quantity demanded substantially, which means that the demand is elastic.

9. **a** Moving upward along a linear demand curve, the price elasticity of demand falls in value.

10. **d** If demand is unit price elastic, a change in the price of the product creates an offsetting change in the quantity demanded so that total revenue does not change.

11. **c** If the demand is inelastic, the percentage rise in price exceeds the percentage decrease in the quantity demanded, so total revenue from sales of the good increases.

12. **b** When the demand is elastic, the percentage increase in the quantity demanded exceeds the percentage fall in the price, so total revenue rises.

13. **a** When demand is elastic, a rise in the price of the product decreases the quantity demanded by

proportionally more, so that total revenue falls when the price is boosted.

14. **d** When an increase in the price of a product increases your expenditure on the product, your demand for the product is inelastic.

More Elasticities of Demand

15. **d** The cross elasticity of demand is positive for substitutes. Beef and chicken are substitutes, so their cross elasticity of demand is positive.

16. **c** The cross elasticity of demand equals the percentage change in the quantity of Coca Cola divided by the percentage change in the price of a Pepsi. Hence the cross elasticity of demand equals (50 percent)/(10 percent) = 5.0.

17. **a** The cross elasticity of demand is calculated as $(\Delta Q/Q_{ave})/(\Delta P/P_{ave})$, in which the "quantity" refers to magazines and the "price" to paperback books. Using the formula for the cross elasticity gives $(-200/1,000)/(-\$2/\$5) = 0.5$.

18. **d** If the income elasticity is negative, the product is an inferior good.

19. **c** For an inferior good an increase in income decreases demand; for a normal good an increase in income increases demand.

20. **c** The income elasticity of demand equals in this case equals (3 percent)/(10 percent) or 0.3.

21. **d** An increase in income increases the demand for a normal good.

Elasticity of Supply

22. **c** Rearranging the formula for the price elasticity of supply gives (percentage change in quantity supplied) = (price elasticity of supply) × (percentage change in price) = (0.1) × (20 percent) = 2 percent.

23. **b** Analogous to the price elasticity of demand, the elasticity of supply is $(\Delta Q/Q_{avg})/(\Delta P/P_{avg})$, or $(2,000,000/40,000,000)/(\$2/\$14) = 0.35$.

24. **d** When the supply is perfectly elastic, an increase in demand has no effect on the equilibrium price. This result is illustrated in Figure 4.3, in which the increase in demand from D_0 to D_1 leaves the price constant at $50 a ton.

25. **b** The proportion of income spent on the product affects the price elasticity of demand, *not* the price elasticity of supply.

FIGURE 4.3
Multiple Choice Question 24

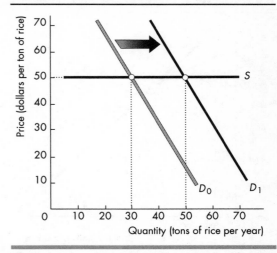

■ Answers to Short Answer Problems

1. Rearranging the formula for the price elasticity of demand gives (price elasticity of demand) × (percentage change in price) = (percentage change in quantity). The price rise is 10 percent, so the amount by which the quantity must be restricted in the short run is (0.2) × (10 percent) = 2 percent.

   In the long run, the price elasticity of demand is 0.8, so the decrease in the quantity is (0.8)(10 percent) = 8 percent. To raise the price by 10 percent, the long-run decrease in the quantity must be four times the short-run decrease.

2. The demand represented by D_A is more elastic than the demand given by D_B. To see why, recall the formula for the price elasticity of demand

$$\frac{\text{(percentage change in quantity demanded)}}{\text{(percentage change in price)}}$$

   Along both demand curves, the percentage change in the price from $10 to $8 is the same. But Figure 4.4 (on the next page) shows that the percentage change in the quantity demanded is greater along D_A where the quantity demanded increases from 30 to 50, a 50 percent increase, whereas along D_B the quantity demanded increases to 40, only a 29 percent increase. Because the percentage increase in the quantity demanded is greater along D_A the price elasticity of demand over this price range is higher for D_A.

FIGURE **4.4**

Short Answer Problem 2

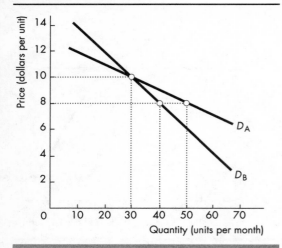

3. The larger the fraction of their income that consumers spend on a product, the greater the price elasticity of demand. People in poor nations spend a larger proportion of their income on food than do people in wealthy nations, so the price elasticity of demand for food is larger in poor nations.

FIGURE **4.5**

Short Answer Problem 4

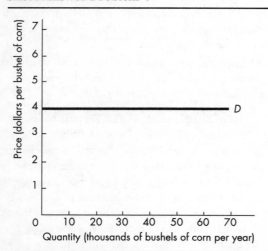

4. A perfectly elastic demand is illustrated in Figure 4.5. Demand is perfectly elastic when demanders can find perfect substitutes for a product. For exam-

ple, consider corn grown by one farmer. Other farmers' corn is a perfect substitute for the first farmer's corn. If there are perfect substitutes for the product, even the smallest rise in the price of the product leads the quantity demanded to decrease to 0. The horizontal demand curve in Figure 4.5 indicates that any rise in the price above $4 a bushel will decrease the quantity demanded to 0.

FIGURE **4.6**

Short Answer Problem 5 (a)

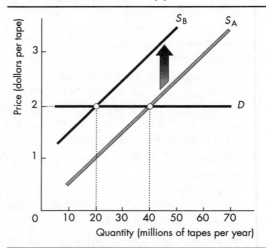

5. a. In Figure 4.6 the rise in costs shifts the supply curve from S_A to S_B. The arrow indicates $1, the amount by which the new supply curve lies above the old supply curve. The price stays at $2; in other words, the price does not rise. The quantity, however decreases from 40 million to 20 million per year.

   b. In Figure 4.7 (on the next page), the supply curve again shifts from S_A to S_B and the length of the arrow again indicates $1. In this case, when the demand is perfectly inelastic, the price rises by the full amount indicated by the arrow; that is, the price climbs from $2 to $3 a tape, which is a rise of exactly $1. The quantity, however, remains constant at 40 million tapes.

   c. As Figures 4.6 and 4.7 show, the rise in costs increases the price the most when demand is inelastic. When demand is perfectly inelastic, the price goes up by the full amount of the rise in costs. Then, as demand becomes more elastic, the price rises by less. At the other extreme,

FIGURE **4.7**

FIGURE **4.7**

Short Answer Problem 5 (b)

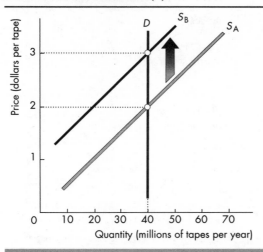

when demand is perfectly elastic, the price does not change.

The quantity decreases most when demand is perfectly elastic. As demand becomes less elastic, the change in the quantity becomes smaller.

FIGURE **4.8**

Short Answer Problem 6 (a)

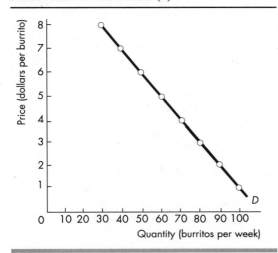

6. a. Figure 4.8 shows the demand curve.
    b. Table 4.4 contains the price elasticities of demand. To see how these elasticities are calculated, take the elasticity between $1 and $2 as

TABLE **4.4**

Short Answer Problem 6 (b)

Prices	Elasticity
$7 to $8	2.14
6 to 7	1.44
5 to 6	1.00
4 to 5	0.69
3 to 4	0.47
2 to 3	0.29
1 to 2	0.16

TABLE **4.5**

Short Answer Problem 6 (c)

Price	Total Revenue
$8	$240
7	280
6	300
5	300
4	280
3	240
2	180
1	100

an example. The elasticity of demand is defined as $(\Delta Q/Q_{ave})/(\Delta P/P_{ave})$, which in this case gives $(10/95)/(\$1/\$1.50) = 0.16$.

c. The total revenues are given in Table 4.5. Total revenue equals $(P)(Q)$, so at a price of $6, $(\$6)(50) = \$300$.

d. Moving along the demand curve from $8 to $1 results in the elasticity falling, from 2.14 when the price is between $8 and $7, to 0.16 when the price is between $2 and $1. When demand is elastic, between $8 and $6, a fall in price (with its corresponding increase in sales) raises total revenue. When demand is unit elastic, between $6 and $5, total revenue is at its maximum and a drop in price (with the increase in sales) does not change the total revenue. Finally, over the range when demand is inelastic, from a price of $5 to a price of $1, even though a fall in price raises the quantity sold, it does so by a smaller percentage so that in this range the fall in price lowers total revenue.

FIGURE **4.9**

Short Answer Problem 7 (a)

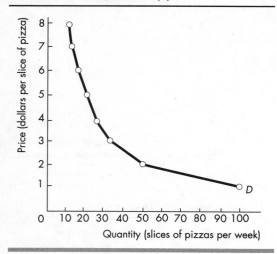

7. a. Figure 4.9 illustrates the demand curve.

b. Table 4.6 contains the price elasticities of demand. For example, at a price between $4 and $5, the price elasticity of demand equals $(\Delta Q/Q_{ave})/(\Delta P/P_{ave}) = (5/22.5)/(\$1/\$4.50) = 1.00$.

c. Total revenues are in Table 4.7. Total revenue equals $(P)(Q)$. Thus to calculate the total revenue at a price of, say, $2, multiply the price times the quantity, or $(\$2)(50) = \$100$.

d. The price elasticity of demand along this demand curve always equals 1.00. In other words, this demand is always unit elastic. With unit elasticity, changes in price do not change total revenue, which is precisely what Table 4.7 illustrates.

TABLE **4.6**

Short Answer Problem 7 (b)

Prices	Elasticity
$7 to $8	1.00
6 to 7	1.00
5 to 6	1.00
4 to 5	1.00
3 to 4	1.00
2 to 3	1.00
1 to 2	1.00

TABLE **4.7**

Short Answer Problem 7 (c)

Price	Total Revenue
$8	$100
7	100
6	100
5	100
4	100
3	100
2	100
1	100

8. The demand for the meals is elastic. Why? When the demand is elastic, a fall in price raises total revenue, which is precisely what you have observed.

9. The elasticity of supply increases as time passes after a price change because making changes in the production process becomes easier. For instance, to meet a permanent increase in the demand for automobiles, initially automakers might only be able to add an additional shift of workers at existing factories. But with the passage of time, the companies can make larger changes, such as building more factories. As more capacity is added, more cars will be manufactured, increasing the elasticity of supply.

FIGURE **4.10**

Short Answer Problem 10

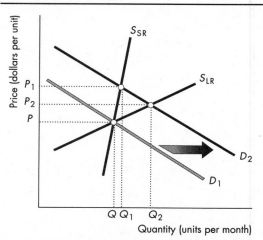

10. The price of the product rises the most immediately after the increase in demand, and the quantity increases the most in the long run. These results are

illustrated in Figure 4.10. Here the short-run supply curve is labeled S_{SR} and the long-run supply curve is labeled S_{LR}. Demand increases from D_1 to D_2. Immediately after the increase, the price rises from P to P_1 and the quantity increases from Q to Q_1. In the long run, supply becomes more elastic and so the long run supply curve, S_{LR}, becomes relevant. Hence the price rises ultimately only to P_2 while the quantity increases all the way to Q_2.

■ You're the Teacher

1. "This is not so hard if you think about it the right way! The formula is price elasticity of demand =

$$\frac{\text{(percentage change in quantity demanded)}}{\text{(percentage change in price)}}$$

This formula contains three numbers: price elasticity of demand, (percentage change in quantity demanded), and (percentage change in price). Now, just so you can really see these as symbols and numbers, let me call the (percentage change in price) $\%\Delta P$ and the (percentage change in quantity demanded) $\%\Delta Q$. I think that by using these symbols, it makes the formulas even clearer.

"Now, the whole deal is that if you have any two of the numbers, you can solve for the third. For instance, if you have the $\%\Delta Q$ and $\%\Delta P$, you can determine the price elasticity of demand. Similarly, if you know the price elasticity of demand and $\%\Delta Q$, you can quickly rearrange the basic elasticity formula to solve for $\%\Delta P$, as $\%\Delta P = (\%\Delta Q)/(\text{Price elasticity of demand})$. Finally, if you have the price elasticity of demand and $\%\Delta P$, you can calculate $(\%\Delta Q)$ by rearranging the basic formula to get

$\%\Delta Q = (\text{Price elasticity of demand})(\%\Delta P)$. Just plug the numbers into these formulas and that's all there is to it!"

TABLE **4.8**

You're the Teacher Question 2

Price	Quantity	Price	Quantity
$1.00	11	100¢	11
2.00	10	200	10

2. "You're basically right: All elasticity does is measure how strongly a relationship responds to some sort of change. But you're missing an important point about the slope. The slope of, say, the demand curve depends on the units involved and changes when the units used change. For example, two points on a demand curve are presented in different units in Table 4.8. In one case the prices are in dollars and in the other case the prices are in cents. The magnitude of the slope of the demand curve ($\Delta P/\Delta Q$) in the first part of the table is 1.00 and in the second part is 100.0. If the measure of elasticity changed every time we changed units, we would have a problem. For instance, we couldn't easily compare, say, the price elasticity of demand for food in Japan, where prices are stated in yen, with that in the United States, where they are stated in dollars. Using percentages, however, avoids this problem. In each of the two columns, the price elasticity of demand is the same: 0.14. That's why percentages are used in the elasticity formulas, not because economists want to make us study more in order to understand elasticity!"

Chapter Quiz

1. On a supply and demand diagram, the total revenue from sales of a good is shown as
   a. a vertical distance.
   b. a horizontal distance.
   c. the area of a triangle.
   d. the area of a rectangle.

2. The fewer substitutes available for a good, the
   a. larger is the income elasticity of demand.
   b. smaller is the income elasticity of demand.
   c. larger is the price elasticity of demand.
   d. smaller is the price elasticity of demand.

3. If the price elasticity of demand exceeds 1.0 but is less than infinity, demand is
   a. inelastic.
   b. unit elastic.
   c. elastic.
   d. perfectly elastic.

4. If the price elasticity of demand is _____, the demand curve is _____
   a. infinity; horizontal
   b. infinity; vertical
   c. one; horizontal
   d. one; vertical

5. A fall in the price of lemons from $10.50 per bushel to $9.50 increases the quantity demanded from 19,200 bushels to 20,800. The price elasticity of demand in this range of the demand is
   a. 0.80.
   b. 1.20.
   c. 1.25.
   d. 8.00.

6. If an increase in the price of corn increases the total expenditure on corn, then it is definitely the case that the
   a. supply of corn is elastic.
   b. supply of corn is inelastic.
   c. demand for corn is elastic.
   d. demand for corn is inelastic.

7. If the demand for a product is price inelastic, but *not* perfectly price inelastic, then a 10 percent decrease in its price causes the quantity demanded to increase by
   a. more than 10 percent.
   b. 10 percent.
   c. less than 10 percent.
   d. 0 percent.

8. If two different goods are complements, their
   a. cross elasticity of demand is negative.
   b. cross elasticity of demand is positive.
   c. income elasticity of demand is negative.
   d. income elasticity of demand is positive.

9. The price elasticity of supply measures
   a. how often the price of the good changes.
   b. the slope of the supply curve.
   c. how sensitive the quantity supplied is to changes in supply.
   d. how sensitive the quantity supplied is to changes in the price.

10. The supply of a product such as fresh fish is usually least elastic in the
    a. momentary period.
    b. short run.
    c. long run.
    d. competitive period.

The answers for this Chapter Quiz are on page 367

Chapter 5 EFFICIENCY AND EQUITY

■ Efficiency: A Refresher

An **efficient allocation** of resources occurs when the goods and services produced are those that people value most highly.

♦ **Marginal benefit** — the benefit a person receives from consuming one more unit of a good or service. The marginal benefit of a product is the amount of other goods and services the person is willing to give up to get one more unit of the product. As the quantity of the good consumed increases, its marginal benefit decreases.

♦ **Marginal cost** — the opportunity cost of producing one more unit of a good or service. As more of a product is produced, its marginal cost increases.

The efficient amount of a good is produced when the marginal benefit from the good equals its marginal cost.

♦ If the marginal benefit exceeds the marginal cost, the benefit of another unit exceeds the cost to produce the unit, so resources should be used to produce the unit.

♦ If the marginal cost exceeds the marginal benefit, the benefit of the last unit being produced is less than the cost of producing it, so the unit should not be produced.

■ Value, Price, and Consumer Surplus

The **value** of one more unit of a good is its marginal benefit. Marginal benefit can be measured as the

FIGURE **5.1**
Consumer Surplus

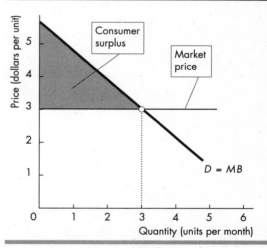

maximum that someone is willing to pay for another unit of the good. The demand curve shows the maximum someone is willing to pay for each unit of a good, so the demand curve for a good is its marginal benefit curve.

The value of a good can be different than the good's price. **Consumer surplus** is the value of a good minus the price paid for it.

♦ Because the demand curve shows the marginal benefit or value for each unit of a good, consumer surplus is the area under the demand curve (the value) and above the market price. Figure 5.1 shows the consumer surplus for the good as the darkened triangle under the demand curve and above the market price.

■ Cost, Price, and Producer Surplus

The cost of producing a good is what the producer pays to produce it; the price of a good is what the producer receives for it. The marginal cost of a good is the minimum price a producer must receive to produce the unit of the good because this amount just covers all the opportunity costs of producing it. Because a supply curve shows the minimum price a producer must receive to produce another unit of a product, a product's supply curve is also its marginal cost curve.

If a firm sells a good for more than it costs to produce it, the firm receives a producer surplus. **Producer surplus** is the price of the good minus the opportunity cost of producing it.

♦ Because the supply curve is the marginal cost curve, producer surplus equals the area below the market price of the product and above the supply curve. Figure 5.2 shows a producer surplus.

FIGURE **5.2**
Producer Surplus

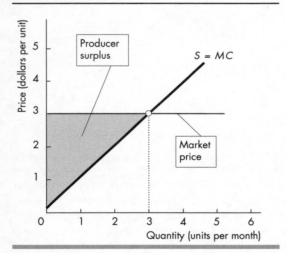

■ Is the Competitive Market Efficient?

♦ The price in a competitive market is the equilibrium price; the quantity is the equilibrium quantity. In Figure 5.3, the price is $3 and the quantity produced is 3 units, determined by the *D* and *S* curves.

♦ A competitive market is efficient because the quantity produced is the same as the efficient quantity, that is, the quantity that sets the marginal benefit

FIGURE **5.3**
Efficiency of Perfect Competition

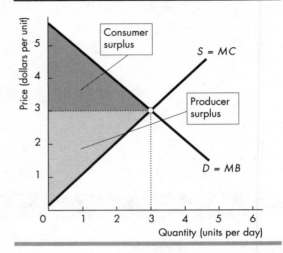

equal to the marginal cost, *MB* = *MC*. In Figure 5.3, the efficient quantity is 3 units, determined by the *MB* and *MC* curves.

♦ When the market is using resources efficiently, the sum of consumer surplus plus producer surplus is as large as possible, as illustrated in Figure 5.3.

♦ Adam Smith's historical idea of the invisible hand concludes that competitive markets send resources to their highest valued use, that is, Adam Smith concluded that competitive markets are efficient.

Contrary to the invisible hand idea, markets are not always efficient. There are five major obstacles that can lead to inefficiency in which the market overproduces or underproduces the good:

♦ *Price ceilings and floors* — government regulations that set the highest price legal to charge (a price ceiling) or the lowest price legal to charge (a price floor). Price ceilings and floors can prevent the market from reaching its free market equilibrium price and quantity.

♦ *Taxes, subsidies, and quotas* — taxes increase the price paid by buyers and lower the price received by sellers; subsidies decrease the price paid by buyers and raise the price received by sellers; and quotas directly limit the production that can occur.

♦ *Monopoly* — a **monopoly** is a single firm that controls the entire market. A monopoly decreases the output it produces in order to raise its price and increase its profit.

◆ *Public goods* — a **public good** is a good or service that can be consumed simultaneously by everyone regardless of whether they paid for it. Public goods create a free rider problem, in which people are unwilling to pay for the product.

◆ *External costs and external benefits* — an **external cost** is a cost imposed on someone other than the producer of the product; an **external benefit** is a benefit that goes to someone other than the buyer of the good.

When a market underproduces or overproduces a good, a deadweight loss is created. **Deadweight loss** is decrease in consumer surplus and producer surplus that results from an inefficient level of production.

◆ The deadweight loss is inflicted on the entire society; it is not something that the producer gains at the expense of the consumer or vice versa.

◆ Figure 5.4 illustrates the deadweight loss triangles from overproduction (producing 4 units rather than 3) and underproduction (producing 2 units rather than 3).

FIGURE **5.4**
Deadweight Loss

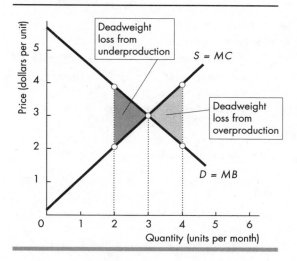

■ Is the Competitive Market Fair?

The two approaches to fairness are "It's not fair if the result isn't fair" and "It's not fair if the rules aren't fair."

◆ **Utilitarianism** — aims for "the greatest happiness for the greatest number of people." Utilitarianism looks at the results of the process. Redistribution to achieve equality in incomes (the "fair" outcome) leads to the **big tradeoff**, the tradeoff between efficiency and fairness. Redistribution weakens the incentive to work so that a more equal income distribution leads to inefficiency.

◆ **Symmetry Principle** — the requirement that similar people should be treated the same. The symmetry principle looks at the rules of the process. If the market is efficient (there are no price ceilings, price floors, subsidies, quotas, monopolies, public goods, external benefits, or external costs), competitive markets are fair according to the symmetry principle.

Helpful Hints

1. **WHY *MB* = *MC* IS EFFICIENT :** Efficiency requires producing the level of output such that $MB = MC$. It might seem more reasonable to produce where $MB > MC$. However, this presumption is wrong. Why? As long as people value another unit of the good more than it costs to produce the good, that is, $MB > MC$, society's total surplus increases if the good is produced. Look at Figure 5.5. The first unit has a large difference between MB and MC, equal

FIGURE **5.5**
Efficiency and $MB = MC$

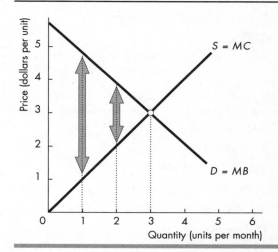

to the length of the long gray arrow. The second unit also has MB greater than MC but by less than the first unit, as indicated by the shorter gray arrow. However, producing this unit still adds to society's *total* net surplus; it just adds less than the first unit. As long as *MB* is larger than *MC*, the unit has a greater value to someone than its cost of production, so the unit should be produced. Only when *MB* = *MC* should production stop expanding because beyond this point the marginal benefit from more units falls short of the marginal cost.

2. **MARGINAL BENEFIT AND MARGINAL COST :** In casual conversation we talk about "how much a good cost us". We also talk about "how much a firm benefited by selling us the good." But be careful not to confuse conversation with the precise language of economic science. In particular, the marginal benefit from a good is received by the consumer and the marginal cost is paid by the producer. It is that the consumer of the good who benefits from the product. You, when you drive your car, benefit from your car. It is the producer of the good who pays for the production. The firm that manufactured your car paid the steel mill for the steel used to produce it.

Questions

■ True/False and Explain

Efficiency: A Refresher

1. Resource use is efficient when the goods with the lowest opportunity cost are produced.

2. As more of a product is consumed, its marginal benefit decreases.

3. The marginal cost of the one millionth pizza is the total cost of producing all million pizzas.

4. If the marginal benefit from a good exceeds its marginal cost, resources are used more efficiently if less of the good is produced.

5. Resource efficiency requires that the marginal benefit of a good equal its marginal cost.

Value, Price, and Consumer Surplus

6. The price of a product always equals its value.

7. The demand curve for tacos shows the maximum someone is willing to pay for the ten millionth taco.

8. Consumer surplus equals the area above the demand curve and below the market price.

Cost, Price, and Producer Surplus

9. Cost and price are the same thing.

10. The supply curve and the marginal benefit curve are the same.

11. Producer surplus equals the price of the good minus the opportunity cost of producing the unit.

Is the Competitive Market Efficient?

12. A competitive market is always efficient.

13. When producing the efficient quantity of a good, the sum of consumer surplus plus producer surplus is as large as possible.

14. Deadweight loss is comprised of a loss of consumer surplus and/or producer surplus.

Is the Competitive Market Fair?

15. Utilitarianism says that a competitive market producing the efficient quantity is always fair.

16. The idea of making the poorest as well off as possible uses the "results" to judge fairness.

17. The symmetry principle states that people should have identical, this is, "symmetric" incomes.

■ Multiple Choice

Efficiency: A Refresher

1. In general, resources are used efficiently when the
   a. opportunity cost of the goods being produced is as low as possible.
   b. marginal benefit from a good exceeds its marginal cost by as much as possible.
   c. goods produced are those valued most highly.
   d. None of the above.

2. Susan is eating two slices of pizza. Which of the following statements is necessarily true?
   a. Susan's marginal benefit from the second slice of pizza is equal to the sum of the benefit she gets from the first slice plus her benefit from the second slice.
   b. Susan's marginal benefit from the second slice of pizza equals the maximum she is willing to pay for the second slice.
   c. Susan has no consumer surplus from the second slice of pizza.
   d. Susan has some consumer surplus from the second slice of pizza.

FIGURE **5.6**
Multiple Choice Question 3

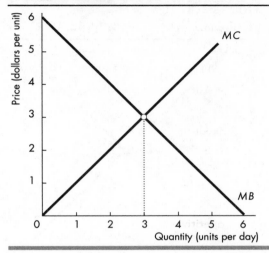

3. What is the efficient amount of output in Figure 5.6?

   a. 0 units, where *MB* exceeds *MC* by as much as possible.
   b. 3 units, where *MB* equals *MC*.
   c. 6 units, where *MC* exceeds *MB* by as much as possible.
   d. None of the above.

Value, Price, and Consumer Surplus

4. Which of the following statements is <u>FALSE</u>?

   a. The value of one more unit of a good is the good's marginal benefit.
   b. A good's marginal benefit is the maximum price people are willing to pay for another unit.
   c. The maximum price people are willing to pay for one more unit of a good is its value.
   d. None of the above because all the statements are true.

5. The marginal benefit curve for a product is the same as the good's

   a. marginal cost curve.
   b. supply curve.
   c. demand curve.
   d. consumer surplus curve.

6. Susan is willing to pay $3.00 for the second slice of pizza she eats. The price she actually pays is $2.00. Susan's consumer surplus for this slice of pizza equals

   a. $3.00.
   b. $2.00.
   c. $1.50.
   d. $1.00.

7. Because of decreasing marginal benefit, the consumer surplus from the first unit of a good is _____ the consumer surplus from the second unit.

   a. greater than
   b. equal to
   c. less than
   d. not comparable to

Cost, Price, and Producer Surplus

8. The cost of producing one more unit of a good is the good's

   a. price.
   b. marginal benefit.
   c. marginal cost.
   d. producer surplus.

9. The supply curve shows the

   a. minimum price suppliers must receive in order to produce another unit of the good.
   b. maximum price suppliers must receive in order to produce another unit of the good.
   c. amount of producer surplus suppliers receive.
   d. profit that suppliers receive from producing another unit of the good.

10. The producer surplus from a good is equal to the

   a. maximum amount a consumer is willing to pay for the good minus the price that actually must be paid.
   b. actual price of the good minus the maximum amount a consumer is willing to pay for the good.
   c. opportunity cost of producing the good minus its price.
   d. price of the good minus its opportunity cost of production.

Is the Competitive Market Efficient?

Figure 5.7 illustrates a perfectly competitive market without any external costs, external benefits, taxes, subsidies, quotas, price ceilings, or price floors. Use Figure 5.7 for the next two questions.

FIGURE **5.7**

Multiple Choice Questions 11 and 12

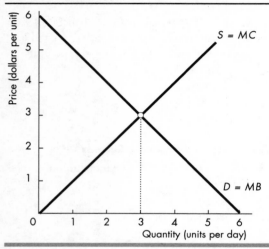

11. The equilibrium quantity produced equals
    a. 0 units.
    b. 3 units.
    c. 6 units.
    d. None of the above.

12. The efficient quantity equals
    a. 0 units.
    b. 3 units.
    c. 6 units.
    d. None of the above.

13. Which of the following is <u>NOT</u> a potential source of inefficiency?
    a. External costs
    b. Decreasing marginal benefit
    c. Monopoly
    d. A tax

Use Figure 5.8, and the areas illustrated in it, for the next four questions.

FIGURE **5.8**

Multiple Choice Questions 14, 15, 16, 17

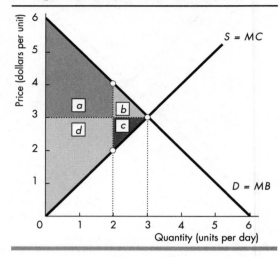

14. When production is 3 units with a price of $3, consumer surplus in the market illustrated in Figure 5.8 equals
    a. area *a*.
    b. area *b*.
    c. area *a* + *b*.
    d. area *a* + *d*.

15. When production is 3 units with a price of $3, producer surplus in this market equals
    a. area *a* + *b*.
    b. area *c*.
    c. area *c* + *d*.
    d. area *a* + *c*.

16. If the quantity is restricted to 2, then the deadweight loss equals
    a. area *c*.
    b. area *c* +*d*.
    c. area *a* +*b*.
    d. area *b* + *c*.

17. How does the sum of the consumer surplus and producer surplus when 3 units are produced compare to the sum when 2 units are produced?
    a. The sum is larger when 3 units are produced.
    b. The sum is the same.
    c. The sum is larger when 2 units are produced.
    d. The sum cannot be compared between these two situations.

FIGURE **5.9**

Multiple Choice Question 18

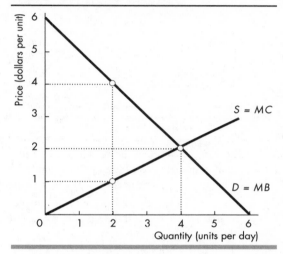

18. In Figure 5.9, when 2 units are produced, what is the dollar value of the deadweight loss?
    a. $0
    b. $2
    c. $3
    d. $8

19. A deadweight loss
    a. is possible only if the good is underproduced but is not possible if the good is overproduced.
    b. subtracts only from producer surplus.
    c. is a loss to consumers and a gain to producers.
    d. is a loss inflicted on the entire society.

20. Suppose consumers decide they value a product more highly than before. Then the efficient quantity to produce of that product ____.
    a. increases.
    b. does not change.
    c. decreases.
    d. perhaps changes, but without more information the direction of the change cannot be told.

21. Suppose the marginal cost of producing a product rises. Then, the efficient quantity to produce of that product ____.
    a. increases.
    b. does not change.
    c. decreases.
    d. perhaps changes, but without more information the direction of the change cannot be told.

Is the Competitive Market Fair?

22. Susan thinks the only fair outcome is one in which she has three slices of pizza a week. Susan is using a ____ concept of fairness.
    a. "it's not fair if the result isn't fair"
    b. "it's not fair if the rules aren't fair"
    c. "big tradeoff"
    d. "symmetry principle"

23. The assertion that if resources are allocated efficiently, they also are allocated fairly is made by
    a. all utilitarians.
    b. John Rawls, who proposed making the poorest as well off as possible.
    c. Robert Nozick, who believes that equality of opportunity is fair.
    d. all economists who understand the big tradeoff.

■ **Short Answer Problems**

1. a. Table 5.1 presents the marginal benefit and marginal cost schedules for video games. There are no external costs or benefits. Based on Table 5.1, complete Table 5.2 (on the next page).

TABLE **5.1**

Marginal Benefit and Marginal Cost of Video Games

Quantity (millions of video games)	Marginal benefit (dollars per game)	Marginal cost (dollars per game)
1	50	10
2	40	20
3	30	30
4	20	40
5	10	50

TABLE **5.2**

Short Answer Problem 1 (a)

Quantity (millions of video games)	Marginal benefit minus marginal cost
1	――
2	――
3	――
4	――
5	――

FIGURE **5.10**

Short Answer Problems 1 and 2

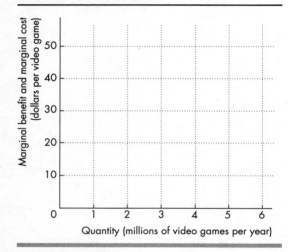

b. In Figure 5.10 draw the marginal benefit and marginal cost curves from Table 5.1.

c. What is the efficient number of video games to produce?

2. a. Using the data in Table 5.1, in Figure 5.10 now draw the demand curve for video games and the supply curve for video games.

  b. There are no price ceilings, price floors, taxes, subsidies, or quotas in this market. The market also is competitive, that is, it is not a monopoly. What quantity of video games will be produced?

  c. Compare your answer to part (c) of problem 2 with your answer to part (c) of problem 1.

3. What is the relationship between the marginal benefit of a good, its value, and the maximum amount that a consumer is willing to pay for the good?

FIGURE **5.11**

The Demand For Jeans

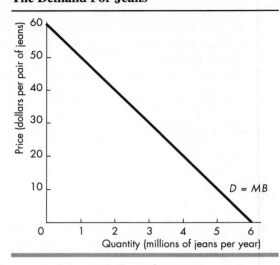

4. a. Figure 5.11 shows the market demand curve for jeans. In the figure, indicate consumer surplus if the market price is $40 for a pair of jeans. What dollar amount does the consumer surplus equal?

  b. In Figure 5.11, indicate the consumer surplus if the market price is $30 for a pair of jeans. What does the consumer surplus now equal?

  c. When is the consumer surplus larger?

FIGURE **5.12**

The Supply Of Jeans

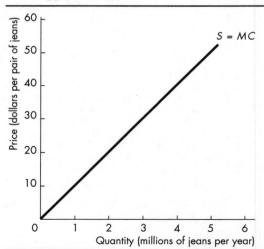

5. a. Figure 5.12 shows the market supply curve for jeans. In the figure, indicate the producer sur-

plus if the market price is $40 for a pair of jeans. What dollar amount does the producer surplus equal?

b. In Figure 5.12, indicate the producer surplus if the market price is $30 for a pair of jeans. What does the producer surplus now equal?

c. When is the producer surplus larger?

FIGURE 5.13
Short Answer Problem 6 (a)

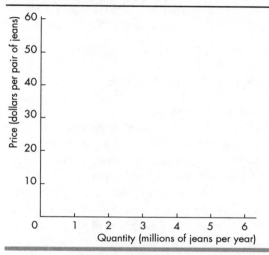

6. a. Using the demand curve from Figure 5.11 and the supply curve from Figure 5.12, in Figure 5.13 determine the equilibrium price and quantity of jeans.

b. In Figure 5.13 illustrate the consumer surplus and the producer surplus. What are the dollar amounts of consumer surplus and producer surplus? What do the total gains from trade equal?

c. Suppose that output is restricted to 2 million pairs of jeans. In a figure similar to Figure 5.13, show the deadweight loss. What does the deadweight loss equal? What do the total gains from trade now equal?

d. Suppose that output is equal to 4 million pairs of jeans. In another figure similar to Figure 5.13, show the deadweight loss. What does the deadweight loss equal? What do the total gains from trade equal?

e. When are the gains from trade the largest: When 2 million jeans are produced? When 4 million jeans are produced? Or when the efficient quantity of jeans is produced?

7. What is a deadweight loss?

8. a. Igor has a job as Minister of Agriculture. He is interested in the market for mushrooms because he has a fondness for mushrooms. Igor realizes that this market is competitive. He also knows that there are no external benefits or external costs and that there are no government policies, such as taxes or subsidies, affecting the market. The equilibrium quantity of mushrooms is 10 million pounds a year. Igor wants to know what would be the quantity produced if resources are being used efficiently. Based on the information given, what is the efficient quantity of mushrooms?

b. Igor can't believe that the efficient quantity is as low as you answered. (He *really* likes mushrooms!) Igor asks: What would be the loss if 11 million pounds of mushrooms are grown? In a diagram, show Igor the loss.

c. Igor now claims that the efficient quantity isn't fair because it is too small. What concept of fairness is Igor using?

d. Given Igor's view in the previous question, is Igor likely to agree that "it isn't fair if the rules aren't fair?" Why or why not?

■ You're the Teacher

1. "You know, there's one point about this chapter that bugs me. I can't understand how it's possible to have too much of a good. After all, in Chapter 3 we talked a lot about scarcity and about how there aren't enough resources available to produce enough stuff so that everyone's wants are met. Now here's this chapter that says we can produce too much of a product. What is going on?" Explain to your friend why it is possible to "overproduce" a product and, if you feel ambitious, further explain how the fact that resources *are* scarce implies that such overproduction harms society.

Answers

True/False Answers

Efficiency: A Refresher

1. **F** Resources are used efficiently when they produce the goods valued most highly.

2. **T** The principle of decreasing marginal benefit states that as more of a good is consumed, its marginal benefit decreases.

3. **F** The marginal cost of the one millionth pizza is the cost of producing only the one millionth pizza.

4. **F** If the marginal benefit exceeds the marginal cost, resources are used more efficiently if production of the good is increased.

5. **T** The equality between marginal benefit and marginal cost signals that resources are being used efficiently.

Value, Price, and Consumer Surplus

6. **F** The value of a product equals the maximum that someone is willing to pay for it, which often exceeds the price.

7. **T** Because the demand curve shows the maximum someone is willing to pay for each unit, the demand curve is the same as the marginal benefit curve.

8. **F** Consumer surplus in a market equals the area *under* the demand curve and *above* the price.

Cost, Price, and Producer Surplus

9. **F** Cost is what a producer pays to produce a good; price is what a producer receives when the good is sold.

10. **F** The supply curve is the same as the marginal cost curve.

11. **T** The statement defines producer surplus.

Is the Competitive Market Efficient?

12. **F** If the government has imposed a tax, a subsidy, a quota, a price ceiling, or a price floor, or if there are external costs or benefits, or if the good is a public good, the market will not necessarily be efficient.

13. **T** The fact that the sum of consumer surplus and producer surplus is as large as possible indicates that the gains from trade are as large as possible.

14. **T** A deadweight loss is a total loss to society; no one benefits from a deadweight loss.

Is the Competitive Market Fair?

15. **F** Utilitarianism argues that income should be taken from the rich and given to the poor. It does *not* claim that efficiency is fair.

16. **T** Making the poorest as well off as possible changes the economic game's results after the game is over.

17. **F** The symmetry principle is the assertion that people in similar circumstances should be treated similarly.

Multiple Choice Answers

Efficiency: A Refresher

1. **c** Efficiency occurs when the goods people value most highly are the goods being produced.

2. **b** The marginal benefit from the second slice of pizza is measured as the maximum Susan is willing to pay for the slice.

3. **b** Producing the quantity that sets *MB* equal to *MC* gives the efficient level of production.

Value, Price, and Consumer Surplus

4. **d** All of the statements are correct. Thus the value of a good equals the marginal benefit of the good equals the maximum amount consumers are willing to pay for another unit of the good.

5. **c** Because the marginal benefit is the maximum amount someone is willing to pay for another unit of the good, the demand curve, which shows this maximum price, is the same as the marginal benefit curve.

6. **d** Susan's consumer surplus equals the maximum she is willing to pay for the slice, $3, minus what she actually pays, $2.

7. **a** With decreasing marginal benefit, the maximum a consumer is willing to pay for the first unit of a good consumed exceeds the maximum the consumer will pay for the second unit.

Cost, Price, and Producer Surplus

8. **c** The question gives the definition of marginal cost.

9. **a** For any unit of output, the supply curve shows the minimum price for which that unit will be

produced and sold. Because the minimum price is the marginal cost of the unit, the supply curve is the same as the marginal cost curve.

10. **d** Producer surplus accrues to suppliers, and answer d is the definition of producer surplus.

Is the Competitive Market Efficient?

11. **b** The quantity produced is determined by the intersection of supply and demand curves.

12. **b** The efficient quantity is determined by the intersection of the marginal benefit, *MB*, and marginal cost, *MC*, curves. In comparison with the last answer, when demand equals the marginal benefit and supply equals the marginal cost, the amount produced is the efficient amount.

13. **b** Decreasing marginal benefit simply implies that the value of the initial units consumed exceeds the value of last units consumed.

14. **c** Consumer surplus equals the area under the demand curve and above the price.

15. **c** Producer surplus is the area above the supply curve and below the price.

16. **d** The deadweight loss is the sum of the lost consumer surplus (area *b*) plus the lost producer surplus (area *c*).

17. **a** When 3 units are produced, the sum of consumer surplus plus producer surplus is the area *a + b + c + d*; when 2 units are produced, the sum is only the area *a + d*.

FIGURE 5.14
Multiple Choice Question 18

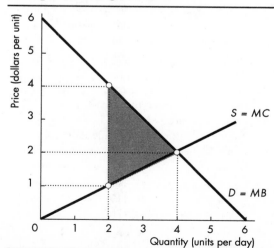

18. **c** The deadweight loss is the area of the darkened triangle in Figure 5.14. The area of a triangle equals (½)(base)(height). The base equals 4 units minus 2 units, or 2. The height equals $4 per unit minus $1 per unit, or $3. Hence the deadweight loss is (½)(2)($3) = $3.

19. **d** *No one* benefits from a deadweight loss.

20. **a** When a product is valued more highly, the marginal benefit increases and so efficiency requires that more of the product be produced.

21. **c** If the marginal cost of producing a product rises, efficiency requires that less be produced.

Is the Competitive Market Fair?

22. **a** Susan is judging fairness by looking at the outcome — she must have three slices of pizza a week — so she is using a "it's not fair if the result isn't fair" approach.

23. **c** Robert Nozick asserts that the government must establish and protect private property and that all exchanges must be voluntary, in which case the resulting outcome is efficient and fair.

■ Answers to Short Answer Problems

TABLE 5.3
Short Answer Problem 1 (a)

Quantity (millions of video games)	Marginal benefit minus marginal cost
1	40
2	20
3	0
4	−20
5	−40

1. a. See the completed Table 5.3. For each quantity, the answer in the table is obtained by subtracting the marginal benefit from the marginal cost.

   b. Figure 5.15 (on the next page) shows the marginal benefit and marginal cost schedules.

   c. Both the table and the figure demonstrate that the efficient number of video games is 3 million because this quantity sets the marginal benefit from an additional game equal to the game's marginal cost.

FIGURE **5.15**

Short Answer Problem 1

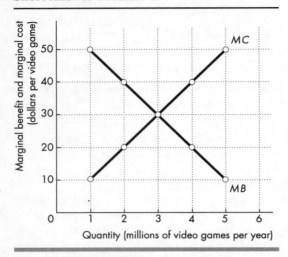

FIGURE **5.16**

Short Answer Problem 2

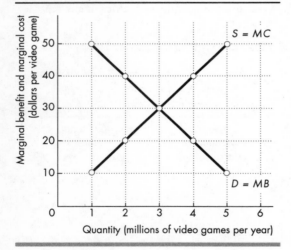

2. a. Figure 5.16 shows the demand and supply
        curves for video games. The key point in draw-
        ing Figure 5.16 is the fact that the demand
        curve, D, is the same as the marginal benefit
        curve, MB, and the supply curve, S, is the same
        as the marginal cost curve, MC. These equiva-
        lencies are noted in the figure.

    b. The quantity produced is 3 million video games,
        determined by where the supply and demand
        curves cross.

c. The two answers are identical, 3 million video
    games. In other words, the efficient quantity of
    video games is the same as the quantity actually
    produced.

3. All three concepts are the same. In other words, the
    marginal benefit of a good is defined as the good's
    value. And the value of a good is the maximum
    amount that someone is willing to pay for it. Hence
    all three terms are interchangeable.

FIGURE **5.17**

Short Answer Problem 4 (a)

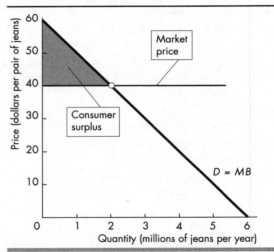

4. a. Figure 5.17 shows the consumer surplus as the
        area of the shaded triangle. The amount of con-
        sumer surplus is equal to the area of the triangle.
        Use the formula for the area of a triangle,
        ($\frac{1}{2}$)(base)(height). The base equals 2 million
        pairs of jeans, the quantity demanded. The
        height is $20 per jean. Thus consumer surplus is
        ($\frac{1}{2}$)(2 million jeans)($20 per jean) or $20 mil-
        lion.

    b. Figure 5.18 (on the next page) shows the con-
        sumer surplus when the price of jeans is $30 a
        pair. The consumer surplus in this case is $45
        million, from ($\frac{1}{2}$)(3 million jeans)($30 per
        jean). As the price falls, the consumer surplus
        rises.

    c. Consumer surplus is larger when the price is
        lower. This result reflects the conclusion that
        consumers are better off when the prices of the
        products they buy are lower.

FIGURE 5.18
Short Answer Problem 4 (b)

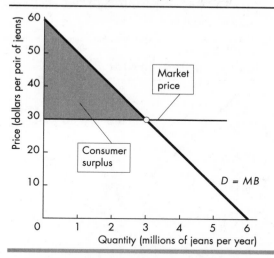

FIGURE 5.19
Short Answer Problem 5 (a)

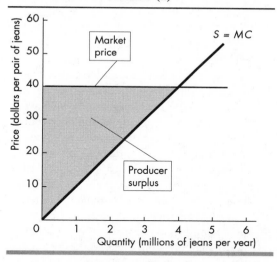

5. a. Figure 5.19 shows the producer surplus as the area of the shaded triangle. The amount of the producer surplus can be determined by using the formula for the area of a triangle, specifically (½)(base)(height). The base equals 4 million pairs of jeans, the quantity supplied. The height equals $40 per jean. Producer surplus is (½)(4 million jeans)($40 per jean) or $80 million.

b. Figure 5.20 shows the producer surplus when the price of a pair of jeans is $30. Producer surplus equals (½)(base)(height) or, in this case,

FIGURE 5.20
Short Answer Problem 5 (b)

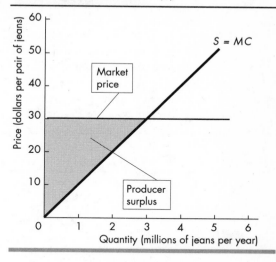

(½)(3 million jeans)($30 per jean) = $45 million.

c. Producer surplus is larger when the price is higher. This result illustrates the fact that producers are better off when the price of the product they sell is higher.

FIGURE 5.21
Short Answer Problem 6 (a) and 6 (b)

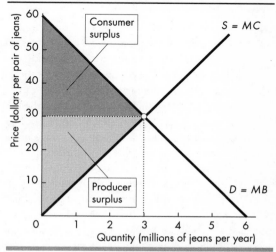

6. a. Figure 5.21 demonstrates that the quantity is 3 million jeans and the price is $30 a pair.

b. Consumer surplus and producer surplus are illustrated in Figure 5.21. The price of a pair of jeans is $30. Hence from Problem 4 (b), the consumer surplus is $45 million. From Problem 5 (b), producer surplus is $45 million. (The result that the consumer surplus equals the producer surplus is a coincidence; in general there is no particular relationship between the amount of consumer surplus and the amount of producer surplus.) The total gains from trade equal the sum of consumer surplus plus producer surplus, so the total gains from trade are $90 million.

FIGURE **5.22**
Short Answer Problem 6 (c)

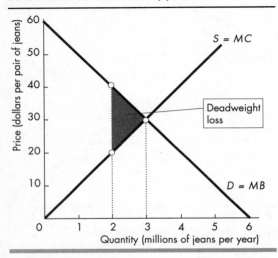

c. When the production of jeans is limited to 2 million pairs of jeans, Figure 5.22 illustrates the situation. The deadweight loss is the dark triangle in the figure. The deadweight loss can be calculated by using the formula for the area of a triangle, (½)(base)(height). In this case, the base is 1 million pairs of jeans (the difference between the efficient amount, 3 million, and the amount produced, 2 million). The height is $20 per jean, the difference between what consumers are willing to pay for another pair of jeans, $40, and the amount suppliers need to receive to produce an additional pair, $20. Thus the deadweight loss equals (½)(1 million jeans)($20 per jean) or $10 million. The total gains from trade are most easily calculated by subtracting the deadweight loss from the gains from trade when the market is allowed to produce the efficient quantity of jeans. From part (b) of this problem, the gains from trade when the market is efficient is $90

million. Therefore when the market underproduces by producing only 2 million pairs of jeans, the total gains from trade equal $90 million minus $10 million or $80 million.

FIGURE **5.23**
Short Answer Problem 6 (d)

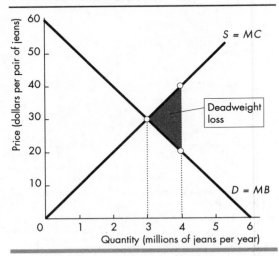

d. Figure 5.23 shows the situation when 4 million pairs of jeans are produced. The deadweight loss is again illustrated by the dark triangle. The amount of deadweight loss equals the area of the triangle, or (½)(base)(height). The base is 1 million pairs of jeans, the amount of overproduction. The height is $20, the difference between the marginal cost of another pair of jeans and the marginal benefit from another pair. Hence the deadweight loss is equal to (½)(1 million jeans)($20 per jean) = $10 million. The result that the deadweight loss in part (d) from overproducing 1 million pairs of jeans equals the deadweight loss from underproducing 1 million pairs of jeans, in part (c), is a coincidence. In general these amounts are not equal. The total gains from trade in this situation of overproduction equal the total gains from trade when the efficient quantity is produced, $90 million, minus the deadweight loss, $10 million, leaving total gains from trade of $80 million.

e. The total gains from trade are largest when the efficient quantity of jeans is produced, namely when 3 million pairs of jeans are produced.

7. A deadweight loss is the loss to society when resources are used inefficiently. When resources are

used efficiently, the total gains from trade are as large as possible. Any sort of inefficiency decreases the total gains from trade, and the decrease is the deadweight loss. It is important to note that a deadweight loss is a loss to *society* as a whole. In other words, no one benefits from a deadweight loss.

8. a. Based on the data in the question, the efficient quantity of mushrooms to produce is 10 million pounds a year. Why? The mushroom market meets all the criteria to be efficient: It is a competitive market, there are no externalities, and there are no government policies (such as price controls or taxes) that lead the amount produced to differ from the equilibrium quantity. So the amount produced, the equilibrium quantity, is the efficient amount.

FIGURE 5.24
Short Answer Problem 8 (b)

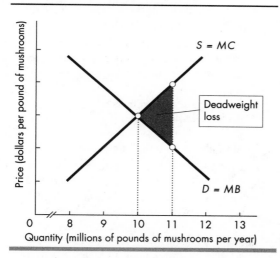

b. Figure 5.24 shows the deadweight loss from producing 11 million pounds of mushrooms. The deadweight loss exists because past 10 million pounds of mushrooms, the value people place on an additional pound of mushrooms — their marginal benefit — is less than the cost to produce an additional pound — the marginal cost. Hence all the pounds past 10 million subtract from the gains from trade, and the amount subtracted is equal to the deadweight loss.

c. Igor thinks that too few mushrooms are produced. Hence, Igor is using the result (not

enough mushrooms) to judge fairness. Thus Igor is using the concept of "it's not fair if the result isn't fair."

d. Igor is unlikely to agree that "it isn't fair if the rules aren't fair" because when the rules are "fair", that is, when there is no government interference in the market, Igor does not like the outcome. Basically, Igor wants to bend the rules so that more mushrooms are grown, perhaps by giving growers a subsidy to encourage more production.

■ You're the Teacher

1. "Yeah, I know what you mean that there seems to be a contradiction between the idea that 'resources are limited and therefore not everyone can have everything they want' and a lesson in this chapter that 'it is possible to produce too much of a product'. But, once you think about it a bit, the two ideas actually fit together okay.

"Think about sodas. We both drink a lot of them, but you know we'd both like to drink more. The fact that we'd like more shows us that sodas are 'scarce,' that is, some of our wants for more sodas won't be satisfied. But now suppose that 100 times more sodas were produced. We'd have soda coming out of our ears! We'd have plenty to drink, but we'd have to brush our teeth in it and use it in the shower. I like soda as much as anybody, but taking a bath in soda sounds gross! In this situation obviously too much soda is being produced. We'd be a lot better off if production was cut back.

"In fact, in some sense it's precisely because resources are limited that we can overproduce a product. Look, if society produced 100 times the amount of soda we produce now, the fact that our resources are limited means that we'd have to give up a bunch of other things: We'd have no cars because all the metal was being used to make soda cans; we'd have no books or magazines because all the paper was being used to make six-pack holders; we'd lose a *lot* of stuff because the resources were devoted to making soda. If we had unlimited resources, we would not lose anything and so in this case, we really couldn't overproduce a good. But, because our resources are limited, we want to use them the best we can, which means we want to produce the efficient amount of each good!"

Chapter Quiz

1. If the marginal cost of the sixth slice of pizza is greater than the marginal benefit, then the output level is
   a. efficient and more pizza should be produced.
   b. efficient and less pizza should be produced.
   c. inefficient and more pizza should be produced.
   d. inefficient and less pizza should be produced.

2. If the total cost of producing 5 books is $30 and the total cost of producing 6 books is $42, the marginal cost of the sixth book is
   a. $6.
   b. $7.
   c. $12.
   d. $42.

3. A person's demand curve for pizza
   a. lies above the person's marginal benefit curve for pizza.
   b. lies below the person's marginal benefit curve for pizza.
   c. is the same as the person's marginal benefit curve for pizza.
   d. has one point in common with the person's marginal benefit curve for pizza.

4. The value of a good minus the price paid for it is the
   a. producer surplus from the good.
   b. consumer surplus from the good.
   c. total surplus from the good.
   d. exchange surplus from the good.

5. Which of the following is a source of economic inefficiency?
   a. Competition
   b. Taxes
   c. Markets
   d. None of the above are sources of economic inefficiency.

6. Competitive markets will generally
   a. produce too much of a public good.
   b. produce too little of a public good.
   c. produce the efficient amount of a public good.
   d. produce too much, too little, or the efficient amount of a public good depending on whether the market demand curve accurately reflects the marginal benefit.

7. Which of the following statements about a deadweight loss is correct?
   a. The deadweight loss is largest in a perfectly competitive market producing a product with no external costs or benefits.
   b. A deadweight loss is a loss to consumers and a gain to producers.
   c. A deadweight loss is a loss to consumers and producers.
   d. None of the above are correct.

8. If the marginal cost of the last unit of a good produced exceeds the marginal benefit, then
   a. the amount produced is efficient.
   b. less than the efficient amount is being produced.
   c. more than the efficient amount is being produced.
   d. as time passes, consumers will increase their benefit from the good.

9. Deadweight loss can be the result of
   a. overproduction but not underproduction.
   b. underproduction but not overproduction.
   c. both overproduction and underproduction.
   d. neither overproduction nor underproduction.

10. The "Big Tradeoff" points out that
    a. the symmetry principle is not fair.
    b. taking income from rich people and giving it to poor people can create inefficiency.
    c. making the poorest as well off as possible is not compatible with fairness.
    d. utilitarianism is fair.

The answers for this Chapter Quiz are on page 367

Chapter 6 MARKETS IN ACTION

Key Concepts

■ Housing Markets and Rent Ceilings

The response of the housing market to shocks depends on whether the market is regulated. Suppose that the supply decreases, perhaps because of an earthquake. In an unregulated market:

♦ In the short run the equilibrium rent rises and there is no shortage. This outcome is demonstrated in Figure 6.1, which shows what happened in San Francisco after the 1906 earthquake. Supply decreased and demand did not change. Rents rose from $16 to $20 and the equilibrium quantity of apartments decreased to 74,000 units.

♦ The higher rent encourages building activity, so as time passes supply increases and the short-run supply curve shifts rightward.

♦ In the long run the rent and quantity of apartments rented return to their original levels.

The government might regulate a market. A **price ceiling** is a regulation that makes it illegal to charge a price higher than a specified amount. A price ceiling imposed in a housing market is called a rent ceiling. A **rent ceiling** prohibits charging rent that exceeds the ceiling amount. Rent ceilings alter the market's behavior to a supply shock:

♦ Figure 6.1 shows that with a rent ceiling of $16, after the decrease in supply the rent stays at $16 and a shortage of 56,000 units (100,000 demanded minus 44,000 supplied) emerges.

FIGURE **6.1**

The Housing Market in San Francisco

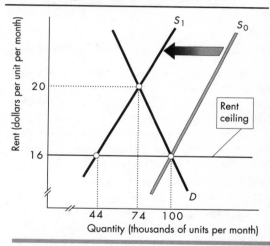

The existence of a shortage leads to:

♦ **search activity** — time spent looking for someone with whom to do business.

♦ **black markets** — an illegal market in which the price exceeds the legally imposed price ceiling.

Rent ceilings create inefficiency and a deadweight loss. Figure 6.2 (on the next page) illustrates the deadweight loss created by a rent ceiling. In the absence of a rent ceiling, in the figure the equilibrium rent would be $300 per month and the quantity of apartments would be 3,000. With a rent ceiling of $200 per month, the quantity of apartments decreases to 2,000, a shortage exists, and a deadweight loss — the gray triangle — is created.

FIGURE **6.2**

The Deadweight Loss from a Rent Ceiling

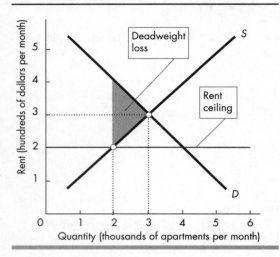

FIGURE **6.3**

The Effect of a Tax

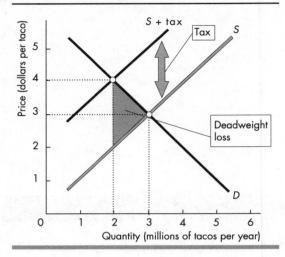

■ The Labor Market and the Minimum Wage

In an unregulated labor market, in the short run a decrease in the demand for a type of labor lowers the wage rate for that type of labor. The lower wage rate influences workers to leave this labor market, which decreases the supply of this type of labor, which offsets the initial fall in the wage rate and further decreases employment in this labor market decreases.

A **price floor** is a regulation that makes it illegal to buy or sell at a price lower than the specified level. A **minimum wage law** is a price floor that makes hiring workers for less than the specified wage rate illegal.

♦ In a regulated labor market, when the demand for labor decreases minimum wage laws create lower employment and create unemployment.

♦ Most economists believe that minimum wage laws contribute to high unemployment among low-skilled young workers.

♦ Minimum wage laws create economic inefficiency. They result in unemployment and excessive job search.

■ Taxes

A sales tax decreases the supply of the taxed good, so the supply curve shifts leftward. The vertical distance between the supply curve with the tax and without it equals the amount of the tax. The equilibrium price,

including the tax, rises and the equilibrium quantity decreases, as illustrated in Figure 6.3. After the tax of $2 per taco (which equals the length of the double-headed arrow) is imposed, the quantity of tacos decreases from 3 million to 2 million and the price paid by buyers rises from $3 to $4 per taco. Sellers receive the price, $4, minus the tax, $2, so suppliers keep $2 per taco. After a tax is imposed, buyers pay more for the product and sellers keep less.

The division of the tax depends on the elasticities of demand and supply. The more inelastic the demand, the more demanders pay of the tax.

♦ Perfectly inelastic demand — buyers pay all the tax.

♦ Perfectly elastic demand — sellers pay all the tax.

The more inelastic the supply, the more sellers pay of the tax.

♦ Perfectly inelastic supply — sellers pay all the tax.

♦ Perfectly elastic supply — buyers pay all the tax.

Usually products with inelastic demands are taxed because the tax does not reduce the quantity purchased by as much as taxing goods with elastic demands. So taxing a good with an inelastic demand results in more tax revenue and a smaller deadweight loss than taxing a good with an elastic demand.

♦ In general, imposing a tax on a product creates a deadweight loss, as illustrated in Figure 6.3. (If the demand or supply is perfectly inelastic, imposing the tax creates no deadweight loss.)

Markets for Illegal Goods

The purchase and sale of some goods is illegal. Penalties can be levied on sellers and/or buyers.

Compared to the situation if the product was legal, if sellers are penalized:

♦ The cost of selling the product rises, so the supply curve shifts leftward.

♦ These penalties boost the price and decrease the quantity.

Compared to the situation if the product was legal, if buyers are penalized:

♦ The perceived benefits from the product fall, so the demand curve shifts leftward.

♦ These penalties lead to a fall in the price and a decrease in the quantity.

If buyers and sellers are each penalized:

♦ Both the demand and supply curves shift leftward.

♦ The quantity definitely decreases. The price rises if the decrease in supply is larger and falls if the decrease in demand is larger.

A policy of decriminalizing and then taxing the product might be able to achieve the same consumption levels as prohibition. But:

♦ The required tax rate might be high, leading to substantial tax evasion.

♦ Legalization might send the wrong signal to potential consumers.

Stabilizing Farm Revenues

The demand for farm products is inelastic, so variations in the harvest results in wide price and revenue swings. In an unregulated market, a poor harvest leads to a large increase in price and raises total farm revenue; a bumper crop results in a large fall in price and lowers total farm revenue. Speculative markets and farm price stabilization policies can change these results.

♦ Farm prices can be stabilized through speculation by inventory holders, who buy at low prices (thereby boosting the price) to sell at high prices (thereby lowering the price). Inventory holding reduces price fluctuations but it does not stabilize farm revenues.

♦ Farm stabilization agencies of the government also limit price fluctuations by setting production limits (quotas), setting price floors, and buying any resulting surplus.

1. **THE EFFECT OF AN EARTHQUAKE ON THE DEMAND FOR HOUSING :** An earthquake destroys apartments and thereby decreases the supply of housing. People are made homeless; why doesn't this effect then increase the demand for housing? To see why, suppose that before the earthquake there are 100,000 apartments rented at $400 a month. Thus the quantity of apartments demanded at a rent of $400 a month is 100,000 and all 100,000 families demanding an apartment have one. Suppose an earthquake destroys 60,000 apartments so that 60,000 families are homeless. At the rent of $400 a month, there are *still* 100,000 apartments demanded but now of the 100,000 families demanding an apartment, only 40,000 have one; 60,000 are homeless. The key point is that the demand has not changed. At the rent of $400 a month, the *same* number of apartments are demanded before and after the earthquake.

2. **THE HARM FROM RENT CEILINGS :** Whenever some influence disturbs an equilibrium in an unregulated (free) market, the differing desires of buyers and sellers are brought back into balance by price movements. If prices are controlled by government regulation, however, the price mechanism no longer can serve this purpose. In the case of price ceilings, increased search activity will emerge.

By creating increased search, price ceilings waste society's scarce resources. For instance, with rent controls, would-be apartment dwellers, fruitlessly driving around the city searching for an apartment, accomplish nothing from a social perspective. The time and energy that these people dissipate in futile search activity creates nothing socially useful.

In addition, price ceilings deliver the wrong signals to suppliers. In a free market, a shortage of apartments means rents are driven higher. Higher rents give apartment owners the incentive to increase the number of apartments they rent, which helps overcome the initial shortage. With rent controls, rents do not rise. Hence apartment owners have no incentive to increase the number of apartments they rent.

3. **INTUITIVE EXPLANATION OF WHO PAYS A TAX :** Consider the intuition of how the demand elasticity affects the division of the tax. Suppliers always want

to pass all of the tax along to buyers in the form of a higher price. But if the demand for the product is very elastic, consumers can find good substitutes for the product being taxed. So, if sellers tried to stick demanders with a large part of the tax, buyers would substitute other products, and suppliers would find themselves unable to sell anything. In this case, suppliers absorb a large portion of the tax. However, if the demand for the good is inelastic, consumers cannot readily find anything to take the product's place. In this situation, consumers pay a large part of the tax.

Similar reasoning applies to the elasticity of supply. If supply is very elastic, suppliers can find other products to produce and so buyers wind up paying most of the tax. However, if the supply is inelastic, producers cannot easily switch to producing another product. Buyers do not have to pay much in this case because suppliers can't find anything else to produce.

Questions

■ True/False and Explain

Housing Markets and Rent Ceilings

1. In an unregulated housing market, higher rents increase the quantity of housing supplied.

2. With a rent ceiling set below the equilibrium rent, there is no way to allocate apartments among potential renters.

3. Suppose that price controls are holding the price of gasoline below its equilibrium level. When controls are abolished and the price rises, the amount of gasoline purchased by consumers will decrease.

4. A rent ceiling below the equilibrium rent increases economic efficiency and decreases the deadweight loss because more people can afford apartments.

The Labor Market and the Minimum Wage

5. In an unregulated labor market, a decrease in the demand for low-skilled labor leads to a fall in the wage rate for low-skilled workers.

6. If the minimum wage is above the equilibrium wage, raising the minimum wage decreases the number of workers employed.

7. Most economists believe that raising the minimum wage has no effect on unemployment.

Taxes

8. Levying a tax on a product shifts its supply curve so that the supply curve with the tax lies below the supply curve without the tax.

9. Buyers always pay a larger amount of a sales tax than do sellers.

10. If the demand for Exxon gasoline is perfectly elastic, imposing a tax on Exxon gasoline raise its price.

11. The more elastic the demand for a product, the larger is the amount of a sales tax paid by consumers.

Markets for Illegal Goods

12. Imposing penalties on sellers of an illegal product raises the price of the illegal product.

13. Imposing penalties on *both* buyers and sellers of an illegal product always raises the price of the illegal product.

Stabilizing Farm Revenue

14. If demand for a farm product is inelastic, in the absence of inventories or government programs, a crop failure decreases farmers' total revenue.

15. If the current price is higher than an inventory holder's expected future price, the inventory holder sells goods from his or her inventory.

16. Farm stabilization agencies generally create large shortages of farm products.

■ Multiple Choice

Housing Markets and Rent Ceilings

1. The short-run supply curve for rental housing is positively sloped because
   a. the supply of housing is fixed in the short run but not the long run.
   b. the current stock of buildings will be used more intensively as rents rise.
   c. the cost of constructing new buildings rises as the number of buildings increases.
   d. new buildings will be constructed as rents rise.

2. In an unregulated market, which of the following will <u>NOT</u> happen as result of the sudden destruction of a large proportion of the stock of housing?

a. Higher rents
b. A persisting shortage of rental housing
c. More basement apartments offered for rent
d. More families sharing living quarters

3. If the government sets a price ceiling on pizza that is below the equilibrium price of a pizza, then

a. there is a shortage of pizza.
b. there is a surplus of pizza.
c. existing firms will expand their production to meet the increased quantity demanded.
d. new firms will enter the market to meet the increase in the quantity demanded.

For the next five questions, use Table 6.1, which shows the supply and demand schedules for apples.

TABLE **6.1**

Multiple Choice Questions 4, 5, 6, 7, 8

Price (dollars per pound)	Quantity demanded (tons per year)	Quantity supplied (tons per year)
$1.10	24	30
1.00	28	28
0.90	32	26
0.80	36	24
0.70	40	22

4. What is the equilibrium price of an apple?

a. $1.10 per pound
b. $1.00 per pound
c. $0.80 per pound
d. $0.60 per pound

5. What is the equilibrium quantity of apples?

a. 24 tons
b. 28 tons
c. 32 tons
d. 36 tons

6. The government imposes a price ceiling of 80¢ per pound. At this price, how many apples are supplied?

a. 24 tons
b. 28 tons
c. 32 tons
d. 36 tons

7. At the ceiling price of 80¢ per pound, how many apples are consumed?

a. 24 tons
b. 28 tons
c. 32 tons
d. 36 tons

8. At the ceiling price of 80¢ per pound of apples, what is the shortage of apples?

a. 0 tons
b. 12 tons
c. 24 tons
d. 36 tons

FIGURE **6.4**

Multiple Choice Questions 9 and 10

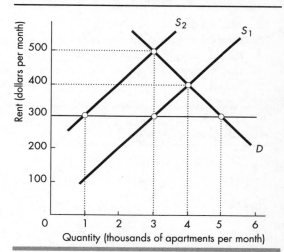

9. In Figure 6.4, with the supply curve of housing S_1 and with a rent ceiling of $300 a month, there is

a. a surplus of $100 a month.
b. a shortage of 5,000 apartments a month.
c. a shortage of 2,000 apartments a month.
d. neither a shortage nor surplus of apartments.

10. In Figure 6.4 a disaster strikes so that the supply curve shifts to S_2. If the rent ceiling remains at $300, there is a

a. surplus of $200 a month.
b. shortage of 5,000 apartments a month.
c. shortage of 4,000 apartments a month.
d. shortage of 1,000 apartments a month.

11. Which of the following is an example of a black market?

    a. A market where legal transactions take place at prices lower than a government imposed price ceiling.
    b. A market where illegal transactions take place at prices higher than a government imposed price ceiling.
    c. A legal market where buyers and sellers search for each other.
    d. An illegal market in which the lights are not turned on.

The Labor Market and the Minimum Wage

12. In a labor market without a minimum wage, the demand for labor decreases. As a result, the wage rate _____ and as time passes _____.

    a. falls; the demand for labor increases
    b. rises; the supply of labor increases
    c. falls; the supply of labor decreases
    d. falls; neither the supply of nor demand for labor changes

FIGURE **6.5**
Multiple Choice Questions 13 and 14

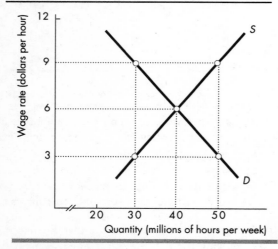

13. In Figure 6.5 if the minimum wage was set at $3 per hour, what would be the level of unemployment in millions of hours?

    a. 50.
    b. 40.
    c. 20.
    d. 0.

14. In Figure 6.5 if the minimum wage was set at $9 per hour, what would be the level of unemployment?

    a. 50 million hours
    b. 40 million hours
    c. 20 million hours
    d. 0 hours

15. Suppose the government imposes a minimum wage *above* the equilibrium wage rate for low-skilled workers. When will more workers be employed?

    a. When the minimum wage is in effect.
    b. When the minimum wage is NOT in effect.
    c. Employment is the same regardless of the presence or absence of this minimum wage.
    d. The question cannot be answered without knowledge of the actual amounts of the minimum wage and equilibrium wage rate.

Taxes

FIGURE **6.6**
Multiple Choice Questions 16, 17, 18

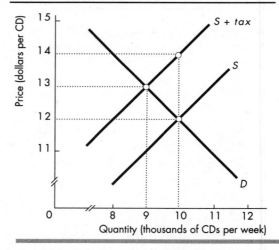

16. In Figure 6.6 what is the amount of the tax on CDs?

    a. $14 per CD
    b. $13 per CD
    c. $2 per CD
    d. $1 per CD

17. In Figure 6.6, how much of the tax is paid by buyers?

    a. $14 per CD
    b. $13 per CD
    c. $2 per CD
    d. $1 per CD

18. In Figure 6.6, how much of the tax is paid by suppliers?
    a. $14 per CD
    b. $13 per CD
    c. $2 per CD
    d. $1 per CD

19. The division of a tax falls heaviest on consumers when
    a. demand is perfectly elastic.
    b. demand is inelastic but not perfectly inelastic.
    c. demand is perfectly inelastic.
    d. supply is perfectly inelastic.

20. Suppose that the government wants to discourage the use of cigarettes. If it imposes a tax on cigarettes, the equilibrium quantity decreases the most when the elasticity of demand equals
    a. 2.00.
    b. 1.00.
    c. 0.50.
    d. 0.

21. The more elastic the supply, the
    a. more likely the government is to tax the product.
    b. more likely the government is to impose a price ceiling.
    c. smaller the amount of any tax imposed on the product paid by the suppliers.
    d. more elastic is the demand.

Markets for Illegal Goods

22. By imposing sanctions on buyers of an illegal good, the government shifts the good's
    a. demand curve rightward.
    b. demand curve leftward.
    c. supply curve leftward.
    d. supply curve rightward.

23. If sanctions are imposed on sellers but not users of an illegal good, the
    a. price falls and the quantity decreases.
    b. price rises and the quantity increases.
    c. price rises and the quantity decreases.
    d. price falls and the quantity increases.

24. If the government wants to discourage consumption of a good, it can
    a. impose penalties on buyers of the good.
    b. impose penalties on sellers of the good.
    c. tax the product.
    d. do all of the above because all the policies serve to decrease consumption of the good.

Stabilizing Farm Revenues

25. Which of the following combinations would yield the greatest price fluctuation?
    a. Large shifts in the supply curve and inelastic demand
    b. Large shifts in the supply curve and elastic demand
    c. Large shifts in the supply curve and perfectly elastic demand
    d. Small shifts in the supply curve and elastic demand

26. Inventory holders buy when the current price is
    a. higher than the future expected price.
    b. equal to the future expected price.
    c. lower than the future expected price.
    d. None of the above because the future expected price has nothing to do with when speculators buy.

27. Speculative markets in inventories
    a. always raise the price paid by consumers of the product.
    b. always lower the price received by suppliers of the product.
    c. can help limit fluctuations in the price of the product.
    d. Both answers (a) and (b) are correct.

28. You notice that a bumper crop of soy beans has no effect on the price of soy beans and that the incomes of farmers who grow soy beans increase. This set of observations can be the result of
    a. a perfectly inelastic demand for soy beans.
    b. an inelastic but not necessarily perfectly inelastic demand for soy beans.
    c. speculators holding inventories of soy beans.
    d. the supply curve of soy beans being downward sloping.

29. The European Union countries have been accumu-
    lating butter mountains and wine lakes. These sur-
    pluses are the result of
    a. price floors for agricultural products that are
       below equilibrium market prices.
    b. price floors for agricultural products that are
       above equilibrium market prices.
    c. price ceilings for agricultural products that are
       below equilibrium market prices.
    d. price ceilings for agricultural products that are
       above equilibrium market prices.

30. Which of the following creates a deadweight loss?
    a. A housing market with a rent ceiling below the
       equilibrium rent
    b. A labor market with a minimum wage above the
       equilibrium wage
    c. A farm market in which the government has
       imposed quotas
    d. All of the above create a deadweight loss

■ Short Answer Problems

1. Suppose that there is a significant decrease in the
   supply of timber. Explain how an unregulated market adjusts. What induces consumers to decrease
   their consumption of timber?

TABLE **6.2**
Short Answer Questions 2, 3

Price (dollars per gallon)	Quantity demanded (millions of gallons per year)	Quantity supplied (millions of gallons per year)
1.40	8	24
1.30	10	22
1.20	12	20
1.10	14	18
1.00	16	16
0.90	18	14

2. Table 6.2 presents the supply and demand schedules for gasoline.
   a. With no government intervention in the mar-
      ket, what is the equilibrium price of gasoline?
      The equilibrium quantity?
   b. If there is a deadweight loss, what does it equal?

c. Suppose that the government imposes a price
   ceiling of 90¢ a gallon. Now what is the quantity demanded? The quantity supplied?
d. With the price ceiling of 90¢ a gallon, how
   much gasoline do consumers buy? What is the
   amount of the shortage?
e. If there is a deadweight loss, what does it equal?

3. Suppose that the supply schedule of gasoline in
   Table 6.2 suddenly decreases, perhaps because of
   events in the Middle East. In particular, suppose
   that at every possible price of gasoline, the quantity
   supplied is now 8 million gallons less per year.
   a. If the government did not impose any price
      controls, what is the new equilibrium price of
      gasoline? The new equilibrium quantity? How is
      the gasoline allocated now among potential con-
      sumers?
   b. Suppose that the government imposed a price
      ceiling of 90¢. Now what is the quantity de-
      manded? The quantity supplied?
   c. With a price ceiling of 90¢ in place, how much
      gasoline do consumers buy? What is the amount
      of the shortage? How is gasoline allocated
      among potential consumers?
   d. When are demanders able to consume more
      gasoline? When the price is controlled at 90¢ a
      gallon, or when the price is left free to reach its
      equilibrium? Explain.

4. Suppose that policymakers decide that the price of
   a pizza is too high and that not enough people can
   afford to buy pizza. As a result, they impose a price
   ceiling on pizza that is below the current equilibrium price. When are consumers able to buy more
   pizza: before the price ceiling or after? Use a demand and supply diagram to support your answer.

5. Table 6.3 presents the demand and supply schedules for bushels of corn.
   a. Plot the demand and supply curves in Figure
      6.7.
   b. What is the equilibrium price of a bushel of
      corn? The equilibrium quantity?
   c. Suppose the government imposes a price ceiling
      of $3.90 per bushel of corn. On your diagram,
      show the quantities demanded and supplied and
      identify any shortage or surplus. Illustrate the
      deadweight loss.

TABLE **6.3**

Short Answer Problems 5, 6, 7

Price (dollars per bushel)	Quantity demanded (millions of bushels per year)	Quantity supplied (millions of bushels per year)
4.20	30	42
4.10	34	40
4.00	38	38
3.90	42	36
3.80	46	34
3.70	50	32

FIGURE **6.7**

Short Answer Problem 5

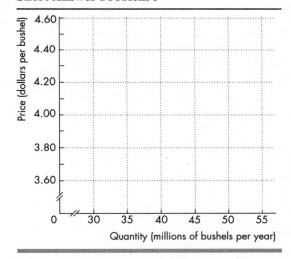

FIGURE **6.8**

Short Answer Problem 6

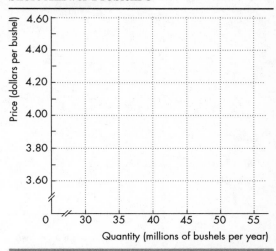

6. Use the demand and supply schedules in Table 6.3. Suppose that the government decides to impose a tax of 30¢ per bushel of corn.

   a. Plot the demand and supply curves in Figure 6.8 (on the next page) and show how the tax affects the supply curve.

   b. After the tax is imposed, what is the equilibrium price of corn? The equilibrium quantity?

   c. What does the deadweight loss equal?

7. The government makes one more attempt to alter the equilibrium in the corn market, given by the demand and supply schedules in Table 6.3. The government decides to impose a price floor of $4.10. It does so by promising farmers that it will buy the amount of corn necessary to keep the price pegged at no less than $4.10 a bushel.

   a. In Figure 6.9 plot the demand and supply schedules and the price floor.

   b. With the price floor in place, what is the amount of corn consumed by private demanders? How much corn do farmers grow?

   c. How much corn does the government buy? How much does keeping the price at $4.10 a bushel cost the government?

8. After graduating, you land a plush job advising the president on economic matters. One day the president asks you for your suggestions about products to tax.

   a. The president asks you to produce a list of items to be taxed that will yield substantial tax revenue to the government and for which consumers pay a large amount of the tax. Without trying to name specific products, what is the general characteristic of the demand for the products that you will suggest be taxed? Why?

   b. After you discuss this first list with the president, the president realizes that this year is an election year. As a result, the president changes your assignment a bit. Now the president asks you for a list of products that will still yield a lot of revenue for the government, but whose tax will fall more heavily on producers. Again without trying to name specific products, what is

FIGURE **6.9**

Short Answer Problem 7

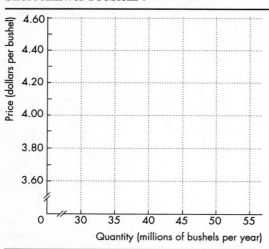

the general characteristic of the supply of the products that would comprise your second list? Why?

9. You are in charge of combating illegal drug use in the United States. You must decide between imprisoning users or imprisoning sellers of drugs.

   a. If you decide to imprison users, what effect do you expect this policy to have on the price and quantity of illegal drugs?

   b. If you decide to imprison sellers, what effect do you think this policy will have on the price and quantity of illegal drugs?

   c. Without knowing which policy is being followed, can changes in the price of illegal drugs alone determine the success of a policy designed to reduce the consumption of illegal drugs?

10. Suppose that demand for a good is subject to unpredictable fluctuations so that sometimes the demand increases and other times the demand decreases. Explain how inventory holders reduce the price variability of the good.

■ **You're the Teacher**

1. "I don't get this stuff about how suppliers and demanders split the sales tax. Every time *I* go to the store, I pay *all* the sales tax. I have never seen a store that offered to split the tax with me. So, how can our text say that suppliers usually have to pay part of a tax? I'm lost; can you help me out?" Your classmate is befuddled. Point your friend in the right direction.

Answers

■ True/False Answers

Housing Markets and Rent Ceilings

1. **T** The supply curve has a positive slope: As the rent rises, the quantity supplied of apartments increases.

2. **F** Lines and payments on the black market are devices that help allocate apartments among potential renters.

3. **F** With the price control, there was a shortage of gasoline; when the price rises, suppliers produce more gasoline and demanders are able to buy more.

4. **F** A rent ceiling below the equilibrium rent creates inefficiency and a deadweight loss.

The Labor Market and the Minimum Wage

5. **T** The fall in the wage rate signals workers to substitute other endeavors or other labor markets where the demand for their effort has not decreased.

6. **T** By raising the wage that firms must pay, firms respond by decreasing the quantity of workers they demand, that is, decreasing the number of workers they will hire.

7. **F** Most economists believe that a rise in the minimum wage increases unemployment.

Taxes

8. **F** The supply curve shifts so that the new supply curve lies above the initial supply curve and the vertical distance between the two curves is the amount of the tax.

9. **F** The amount paid by buyers depends on the relative elasticities of demand and supply.

10. **F** If the demand for a product is perfectly elastic, a tax has no effect on its price.

11. **F** The more elastic the demand, the larger the amount of the tax paid by suppliers.

Markets for Illegal Goods

12. **T** The penalties increase the cost of supplying the good, thereby decreasing the supply and causing a rise in the price.

13. **F** The price rises if the penalties are more severe on sellers and falls if they are more severe on buyers.

Stabilizing Farm Revenues

14. **F** The crop failure raises the price of the crop and, because the demand for it is inelastic, boosts farmers' total revenue.

15. **T** The inventory holder will sell to take advantage of the temporarily higher price.

16. **F** Stabilization programs almost always result in large surpluses, not shortages.

■ Multiple Choice Answers

Housing Markets and Rent Ceilings

1. **b** As rents rise, building owners are motivated to make more space available for use as apartments.

2. **b** Any incipient shortage is eliminated by the higher rents that result.

3. **a** When a price ceiling is below the equilibrium price, the quantity demanded exceeds the quantity supplied and a shortage results.

4. **b** At this price, the quantity supplied of apples equals the quantity demanded.

5. **b** When apples are $1 per pound, 28 tons of apples are demanded and supplied.

6. **a** At a price of 80¢ a pound, the supply schedule shows that producers supply 24 tons per year.

7. **a** Although consumers demand 36 tons of apples, only 24 tons are produced, so only 24 tons can be consumed.

8. **b** The shortage equals the quantity of apples demanded, 36 tons, minus the quantity of apples supplied, 24 tons.

9. **c** The shortage equals the quantity demanded at the ceiling price (5,000) minus the quantity supplied at that price (3,000).

10. **c** The shortage increases because the quantity demanded remains at 5,000 while the quantity supplied falls to 1,000.

11. **b** Black markets are illegal markets wherein people conduct transactions at prices forbidden by the government.

The Labor Market and the Minimum Wage

12. **c** In the short run, the decrease in demand lowers the wage rate. Then, as time passes, the lower wage rate creates an incentive for workers to move to other markets, and so the supply of labor decreases.

13. **d** A minimum wage of $3 falls below the equilibrium wage, so no unemployment is created.

14. **c** If the minimum wage is raised to $9, the quantity of labor supplied, 50 million hours, exceeds the quantity demanded, 30 million hours, by 20 million hours.

15. **b** The fact that the minimum wage rate exceeds the equilibrium wage rate means that firms will decrease the quantity of employment that they demand, thereby decreasing employment.

Taxes

16. **c** The supply curve with the tax lies above the supply without the tax by a distance equal to the amount of the tax. The vertical distance in Figure 6.6 is $2, so this amount is the tax.

17. **d** The total price paid by consumers climbs from $12 to $13, so demanders pay $1 of the tax.

18. **d** The receipts per CD fall from $12 to $11, so suppliers pay $1 of the tax.

19. **c** When demand is perfectly inelastic, the price of the product rises by the entire amount of the tax so consumers pay the entire tax.

20. **a** The greater the elasticity of demand, the more the tax decreases the equilibrium quantity consumed.

21. **c** The more elastic the supply, the greater the amount of a tax paid by consumers.

Markets for Illegal Goods

22. **b** The sanctions decrease the benefits buyers receive from the good, thereby decreasing demand for the product.

23. **c** The sanctions shift the supply curve leftward, thereby raising the price and decreasing the quantity.

24. **d** All of the policies decrease the quantity so all could be used to discourage consumption of a good.

Stabilizing Farm Revenues

25. **a** This set of factors describes the situation in many agricultural markets, so in the absence of regulation, agricultural prices would be subject to large fluctuations.

26. **c** By purchasing when the price is currently low, inventory holders expect to profit by selling when the price rises in the future.

27. **c** Inventory holders buy when the current price otherwise would be low, thereby raising the price, and sell when the current price otherwise would be high, thereby lowering the price.

28. **c** Speculators buy a large part of the crop, so the price does not fall and their purchases boost the incomes of soy bean farmers.

29. **b** The floor price being above the equilibrium price gives producers the incentive to increase their production of butter and wine. Meanwhile, demanders have the incentive to decrease their consumption, so the European Union nations must buy the resulting surplus.

30. **d** Rent ceilings, minimum wages, and quotas all create deadweight losses.

■ **Answers to Short Answer Problems**

1. If the timber market is in equilibrium initially and there is a significant decrease in supply, an excess quantity will be demanded at the existing price. As a result, the price of timber rises, which causes movements along the new supply and the demand curve. The rising price results in a price-induced increase in the quantity supplied and a price-induced decrease in the quantity demanded. The price continues to rise until the excess quantity demanded is eliminated. The price hike causes consumers to decrease their desired consumption of timber and substitute other products, such as brick or plaster. Note how price adjustments coordinate people's decisions in this unregulated market.

2. a. The equilibrium price of gasoline is $1.00 a gallon because that price equates the quantity supplied to the quantity demanded. The equilibrium quantity is 16 million gallons a year.

    b. There is no deadweight loss in this unregulated market.

    c. If the government imposes a price ceiling of 90¢ a gallon, the demand schedule shows that consumers demand 18 million gallons of gasoline a year. At the ceiling price, the supply schedule indicates that producers supply 14 million gallons of gasoline a year.

    d. With the price ceiling, only 14 million gallons of gasoline are available. Thus even though consumers would be willing to purchase 18 million gallons, all they can actually buy is 14 million gallons. The shortage equals the amount con-

FIGURE **6.10**

Short Answer Problem 2 (e)

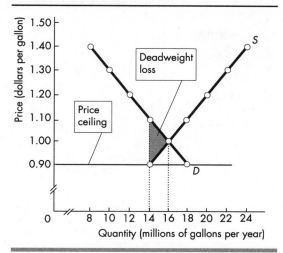

TABLE **6.4**

Short Answer Question 3

Price (dollars per gallon)	Quantity demanded (millions of gallons per year)	New quantity supplied (millions of gallons per year)
$1.40	8	16
1.30	10	14
1.20	12	12
1.10	14	10
1.00	16	8
0.90	18	6

c. With the price ceiling, consumers are able to purchase only the amount of gasoline actually made available. That is, consumers can buy only 6 million gallons of gasoline, and there is a shortage of 12 million gallons (18 million gallons – 6 million gallons). Because the price cannot allocate gasoline among consumers, other mechanisms come into play. Long lines will exist at gasoline stations, so people willing and able to wait in the lines will buy gasoline. Black markets, where bribes and other side payments are made to suppliers by consumers, will spring up. Thus consumers willing and able to participate in black markets will buy gasoline.

d. When the price is left free to reach its equilibrium, consumers can buy and use 12 million gallons of gasoline. With the price ceiling, consumers can buy only 6 million gallons of gasoline. Hence, as a group, consumers are able to consume more gasoline when the market is left unregulated.

sumers are willing to buy (18 million gallons) minus the amount actually available (14 million gallons), or 4 million gallons.

e. The easiest way to calculate the deadweight loss uses Figure 6.10, which shows the deadweight loss triangle. The height of the triangle is $0.20 per gallon (= $1.10 – $0.90) and the base of the triangle is 2 million gallons (= 16 million gallons – 14 million gallons). Using the formula for the area of a triangle, the deadweight loss therefore equals (½)($.20 per gallon)(2 million gallons), or $200,000.

3. a. Table 6.4 makes answering this question easier. It shows the new supply schedule after the decrease in supply. Note that the demand schedule is unchanged. The new equilibrium price is $1.20 a gallon, and the new equilibrium quantity is 12 million gallons a year. The gasoline is allocated among consumers by price. Faced with the higher price, consumers will decrease the quantity they demand. Essentially, those consumers willing and able to pay the higher price buy gasoline and consumers either unwilling or unable to pay the higher price do not.

b. If the government imposes a price ceiling of 90¢ a gallon, the demand schedule shows that the quantity demanded is 18 million gallons. The quantity supplied at the ceiling price is 6 million gallons.

4. Figure 6.11 (on the next page) illustrates the pizza market before and after the price ceiling has been imposed. Before a price ceiling of, say, $11 is imposed, the equilibrium price is $12 a pizza and the quantity produced and consumed is 3 million per month. With the price ceiling of $11 a pizza, suppliers are willing to produce only 2 million pizzas a month. Consumers would like to buy more pizza, 4 million a month, but they cannot buy what is not produced. Thus only 2 million pizzas rather than 3 million are consumed after the price ceiling. So even though the price ceiling might have been imposed to give more consumers the ability to afford to buy pizza, in aggregate more pizza is consumed without the price ceiling than with it.

FIGURE **6.11**
Short Answer Problem 4

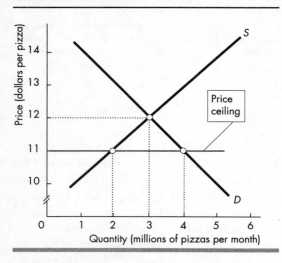

FIGURE **6.12**
Short Answer Problem 5

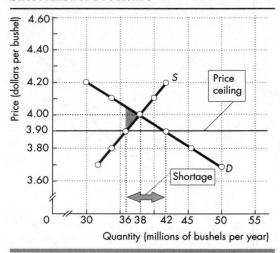

5. a. Figure 6.12 presents graphs of the demand and
       supply schedules.

    b. The equilibrium price of corn is $4.00 a bushel,
       where the demand and supply curves cross. The
       equilibrium quantity is 38 million bushels per
       year.

    c. Figure 6.12 shows that, with a price ceiling of
       $3.90, the quantity demanded is 42 million
       bushels of corn and the quantity supplied is 36
       million bushels of corn. Thus the shortage is 6
       million bushels of corn. The deadweight loss is
       the area of the gray triangle.

6. a. Figure 6.13 illustrates the demand curve and the
       supply curves (with and without the tax). The
       tax shifts the supply curve so that it lies above
       the old supply curve by the amount of the tax, or
       30¢ a bushel.

    b. As Figure 6.13 shows, the equilibrium price after
       the tax is imposed is $4.10 a bushel because the
       demand curve and the supply plus tax curve
       cross at this price. The equilibrium quantity is
       34 million bushels.

    c. The deadweight loss equals the area of the gray
       triangle in Figure 6.13. The height of the trian-

FIGURE **6.13**
Short Answer Problem 6

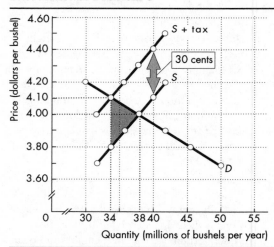

gle is $.30 per bushel ($4.10 bushel – $3.80
bushel) and the base of the triangle is the decrease in production, 4 million bushels (38 million bushels – 34 million). Thus using the
formula for the area of a triangle give
(½)($.30)(4 million bushels) or $600,000.

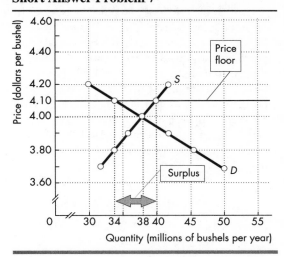

FIGURE **6.14**
Short Answer Problem 7

7. a. Figure 6.14 shows the market with the price floor of $4.10 a bushel.

  b. With the price floor in place, private demanders buy only 34 million bushels of corn, but farmers supply 40 million bushels.

  c. Without any government action, a price of $4.10 a bushel creates a surplus of 6 million bushels of corn. To keep the price at $4.10 a bushel, the government must buy this surplus. Hence the government spends ($4.10/bushel) (6 million bushels), or $24,600,000.

8. a. You want to find products for which the demand is relatively inelastic. Taxing products with inelastic demands has two effects. First, the decrease in the equilibrium quantity is less than it would be if a good with an elastic demand were taxed; and, second, the amount of the tax paid by consumers is higher for goods with inelastic demands. Because the president wants the taxes to fall most heavily on consumers, the second effect directly achieves the president's second goal. In addition, the president also wants to generate substantial tax revenues. Because the equilibrium quantity is not decreased much, more of this product will be bought and sold. Thus with more transactions, the government will collect more tax. So the first effect means that the government will collect significant tax revenues — the president's first goal.

  b. You will recommend that the government tax products with relatively inelastic supplies. First a relatively inelastic supply means that a tax does not reduce the equilibrium quantity by much. As a result, the government will collect more tax revenues than if it taxed products with elastic supplies. Second, the amount of the tax paid by suppliers increases as the supply becomes less elastic. So by taxing products with inelastic supplies, the producers will pay a larger part of the tax.

9. a. Imposing sanctions on consumers shifts the demand curve for illegal drugs leftward. That lowers the price and decreases the quantity of illegal drugs consumed.

  b. If sellers are penalized, the supply curve shifts leftward. In this case, the price of illegal drugs rises and the quantity consumed decreases.

  c. The answers to parts (a) and (b) illustrate that the price of illegal drugs alone cannot be used to judge the success of a policy against drugs. For instance, if the price rises when sanctions are imposed against sellers, such as imprisoning sellers, the policy is effective. However, if the price rises when sanctions are imposed against users, the policy is failing because even with the sanctions demand is increasing enough so that consumption is rising. Hence to use price changes as a signal of the success or failure of a policy also requires knowledge of what type of policy is being pursued.

10. Inventory holders buy the product to exploit any potential profit opportunities. In particular, they aim to sell the good from their inventories if the current price is higher than the expected future price and they strive to buy the good to be added to their inventories if the current price is below the expected future price. The first profit opportunity — selling when the current price is higher than the expected future price — reduces the current price. The second profit opportunity — buying when the current price is lower than the expected future price — raises the current price. Selling, if the price is higher than, or buying, if the price is lower than the expected future price, means that the price will not deviate much from the expected future price. Thus speculative markets in inventories reduce price fluctuations and make the price less variable.

■ You're the Teacher

1. "You're getting a bit confused. It's easiest to explain this concept with a concrete example: I'm hungry so let's think about pizza. Suppose that the government did not tax pizza and that the equilibrium price was $11 per pizza. Okay, now suppose that the government slaps a $2 per pizza tax on pizza. What our textbook has shown me is that this tax will raise the price, say, to $11.50 per pizza. In other words, the price — *including* the tax — will be $11.50 per pizza. That also means that the price without the tax falls to $9.50 per pizza. So when we call the people at the pizza shop on the phone, they tell us that the price is $9.50 plus $2 tax, or $11.50. So, it looks like we're getting stuck with the entire $2 tax. But we're not. Actually, after the tax is imposed, we pay only $0.50 more because the price we pay rises only from $11.00 to $11.50. The pizza makers wind up paying $1.50 of this tax: Before the tax they got to keep $11.00 per pizza, but after the tax they get to keep only $9.50 per pizza. The moral here is that appearances can be deceiving. Another moral is that you need to study your economics more!"

Chapter Quiz

1. In the short run, a shock that increases the supply results in a _____ equilibrium quantity and a _____ market price.
   a. smaller; lower
   b. smaller; higher
   c. larger; lower
   d. larger; higher

2. Effective rent controls
   a. increase search activity.
   b. increase the long-run housing supply.
   c. have no effect on the quantity of apartments rented.
   d. increase the vacancy rate of apartments.

3. How does an earthquake affect the housing market?
   a. It shifts the supply curve leftward and does not shift the demand curve.
   b. It shifts the demand curve leftward and does not shift the supply curve.
   c. It shifts both the supply and demand curves leftward.
   d. It shifts the supply curve leftward and the demand curve rightward.

4. A price floor set below the equilibrium price
   a. decreases only the quantity demanded.
   b. decreases only the quantity supplied.
   c. decreases both the quantity supplied and the quantity demanded.
   d. has no effect.

5. The minimum wage boosts firms' incentive to
   a. hire more workers.
   b. increase output.
   c. use labor-saving technology.
   d. hire teens.

6. In the market for skilled-labor, a rightward shift of the demand curve directly
   a. raises the equilibrium wage rate.
   b. lowers the equilibrium wage rate.
   c. increases the supply of high-skilled labor.
   d. decreases the supply of high-skilled labor.

7. In the market for low-skilled labor, labor saving technology directly shifts the
   a. labor supply curve rightward.
   b. labor supply curve leftward.
   c. labor demand curve rightward.
   d. labor demand curve leftward.

8. The supply and demand for a good are neither perfectly elastic nor perfectly inelastic. Hence imposing a tax on the good harms
   a. only buyers.
   b. only sellers.
   c. both buyers and sellers.
   d. neither buyers nor sellers.

9. If the government declares that selling certain drugs is illegal, then the
   a. demand curve shifts rightward.
   b. demand curve shifts leftward.
   c. supply curve shifts rightward.
   d. supply curve shifts leftward.

10. If inventory holders are present, a bumper farm crop will _____ the price of the product and _____ the total revenue collected by farmers.
    a. lower; decrease
    b. lower; not change
    c. not change; increase
    d. not change; decrease

The answers for this Chapter Quiz are on page 367

2 HOW MARKETS WORK

Reading Between the Lines

GOLD SURGES ABOVE $300

On March 28, 2002 the price of gold rose above $300 per ounce, to $303.30 per ounce. After being below $300 an ounce for most of the past five years, gold first rose above $300 in February 2002. The price then fell below $300 an ounce but in March it rose above $300 once again. The article noted some Japanese buyers had been purchasing gold because they were worried about their nation's banking system. The article also commented that some U.S. investors were potentially interested in buying gold. However, U.S. investors had not yet begun to purchase gold in large numbers.

For details, go to The Economics Place web site, the Economics in the News archive, www.economicsplace.com/econ5e/einarchives.html

■ **Analyze It**

Gold is traded in a market and its price is determined by supply and demand. Gold set a record high price of over $800 an ounce in 1980 but since then the price has generally fallen, to a low of around $260 an ounce in 2000. While gold mines were closed in the 1990s, in more recent years there has been little movement to close additional mines.

1. In a supply and demand diagram, illustrate the most likely reason why the price of gold has risen to exceed $300 an ounce in 2002.

2. If U.S. investors also decide to buy gold, what will be the impact on the price of gold?

Mid-Term Examination

■ **Chapter 3**

1. The law of demand states that, other things remaining the same, the higher the price of a good, the
   a. smaller will be the demand for the good.
   b. larger will be the demand for the good.
   c. smaller will be the quantity of the good demanded.
   d. larger will be the quantity of the good demanded.

2. Which of the following shifts the supply curve?
   a. An increase in income but only if the good is a normal good.
   b. An increase in income regardless of whether the good is normal or inferior.
   c. A rise in the price of the good.
   d. An increase in the cost of producing the product.

3. A surplus
   a. shifts the demand curve leftward.
   b. shifts the supply curve rightward.
   c. leads to the price falling.
   d. leas to the price rising.

4. When supply increases, the equilibrium quantity
   a. increases and the price rises.
   b. decreases and the price falls.
   c. increases and the price falls.
   d. decreases and the price rises.

■ **Chapter 4**

5. If a rightward shift of the supply curve leads to a 5 percent decrease in price and a 10 percent increase in quantity, then the price elasticity of demand is
   a. 0.50.
   b. 2.0.
   c. 5.0.
   d. 10.0.

6. If the price elasticity of demand exceeds 1, then demand is
   a. elastic.
   b. unit elastic.
   c. inelastic.
   d. positively related to the price of the product.

7. The elasticity of demand for Pizza Hut pizza is
   a. lower than the elasticity of demand for pizza in general and probably inelastic.
   b. larger than the elasticity of demand for pizza in general and probably inelastic.
   c. larger than the elasticity of demand for pizza in general and probably elastic.
   d. lower than the elasticity of demand for pizza in general and probably elastic.

8. A fall in the price of rutabagas from $10.50 to $9.50 a bushel raises the quantity demanded from 19,200 bushels to 20,800 bushels. The price elasticity of demand in this part of the demand curve is
   a. 0.80.
   b. 1.20.
   c. 1.25.
   d. 8.00.

■ **Chapter 5**

9. Resource use is efficient when
   a. it is possible to rearrange production and make everyone better off.
   b. it is not possible to rearrange production.
   c. the goods and services produced are those valued most highly.
   d. whenever supply equals demand.

10. As more of a good is consumed and produced, the marginal benefit _____ and the marginal cost _____.
    a. increases; increases
    b. increases; decreases
    c. decreases; increases
    d. decreases; decreases

11. If the marginal benefit exceeds the marginal cost of producing a unit of output
    a. resource use is efficient.
    b. resource use is inefficient and less should be produced.
    c. resource use is inefficient and more should be produced.
    d. it is impossible to determine if resource use is efficient without information about the demand and supply.

12. In a perfectly competitive market with no external costs or benefits, the marginal benefit curve is the same as the demand curve. In the same situation, the marginal cost curve is the same as the supply curve.
    a. Both sentences are true.
    b. The first sentence is true and the second sentence is false.
    c. The first sentence is false and the second sentence is true.
    d. Both sentences are false.

■ **Chapter 6**

13. A good has an upward sloping supply curve and a perfectly elastic demand. Imposing a sales tax on this good shifts the supply curve

    a. leftward and the buyer pays the entire amount of the tax.
    b. rightward and the buyer pays the entire amount of the tax.
    c. rightward and the seller pays the entire amount of the tax.
    d. leftward and the seller pays the entire amount of the tax.

14. If buying a drug is declared illegal, the demand curve shifts

    a. leftward and the price falls.
    b. leftward and the price rises.
    c. rightward and the price falls.
    d. rightward and the price rises.

15. If demand is inelastic, a rightward shift of the supply curve will

    a. decrease total revenue.
    b. increase total revenue.
    c. have no effect on total revenue.
    d. reduce the demand for the product.

16. The cross elasticity of demand is

    a. positive for complements.
    b. positive for substitutes.
    c. positive for normal goods.
    d. positive for inferior goods.

Answers

■ Reading Between the Lines

1. The price of gold rose in March because the demand for gold increased (recall the Japanese citizens who were now buying gold) and shifted the demand curve rightward. The supply has not changed in recent years, so the supply curve did not shift. Figure 1 illustrates the result. The demand curve shifts rightward and the supply curve does not shift. (There is, however, a movement along the supply curve.) The equilibrium price of gold rises, in the figure, and on March 28, to $303.30 per ounce.

2. If U.S. investors decided to buy gold, the demand for gold would increase still more. With a further increase in demand, the demand curve would shift further to the right and the price of gold would rise still higher.

FIGURE 1

The Gold Market

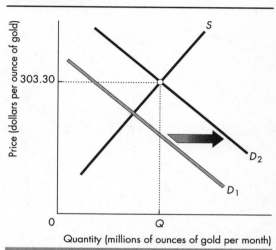

■ Mid-Term Exam Answers

1. c;   2. d;   3. c;   4. c;   5. b;   6. a;   7. c;   8. a;   9. c;   10. c;   11. c;   12. a;   13. d;   14. a;   15. a;   16. b.

Chapter 7

UTILITY AND DEMAND

Key Concepts

Household Consumption Choices

Consumption choices are determined by the interaction of the household's consumption possibilities and its preferences.

- Consumption possibilities — the household's purchases are limited by its income and by the prices of the goods and services. A *budget line*, as illustrated in Figure 7.1, shows the limits to what the household can purchase.
- *Preferences* — an individual's likes and dislikes.

Preferences are measured by utility. **Utility** is the benefit or satisfaction from consumption of a good or service.

- **Total utility** is the *total* benefit from consumption of goods and services.
- **Marginal utility** (*MU*) is the *change* in total utility from a one-unit increase in the quantity of a good consumed. *MU* is positive, but because of **diminishing marginal utility**, falls as the consumption of the good increases.

Maximizing Utility

Consumers strive to obtain the most total utility possible; they maximize their total utility. A **consumer equilibrium** occurs when all the consumer's income is allocated among different products so that the combination of products maximizes the consumer's total utility.

Total utility is maximized when:

- all the consumer's income is spent; and

FIGURE **7.1**
A Budget Line

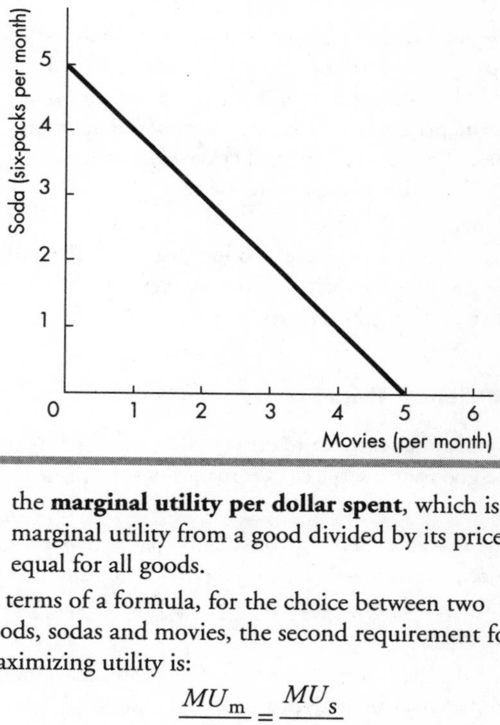

- the **marginal utility per dollar spent**, which is the marginal utility from a good divided by its price, is equal for all goods.

In terms of a formula, for the choice between two goods, sodas and movies, the second requirement for maximizing utility is:

$$\frac{MU_m}{P_m} = \frac{MU_s}{P_s}$$

with MU_m the marginal utility from an additional movie, P_m the price of a movie, and MU_s and P_s the analogous variables for soda.

Equating the marginal utilities per dollar is an example of *marginal analysis*. Marginal analysis says that if the marginal gain from an action exceeds the marginal loss, take the action.

■ Predictions of Marginal Utility Theory

♦ A fall in the price of a movie raises the marginal utility per dollar spent on movies. Consumers increase the quantity of movies viewed as they substitute movies for sodas. There is a movement along the downward sloping demand curve for movies. The demand curve for soda, a substitute for movies, shifts leftward.

♦ A rise in the price of soda results in a decrease in the quantity of sodas consumed. There is an upward movement along the negatively sloped demand curve for soda. The demand curve for movies, a substitute for soda, shifts rightward.

♦ Movies and soda are normal goods, so an increase in income increases the consumption of both products and thereby increases the demand for both products.

The *individual demand* is the relationship between the price of an item and the quantity demanded by an individual. The **market demand** is the relationship between the price of an item and the *total* quantity demanded. The market demand curve is the horizontal sum of the individual demand curves.

If the marginal utility of a product diminishes only a little as the quantity consumed increases, the demand for the product is elastic; if it diminishes rapidly as the quantity consumed increases, the demand is inelastic.

■ Efficiency, Price, and Value

♦ A consumer is using resources efficiently by buying the goods and services that maximizes his or her utility.

♦ The marginal benefit from a good is the maximum price a consumer is willing to pay for another unit of the good when the consumer is maximizing his or her utility.

♦ The distinction between total utility and marginal utility solves the paradox of value. Diamonds are less useful than water (that is, they have lower total utility), but diamonds have a higher price since they have higher *marginal* utility because most people have only a few diamonds. Water is more useful (it has higher total utility), but has a lower price since it has a lower *marginal* utility because the quantity of water consumed is large.

Helpful Hints

1. **THE MEANING OF CONSUMER EQUILIBRIUM :** This chapter introduces another equilibrium, namely, the consumer equilibrium. What does consumer equilibrium mean? Recall that the general definition of equilibrium is a situation "where opposing forces balance." When that occurs, there is no incentive for any changes. In the supply and demand model, equilibrium is attained at the price at which the quantity supplied equals the quantity demanded. At that price neither demanders nor suppliers have an incentive to change their behavior. Consumer equilibrium is similar. When the equilibrium conditions are satisfied, the consumer has the most total utility that can be attained. The consumer therefore has no incentive to change the combination of goods consumed.

2. **THE MARGINAL UTILITY PER DOLLAR FORMULA :** One condition for consumer equilibrium is that the marginal utility per dollar spent on a good must equal the marginal utility per dollar of the other goods. In terms of a formula, for two goods, X and Y, the requirement is that the consumer allocate his or her income so that

$$\frac{MU_X}{P_X} = \frac{MU_Y}{P_Y}.$$

Why is this condition necessary for consumer equilibrium? Recall that the term MU_X/P_X is the marginal utility per dollar spent on good X so it is the utility gained if spending on X is increased a dollar or the utility lost if spending on X is decreased by a dollar. MU_Y/P_Y tells us similar information about Y. Anytime there is an inequality between the marginal utility per dollar spent on different goods, the consumer can increase his or her total utility by buying less of the product with the low MU/P and by buying more of the good with the high MU/P. Only when the marginal utilities per dollar are equal does the consumer not gain by rearranging the consumption bundle. As a result, only when this equality holds (and the consumer spends all his or her income) is the consumer in equilibrium by obtaining the maximum possible total utility.

Questions

■ True/False and Explain

Household Consumption Choices

1. A budget line shows the different combinations of goods and services a consumer can afford to buy.

2. Utility measures a consumer's level of satisfaction.

3. Marginal utility measures the *additional* utility from consuming an *additional* unit of a good.

4. As more of a good is consumed, diminishing marginal utility means that the total utility from the good diminishes.

Maximizing Utility

5. Economists assume that households choose their consumption to maximize their marginal utility per dollar spent.

6. The marginal utility per dollar spent on a soda is MU_s/P_s where MU_s is the marginal utility from a soda and P_s is the price of a soda.

7. If the marginal utilities from consuming two goods are equal and the consumer is spending all of his or her income, the consumer is in equilibrium.

8. A household is maximizing its utility if the marginal utility per dollar spent is equal for all goods and the household spends all its income.

9. If the marginal utility per dollar spent on pizza exceeds the marginal utility per dollar spent on tacos, total utility rises by increasing consumption of pizza and decreasing consumption of tacos.

Predictions of Marginal Utility Theory

10. Marginal utility theory predicts that when the price of a product rises, a consumer buys more because the marginal utility from the product is larger.

11. An individual demand curve shows the total market demand for an individual product.

12. The market demand curve is the horizontal sum of all individual demand curves.

13. If the marginal utility from a good diminishes rapidly as more is consumed, demand for the good is inelastic.

Efficiency, Price, and Value

14. Marginal utility theory shows that goods with high prices (such as diamonds) have high total utilities.

15. By maximizing his or her utility, a consumer uses his or resources efficiently.

■ Multiple Choice

Household Consumption Choices

1. A household's consumption choices are determined by
   a. prices of goods and services.
   b. its income.
   c. its preferences.
   d. all of the above.

2. A household's consumption is limited by
   a. its preferences.
   b. only its income.
   c. only the prices it pays for what it buys.
   d. both its income and the prices it pays for what it buys.

3. Which of the following is <u>NOT</u> an assumption of marginal utility theory?
   a. People derive utility from their consumption.
   b. More consumption yields more total utility.
   c. Marginal utility diminishes with more consumption.
   d. Utility can be measured and the units of utility are precisely defined.

4. As more of a good is consumed,
   a. both the marginal utility and total utility from the good rise.
   b. the marginal utility from the good rises and the total utility falls.
   c. the marginal utility from the good falls and the total utility rises.
   d. both the marginal utility and total utility from the good fall.

Maximizing Utility

5. Economists assume that consumers' objective is to
   a. maximize their total utility.
   b. maximize their marginal utility.
   c. maximize their income.
   d. none of the above.

6. Andrew finds that the marginal utility from a BMW exceeds that from a slice of pizza. Andrew is spending all of his income. These conditions mean that Andrew
   a. is not maximizing his utility.
   b. is maximizing his utility.
   c. must increase his income in order to maximize his utility.
   d. might be maximizing his utility, but we cannot tell without more information.

7. When Kelly maximizes her utility, she spends all of her income and makes sure that the
   a. marginal utility of each good she buys is as high as possible.
   b. marginal utility of each good she buys is equal.
   c. amount of each good she buys is the same.
   d. marginal utility of a good divided by its price is equal for each good she buys.

Use the following table for the next four questions.

TABLE **7.1**

Multiple Choice Questions 8, 9, 10, 11

	Marginal utility	
Quantity	Law books	Paper pads
1	12	16
2	10	12
3	8	8
4	6	4
5	4	2

8. Amy spends her entire income of $10 on law books and yellow paper pads. Law books cost $2 and paper pads cost $4. The marginal utility of each good is given in Table 7.1. If Amy is maximizing her utility, how many yellow paper pads does she buy?
   a. 0
   b. 1
   c. 2
   d. 3

9. Amy's total utility at her consumer equilibrium is
   a. 82
   b. 48
   c. 46
   d. 40

10. Amy's income rises to $16. She continues to buy only law books and yellow paper pads and she continues to maximize her utility. How many yellow paper pads does she buy after her income increases?
    a. 0
    b. 1
    c. 2
    d. 3

11. After Amy's income rises to $16, what is her total utility?
    a. 82
    b. 64
    c. 40
    d. 36

12. Bobby buys only soda and pizza and is buying the amounts that maximize his utility. The marginal utility from a soda is 10, and the price of the soda is $1. The marginal utility from a slice of pizza is 20. The price of a slice of pizza must be
    a. $20.
    b. $2.
    c. $1.
    d. some amount that cannot be calculated without more information.

13. Meg buys only soda and pizza and is buying the amounts that maximize her utility. The marginal utility from a soda is 30 and the price of the soda is $1. The marginal utility from a slice of pizza is 60. The price of a slice of pizza must be
    a. $20.
    b. $2.
    c. $1.
    d. some amount that cannot be calculated without more information.

14. If Soula is maximizing her utility, when two goods have the same price she will
    a. buy only one.
    b. buy equal quantities of both.
    c. get the same marginal utility from each.
    d. get the same total utility from each.

Predictions of Marginal Utility Theory

15. Marginal utility theory predicts that a rise in the price of a banana leads to

    a. the demand curve for bananas shifting rightward.
    b. the demand curve for bananas shifting leftward.
    c. a movement upward along the demand curve for bananas.
    d. a movement downward along the demand curve for bananas.

16. Lisa buys only compact discs and tapes and spends all her income. The marginal utility from a compact disc is 30 and the marginal utility from a tape is 20. The price of a compact disc is $15 and the price of a tape is $10. To maximize her utility, Lisa should

    a. increase her consumption of compact discs.
    b. increase her consumption of tapes.
    c. not change her consumption of compact discs and tapes.
    d. lower the price of a tape.

17. Michael consumes only steak and lobster. Suppose that the price of a steak rises but Michael's income does not change. After he is back at a consumer equilibrium, compared to the situation when steak was cheaper, the marginal utility from the last steak will

    a. have increased.
    b. have not changed.
    c. have decreased.
    d. not be comparable with the marginal utility from before the price hike.

18. Michael consumes only steak and lobster. Both are normal goods. Michael's income increases but the prices of neither steak nor lobster change. After he is back at equilibrium, compared to the situation when Michael's income was less, the marginal utility from the last steak will

    a. have increased.
    b. have not changed.
    c. have decreased.
    d. not be comparable with the marginal utility from before the increase in income.

19. Which of the following statements is true?

    a. Marginal utility theory predicts that an increase in a consumer's income increases consumption of *all* goods.
    b. It is possible to derive the law of demand — that a higher price decreases the quantity demanded — using marginal utility theory.
    c. Marginal utility theory makes no prediction about a consumer's responses to hikes in the prices of the goods and services he or she consumes.
    d. Marginal utility theory predicts that all goods are normal goods and that all goods are substitutes for each other.

20. The marginal utility from gasoline diminishes very rapidly. As a result, the

    a. demand curve for gasoline is upward sloping and very steep.
    b. demand for gasoline is price inelastic.
    c. demand for gasoline is price elastic.
    d. consumer surplus from gasoline is likely to be nonexistent.

Efficiency, Price, and Value

21. The fact that rubies are more expensive than milk reflects the fact that for most consumers

    a. the total utility from rubies exceeds that from milk.
    b. the marginal utility from rubies equals that from milk.
    c. more milk is consumed than rubies.
    d. a quart of rubies is prettier than a quart of milk.

22. The principle of diminishing marginal utility means that the consumer surplus from the second slice of pizza is

    a. greater than that from the first.
    b. equal to that from the first.
    c. less than that from the first.
    d. not comparable to that from the first.

FIGURE 7.2
Multiple Choice Question 23

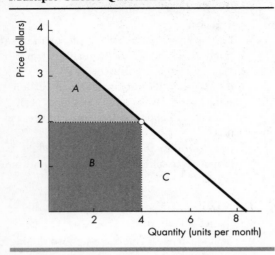

23. In Figure 7.2 the consumer is buying 4 units at a price of $2 each. Consumer surplus is the area marked
    a. *A*
    b. *B*
    c. *C*
    d. None of the above.

■ Short Answer Problems

1. Explain how the consumer equilibrium condition and the principle of diminishing marginal utility can be used to derive the law of demand.

2. Jake consumes only fish sticks and broccoli. He is initially maximizing his utility, so he spends all of his income on fish sticks and broccoli and sets

$$\frac{MU_{FS}}{P_{FS}} = \frac{MU_B}{P_B}$$

   with MU_{FS} the marginal utility from fish sticks; P_{FS} the price of fish sticks; MU_B the marginal utility from broccoli; and P_B the price of broccoli. The price of fish sticks rises (from 70 cents a pound to 80 cents) as a result of the shift in the supply curve shown in Figure 7.3. Use the condition for utility maximization to explain how Jake will move to a new utility-maximizing consumer equilibrium. Also show the connection between your explanation and the change in the figure from 11,000 pounds of fish sticks being consumed to 10,000 pounds.

FIGURE 7.3
Short Answer Problem 2

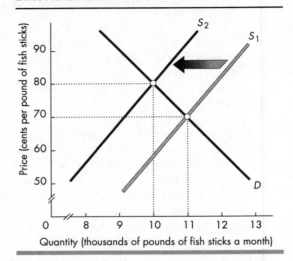

3. Loren is in equilibrium, spending her income of $200 buying 2 video games at a price of $40 each and 8 compact discs at a price of $15 each. Then, inflation causes the price of a compact disc and a video game to double (to $80 and $30, respectively) while Loren's income also doubles (to $400). What happens to Loren's purchases of video games and compact discs: Do both increase, decrease, not change, or change in some direction that cannot be determined?

TABLE 7.2
Short Answer Problem 4

Quantity	Marginal utility Bats	Marginal utility Lizards
1	20	50
2	18	44
3	14	36
4	8	26

4. Igor maximizes his utility by spending his entire income of $16 on bats and lizards. Table 7.2 has Igor's marginal utility from each good. The price of a bat is $2, and he buys 2 bats. The marginal utility from the last lizard he buys is 36.
   a. Calculate the price of a lizard *two* ways.
   b. What is Igor's total utility?
   c. Igor could buy 4 lizards. If he did so and also purchased the maximum number of bats possi-

ble given his income, what would be his total utility then?

d. The marginal utility of even the fourth lizard exceeds the marginal utility from the first bat; yet when maximizing his utility, Igor nonetheless buys some bats. Explain why Igor buys some bats. (Hint: Igor is not batty.)

TABLE **7.3**

Liz's Utility from Popcorn

Bags of popcorn	Total utility	Marginal utility from last bag
0	0	XX
1	20	20
2	36	16
3	50	___
4	___	12
5	72	___
6	80	___

TABLE **7.4**

Liz's Utility from Candy Bars

Candy bars	Total utility	Marginal utility from last bar
0	0	XX
1	14	14
2	26	12
3	___	10
4	44	___
5	51	___
6	57	___

5. Tables 7.3 and 7.4 give Liz's utility from her consumption of popcorn and candy.

a. Complete Tables 7.3 and 7.4.

b. Suppose that the price of a bag of popcorn is $1 and that the price of a candy bar is $0.50. Use the information in Tables 7.3 and 7.4 to complete Table 7.5. There *MU/P* means marginal utility divided by price, which is equivalent to marginal utility per dollar spent.

c. Liz's weekly allowance is $4. If she spends her entire allowance on popcorn and candy, how much popcorn and how many candy bars will Liz consume each week?

TABLE **7.5**

Liz's Marginal Utilities per Dollar

Bags of popcorn	MU/P	Candy bars	MU/P
1	___	1	___
2	___	2	___
3	___	3	___
4	___	4	___
5	___	5	___
6	___	6	___

d. In part (c), what is Liz's total utility?

e. Now suppose that Liz consumes 3 bags of popcorn and 2 candy bars. Explain why she is not maximizing her utility. Be sure to compare her total utilities for the two consumption bundles — your answer to part (c) and the 3 bags of popcorn, 2 candy bars used in this question. Also use the *MU/P* terms to explain why consuming 3 bags of popcorn and 2 candy bars is not optimal.

6. Suppose that Liz's utility remains as it is in Problem 5 but the price of a candy bar doubles to $1. The price of a bag of popcorn, however, does not change — it remains equal to $1 per bag.

a. Construct a new table (similar to Table 7.5) of the marginal utility per dollar for popcorn and candy bars.

b. Liz's allowance continues to be $4. After the price change, how much popcorn and how many candy bars will she consume each week?

c. Are popcorn and candy bars substitutes or complements for Liz? Why?

d. Based on the information you have obtained, draw Liz's demand curve for candy bars.

7. Lori has $40 a week that she spends on playing tennis and buying comic books. A set of tennis costs $1 and a comic book costs $2. One week when Lori spent all her income, she found that the marginal utility from the last set of tennis was 16 and that the marginal utility from the last comic book was 20.

a. Show that Lori's choice of tennis sets and comic books was not optimal.

b. To increase her utility, which good should Lori consume more of and which less?

TABLE **7.6**
Short Answer Problem 8

Price (dollars per pound)	Quantity demanded (pounds per week)			
	Alice	Bob	Carol	Market
$0.50	10	4	10	____
0.75	9	2	7	____
1.00	8	0	4	____
1.25	7	0	1	____

8. Table 7.6 shows Alice's, Bob's, and Carol's demand schedules for rutabagas (a turnip-like vegetable that is one of Canada's main exports).

   a. Assume that Alice, Bob, and Carol comprise the entire market and complete the table by calculating the market demand schedule.

   b. On a single diagram, draw the individual demand curves for Alice, Bob, and Carol, as well as the market demand curve.

9. What is the relationship between price elasticity and how rapidly marginal utility diminishes as more of a good is consumed? Why does this relationship exist?

10. How does marginal utility theory resolve the diamond / water paradox of value?

■ **You're the Teacher**

1. "This whole idea of marginal utility is stupid. I mean, after all, who goes into a store and calculates the marginal utility from something before deciding to buy it? I just look at something, look at the price, think about how much money I've got in my pocket, and then decide whether or not to buy the thing. No one I know calculates marginal utilities when they go shopping, so why do I have to learn this stuff?" What response do you make to your classmate? (*Don't* agree!)

2. "One thing I don't understand about all this material dealing with consumers and their choices is how I am supposed to think about products like apartments. Suppose that the rent in my apartment goes up. Marginal utility theory says that I will consume fewer apartments. But what does this mean? I'll still rent *one* apartment. And, if rent goes down, I sure won't go out and rent two! How does marginal utility theory account for this fact?" Your friend has come up with a good question; provide an equally good explanation to help your friend understand this point.

Answers

■ True/False Answers

Household Consumption Choices

1. **T** The budget line shows the limits to what a consumer can afford to purchase.

2. **T** Utility measures an individual's satisfaction without any regard to the prices of the items or the person's income.

3. **T** As this definition stresses, marginal utility is the extra utility from an extra unit of a good.

4. **F** The principle of diminishing marginal utility implies that the *marginal* utility from additional units declines.

Maximizing Utility

5. **F** Economists assume that households maximize their total utility.

6. **T** The question presents the definition of marginal utility per dollar.

7. **F** To be in equilibrium, the marginal utilities divided by the prices, MU/P, must be equal.

8. **T** These are the two conditions necessary for a household to maximize its utility.

9. **T** In this case, the gain in utility from consuming one dollar more of pizza exceeds the loss in utility from consuming one dollar less of tacos.

Predictions of Marginal Utility Theory

10. **F** Marginal utility theory predicts that the quantity demanded of a product decreases when its price rises.

11. **F** An individual demand curve shows one individual's demand for a product.

12. **T** The market demand shows the demand from *all* individuals.

13. **T** If the marginal utility declines rapidly, then when the price of the good changes it requires only a small change in consumption of the good to restore its marginal utility per dollar back to equality with the marginal utility per dollar for other goods.

Efficiency, Price, and Value

14. **F** Products with high prices must have high marginal utilities, not necessarily high total utilities.

15. **T** By maximizing his or her utility, the person is consuming the combination of goods and services that gives him or her the highest value, which means no resources are wasted.

■ Multiple Choice Answers

Household Consumption Choices

1. **d** A household's consumption is determined by its preferences, its income, and prices of goods.

2. **d** A household's consumption purchases are limited by its budget, which depends on the household's income and the prices of the goods and services it buys.

3. **d** Utility cannot be measured, so its units cannot be precisely defined.

4. **c** The marginal utility diminishes and, as a result, total utility increases but by less as each additional unit of the good is consumed.

Maximizing Utility

5. **a** By maximizing their total utilities, people make themselves as well off as possible.

6. **d** If Andrew is maximizing his utility, we know that $MU_{pizza}/P_{pizza} = MU_{BMW}/P_{BMW}$ but without information about the price of a BMW and a pizza, we cannot determine whether this condition is satisfied.

7. **d** To maximize her utility, Kelly consumes the amounts of the different goods that equalize the marginal utility per dollar of each good.

8. **b** When Amy buys 1 yellow paper pad, she can buy 3 books. With this consumption bundle, $MU_{pad}/P_{pad} = 4$ and $MU_{book}/P_{book} = 4$.

9. **c** Amy receives utility of 16 from yellow paper pads and 30 (12 + 10 + 8) from law books, for total utility of 46.

10. **c** Amy now buys 2 paper pads and 4 law books because this combination of pads and books uses all her income and sets $MU_{pad}/P_{pad} = MU_{book}/P_{book} = 3$.

11. **b** Amy has utility of 28 (16 +12) from yellow paper pads and 36 (12 + 10 + 8 + 6) from law books for total utility of 64.

12. **b** To maximize his utility, Bobby must set $MU_{soda}/P_{soda} = MU_{pizza}/P_{pizza}$. Because

$MU_{soda}/P_{soda} = 10/1 = 10,$ in order for MU_{pizza}/P_{pizza} also to equal 10, with $MU_{pizza} = 20,\ P_{pizza} = \$2$.

13. **b** The same reasoning outlined in the answer to Question 12 applies and $P_{pizza} = \$2$. Even though Bobby's and Meg's marginal utilities are not the same, nonetheless to maximize their utility, both set MU_{soda}/P_{soda} equal to MU_{pizza}/P_{pizza}.

14. **c** Because MU/P is equal for all goods, if two products have the same P, they must have the same MU.

Predictions of Marginal Utility Theory

15. **c** With a higher price for a banana, consumers decrease the quantity they consume, which raises the marginal utility of bananas.

16. **c** $MU_{CDs}/P_{CDs} = MU_{tape}/P_{tape}$. Lisa is already maximizing her utility.

17. **a** Michael consumes fewer steaks, so the marginal utility from the last steak he consumes is higher.

18. **c** Michael consumes more steak because steak is a normal good. Because he consumes more steak, the marginal utility from the last steak he consumes is lower than before.

19. **b** By making assumptions about people's behavior — that they aim to obtain the maximum total utility and that their marginal utility diminishes as they consume more of a product — it is possible to derive the law of demand.

20. **b** Consider a large fall in the price of gasoline. To bring MU_{gas}/P_{gas} back to equality with MU/P for other goods, more gasoline will be consumed, which lowers MU_{gas}. If the marginal utility declines rapidly as more gasoline is consumed, only a little more gasoline is consumed before MU_{gas} falls enough so that MU_{gas}/P_{gas} equals MU/P for everything else. As a result, the large fall in the price of gasoline leads to only a small increase in the quantity demanded.

Efficiency, Price, and Value

21. **c** Because more milk is consumed, the MU from milk is lower than the MU from rubies.

22. **c** Because the second slice of pizza is valued less than the first because of diminishing marginal utility, consumer surplus from the second slice is less than that from the first.

23. **a** Consumer surplus is the area under the demand curve and above the price paid.

■ Answers to Short Answer Problems

1. Suppose that an individual in consumer equilibrium consumes only two goods, X_0 units of good X and Y_0 units of good Y. Therefore at consumption levels X_0 and Y_0, the marginal utility per dollar spent on X equals the marginal utility per dollar spent on Y. If the price of X rises, how does the consumer respond? The marginal utility per dollar spent on X declines and becomes less than the marginal utility per dollar spent on Y. To restore equilibrium, the consumer must increase the marginal utility of X and decrease the marginal utility of Y. From the principle of diminishing marginal utility, the only way to do so is to decrease the consumption of X and increase the consumption of Y. This action, then, demonstrates the law of demand: A rise in the price of X results in a decrease in the consumption of X.

2. When the price of a fish stick rises,

$$\frac{MU_{FS}}{P_{FS}} < \frac{MU_B}{P_B}.$$

Jake no longer is in equilibrium because the utility per dollar spent on fish sticks is less than that for broccoli. So Jake increases his total utility by spending fewer dollars on fish sticks and more on broccoli. These changes make MU_{FS} rise and MU_B fall, which will eventually result in equality between the marginal utility per dollar spent on fish sticks and broccoli. Jake's decreased consumption of fish sticks moves him along his individual demand curve for fish sticks. Indeed, consumers in general decrease the quantity of fish sticks they consume, which accounts for the movement along the market demand curve in the figure from the initial equilibrium (with 11,000 pounds of fish sticks produced and consumed) to the new equilibrium (with only 10,000 pounds of fish sticks produced and consumed).

3. After the inflation Loren still purchases 2 video games and 8 compact discs. Loren buys the combi-

nation of games and CDs that maximizes her utility, setting $MU_{games}/P_{games} = MU_{CDs}/P_{CDs}$ and spending all her income. For the first requirement, before the inflation the combination of 2 games and 8 CDs maximized Loren's utility so that it was the case that $MU_{games}/P_{games} = MU_{CDs}/P_{CDs}$. After the inflation, the marginal utilities do not change, but the prices double. So, MU/P for games equals $MU_{games}/(2 \times P_{games})$ and MU/P for CDs equals $MU_{CDs}/(2 \times P_{CDs})$. The MU/P for video games is half what it was before, as is the MU/P for compact discs. Because they were equal before the inflation, dividing each by 2 does not change their equality; that is, after the inflation the equality of the marginal utilities per dollar condition for utility maximization is still met. For the second condition, that all income is spent, after the inflation, buying 2 video games and 8 compact discs uses up all of Loren's income, so the second criteria is met. The combination of 2 games and 8 CDs continues to maximize Loren's utility, so that is the combination she will purchase.

4. a. One of two methods for calculating the price of a lizard is based on the fact that Igor spends all his income on bats and lizards. This fact means that:

$$Y = P_b \times Q_b + P_l \times Q_l$$

where Y is Igor's income, P_b is the price of a bat, Q_b is the quantity of bats bought, P_l is the price of a lizard, and Q_l is the quantity of lizards purchased. We know that $Y = \$16$, $P_b = \$2$, $Q_b = 2$, and, if the marginal utility of the last lizard is 36, that $Q_l = 3$. Substituting these values, we solve for P_l:

$$\$16 = \$2 \times 2 + P_l \times 3$$
$$\$12 = P_l \times 3$$
$$\$4 = P_l$$

The second way to determine the price of a lizard uses the condition for utility maximization, that the marginal utility per dollar spent on a lizard equals the marginal utility per dollar spent on a bat. In terms of a formula, we have that

$$\frac{MU_l}{P_l} = \frac{MU_b}{P_b}.$$

We know that $MU_l = 36$, $P_b = \$2$, and, if Igor buys 2 bats, that $MU_b = 18$. Substituting these values, we solve for P_l:

$$\frac{36}{P_l} = \frac{18}{\$2}$$
$$\frac{36}{9} = P_l$$
$$\$4 = P_l$$

b. Igor receives total utility of 38 from his bats (20 + 18) and total utility of 130 from his lizards (50 + 44 + 36). Igor's overall total utility from bats and lizards is 168.

c. If Igor buys 4 lizards, because each lizard costs $4, he spends all his income and so can purchase no bats. In this case, Igor's total utility is 156 (50 + 44 + 36 + 26).

d. Even though each bat returns less marginal utility than a lizard, bats are less expensive then lizards. So when Igor is selecting his utility-maximizing combination of bats and lizards, the cheapness of bats means that he will buy some. For example, compare Igor's total utility when he buys 2 bats and 3 lizards, given in part (b) as 168, with his total utility when he buys 0 bats and 4 lizards, computed in part (c) as 156. Clearly Igor's *total* utility is higher when he buys 2 bats and 3 lizards than when he concentrates solely on lizards by purchasing 4 lizards and 0 bats.

5. a. Tables 7.7 and 7.8 (on the next page) are completed versions of Tables 7.3 and 7.4, respectively.

b. Table 7.9 (on the next page) completes Table 7.5.

TABLE 7.7

Liz's Utility from Popcorn

Bags of popcorn	Total utility	Marginal utility from last bag
0	0	XX
1	20	20
2	36	16
3	50	14
4	62	12
5	72	10
6	80	8

TABLE 7.8
Liz's Utility from Candy Bars

Candy bars	Total utility	Marginal utility from last bar
0	0	XX
1	14	14
2	26	12
3	36	10
4	44	8
5	51	7
6	57	6

TABLE 7.9
Liz's Marginal Utilities Per Dollar

Bags of popcorn	MU/P	Candy bars	MU/P
1	20	1	28
2	16	2	24
3	14	3	20
4	12	4	16
5	10	5	14
6	8	6	12

c. 2 bags of popcorn and 4 candy bars. This combination uses up all of Liz's income and also equates the marginal utility per dollar spent on popcorn and candy bars (16).

d. Total utility is the utility from the consumption of 2 bags of popcorn (36) plus the utility from the consumption of 4 candy bars (44) or 80.

e. If Liz consumed 3 bags of popcorn and 2 candy bars, total utility would be 76, less than 80, the total utility from the consumption of 2 bags of popcorn and 4 candy bars. For the combination of 3 bags of popcorn and 2 candy bars, MU/P for popcorn is 14 and MU/P for candy bars is 24. Because MU/P is not the same for both goods, this combination does not maximize Liz's utility. More specifically, Liz could decrease her consumption of popcorn by a dollar, use the dollar to buy more candy bars, and thereby would raise her total utility. This marginal analysis shows that Liz can increase her total utility by consuming less popcorn and more candy whenever the MU/P from popcorn is less than the MU/P from candy bars.

TABLE 7.10
Liz's (New) Marginal Utilities Per Dollar

Bags of popcorn	MU/P	Candy bars	MU/P
1	20	1	14
2	16	2	12
3	14	3	10
4	12	4	8
5	10	5	7
6	8	6	6

6. a. Table 7.10 shows Liz's MU/P for popcorn and candy after the price hike for candy. The price rise did not change Liz's MUs.

b. Liz will consume 3 bags of popcorn and 1 candy bar. This combination of popcorn and candy spends all of Liz's income ($4), and the marginal utility per dollar spent is the same for popcorn and candy bars (14).

c. Popcorn and candy bars are substitutes for Liz because a rise in the price of a candy bar leads to an increase in the demand for popcorn.

d. Two points on Liz's demand curve have been identified. When the price of a candy bar is $1, 1 candy bar will be demanded, and when the price is $0.50, 4 candy bars will be demanded. The demand curve is a line through these two points, as illustrated in Figure 7.4.

FIGURE 7.4
Short Answer Problem 6

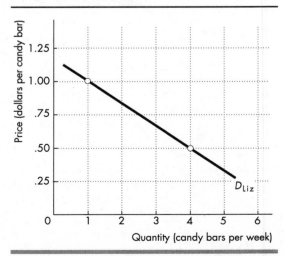

7. a. Lori is not maximizing her utility because the marginal utility per dollar spent on the set of tennis ($16/\$1 = 16$) is not the same as the marginal utility per dollar spent on comic books ($20/\$2 = 10$).

   b. To equate the marginal utilities per dollar spent (and by so doing increase her total utility), Lori will increase her consumption of tennis and decrease her consumption of comic books. To show that this change raises her utility, we can use marginal analysis. By cutting back a dollar on comic books, Lori loses 10 units of utility; but by then spending the dollar on tennis, Lori gains 16 units. Therefore on net, Lori gains 6 units of utility (16 gained from tennis minus 10 lost from comic books) by changing her consumption bundle.

TABLE **7.11**

Short Answer Problem 8

Price (dollars per pound)	Market demand
0.50	24
0.75	18
1.00	12
1.25	8

8. a. Table 7.11 gives the market demand. For an example of how to calculate these answers, at the price of $0.50 per pound, the market demand is 24, with 10 demanded by Alice plus 4 demanded by Bob plus 10 demanded by Carol.

   b. Figure 7.5 shows the three individual demand curves and the market demand curve, the sum of Alice's plus Bob's plus Carol's demand.

9. The more rapidly the marginal utility from a good diminishes as more of the good is consumed, the less elastic is the demand for the product. Conversely, the less rapidly the marginal utility diminishes, the more elastic is the demand for the product. For an example, take the case of sugar. The marginal utility of sugar diminishes rapidly as more units of it are consumed. Initially consumers set the MU/P from sugar equal to the MU/P for all other products. Suppose that the price of sugar falls by a substantial amount. This change causes the marginal utility per dollar spent on sugar, MU/P,

FIGURE **7.5**

Short Answer Problem 8

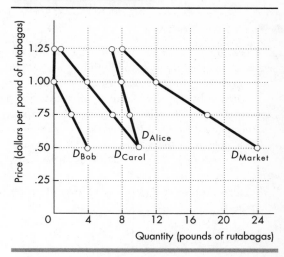

to rise (a lot) because P falls (a lot). In response to the increase in the marginal utility per dollar spent on sugar, people consume more sugar. This increase in consumption reduces sugar's marginal utility, and the MU/P from sugar falls. Enough additional sugar will be consumed so that the MU/P from sugar falls back to equality with the MU/P from all other products. How much additional sugar consumption is required? Because the marginal utility from sugar falls rapidly as more sugar is consumed, not very much more sugar must be consumed in order to reduce substantially the MU/P of sugar. So when the marginal utility from a good diminishes rapidly as more is consumed, a large price change brings only a small change in the quantity demanded, which means that the demand for the product is price inelastic.

10. The paradox of value is resolved by recognizing the difference between the total utility from a product and its marginal utility. For instance, the total utility from consumption of water is large but because we consume a lot of water, the marginal utility from the last gallon of water is small. The total utility from the consumption of diamonds is small, but because we consume few diamonds, the marginal utility of the last diamond is large. In consumer equilibrium, because the marginal utility per dollar spent is the same for water and diamonds, the price of water must be low and the price of a diamond must be high. The paradox of value is solved because it is the

marginal utilities — not the total utilities — that are related to the price of diamonds and water.

■ You're the Teacher

1. "You're right that no one goes into a store and calculates marginal utility before deciding whether to buy something. But that is missing the point of marginal utility theory. Marginal utility theory is *not* trying to explain how people make decisions about what to buy. Instead, it is based on the assumption that people make themselves as well off as possible — maximize their utility — to explain how people respond to changes in prices and incomes. It's not a theory of people's thoughts. It's a theory of people's actions."

2. "What you are missing is the fact that apartments are not all identical. My apartment is larger than yours. If the price of an apartment rose — rents go up — I'd move to a smaller apartment. Or, if the price went down, I wouldn't rent two apartments, but I'd move to a still larger one. So think about it this way: If the price of an apartment goes up, we'll consume 'fewer' apartments by renting smaller apartments; and, if the price goes down, we'll consume 'more' apartments by renting larger ones."

Chapter Quiz

1. As Sam's consumption of rice decreases, his
   a. average utility from rice falls.
   b. total utility from rice falls.
   c. marginal utility from rice decreases.
   d. elasticity of utility from rise increases.

2. When Romona is in consumer equilibrium,
   a. her marginal utilities from all goods are equal.
   b. her total utilities from all goods are equal.
   c. her total utility per dollar from all goods are equal.
   d. her marginal utility per dollar from all goods are equal.

3. According to marginal utility theory, consumers
   a. maximize their total utility and minimize their marginal utility.
   b. maximize their total utility given the prices of goods and their income.
   c. maximize their income.
   d. spend the most on least expensive goods.

4. The price of a soda is $1 and the price of a movie is $5. Bobby spends all of his income on sodas and movies. If Bobby's marginal utility from a soda is 10 and his marginal utility from a movie is 20, to maximize his utility Bobby definitely _____ the number of movies he sees and _____ his consumption of sodas.
   a. increases; increases
   b. increases; decreases
   c. decreases; increases
   d. decreases; decreases

5. When economists talk of inferior goods they mean only goods for which
   a. the demand curve slopes downward.
   b. marginal utility falls as more of the good is consumed.
   c. marginal utility is always negative.
   d. demand decreases when income rises.

6. The statement that more consumption yields more utility is
   a. a prediction of marginal utility theory.
   b. an assumption of marginal utility theory.
   c. a fallacy disproven by marginal utility theory.
   d. true of goods but not of services.

7. Marginal utility theory predicts that an increase in the price of a good _____ the quantity demanded.
   a. increases
   b. has no effect on
   c. decreases
   d. perhaps increases, has no effect on, or decreases, depending on whether the good is a normal good or inferior good.

8. The market demand curve for rutabagas is
   a. used to derive the individual demand curves.
   b. the sum of the quantity demanded by each individual at each price.
   c. more elastic than any individual demand curve.
   d. less elastic than any individual demand curve.

9. Kathy is in consumer equilibrium and consumes many goods. For her, purses are a normal good. An increase in her income changes her to a new equilibrium in which her consumer surplus from purses is
   a. zero, as it was in the old equilibrium.
   b. positive and equal to what it was in the old equilibrium.
   c. lower than in the old equilibrium.
   d. higher than in the old equilibrium.

10. Megan buys only soda and pizza and is buying the amounts that maximize her utility. The marginal utility from a soda is 10 and the price of a soda is $1. The marginal utility from a pizza is 80. Hence the price of a pizza must be
    a. $80.
    b. $10.
    c. $8.
    d. $4.

The answers for this Chapter Quiz are on page 367

Chapter 8 POSSIBILITIES, PREFERENCES, AND CHOICES

Consumption Possibilities

The **budget line** shows the limits to a household's consumption. Figure 8.1 graphs a budget line; the formula for the budget line in this figure is:

$$Q_{soda} = \frac{y}{P_{soda}} - \left(\frac{P_{movies}}{P_{soda}}\right)Q_{movies}$$

♦ A household's **real income** is the income expressed as a quantity of goods the household can afford to buy. In terms of soda, (y/P_{soda}) is the household's real income. An increase in income (y) shifts the budget line rightward but does not change its slope.

♦ The magnitude of the slope of the budget line (P_{movies}/P_{soda}) is the **relative price** of a movie in terms of a soda.

♦ Changes in the relative price rotate the budget line. A fall in the price of movies, the product on the horizontal axis, rotates the budget line outward so that it becomes flatter.

Preferences and Indifference Curves

An **indifference curve** is a curve showing combinations of goods among which a person is indifferent. Figure 8.2 illustrates a family of indifference curves.

♦ Indifference curves farther from the origin are preferred over those closer to the origin.

The **marginal rate of substitution** (MRS) is the rate at which the household is willing to give up the good on the vertical axis (soda) for an additional unit of the good on the horizontal axis (movies) and still remain indifferent. The magnitude of the slope of the indifference curve equals the MRS.

♦ The **diminishing marginal rate of substitution** is the tendency for a person to be willing to give up

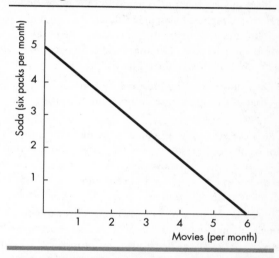

FIGURE **8.1**
The Budget Line

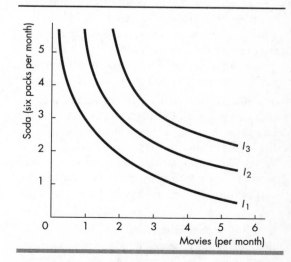

FIGURE **8.2**
Indifference Curves

133

less of the good on the vertical axis to get one more unit of the good on the horizontal axis, while remaining indifferent (that is, on the same indifference curve) as the quantity of the good on the horizontal axis increases.

♦ Goods that are substitutes have straighter indifference curves; goods that are complements have more bowed indifference curves.

■ Predicting Consumer Behavior

The household chooses the best affordable point. This point is the combination of goods on the budget line and on the highest possible indifference curve. Figure 8.3 illustrates the best affordable point, where the household consumes M movies and S six-packs of soda per month. At this optimal point:

♦ the budget line and indifference curve are tangent so that the marginal rate of substitution equals the relative price.

The **price effect** is the change in the quantity consumed of a good resulting from a change in its price. When the price of a movie falls, the budget line rotates as shown in Figure 8.4 and the consumption of movies increases from M_1 to M_2.

The fall in the price of a movie increases the quantity of movies demanded, which shows how this analysis can be used to derive the demand curve for movies.

The price effect can be divided into the substitution effect plus the income effect.

♦ The **income effect** is the change in consumption resulting from a change in income. For normal goods, higher income increases consumption and the demand curve shifts rightward; for inferior goods, higher income decreases consumption and the demand curve shifts leftward.

♦ The **substitution effect** is the change in consumption resulting from a change in price accompanied by a (hypothetical) change in income that leaves the household indifferent (on the same indifference curve) between the initial and new situations. For all goods, the substitution effect of a price fall increases consumption of the good.

♦ For normal goods, the substitution and income effects from a price change work in the same direction, so a lower price unambiguously increases consumption. For inferior goods, the substitution and income effects work in opposite directions.

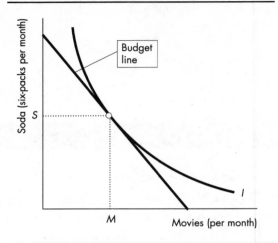

FIGURE **8.3**
The Best Affordable Point

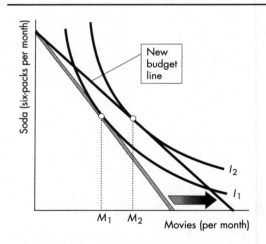

FIGURE **8.4**
A Fall in the Price of a Movie

■ Work-Leisure Choices

Labor supply decisions can be analyzed using an indifference curve/budget line approach.

♦ A budget line and the indifference curves exist between leisure and consumption of other goods.

♦ A rise in the wage rate changes the slope of the budget line, creating income and substitution effects. The substitution effect leads to more hours spent working, but the income effect leads to fewer hours spent working.

Helpful Hints

1. **A PERSPECTIVE ON THE CHAPTER :** The analysis in this chapter clarifies economists' general view that people strive to make themselves as well off as possible. However, people face constraints. These constraints, which limit the range of possible choices, depend on income and the prices of goods and are represented graphically by the budget line. Doing the best means finding the most preferred outcome consistent with those constraints.

   Graphically, the problem is to find the highest indifference curve attainable given the budget line. To make graphical analysis feasible, we restrict ourselves to choices between only two goods, but the same principles apply in the real world to a broader array of choices.

2. **INCOME, PRICES, AND INDIFFERENCE CURVES :** Indifference curves plot people's preferences and do not depend on their incomes or the prices of the goods. For example, an indifference curve indicates how much a person likes (or dislikes) lobster without regard to the price of a lobster or the person's income. When the price of a lobster or the individual's income changes, the budget line changes, but the indifference curves do not change. If lobster is a normal good, higher income leads to more lobster being consumed. But the reason that more lobster is consumed is that the budget line has shifted outward, making more combinations of goods affordable.

5. Indifference curves farther from the origin are preferred to those closer to the origin.

6. The magnitude of the slope of a person's indifference curve is the marginal rate of substitution.

7. The marginal rate of substitution falls when moving upward along an indifference curve.

8. Goods that are perfect substitutes have L-shaped indifference curves.

Predicting Consumer Behavior

9. The best affordable point of consumption is on the budget line and on the highest attainable indifference curve.

10. The law of demand can be derived from an indifference curve diagram by using the diagram to determine the impact changes in price have on the person's consumption bundle.

11. The substitution effect can be divided into the price effect and the income effect.

12. For an inferior good, an increase in income shifts the budget line leftward.

13. When the relative price of a good falls, the income effect always leads to increased consumption of the good.

Work-Leisure Choices

14. The indifference curve/budget line approach shows that a rise in the wage rate definitely increases the quantity of labor supplied.

15. Both the substitution effect and income effect from a higher wage rate lead to an increase in the quantity of labor supplied.

Questions

■ True/False and Explain

Consumption Possibilities

1. The budget line has a negative slope and is linear.

2. The magnitude of the slope of the budget line is a relative price.

3. An increase in income shifts the budget line outward and makes it steeper.

Preferences and Indifference Curves

4. A person is indifferent between any combination of goods on a particular indifference curve.

■ Multiple Choice

Consumption Possibilities

1. Which of the following statements best describes a consumer's budget line?
   a. It shows all combinations of goods among which the consumer is indifferent.
   b. It shows the limits to a consumer's set of affordable consumption choices.
   c. It shows the desired level of consumption for the consumer.
   d. It shows the consumption choices made by a consumer.

2. The magnitude of the slope of the budget line
   a. is defined as marginal rate of substitution.
   b. equals the relative price of the good measured along the horizontal axis.
   c. increases when income increases.
   d. decreases when income increases.

3. The budget line can shift or rotate
   a. only when income changes.
   b. only when prices change.
   c. when either income or prices change.
   d. None of the above because changes in income and prices do not shift or rotate the budget line.

Use Figure 8.5 for the next two questions.

FIGURE **8.5**
Multiple Choice Questions 4 and 5

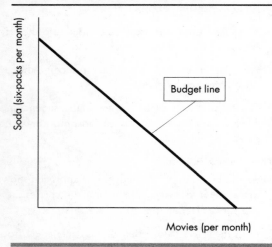

4. Suppose that this consumer's income increases and nothing else changes. As a result, the consumer's budget line
   a. rotates around the vertical intercept and becomes steeper.
   b. rotates around the vertical axis and becomes shallower.
   c. shifts rightward and becomes steeper.
   d. shifts rightward and its slope does not change.

5. Suppose that the price of a movie rises and nothing else changes. This change means the budget line
   a. rotates around the vertical intercept and becomes steeper.
   b. rotates around the vertical axis and becomes flatter.
   c. shifts rightward and becomes steeper.
   d. shifts rightward and does not change its slope.

6. Sue consumes apples and bananas. Suppose that Sue's income doubles *and* that the prices of apples and bananas also double. Sue's budget line will
   a. shift leftward but not change slope.
   b. remain unchanged.
   c. shift rightward but not change slope.
   d. shift rightward and become steeper.

Preferences and Indifference Curves

7. As a consumer moves rightward along an indifference curve, the
   a. consumer remains indifferent among the different combinations of goods.
   b. consumer generally prefers the combinations of goods farther rightward along the indifference curve.
   c. income required to buy the combinations of the goods always increases.
   d. relative price of both goods falls.

8. Indifference curves shift or rotate
   a. only when income changes.
   b. only when prices change.
   c. when either income or prices change.
   d. with none of the above because changes in income and prices do not shift indifference curves.

9. If your local newspaper reported that wearing plaid clothing was a sure way to obtain good grades, students'
   a. budget lines would shift rightward to compensate for the higher price of plaid clothing.
   b. budget lines would rotate so that more plaid clothing would be purchased.
   c. preferences would change in favor of more plaid clothing.
   d. None of the above.

10. Diminishing marginal rate of substitution means that
    a. the budget line has a negative slope.
    b. the budget line does not shift when people's preferences change.
    c. indifference curves might have a positive slope.
    d. indifference curves will be concave.

11. If two goods are perfect substitutes, their
    a. indifference curves are positively sloped straight lines.
    b. indifference curves are negatively sloped straight lines.
    c. indifference curves are L-shaped.
    d. marginal rate of substitution is infinity.

12. If the indifference curves between two goods are L-shaped, the goods are
    a. complementary goods.
    b. substitute goods.
    c. normal goods.
    d. inferior goods.

Predicting Consumer Behavior

Use Figure 8.6 for the next two questions.

FIGURE 8.6
Multiple Choice Questions 13 and 14

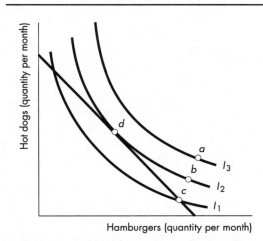

13. Which of the following statements about Figure 8.6 is correct?
    a. Point *a* is preferred to point *d*, but *a* is not affordable.
    b. The consumer is indifferent between points *d* and *c*, but *c* is more affordable.
    c. Point *b* is preferred to point *d*, but *b* is not affordable.
    d. Both points *a* and *d* cost the same, but *a* is preferred to *d*.

14. What is the best affordable point of consumption?
    a. *a*
    b. *b*
    c. *c*
    d. *d*

15. A consumer is in equilibrium when the consumption point is on
    a. the budget line.
    b. an indifference curve.
    c. the highest indifference curve that just touches the budget line.
    d. None of the above.

16. Which of the following is true when the consumer is at the best affordable point?
    a. The point is on the budget line and highest attainable indifference curve.
    b. The slope of the budget line equals the slope of the indifference curve.
    c. The MRS equals the relative price.
    d. All of the above are true at the best affordable point.

17. Which of the following statements is true?
    a. The law of diminishing marginal rate of substitution means that indifference curves are convex (bowed out).
    b. A demand curve can be derived from the indifference curve/budget line analysis.
    c. Demand curves and indifference curves measure the same things.
    d. Demand curves and indifference curves have negative slopes for the same reason.

18. When the price of an orange falls, the income effect
    a. increases the consumption of oranges if oranges are a normal good.
    b. increases the consumption of oranges if oranges are an inferior good.
    c. always increases the consumption of oranges.
    d. always decreases the consumption of oranges.

19. When oranges fall in price, the substitution effect
    a. increases the consumption of oranges if oranges are a normal good.
    b. increases the consumption of oranges if oranges are an inferior good.
    c. always increases the consumption of oranges.
    d. always decreases the consumption of oranges.

Use Figure 8.7 for the next three questions.

FIGURE **8.7**
Multiple Choice Questions 20, 21, 22

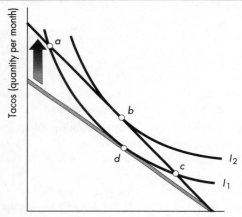

Tacos (quantity per month)

Slices of pizza (quantity per month)

20. The change in the budget line is the result of a(n)
    a. fall in the price of a slice of pizza.
    b. fall in the price of a taco.
    c. increase in income.
    d. None of the above

21. With the change in the budget line, the consumer's real income measured in units of tacos
    a. definitely increased.
    b. definitely decreased.
    c. did not change.
    d. might have changed, but it is impossible to tell from the figure.

22. The new consumer equilibrium is at point
    a. *a.*
    b. *b.*
    c. *c.*
    d. *d.*

23. When you examine the effect from a change in price while (hypothetically) changing income to keep the consumer on the same indifference curve, you are examining the
    a. price effect.
    b. income effect.
    c. substitution effect.
    d. *ceterus paribus* effect.

24. When the price of a normal good falls, the income effect _____ the quantity demanded and the substitution effect _____ the quantity demanded.
    a. increases; increases
    b. increases; decreases
    c. decreases; increases
    d. decreases; decreases

25. An inferior good
    a. has a substitution effect opposite that of a normal good.
    b. has an income effect opposite that of a normal good.
    c. has a price effect opposite that of a normal good.
    d. is one that breaks after its first use.

Work-Leisure Choices

26. The substitution effect from a rise in the wage rate
    a. motivates a decrease in leisure.
    b. motivates an increase in leisure.
    c. has the same effect on leisure as does the income effect.
    d. None of the above.

27. Over the past 100 years, the quantity of labor supplied has decreased as wages have risen. This change indicates that the income effect
    a. and the substitution effect have both discouraged leisure.
    b. and the substitution effect have both encouraged leisure.
    c. encouraging leisure has dominated the substitution effect discouraging leisure.
    d. has not affected the work–leisure choice.

■ Short Answer Problems

1. Why do indifference curves have negative slopes?

2. Jan and Dan eat bread and peanut butter and have the same income. Because they face the same prices, they have identical budget lines. Currently, Jan and Dan consume the same quantities of bread and peanut butter; they have the same best affordable consumption point. Jan views bread and peanut butter as close (though not perfect) substitutes, whereas Dan considers bread and peanut butter to be quite (but not perfectly) complementary. On the same diagram, draw a budget line and representative indifference curves for Jan and Dan. (Measure the quantity of bread on the horizontal axis.)

FIGURE **8.8**
Short Answer Problem 3

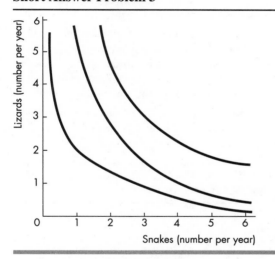

3. Three of Igor's indifference curves are illustrated Figure 8.8.

   a. Suppose that the price of a snake is $10, the price of a lizard is $20, and Igor has $60 to spend on snakes and lizards. Carefully draw his budget line in Figure 8.8. How many snakes does Igor buy? How many lizards?

   b. Suppose that the price of a snake spirals to $20 while the price of a lizard does not change. If Igor's income stays at $60, draw his new budget line in Figure 8.8. Now how many snakes does Igor buy? How many lizards? Are snakes and lizards substitutes or complements?

   c. When is Igor better off: before or after snakes go up in price? How can you tell?

FIGURE **8.9**
Short Answer Problem 4

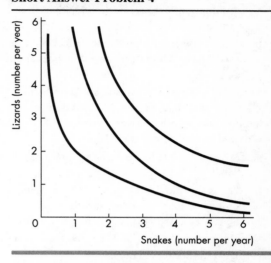

4. Figure 8.9 again shows Igor's indifference curves.

   a. Snakes cost $20, lizards cost $20, and Igor's income is $60. Draw Igor's budget line in Figure 8.9. How many snakes does Igor buy? How many lizards?

   b. For his superior work in finding brains, Igor's master gives him a raise to $120. In Figure 8.9 draw Igor's new budget line. After the raise, how many snakes does Igor buy? How many lizards? For Igor, are snakes and/or lizards a normal good?

5. Ms. Muffet consumes curds and whey. The initial price of curds is $1 per unit, and the price of whey is $1.50 per unit. Ms. Muffet's income is $12.

   a. What is the relative price of curds?

   b. Derive Ms. Muffet's budget equation and draw her budget line on a graph. (Measure curds on the horizontal axis.)

   c. On your graph, draw an indifference curve so that the best affordable point corresponds to 6 units of curds and 4 units of whey.

   d. What is the marginal rate of substitution of curds for whey at this point?

   e. Show that any other point on the budget line is inferior.

6. For the initial situation described in problem 5, suppose that Ms. Muffet's income now increases.

   a. Illustrate graphically how the consumption of curds and whey are affected if both goods are normal. (Precise numerical answers are not necessary here. In your graph, just show whether consumption increases or decreases but do not worry about specific numbers.)

b. Draw a new graph showing the effect of an increase in Ms. Muffet's income if whey is an inferior good.

7. Return to the initial circumstances in problem 5. Now, suppose that the price of curds doubles to $2 a unit while the price of whey remains at $1.50 per unit and income remains at $12.

a. Draw the budget line before and after the price change.

b. Why is the initial best affordable point (label it point *a*) no longer the best affordable point?

c. Use your graph and show the new best affordable point and label it *d*. What has happened to the consumption of curds?

d. Use your graph to illustrate the substitution and income effects from the price change. Label the point created by the substitution effect *b*.

FIGURE **8.10**
Short Answer Problem 8 (a) and 8 (b)

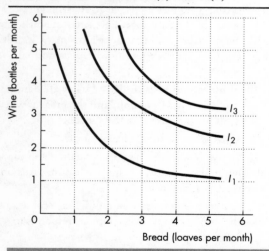

8. Figure 8.10 illustrates Carolyn's indifference map between bread and wine.

a. The price of a bottle of wine is $2, and the price of a loaf of bread is $1. Carolyn has $6 to spend on bread and wine. In Figure 8.10 draw her budget line. How many bottles of wine does Carolyn buy?

FIGURE **8.11**
Short Answer Problem 8 (c)

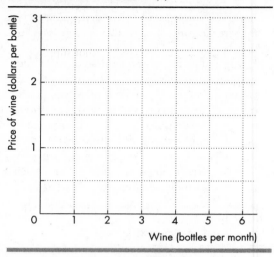

b. The price of a bottle of wine falls to $1. The price of a loaf of bread remains at $1, and Carolyn's income is constant at $6. Draw her new budget line in Figure 8.10. How many bottles of wine does Carolyn now buy?

c. Assume that Carolyn's demand curve is linear. In Figure 8.11 draw Carolyn's demand curve for wine.

FIGURE **8.12**
Short Answer Problem 9

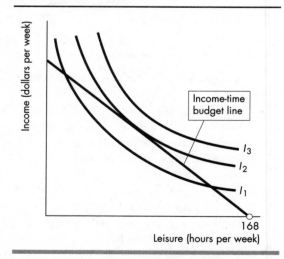

9. In Figure 8.12 indicate the initial hours of leisure this person enjoys. Suppose that the wage rate rises so that the person moves to another of the indiffer-

ence curves already in the figure; that is, the budget line rotates so that another indifference curve is now optimal. Draw the new budget line and show the new equilibrium amount of leisure. How did the amount of leisure change with the higher wage rate? How did the amount of labor supplied change as the wage rate rose? What accounts for your answers to the last two questions?

■ You're the Teacher

1. "I see that we can use this indifference curve/budget line approach to derive demand curves. But why bother? I mean, after all, why not just use the demand curves like we've been doing all along and not worry about this other stuff?" This question is reasonable. Tell your friend why this other stuff is worth bothering about.

2. "I finally understand this chapter: Indifference curves and demand curves are the same thing! My studying is beginning to pay off." Actually your friend is *not* studying enough. Help your friend by explaining why indifference curves and demand curves are not the same.

Answers

■ True/False Answers

Consumption Possibilities

1. **T** The budget line is straight; indifference curves are concave (bowed toward the origin).

2. **T** The magnitude of the slope of the budget line is the relative price of the good on the horizontal axis in terms of the good on the vertical axis.

3. **F** An increase in income shifts the budget line outward, but does not change its slope.

Preferences and Indifference Curves

4. **T** This definition is why a consumer is indifferent between points on a particular indifference curve.

5. **T** Indifference curves farther from the origin have more potential consumption of *all* goods and services and so are preferred.

6. **T** The statement tells how to measure the marginal rate of substitution.

7. **F** The principle of diminishing marginal rate of substitution means that the marginal rate of substitution falls while moving *downward* along an indifference curve.

8. **F** Goods that are complements have L-shaped indifference curves.

Predicting Consumer Behavior

9. **T** The best affordable point is best because it is on the highest indifference curve and is affordable because it is on the budget line.

10. **T** The question tells how a demand curve can be derived.

11. **F** The price effect can be divided into the substitution effect and the income effect.

12. **F** The budget line shifts rightward, but the equilibrium amount of the good consumed decreases.

13. **F** The income effect leads to increased consumption for normal goods and decreased consumption for inferior goods.

Work-Leisure Choices

14. **F** A rise in the wage rate might either increase or decrease labor supply. See the next answer for more details on why this ambiguity occurs.

15. **F** The income effect decreases the quantity of labor supplied, but the substitution effect increases the quantity. The net effect on the supply of labor from the increase in the wage rate is ambiguous.

■ Multiple Choice Answers

Consumption Possibilities

1. **b** The budget line illustrates the different combinations of goods an individual can afford. In this sense it is like a menu, showing what can be purchased. But in order to determine what will be purchased, information is needed on the consumer's preferences about the different combinations of goods.

2. **b** The slope indicates how many units of the good measured on the vertical axis must be given up in order to gain another unit of the good measured on the horizontal axis.

3. **c** Income and price changes shift or rotate the budget line, not indifference curves.

4. **d** Changes in the relative price rotate the budget line; changes in income shift it in a parallel fashion.

5. **a** A rise in the price of a movie does not change the vertical intercept (y/P_{soda}), but the magnitude of the slope (P_{movies}/P_{soda}) increases.

6. **b** The relative price of bananas and apples does not change because both prices doubled, so the slope of the budget line is unchanged. In addition, the intercepts do not change because the higher income matches the higher prices. So, the budget line does not change.

Preferences and Indifference Curves

7. **a** By definition, the consumer is indifferent between any consumption combination on an indifference curve.

8. **d** Only changes in the individual's preferences shift the indifference curves.

9. **c** Preferences change because now students "like" plaid clothing more than before.

10. **d** The diminishing marginal rate of substitution means that an indifference curve becomes flatter while moving rightward along it so that more of the good measured on the horizontal axis is consumed.

11. **b** The more closely two goods substitute for each other, the more closely their indifference curves approach being straight lines.

12. **a** Perfect complements have L-shaped indifference curves.

Predicting Consumer Behavior

13. **a** Point *a* is preferred because it is on a higher indifference curve, but it is not affordable because it lies beyond the budget line.

14. **d** Point *d* is the point on the highest indifference curve that is affordable.

15. **c** The consumption bundle represented by the point on the budget line where the highest indifference curve touches the budget line is the best affordable consumption bundle.

16. **d** All the statements accurately characterize consumer equilibrium.

17. **b** In other words, demand curves are the result of people selecting the best affordable consumption combination.

18. **a** The income effect of a lower price motivates an increase in the consumption of normal goods only. The income effect motivates a *decrease* in the consumption of inferior goods.

19. **c** The substitution effect from a lower price *always* motivates an increase in the consumption of the relatively cheaper good.

20. **b** When the price of a taco falls, the maximum amount of tacos that can be purchased increases, but the maximum amount of pizza slices that can be purchased does not change.

21. **a** Real income increased because more tacos can be purchased.

22. **b** After the price change, point *b* is on the highest affordable indifference curve.

23. **c** This question defines the substitution effect.

24. **a** For normal goods, both the substitution and income effects from a lower price will increase the quantity demanded.

25. **b** Increases in income increase the demand for a normal good and decrease the demand for an inferior good.

Work-Leisure Choices

26. **a** The substitution effect of a higher wage rate increases the quantity of labor supplied.

27. **c** The income effect from a higher wage rate encourages people to spend less time at work and more at leisure; the substitution effect is the opposite, encouraging more time at work and less at leisure.

■ **Answers to Short Answer Problems**

1. An indifference curve shows how much the consumption of one good must increase as the consumption of another good decreases in order to leave the consumer indifferent (no better or worse off).

   It has a negative slope because both goods are desirable. In order to not be made worse off, as the consumption of one good decreases, consumption of the other good must increase. This relationship implies a negative slope.

FIGURE **8.13**
Short Answer Problem 2

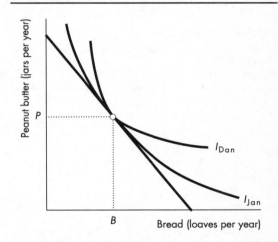

2. Figure 8.13 shows Jan and Dan's budget line and their indifference curves. Because Jan views bread and peanut butter as substitutes and Dan views them as complements, Jan's indifference curve is more linear than Dan's and Dan's is more L-shaped than Jan's.

   In general, the more the goods are viewed as substitutes, the more linear are the indifference curves. The more the goods are viewed as complements, the more L-shaped are the indifference curves.

FIGURE **8.14**
Short Answer Problem 3 (a)

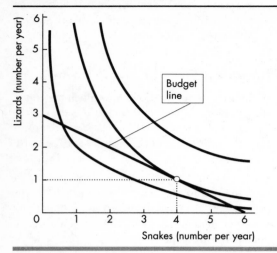

3. a. Figure 8.14 shows the budget line. The point
        with the highest attainable utility is indicated by
        the circle, where the budget line touches the
        highest possible indifference curve. At this point
        Igor buys 4 snakes and 1 lizard.

FIGURE **8.15**
Short Answer Problem 3 (b)

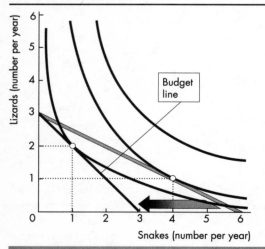

    b. Figure 8.15 illustrates Igor's new budget line.
        After the price hike for snakes, Igor buys 1 snake
        and 2 lizards. Lizards and snakes are substitutes.
        The increase in the price of a snake increases the
        quantity of lizards that Igor buys.

    c. Igor was better off before the price of a snake
        rose. A comparison of Figures 8.14 and 8.15 re-
        veals that Igor was on a higher indifference curve
        before the price of a snake rose, so he preferred
        the situation before snakes rose in price.

FIGURE **8.16**
Short Answer Problem 4 (a)

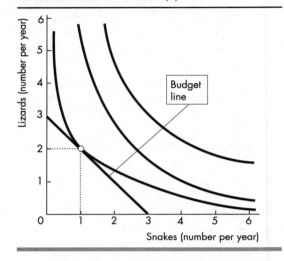

4. a. Figure 8.16 show that Igor buys 1 snake and 2
        lizards.

FIGURE **8.17**
Short Answer Problem 4 (b)

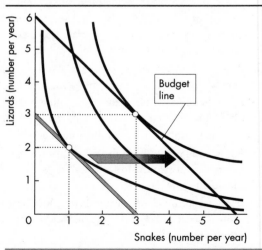

    b. The increase in income shifts Igor's budget line,
        as indicated in Figure 8.17. After his increase in
        income, Igor buys 3 snakes and 3 lizards. For

Igor, both snakes and lizards are normal goods because he buys more of both when his income increases.

5. a The relative price of curds is the money price of curds divided by the money price of whey: ($1 per unit of curds)/($1.50 per unit of whey) or 2/3 whey per curd.

b. Let P_c = the price of curds, P_w = the price of whey, Q_c = quantity of curds, Q_w = quantity of whey, and y = income. The budget equation, in general form, is:

$$Q_w = \frac{y}{P_w} - \left(\frac{P_c}{P_w}\right) Q_c$$

Because P_c = $1, P_w = $1.50, and y = $12, Ms. Muffet's budget equation is specifically given by:

$$Q_w = 8 - \frac{2}{3} Q_c$$

The graph of this budget equation, the budget line, is given in Figure 8.18.

FIGURE **8.18**
Short Answer Problem 5

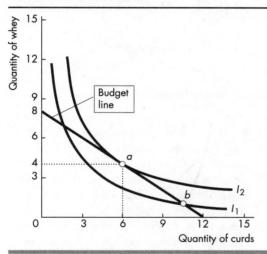

c. Indifference curve I_2 is the indifference curve tangent to the budget line so that Ms. Muffet's best affordable point — that is, her equilibrium point — is point a, with consumption of 6 units of curds and 4 units of whey.

d. The marginal rate of substitution is the magnitude of the slope of the indifference curve at point a. We do not know the slope of the indifference curve directly, but we can easily compute

the slope of the budget line and thereby calculate the marginal rate of substitution. At the best affordable point a, the indifference curve and the budget line have the same slope. (The fact that the slope of the indifference curve equals that of the budget line at the best affordable point is the hallmark of the best affordable point.) So we can obtain the marginal rate of substitution of curds for whey by using the slope of the budget line. Because the slope of the budget line is $-2/3$, the marginal rate of substitution is 2/3. For example, Ms. Muffet is willing to give up 2 units of whey in order to receive 3 additional units of curds.

e. Because indifference curve I_2 lies above the budget line (except at point a), every other point on the budget line is on a lower indifference curve. For example, take point b. Point b lies on indifference curve I_1, which is less preferred than indifference curve I_2. Just like point b, every other point on the budget line lies on a less preferred indifference curve and so every other point is inferior to point a. As a result, point a is the equilibrium point.

FIGURE **8.19**
Short Answer Problem 6 (a)

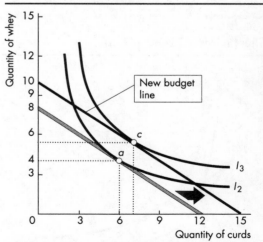

6. a. An increase in income causes a parallel rightward shift of the budget line, as shown in Figure 8.19. If both curds and whey are normal goods, Ms. Muffet moves to a point such as c, at which the consumption of both goods has increased.

FIGURE **8.20**
Short Answer Problem 6 (b)

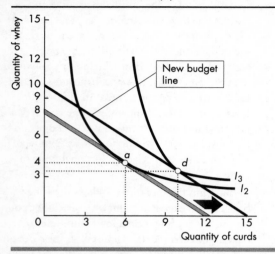

b. If whey is an inferior good, its consumption decreases as income increases, as illustrated in Figure 8.20. Again, the budget line shifts rightward, as in part (a), but Ms. Muffet's preferences are such that her new consumption point is given by a point such as *d*, on indifference curve I_3, where the consumption of whey has declined.

FIGURE **8.21**
Short Answer Problem 7 (a)

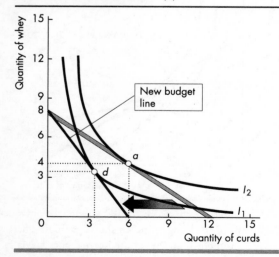

7. a. Ms. Muffet's initial budget line and her initial best affordable point, *a*, are illustrated in Figure 8.21. (The best affordable point is the same

point as in Figure 8.18.) Here the new budget line following a rise in the price of curds to $2 is illustrated.

b. After the price rise, point *a* is no longer the best affordable point because now it is no longer affordable.

c. The new best affordable point (labeled *d* in Figure 8.21) indicates a decrease in the consumption of curds. That is as expected because the price of curds rose.

FIGURE **8.22**
Short Answer Problem 7 (d)

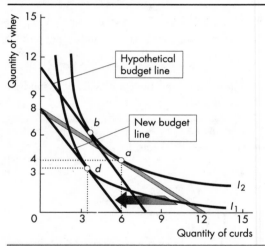

d. The substitution effect is the movement from point *a* to point *b,* and the income effect is the movement from point *b* to point *d.* The key to the substitution effect is that point *b* is on the same indifference curve as point *a.* The hypothetical budget line that determines point *b* has the same slope as the actual new budget line, however Ms. Muffet's income has been (hypothetically) increased along the hypothetical budget line to keep her on the same indifference curve.

The substitution effect *always* leads to a decrease in the consumption of the good whose relative price has risen and an increase in the consumption of a good whose relative price has fallen. In the case at hand, the substitution effect leads to a decrease in the consumption of curds and an increase in the consumption of whey.

FIGURE **8.23**
Short Answer Problem 8 (a)

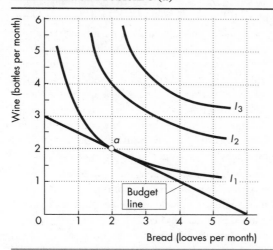

FIGURE **8.25**
Short Answer Problem 8 (c)

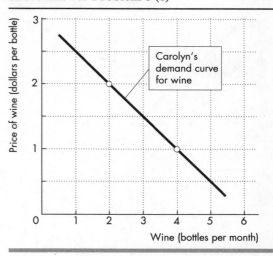

8. a. Figure 8.23 shows Carolyn's budget line. In this figure Carolyn's best attainable point is labeled *a*. She consumes 2 bottles of wine per month.

   b. The reduction in the price of a bottle of wine rotates Carolyn's budget line higher, as illustrated in Figure 8.24. Here her best attainable point is *b* and she consumes 4 bottles of wine per month. Note that indifference curve I_3 continues to remain unaffordable.

   c. When the price of wine is $2 a bottle, part (a) indicates that Carolyn buys 2 bottles of wine. When the price of wine falls to $1 a bottle, part (b) shows that Carolyn buys 4 bottles. These two points on her demand curve are illustrated in Figure 8.25, and her (assumed linear) demand curve is drawn through these points.

FIGURE **8.24**
Short Answer Problem 8 (b)

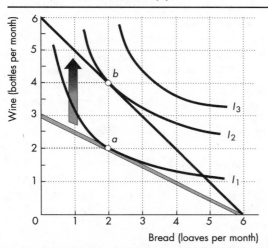

FIGURE **8.26**
Short Answer Problem 9

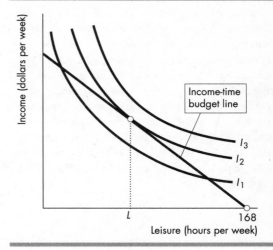

9. Figure 8.26 indicates the initial hours of leisure as *L*. The amount of labor the individual supplies equals 168 hours (the number of hours in a week) minus *L*

FIGURE **8.27**
Short Answer Problem 9

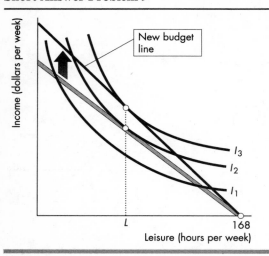

hours of leisure. After the rise in the wage rate, the budget line rotates as shown in Figure 8.27. The total number of hours per week is fixed at 168, so the horizontal intercept cannot change. However the vertical intercept increases because the maximum income that this individual can earn has increased due to the higher wage rate.

The "new" equilibrium amount of leisure the person enjoys is L in Figure 8.27. Leisure remains constant as does the hours of labor supplied.

Why does leisure remain constant? Recall that the impact on leisure is the net result of two forces working in opposing directions: The income effect encourages an increase in leisure, whereas the substitution effect motivates a decrease in leisure. In Figure 8.27, these effects exactly offset each other because the amount of leisure does not change; it remains equal to L. Because the time spent at leisure did not change, neither did this person's labor supply. In other words, the higher wage rate did not change the quantity of hours of labor this individual supplies.

■ **You're the Teacher**

1. "It's certainly true that one of the main goals of budget line/indifference curve analysis is deriving the demand curve. There are a couple of reasons for doing so. First, it's 'nice' to see that we can derive a demand curve by just assuming that people consume the best combination of goods and services they can afford. The idea that people make themselves as well off as possible is the hallmark of economics. This idea represents the basic world view of an economist; if you think it's a reasonable assumption, maybe you ought to major in economics!

"Second, the indifference curve/budget line approach allows us to think about income and substitution effects. These concepts help clarify some important household choices. For instance, without these ideas, understanding why the quantity of labor people supply has declined as wages rose would be difficult. If we didn't know about the income effect, we'd probably think that people were either irrational or stupid for decreasing the quantity of their labor supplied when wage rates rose. So this approach gives us some new insights into how economists view the world and the factors that affect the choices that people make."

2. "Look, you're wrong about this. I know that both indifference curves and demand curves slope downward, but indifference curves and demand curves really are different. In fact, we use indifference curves to help derive demand curves. But, to see the difference, think about a demand curve. It shows us how the price of a good affects how much we will buy. For instance, your demand curve for frozen yogurt cones tells us how much frozen yogurt you'll buy if a cone is $1.50 or how much you'll buy if one is $2.00. Indifference curves are different. They don't give us the relationship between a good's price and how much you'll buy. Indifference curves show us different combinations of two goods that leave you indifferent. You have indifference curves between frozen yogurt cones and ice cream cones. This type of indifference curve shows us all the combinations of yogurt and ice cream cones such that you don't care which combination you get. So, you see, indifference curves and demand curves aren't the same, so don't make this mistake."

Chapter Quiz

1. Tommy's monthly budget line for street hockey balls and books is plotted with books on the horizontal axis. His budget line shifts rightward and its slope does not change. Hence
   a. the price of a street hockey ball has fallen.
   b. the price of a book has fallen.
   c. Tommy's income has risen.
   d. the price of a street hockey ball has fallen and the price of a book has risen.

2. A household's consumption choices are limited by
   a. prices and preferences.
   b. income and preferences.
   c. prices and income.
   d. prices, income, and preferences.

3. Emma has weekly income of $200. A textbook costs $50 and a pad of paper $1. When Emma's budget line is drawn with textbooks on the horizontal axis,
   a. the horizontal intercept is 200 pads of paper.
   b. the slope of the budget line is $200.
   c. the horizontal intercept is 4 textbooks.
   d. the budget line shows that Emma cannot buy 3 textbooks.

4. Preferences
   a. do not depend on what the person can afford.
   b. are shown graphically as a budget line.
   c. change when relative prices change.
   d. show feasible consumption combinations.

5. An indifference curve shows all combinations of two goods that
   a. can be purchased with a given income.
   b. have the same marginal rate of substitution.
   c. are preferred to any other combination of the goods.
   d. among which the consumer is indifferent.

6. Right-hand and left-hand gloves are perfect complements. As a result, the corresponding indifference curves
   a. are L-shaped.
   b. intersect each other.
   c. are straight lines.
   d. are vertical.

7. At the best affordable point,
   a. the indifference curve *crosses* the budget line.
   b. the marginal rate of substitution exceeds the relative price of the goods by as much as possible.
   c. the consumer is on the highest attainable indifference curve.
   d. None of the above.

8. The income effect from a price change
   a. is always greater than the price effect.
   b. is always greater than the substitution effect.
   c. always leads to an increase in the purchase of the good whose relative price has fallen.
   d. None of the above.

9. When the relative price of a normal good falls, the substitution effect results in an _____ in the quantity purchased and the income effect results in an _____ in the quantity purchased.
   a. increase; increase
   b. increase; decrease
   c. decrease; increase
   d. decrease; decrease

10. An increase in the wage rate
    a. has a substitution effect and an income effect.
    b. has a substitution effect but does not have an income effect.
    c. has an income effect but does not have a substitution effect.
    d. has neither a substitution effect nor an income effect.

The answers for this Chapter Quiz are on page 367

GAP SALES FALL

On February 27, 2002 The Gap reported a loss for the important October to December quarter of 2001. The Gap lost money because shoppers did not like the new styles The Gap was selling. The Gap's President was quoted as saying "When we get the product right, we'll get the customers back." He further said that the company's fashion sense had slipped. The Gap planned to return to the styles that had made it a widely popular chain, colorful khakis and t-shirts. But success was far from assured because sales in January continued to fall from the previous year.

For details, go to The Economics Place web site, the Economics in the News archive, www.economicsplace.com/econ5e/einarchives.html

■ Analyze It

People shopping for clothes have choices galore and so if The Gap is to be successful, it must stock clothing that people find fashionable. In the 1990s The Gap had been quite successful at this endeavor and its clothing flew out the door. But in 2001 The Gap tried to sell styles that people did not like, so its sales plummeted. As a result, The Gap suffered a loss for 2001 and the loss continued into the first part of 2002 as The Gap's sales continued to fall. In May, 2002 The Gap's President had resigned. So, The Gap was searching not only for new styles but also a new President.

1. Consumers choose their consumption bundles by equating the marginal utility per dollar of different goods. Think of The Gap's clothing as one good and the clothing of other retailers as the other good. What is the formula that a consumer uses to determine his or her consumer equilibrium?

2. Using the formula from the previous question, how did The Gap's poor selection of styles in 2001 affect the formula and how did consumers respond? What must The Gap accomplish in order to increase its sales and return to profitability?

Mid-Term Examination

■ **Chapter 7**

1. Diminishing marginal utility means that
   a. Ralph will enjoy his first hamburger more than his second.
   b. the utility from one hamburger exceeds the utility from two hamburgers.
   c. the price of two hamburgers is twice the price of one hamburger.
   d. beyond a certain point, total utility falls as income rises.

2. As Sean's consumption of rice decreases, his
   a. average utility from consuming rice falls.
   b. total utility from consuming rice falls.
   c. marginal utility from consuming rice falls.
   d. elasticity of utility from consuming rice falls.

3. Inga's graph of her budget line has apples per week on the vertical axis and loaves of bread per week on the horizontal. An increase in the price of apples shifts the
   a. horizontal intercept left.
   b. horizontal intercept right.
   c. vertical intercept down.
   d. vertical intercept up.

4. Jenny buys sodas and popcorn. Sodas sell for $1 and popcorn sells for $2 a bag. Currently she is in consumer equilibrium with the marginal utility from her last dollar spent on popcorn equal to 50. The marginal utility from her last dollar spent on sodas is
   a. 10.
   b. 15.
   c. 25.
   d. 50.

■ **Chapter 8**

5. A budget line is drawn on a diagram with bus tokens on the horizontal axis and gasoline on the vertical axis. Bus tokens are an inferior good while gasoline is a normal good. As income rises, the best affordable point moves
   a. down and left.
   b. down and right.
   c. up and left.
   d. up and right.

6. Movies are $6 a ticket and videotape rentals are $3 a tape per day. With tapes on the vertical axis, the magnitude of the slope of the budget line is
   a. 0.5.
   b. 2.
   c. 3.
   d. 6.

7. In equilibrium, consumers equate the relative price of two goods to
   a. their money income.
   b. their real income.
   c. their marginal rate of substitution.
   d. relative quantities.

8. For inferior goods, an increase in income
   a. increases the demand.
   b. decreases the demand.
   c. does not change the amount purchased.
   d. changes the slope of the budget line.

Answers

■ Reading Between the Lines

1. When maximizing their utility, consumers will set $\frac{MU_G}{P_G} = \frac{MU_A}{P_A}$ in which MU_G is the marginal utility of clothing from The Gap, P_G is the price of clothing from The Gap, MU_A is the marginal utility of clothing from "All" other retailers, and P_A is the price of clothing from all other retailers.

2. In 2001, when The Gap was stocking clothing consumers did not like, the marginal utility of clothing from The Gap, MU_G, fell. In terms of the consumer equilibrium formula, $\frac{MU_A}{P_A}$ ex-

ceeded $\frac{MU_G}{P_G}$ so that people could gain more utility per dollar by purchasing clothes from retailers other than The Gap. As a result, people's consumer equilibrium changed so that they purchased fewer clothes from The Gap and purchased more clothes from other retailers. The result of this choice was that The Gap's sales fell and The Gap suffered a loss. To return to profitability, The Gap must select clothing that consumers like so that the marginal utility of clothing from The Gap rises. If The Gap is successful in this endeavor, the marginal utility per dollar spent on clothing from The Gap will rise and consumers will respond by purchasing more clothes (khakis and t-shirts!) from The Gap.

■ Mid-Term Exam Answers

1. a;   2. b;   3. c;   4. d;   5. c;   6. b;   7. c;   8. b.

Chapter 9 ORGANIZING PRODUCTION

Key Concepts

■ The Firm and Its Economic Problem

A **firm** is an institution that hires productive resources and uses these resources to produce and sell output.

The firm's goal is to maximize its (economic) profit, which equals its revenue minus its (opportunity) costs. The *opportunity cost* of any action is the highest-valued alternative foregone. A firm's opportunity costs can be separated into explicit costs (costs for which an actual money payment is made) and implicit costs (opportunity costs not paid directly in money). Two common implicit costs are:

- ◆ *Cost of capital* — The **implicit rental rate of capital,** the opportunity cost the business incurs by using its capital rather than renting the capital to another firm, is the sum of economic depreciation plus foregone interest costs. **Economic depreciation** of capital is the change in its market value over a given period.

- ◆ *Cost of owners' resources* — owners supply entrepreneurial ability to the business. Their compensation for this input is profit and the average return for supplying entrepreneurial ability is called **normal profit.**

Economic profit = Total revenue – Opportunity cost.

A business earning an economic profit is earning a profit that exceeds the normal profit.

Three features limit a firm's profit:

- ◆ *Technology constraints* — a **technology** is any method of producing a good or service. Technology limits how a firm can turn resources into output.

- ◆ *Information constraints* — the future is always uncertain and elements of the present (are workers working hard?) are unknown.

- ◆ *Marketing constraints* — how much the firm can sell and at what price are limited by its customers' willingness to buy its products.

■ Technology and Economic Efficiency

- ◆ **Technological efficiency** — when a given output is produced using the least amount of inputs.

- ◆ **Economic efficiency** — when output is produced at the lowest cost possible.

If a business is economically efficient, it must be technologically efficient, but technological efficiency does not necessarily imply economic efficiency.

■ Information and Organization

- ◆ **Command system** — organizes production within a firm using a managerial hierarchy, so that commands go from managers to workers.

- ◆ **Incentive system** — organizes production within a firm using market-like mechanisms, so that incentives are set up to induce workers to maximize the firm's profit.

The **principal–agent problem** is to set rules for compensation so that agents (people employed by others) act in the best interests of the principals (the individuals who employ the agents). Giving managers partial ownership of the company, using incentive pay, and using long-term contracts help overcome the principal-agent problem.

Three forms of business organization are:

- ◆ *Proprietorship* — a single owner with unlimited liability. Profits are taxed once.

- ◆ *Partnership* — two or more owners with unlimited liability. Profits are taxed once.

- ◆ *Corporation* — a business owned by stockholders who have limited liability. Corporate profits are taxed twice: the corporation pays taxes on its profits and its shareholders pay taxes on any dividends they receive. Shareholders also pay tax on capital gains — the income received when a share of stock is sold for a higher price than was paid for it.

There are more proprietorships than any other type of business, but corporations account for the lion's share of total business revenue.

■ Markets and the Competitive Environment

Economists define four market types:

♦ **perfect competition** — a market with many firms and buyers, each firm sells an identical product, and there are no restrictions on entry of new firms.

♦ **monopolistic competition** — a market structure with a large number of firms, and each firm makes a slightly different product. Making a slightly different product is called **product differentiation.**

♦ **oligopoly** — a market structure in which a small number of firms compete.

♦ **monopoly** — an industry that produces a good or service for which no close substitute exists and in which there is one supplier that is protected by a barrier preventing the entry of new firms.

Two measures of market concentration are used:

♦ **Four-firm concentration ratio** — the percentage of an industry's sales made by its four largest firms.

♦ **Herfindahl–Hirschman Index** (HHI) — the sum of the squared market shares of the 50 largest firms in the industry.

A low value for the measure of concentration indicates the presence of extensive competition.

Concentration ratios have limitations:

♦ They are calculated for the national market, but the relevant market for some goods is local and for others is international in scope.

♦ They give no indication of the existence or absence of entry barriers. An industry with a small number of firms may be competitive due to potential entry.

♦ Often the relevant market does not correspond to an industry as defined in the measures.

♦ Many firms operate in several industries.

In the United States, competitive markets account for about 75 percent of the value of goods sold, monopoly accounts for about 5 percent, and oligopoly is near 18 percent.

■ Markets and Firms

Firms coordinate economic activity when they perform the task more efficiently than markets. Firms can have several advantages:

♦ *lower transactions costs* — **transactions costs** are the costs of finding someone with whom to do business.

♦ **economies of scale** — when the cost of producing a unit of output falls as more output is produced.

♦ **economies of scope** — when specialized resources can be used to produce a variety of products.

♦ *economies of team production* — when individuals specialize in tasks that help support each other's production.

Firms can have lower transactions costs than using a market and economies of scale, scope, and team production can mean that production within a firm can be less expensive than using a market.

Helpful Hints

1. **NORMAL PROFIT AS A COST OF DOING BUSINESS:** The idea of a normal profit is important. A normal profit is the (implicit) cost of buying an owner's entrepreneurial ability — for instance, the owner's ability to make sound business decisions.

   Normal profit is part of the firm's opportunity cost of doing business, in the same way that paying workers' wages or interest on debt are opportunity costs to the firm. Think of costs as expenses that *must* be paid; if a company fails to meet its expenses, it will (eventually) close. For example, if a business cannot pay its workers their wages or its debt holders the interest due to them, the firm will have to shut down. Similarly, if it cannot return at least a normal profit to its owners to compensate them for their talents in running the business, eventually the firm will close as the owners take up other endeavors.

2. **ECONOMIC PROFIT AND NORMAL PROFIT :** Economic profit is revenue minus all opportunity costs. Because a normal profit is already part of the firm's opportunity costs, an economic profit signifies a profit over and above the normal profit; that is, an economic profit is an above-normal profit.

Questions

■ True/False and Explain

The Firm and Its Economic Problem

1. A firm's opportunity costs include both its explicit and implicit costs.

2. The wages a firm pays its workers are an implicit opportunity cost of running the business.

3. A firm's normal profit is part of the opportunity costs of running the business.

4. Technology limits a firm's profits.

Technology and Economic Efficiency

5. By definition, a firm is economically efficient whenever it is the case that the business must increase its use of resources in order to increase the amount it produces.

6. If a firm is economically efficient, it must be technologically efficient.

Information and Organization

7. In an incentive system of organizing a business, a manager's commands give the workers the incentive to maximize the firm's profit.

8. A sales associate working in the sportswear department at JCPenney is an example of an "agent."

9. Giving top executives of large corporations stock in their companies is a method of handling a principal-agent problem.

10. If a proprietorship fails, the owner is responsible for *all* the firm's debts.

11. A major advantage of the corporate form of business organization is limited liability.

12. A major disadvantage of the corporate form of business organization is that corporations' profits are taxed twice.

Markets and the Competitive Environment

13. Monopolistic competition occurs when monopolies compete with each other.

14. The four-firm concentration ratio is the sum of the squared market shares of the four largest firms in an industry.

15. A low concentration ratio indicates a low level of competition.

16. Concentration ratios indicate that most of the nation's goods and services are produced in oligopolistic markets.

Markets and Firms

17. Transaction costs are a reason why firms can be more efficient than markets in coordinating economic activity.

18. Markets — rather than firms — likely will coordinate economic activity in situations where there are economies of scale.

■ Multiple Choice

The Firm and Its Economic Problem

1. A firm's goal is to maximize its
   a. revenue.
   b. costs.
   c. profit.
   d. None of the above.

2. Which of the following is an implicit cost of operating a business?
   a. The wages paid to the workers.
   b. The salary paid to the owners.
   c. The interest not earned on funds used to buy capital equipment.
   d. The interest paid on a bank loan the owners incurred to help finance the company.

3. Which of the following is an explicit cost of operating a business?
   a. The firm's normal profit.
   b. The firm's economic profit.
   c. The firm's economic depreciation.
   d. The amount the firm pays to the Post Office to mail its bills.

4. A normal profit is
   a. an explicit opportunity cost of the company.
   b. a cost that is always accurately measured by an accountant.
   c. the amount of profit an accountant calculates for a company.
   d. not the same as the company's economic profit.

5. Which of the following constraints limits a firm's profit?

a. Technology constraints.
b. Information constraints.
c. Market constraints.
d. All of the above limit a firm's profit.

Technology and Economic Efficiency

Use Table 9.1, which shows four methods of producing photon torpedoes, for the next three questions.

TABLE **9.1**

Multiple Choice Questions 6, 7, 8

	Quantities of Resources Used to Produce One Photon Torpedo	
Method	Labor	Capital
1	5	10
2	10	7
3	15	5
4	20	5

6. Which is a technologically inefficient method of making a photon torpedo?

a. Method 1 only
b. Method 2 only
c. Method 3 only
d. Method 4 only

7. If labor costs $10 per unit and capital $20 per unit, which is an economically efficient method of making a photon torpedo?

a. Method 1 only
b. Method 2 only
c. Method 3 only
d. All four methods are economically efficient.

8. If labor costs $10 per unit and capital falls to $15 per unit, which is an economically efficient method of making a photon torpedo?

a. Method 1 only
b. Method 2 only
c. Method 3 only
d. All four methods are economically efficient.

Information and Organization

9. The method of organizing production that uses a managerial hierarchy is a(n)

a. command system.
b. incentive system.
c. principal-agent system.
d. None of the above.

10. The possibility that an employee might not work hard is an example of the

a. problem of opportunity cost.
b. principle of scarcity.
c. limited liability doctrine.
d. principal-agent problem.

11. Most firms are

a. proprietorships.
b. partnerships.
c. corporations.
d. nonprofit.

12. A form of business that is simple to set up, whose profits are taxed only once, and is run by a single owner is a

a. proprietorship.
b. partnership.
c. corporation.
d. either a proprietorship or partnership, depending on other information.

13. The major *disadvantage* of the corporate form of business organization is its

a. limited liability for its owners.
b. unlimited liability for its owners.
c. ability to be run by professional managers.
d. tax liability (its profits are taxed twice).

For the next two questions, suppose that Tracy and Pat start a business. Because of bad decisions by Tracy, the company goes bankrupt, owing a total of $50,000. Tracy is penniless, but Pat is a multimillionaire.

14. If the company were organized as a partnership, Pat would be responsible for

a. $100,000 of debt.
b. $50,000 of debt.
c. $25,000 of debt.
d. $0 of debt.

15. If the company were organized as a corporation, Pat would be responsible for
    a. $100,000 of debt.
    b. $50,000 of debt.
    c. $25,000 of debt.
    d. $0 of debt.

Markets and the Competitive Environment

16. What type of industry structure has many firms, each producing a slightly different good, with no barriers to entry or exit?
    a. Perfect competition
    b. Monopolistic competition
    c. Oligopoly
    d. Monopoly

17. The four-firm concentration ratio measures the share of the largest four firms in total industry
    a. profits.
    b. sales.
    c. cost.
    d. capital.

TABLE **9.2**

Market Shares

Firm	Market Share
Sally's Subs	15%
Samantha's Subs	5%
Susan's Subs	30%
Sydna's Subs	20%
Sheryl's Subs	20%
Shirley's Subs	10%

18. In Table 9.2 what is the four-firm concentration ratio in the submarine sandwich industry?
    a. 100 percent
    b. 85 percent
    c. 70 percent
    d. 30 percent

Markets and Firms

19. Which of the following is <u>NOT</u> a reason for the existence of firms?
    a. Lower transactions costs for firms
    b. Principal-agent problem
    c. Economies of scope
    d. Economies of team production

20. Taco Bell can use its equipment and staff to produce and sell tacos, burritos, and drinks less expensively than would be the case if each had to be purchased separately in a market. This situation demonstrates
    a. economies of scale.
    b. economies of scope.
    c. long-term contracts.
    d. none of the above.

■ Short Answer Problems

1. Contrast how an accountant would measure the following with the opportunity cost approach.
    a. depreciation cost.
    b. the firm borrowing money to finance purchasing its capital.
    c. the firm using its own funds rather than borrowing to purchase its capital.
    d. the value of the business owner's inputs.

2. Frank decides to start a business manufacturing doll furniture. Frank has two sisters: Angela is an accountant and Edith is an economist. Each of the sisters uses the following information to compute Frank's costs and profit for the first year.
    1) *Revenue* — Frank's revenue for his first year was $100,000.
    2) *Alternative job* — Frank took no income from the firm. He has an offer to return to work full time as a bricklayer for $30,000 per year.
    3) *Rent* — Frank rented his machinery for $9,000 a year.
    4) *Garage* — Frank owns the garage in which he works but could rent it out at $3,000 per year.
    5) *Invested funds* — to start the business, Frank used $10,000 of his own money from a savings account that paid 10 percent per year interest. Frank also borrowed $30,000 at 10 percent per year.
    6) *Employee* — Frank hired one employee at an annual salary of $20,000.
    7) *Materials* — the cost of materials during the first year was $40,000.
    8) *Services* — Frank's entrepreneurial services are worth $20,000 to his business.
    a. Set up a table indicating how Angela and Edith would compute Frank's cost.
    b. What is Frank's profit (or loss) as computed by Angela? By Edith?

3. The standard tip in a restaurant is 15 percent. Restaurants *could* raise their prices 15 percent, set a policy of no tipping, and then give their servers the extra 15 percent. Explain why restaurants do not do so by focusing on the principal-agent problem.

4. Is the principal-agent problem between the owner(s) and manager(s) more severe in proprietorships or corporations? Why?

5. Distinguish between technological efficiency and economic efficiency.

6. Considering the geographic scope of markets, how might a concentration ratio understate the degree of competitiveness in an industry? How might it overstate the degree of competitiveness?

7. Markets and firms are alternative ways of coordinating economic activity. Why do both firms and markets exist?

■ You're the Teacher

1. "I don't understand the difference between a 'normal profit' and an 'economic profit'. And, what's more, why should I care? After all, a profit is a profit is a profit!" Explain to your friend the difference and why the difference matters ….especially if you own a business!

2. Answer this question posed to you by a classmate: "How can a situation be technologically efficient and not economically efficient?"

ANSWERS

■ True/False Answers

The Firm and Its Economic Problem

1. **T** Opportunity costs include *all* the costs of running a business.

2. **F** The wages are an explicit cost, that is, a cost paid in money.

3. **T** The normal profit is the payment accruing to an owner for the owner's entrepreneurial ability.

4. **T** Other limiting factors are information and marketing constraints.

Technology and Economic Efficiency

5. **F** The question gives the definition of technological efficiency.

6. **T** Economic efficiency means that the firm necessarily is technologically efficient; technological efficiency, however, does not necessarily mean that the firm is economically efficient.

Information and Organization

7. **F** An incentive system sets up incentives, such as paying sales agents by commission, that give workers the incentive to maximize the firm's profit.

8. **T** The sales associate is (indirectly) hired by the shareholders of JCPenney to help sell sportswear. The associate is an agent for the owners, who are the principals.

9. **T** Because the price of a share of stock generally rises when the company increases its profits, giving executives stock in the company gives executives the incentive to maximize the company's profit.

10. **T** The owners of proprietorships and partnerships face unlimited liability for the debts of their companies.

11. **T** Limited liability means that owners of corporations are not liable for its debts if the company goes bankrupt.

12. **T** Corporate profits are taxed once as income to the corporation. Then, when sent to owners in the form of dividends, they are taxed again as part of the owners' incomes.

Markets and the Competitive Environment

13. **F** Monopolistic competition occurs when many firms, each making a slightly differentiated product, compete with each other.

14. **F** The four-firm concentration is the sum of the market shares of the four largest firms.

15. **F** A low concentration ratio indicates a high degree of competition.

16. **F** Most of the goods and services are produced in competitive markets.

Markets and Firms

17. **T** Doing business with a firm might require only one transaction, whereas conducting the same business in markets might require many transactions.

18. **F** When there are economies of scale — so that the cost of producing an item falls as more are produced — firms will coordinate the activity because they can capture these economies of scale.

■ Multiple Choice Answers

The Firm and Its Economic Problem

1. **c** By maximizing its profit, the firm insures that it has the best chance of surviving and makes its owners as well off as possible.

2. **c** By using the funds to buy capital equipment, interest on them foregone, so the lost interest is an opportunity cost of running the business.

3. **d** An explicit cost is a cost paid in money and only answer (d) is actually paid in money.

4. **d** Economic profit is any profit over and above normal profit.

5. **d** All of the constraints limit the amount of profit a firm can earn.

Technology and Economic Efficiency

6. **d** Method 4 uses more labor and the same capital as method 3; as a result, it is technologically inefficient.

7. **b** Method 2 costs $240 to produce a photon torpedo, whereas methods 1 and 3 cost $250.

8. **a** With the change in input prices, method 1 costs $200, which is less than method 2 ($205) and method 3 ($225).

Information and Organization

9. **a** The question gives the definition of a command system.

10. **d** By loafing, the agent — the employee — takes an action that is not in the best interests of the principal — the owner.

11. **a** Proprietorships are the most numerous type of business organization.

12. **a** Answers (b) and (d) are incorrect because partnerships (which are easy to set up and whose profits are taxed only once) have more than one owner.

13. **d** The income is taxed once when the corporation earns it as a profit and then is taxed again when it is sent by the corporation to the corporation's owners.

14. **b** As a partnership, Pat has unlimited liability for all the firm's debts.

15. **d** If the company is a corporation, Pat's liability is limited to the initial amount invested, so Pat has no additional liability for the $50,000 debt.

Markets and the Competitive Environment

16. **b** Monopolistic competition is similar to perfect competition insofar as there are many firms with no barriers to entry or exit. It is dissimilar in that each firm produces a unique but closely related good.

17. **b** Adding the percentage of the industry's sales made by the four largest firms is the definition of the four-firm concentration ratio.

18. **b** Add the market shares of the four largest firms.

Markets and Firms

19. **b** The principal-agent problem is a *difficulty* that firms must overcome.

20. **b** Economies of scope are present when production of a variety of products lowers the cost of producing each unit.

Answers to Short Answer Problems

1. a. An accountant measures depreciation using IRS specified rules, under which depreciation cost is computed as a prespecified percentage of the original purchase price of the capital good, with no reference to current market value. The opportunity cost approach measures economic de-

preciation, the change in the market value of the capital good over the period in question.

b. If a firm borrows money, the accountant's cost and the opportunity cost are the same; both include the explicit interest payments because the interest expense is the opportunity cost of the loan.

c. If a firm uses its own funds rather than borrowing, the accountant's cost and the opportunity cost differ. The accounting cost is zero because there are no explicit interest payments. The opportunity cost approach recognizes that those funds could have been loaned and so the (implicit) interest income forgone is the opportunity cost.

d. If the owner forgoes the opportunity for other employment, this loss of income is not part of the accounting costs even though it is an opportunity cost. If the owner draws a salary, it will be captured as both an opportunity cost and an accounting cost. In addition, whether or not the owner took money from the business, the cost of the entrepreneurial talent the owner provides to the business is always an opportunity cost — the firm's normal profit.

TABLE **9.3**
Short Answer Problem 2

Item	Accounting cost (Angela's costs)	Economic cost (Edith's costs)
1) Revenue	$100,000	$100,000
2) Alternative job	0	30,000
3) Rent	9,000	9,000
4) Garage	0	3,000
5) Invested funds	3,000	4,000
6) Employee	20,000	20,000
7) Materials	40,000	40,000
8) Services	0	20,000

2. a. Table 9.3 shows how Angela, the accountant, and Edith, the economist, calculate Frank's cost and revenue for each item listed.

b. Accounting profit equals revenue minus accounting cost, and economic profit equals revenue minus opportunity cost. The accounting cost is the sum of the accounting costs listed for items 2 to 8, or $72,000, and the opportunity cost is the sum of the economic costs listed for items 2 to 8, or $126,000. Hence Frank's accounting profit is $28,000 and his economic profit actually is an economic loss of –$26,000.

3. Restaurants are faced with a classic principal-agent problem because servers might provide poor service to the customers. Rather than attempt to have the manager closely monitor each server, delegating the monitoring to customers is more efficient. If the server gives good service, the customer might tip the server 15 percent or more; if the server provides poor service, the customer will easily note this fact and might tip less than 15 percent. Hence the server has the incentive to be a good agent and provide prompt, good service, which is precisely what the principal — the restaurant's owner — wants.

4. The principal-agent problem between owners and managers is more severe in corporations. For a proprietorship, the owner is usually the manager. Because the owner and manager are the same person, there is no principal-agent problem. In corporations, however, the owners are the stockholders. For instance, if you own 100 shares of Microsoft, you are one of many owners of Microsoft. But, most stockholders do not manage the company. Hence the managers and owners are different people. The owners must be concerned that the managers act to maximize the firm's profit rather than pursuing their own goals, such as shirking rather than working diligently.

5. A method is technologically efficient if increasing output without increasing inputs is not possible. A method is economically efficient if the cost of producing a given level of output is as low as possible. Technological efficiency is independent of prices, but economic efficiency depends on the prices of inputs. An economically efficient method of production is always technologically efficient, but a technologically efficient method is not necessarily economically efficient.

6. Concentration ratios are calculated from a national geographic perspective. If the actual scope of the market is not national, the concentration ratio will likely misstate the degree of competitiveness in an industry. If the actual market is global, the concentration ratio will understate the degree of competitiveness. A firm might have a concentration ratio of 100 as the only producer in the nation, but might face a great deal of international competition. For instance, this situation closely resembles the case of certain types of computer memory chips with only one American producer but many producers of the same chip abroad.

When the scope of the market is regional, the concentration ratio will overstate the degree of competitiveness. The concentration ratio includes companies elsewhere in the nation that are not real competitors in the region. Newspapers provide the classic example: A paper published in Maine is hardly a competitor for a newspaper published in San Francisco.

7. As demonstrated by the example in the text, car repair can be coordinated by the market or by a firm. The institution (market or firm) that actually coordinates in any given case is the one that is more efficient. In cases where there are significant transactions costs, economies of scale, or economies of team production, firms are likely to be more efficient and they will dominate the coordination of economic activity. But the efficiency of firms is limited, and there are many circumstances where market coordination of economic activity dominates because it is more efficient. Essentially, if coordination by firms is more efficient, the number of firms increases because doing business with them is cheaper than relying on a market. Conversely, if coordination by the market is more efficient, firms will not be able to compete successfully because doing business with them would be more expensive then relying on a market.

■ **You're the Teacher**

1. "The difference between a 'normal profit' and an 'economic profit' is important. Every business owner supplies some inputs to the business. One of these inputs is entrepreneurial talent — the decisions, leadership, and possibly insight that the owner provides. Normal profit is the payment for these services. Because this payment (perhaps implicitly) is for services rendered, a normal profit is part of the firm's opportunity costs. Essentially, you should think of the normal profit as the standard — average — payment owed to an owner of a business. An economic profit equals the firm's revenues minus its opportunity costs. Because opportunity costs already include normal profit, an economic profit is a profit over-and-above a normal profit. Basically, an economic profit is an above-average profit."

2. "Technological efficiency merely reflects a firm's inputs and resulting output. A situation is technologically efficient when producing more output without using more inputs is impossible. The converse is that technological efficiency occurs whenever decreasing the amount of an input used decreases the amount of output produced. In other words, the firm is not wasting resources.

    "Economic efficiency occurs when the cost of producing a given amount of output is as low as possible. Clearly, if a firm is wasting resources — so that it is possible to reduce the amount of an input without decreasing the amount produced — the business is not economically efficient because decreasing an input will reduce the firm's costs. Hence, if a firm is economically efficient, it must be technologically efficient, too.

    "But a firm can be technologically efficient and not economically efficient if it uses the 'wrong' mix of inputs. For instance, the local McDonald's could hire brain surgeons rather than students to cook its burgers. This move would be technologically efficient because someone is required to cook the burgers. But it would not be economically efficient because the students would work for about $14,000 a year, whereas the brain surgeons command at least $500,000 a year."

Chapter Quiz

1. Which of the following statements is correct?
   a. The firm's goal is to maximize its revenue.
   b. The firm seeks to produce at the lowest possible ratio of labor to capital.
   c. Successful firms have completely overcome the principal-agent problem.
   d. The firm's goal is to maximize its profit.

2. A _____ is an agent and a(n) _____ is its principal.
   a. baseball player; baseball manager
   b. manager of a department at Sears; sales clerk working in the department at Sears
   c. partnership; corporation
   d. movie star; elected official

3. Which of the following is NOT an attempt to overcome a principal-agent problem?
   a. Giving managers long-term contracts.
   b. Paying employees a bonus from the firm's profit.
   c. Granting managers partial ownership of the company.
   d. Granting owners of corporations limited liability.

4. A disadvantage of the corporation over other forms of business organization is that the
   a. owners of a corporation have unlimited liability.
   b. decision-making structure in a corporation is simple.
   c. profits of the corporation are taxed twice.
   d. corporation can be run by professional managers.

5. As a one-quarter partner in a partnership, Sue is legally responsible for
   a. none of its debts.
   b. one-quarter of its debts.
   c. all of its debts.
   d. a fraction of its debts that depends upon how heavily Sue was involved in running the business.

6. The larger an industry's four-firm concentration ratio,
   a. the more competitive the industry.
   b. the less competitive the industry.
   c. the larger the industry's total sales.
   d. the more firms in the industry.

7. A market with only a few firms competing in it is a(n)
   a. perfectly competitive market.
   b. monopolistically competitive market.
   c. oligopoly.
   d. monopoly.

8. Firms typically incur only explicit costs for
   a. the use of capital equipment.
   b. the firm's normal profit.
   c. the owner's time and effort.
   d. the employees' time and effort.

9. Which of the following describes a situation in which a firm rather than a market coordinates economic activity?
   a. There are only a few, low transactions costs of negotiating the buying and selling for a product.
   b. There are no economies of scale present.
   c. There are substantial economies of team production.
   d. If one producer produced a variety of products, its costs quickly and substantially would increase.

10. Both the four-firm concentration ratio and the Herfindahl-Hirschman index attempt to measure
    a. the number of buyers in a market.
    b. the number of sellers in a market.
    c. the extent of competition in a market.
    d. the total economic profit earned by the firms in an industry.

The answers for this Chapter Quiz are on page 367

10 OUTPUT AND COSTS

Key Concepts

■ Decision Time Frames

Firms have two decision time frames:

♦ **Short run** is the time frame in which the quantities of some resources are fixed.

♦ **Long run** is the time frame in which the quantities of *all* resources can be varied.

A **sunk cost** is a past cost. Sunk costs do not affect a firm's decisions.

■ Short-Run Technology Constraint

A firm's short-run technology constraint is described by its:

♦ **Total product** (*TP*) is the total output produced. The total product schedule shows the maximum attainable output with a fixed quantity of capital as the quantity of labor is varied.

♦ **Marginal product** of labor (*MP*) is the change in the total product resulting from a one-unit change in the quantity of labor.

♦ **Average product** of labor (*AP*) — the total product per worker.

Figure 10.1 illustrates the *MP* and *AP* curves for labor. The product curves have the shapes shown because production initially has increasing marginal returns, another worker's marginal product is higher than the previous worker's, followed by **diminishing marginal returns,** another worker's marginal product is less than the previous worker. The **law of diminishing returns** states that as a firm uses more of a variable input, with

FIGURE **10.1**

The Average and Marginal Products

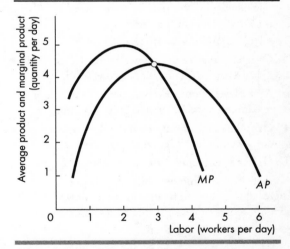

a given quantity of fixed inputs, the marginal product of the variable input eventually diminishes.

This figure also shows the (general) relationship between the marginal product and average product

♦ When the *MP* > *AP*, the *AP* rises.

♦ When the *MP* < *AP*, the *AP* falls.

♦ When *MP* = *AP*, the *AP* is at its maximum.

■ Short-Run Cost

Several important cost concepts are

♦ **Total cost** (*TC*): cost of all resources used, including the normal profit. **Average total cost** (*ATC*) is TC/q.

♦ **Total fixed cost** (*TFC*): cost of the firm's fixed inputs. **Average fixed cost** (*AFC*) is TFC/q.

♦ **Total variable cost** (*TVC*): cost of the firm's variable inputs. **Average variable cost** (*AVC*) is *TVC*/*q*.

♦ **Marginal cost** (*MC*): the increase in total cost resulting from one-unit increase in output or, in terms of a formula, $MC = \Delta TC/\Delta q$.

Two relationships between these costs are:
$$TC = TFC + TVC \quad \text{and} \quad ATC = AFC + AVC.$$

Figure 10.2 shows typical *AVC*, *ATC*, and *MC* curves. The *AVC*, *ATC*, and *MC* curves are U-shaped. The *MC* crosses the *AVC* and *ATC* curves where the *AVC* and *ATC* are at their minimums.

♦ As output initially increases, both *AFC* and *AVC* fall, so *ATC* falls.

♦ As output increases still more, returns will diminish. *AVC* increases as output increases, so eventually *ATC* rises when output increases.

The *MC* and *MP* curves are related.

♦ Over the range of output where the *MP* curve slopes upward, the *MC* curve slopes downward.

♦ At the level of output where the *MP* curve is at its maximum, the *MC* curve is at its minimum.

♦ Over the range of output where the *MP* curve slopes downward, the *MC* curve slopes upward.

The *AP* and *ATC* curves are similarly related.

An increase in technology shifts the firm's product curves upward and shifts its cost curves downward. A rise in resource prices shifts the firm's cost curves upward.

■ Long-Run Cost

The long-run cost is the cost of production when all inputs are adjusted to their economically efficient levels. There are no fixed costs in the long run.

♦ The production function shows the relationship between the maximum attainable output and the quantities of all inputs.

In the long run, because all inputs can be varied, all costs are variable costs. The **long-run average cost curve** (*LRAC*) traces a U-shaped relationship between the lowest attainable average total cost and output

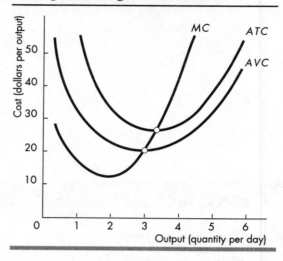

FIGURE 10.2

Average and Marginal Cost Curves

when both the plant size and labor are varied. The long-run average cost curve is derived from the many different (short-run) average total cost curves that reflect different quantities of capital. The long-run average cost shows the lowest average cost to produce any quantity of output.

The ranges of the *LRAC* are:

♦ *Economies of scale* — the range of output over which the *LRAC* falls as output increases. With input prices not changing, economies of scale occur if a change in all inputs leads to a larger percentage change in output.

♦ *Diseconomies of scale* — the range of output over which the *LRAC* rises as output increases. With input prices not changing, diseconomies of scale occur if a change in all inputs leads to a smaller change in output.

Constant returns to scale occur when the long-run average cost is constant as output increases. This can occur when a change in all inputs leads to an equal percentage change in the firm's output. When a firm has constant returns to scale, the long-run average cost curve is horizontal.

The **minimum efficient scale** is the smallest quantity of output at which the long-run average cost is at its lowest level.

Helpful Hints

FIGURE 10.3
Average and Marginal Cost Curves

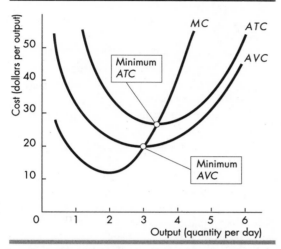

1. **THE MOST IMPORTANT COST CONCEPTS :** Be sure you understand Figure 10.3 thoroughly. Not only is it is the most important graph in the chapter, it is one of the most important graphs in all of microeconomics. You will see it repeatedly in the next several chapters.

   You need to know three important points about Figure 10.3. First, both the *ATC* and *AVC* curves are U-shaped. The *MC* curve also is U-shaped, but the portion that slopes upward is the most important. Second, the *MC* curve intersects the *ATC* and *AVC* curves at their minimum points. In other words, when the *MC* equals the *ATC*, the *ATC* is at its minimum. Third, following the relationship between a marginal and an average, when the *MC* curve is below the *ATC* or *AVC* curves, the *ATC* or *AVC* slope downward. Similarly, when the *MC* curve is above the *ATC* or *AVC* curves, the *ATC* or *AVC* curves slope upward.

2. **MEANING OF THE WORD "MARGINAL" :** Be certain that you understand the difference between "marginal cost" and "average cost." These are *very* different concepts. One way to remember that they are different is to keep in mind that the word "marginal" always means "additional." Economists use the word marginal this way a lot. In this chapter, you already have seen it used in "marginal product" and "marginal cost". You might also have

seen it in Chapter 7 in the discussion of "marginal utility", the additional utility from consuming another unit of a product. In the next few chapters you will encounter the term "marginal revenue," which means additional revenue when output is increased by one unit. In *all* these examples, the word marginal means "additional"!

3. **THE DIFFERENCE BETWEEN ECONOMIES OF SCALE AND DIMINISHING RETURNS :** The later sections of the chapter explain the long-run production function and cost function when the plant size — that is, the capital stock — varies. As the law of diminishing returns is the key to understanding short-run costs, the concept of economies and diseconomies of scale is the key to understanding long-run costs. In the long run, we explore the increase in output relative to the increase in inputs when *all* inputs are increased by the same percentage; diminishing returns are what happens when only *one* resource is changed, with the rest of the inputs being kept constant.

Questions

■ True/False and Explain

Decision Time Frames

1. The short run is the period of time over which only one resource is variable.

2. In the long run, all resources are variable.

Short-Run Technology Constraint

3. If the marginal product of another worker exceeds the marginal product of the previous worker hired, the firm is experiencing economies of scale.

4. The law of diminishing returns implies that the marginal product of an input eventually falls as more of the input is used.

5. If the marginal product of labor exceeds the average product of labor, the average product of labor rises when more workers are hired.

Short-Run Cost

6. Total cost equals fixed cost plus variable cost.

7. Total costs first fall and then, as diminishing returns sets in, total costs rise as the firm expands its output.

8. Total variable costs are always greater than total fixed costs.

9. Marginal cost equals total cost divided by total output.

10. Marginal cost is always greater than average total cost.

11. The average total cost curve, like the average product of labor curve, has an upside-down U-shape.

12. The *ATC* curve always passes through the minimum point of the *MC* curve.

Long-Run Cost

13. In the long run, all costs are variable costs and no costs are fixed cost.

14. No part of any short-run average total cost curve lies below the long-run average total cost curve.

15. Economies of scale occur when an increase in the number of workers employed increases total output.

16. When the long-run average cost (*LRAC*) curve slopes upward, the firm is experiencing economies of scale.

■ Multiple Choice

Decision Time Frames

1. The short run is a time period in which
   a. one year or less elapses.
   b. all inputs are variable.
   c. all inputs are fixed.
   d. there is at least one fixed input and the other inputs can be varied.

2. In the long run,
   a. only the amount of capital the firm uses is fixed.
   b. all inputs are variable.
   c. all inputs are fixed.
   d. a firm must experience diseconomies of scale.

Short-Run Technology Constraint

3. Total product divided by the total quantity of labor employed equals the
   a. average product of labor.
   b. marginal product of labor.
   c. average total cost.
   d. average variable cost.

4. Diminishing marginal returns occurs when
   a. all inputs are increased and output decreases.
   b. all inputs are increased and output increases by a smaller proportion.
   c. a variable input is increased and output decreases.
   d. a variable unit is increased and its marginal product falls.

5. The marginal product of labor equals the average product of labor when
   a. the average product of labor is at its maximum.
   b. the average product of labor is at its minimum.
   c. the marginal product of labor is at its maximum.
   d. None of the above answers are correct because the marginal product of labor never equals the average product of labor.

6. When the marginal product of labor curve is below the average product of labor curve,
   a. the average product of labor curve has a positive slope.
   b. the average product of labor curve has a negative slope.
   c. the total product curve has a negative slope.
   d. the firm experiences diseconomies of scale.

Short-Run Costs

7. Pat's Catering finds that when it caters 10 meals a week, its total cost is $3,000. If, at this level of output, Pat has a total variable cost of $2,500, what is Pat's fixed cost?
   a. $250
   b. $300
   c. $500
   d. $3,000

Use Table 10.1 for the next three questions.

TABLE 10.1
Multiple Choice Questions 8, 9, 10

Output	Total variable cost	Total cost
3	$15	$21
4	18	24

8. The marginal cost of producing the fourth unit is
   a. $6.
   b. $5.
   c. $3.
   d. $2.

9. The average total cost of the fourth unit is
   a. $6.
   b. $5.
   c. $3.
   d. $2.

10. The average *fixed* cost of the third unit is
    a. $6.
    b. $5.
    c. $3.
    d. $2.

11. If the company produces no output, it must pay
    a. no costs.
    b. a small amount of variable cost.
    c. its fixed cost.
    d. its owners a normal profit.

12. The change in total cost from producing another unit of output equals the
    a. average total cost.
    b. variable cost.
    c. average variable cost.
    d. marginal cost.

13. A farmer discovers that the total cost of growing 50 acres of eggplant is $50,000 and that the total cost of growing 51 acres of eggplant is $52,000. The marginal cost of the 51st acre of eggplant is
    a. $52,000.
    b. $50,000.
    c. $2,000.
    d. $1,000.

Use Figure 10.4 for the next four questions.

FIGURE 10.4
Multiple Choice Questions 14, 15, 16, 17

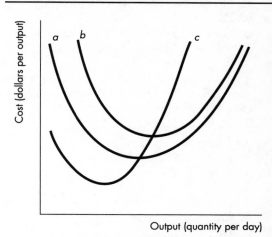

14. In Figure 10.4 the *MC* curve is curve
    a. *a.*
    b. *b.*
    c. *c.*
    d. None of the curves is the *MC* curve.

15. In Figure 10.4 the *ATC* curve is curve
    a. *a.*
    b. *b.*
    c. *c.*
    d. None of the curves is the *ATC* curve.

16. In Figure 10.4 the *AVC* curve is curve
    a. *a.*
    b. *b.*
    c. *c.*
    d. None of the curves is the *AVC* curve.

17. In Figure 10.4 the *AFC* is curve
    a. *a.*
    b. *b.*
    c. *c.*
    d. None of the curves is the *AFC* curve.

18. Which curve intersects the minimum point of the average total cost curve, that is, minimum point of the *ATC* curve?

    a. The marginal cost (*MC*) curve
    b. The average variable cost (*AVC*) curve
    c. The average fixed cost (*AFC*) curve
    d. The marginal product (*MP*) curve

19. If the average total cost (*ATC*) curve slopes downward, then at that level of output the marginal cost (*MC*) curve must be

    a. sloping upward.
    b. sloping downward.
    c. above the *ATC* curve.
    d. below the *ATC* curve.

20. Over the range of output where the *MP* curve slopes upward, the

    a. *MC* curve slopes downward.
    b. *AFC* curve slopes upward.
    c. firm is experiencing economies of scale.
    d. total cost curve slopes downward.

21. A technological advance

    a. shifts the firm's total product curve upward.
    b. does not shift the firm's total product curve.
    c. shifts the firm's total product curve downward.
    d. cannot occur without raising the firm's average total costs and hence shifts the average total cost curve upward.

22. The cost of a variable input, such as the wage paid to workers, rises. This change shifts the

    a. total fixed cost curve upward.
    b. marginal product of labor curve downward.
    c. average variable cost curve upward.
    d. marginal product of labor curve upward.

Long-Run Cost

23. The concept of diminishing returns

    a. applies to both labor and capital.
    b. applies to labor but does not apply to capital.
    c. applies to capital but does not apply to labor.
    d. does not apply to either labor or capital.

24. The *LRAC* curve

    a. equals the minimum points on all the short-run *ATC* curves.
    b. equals the lowest possible marginal cost of producing the different levels of output.
    c. equals the lowest attainable average total cost for all levels of output when all inputs can be varied.
    d. generally lies above the short-run *ATC* curves.

25. The *LRAC* curve generally is

    a. shaped as an upside-down U.
    b. U-shaped.
    c. upward sloping.
    d. downward sloping.

26. When a firm is experiencing economies of scale,

    a. the *MP* curve slopes upward.
    b. the *LRAC* curve slopes downward.
    c. diminishing returns to labor have been suspended.
    d. the *MC* curve slopes downward.

27. Constant returns to scale means that as all inputs are increased,

    a. total output remains constant.
    b. average total cost rises.
    c. average total cost rises at the same rate as do the inputs.
    d. total output increases in the same proportion as do the inputs.

■ Short Answer Problems

1. Where does the marginal product curve intersect the average product curve? Why?

2. a. Table 10.2 (on the next page) gives the total weekly output of turkeys at Al's Turkey Town. Complete this table. (The marginal product is entered midway between rows to emphasize that it is the result of changing inputs — moving from one row to the next. Average product corresponds to a fixed quantity of labor and so is entered on the appropriate row.)

   b. In Figure 10.5 (on the next page) label the axes and draw a graph of the total product curve (*TP*).

   c. In Figure 10.6 (on the next page) label the axes and draw a graph of the marginal product (*MP*) and the average product (*AP*). (As in Table 10.2,

TABLE 10.2
Short Answer Problem 2 (a)

Labor	Quantity (turkeys per week)	Average product of labor (AP)	Marginal product of labor (MP)
0	0	XX	
			100
1	100	100	
			____
2	300	____	
			____
3	450	____	
			110
4	____	____	
			____
5	630	____	
			____
6	____	110	

FIGURE 10.5
Short Answer Problem 2 (b)

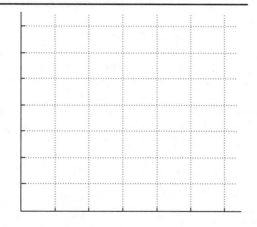

plot the marginal products midway between the units of labor and the average products directly above the units of labor.) Where do the *AP* and *MP* curves cross?

FIGURE 10.6
Short Answer Problem 2 (c)

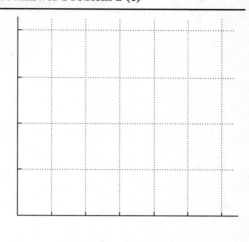

3. a. Now let's examine Al's short-run cost of growing turkeys. The first two columns of Table 10.2 are reproduced in the first two columns of Table 10.3. The cost of 1 worker (the only variable input) is $2,000 per month. Total fixed cost is $4,000 per month. Complete Table 10.3 by using your answers from Table 10.2 and by computing total variable cost and total cost.

TABLE 10.3
Total Cost of Growing Turkeys

Labor	Quantity (turkeys per week)	Total variable cost (TVC)	Total cost (TC)
0	0	____	$4,000
1	100	2,000	____
2	300	____	____
3	450	____	____
4	____	____	12,000
5	630	____	____
6	____	12,000	____

FIGURE **10.7**
Short Answer Problem 3 (b)

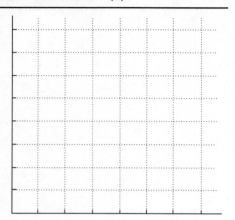

FIGURE **10.8**
Short Answer Problem 3 (d)

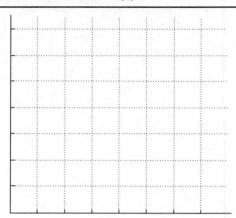

b. In Figure 10.7 label the axes and draw the *TC* and *TVC* curves. What is the relationship between these two curves?

c. Table 10.4 contains spaces for some of Al's other costs, the average total cost (*ATC*), average variable cost (*AVC*), and marginal cost (*MC*). Complete this table by using your answers from Table 10.3 and calculating the new costs called for in Table 10.4.

d. In Figure 10.8 label the axes and draw the *ATC*, *AVC*, and *MC* curves. Be sure to plot the values for the *MC* between the relevant levels of output. What is the relationship between the *ATC* and *AVC* curves? Between the *MC* and *AVC* curves?

4. a. Suppose Al discovers new technology that boosts the productivity of his workers so that more turkeys can be grown than before. Complete Table 10.5, which presents production data with the new technology.

TABLE **10.4**
Other Costs of Growing Turkeys

Quantity (turkeys per week)	Average variable cost (*AVC*)	Average total cost (*ATC*)	Marginal cost (*MC*)
0	XX	XX	
			$20.00
100	$20.00	____	
			____
300	____	____	
			____
450	____	____	
			____
____	____	21.43	
			____
630	____	____	
			66.67
____	____	____	

TABLE **10.5**
New Technology

Labor	Quantity (turkeys per week)	Average product of labor (*AP*)	Marginal product of labor (*MP*)
0	0	XX	
			120
1	120	120	
			____
2	360	____	
			____
3	540	____	
			____
4	672	____	
			____
5	756	____	
			____
6	792	____	

b. Al's fixed cost remains at $4,000 and he can continue to hire workers at a wage rate of $2,000. Use the new technology production data to complete Table 10.6, which has the total cost, and Table 10.7, which has (some of) the average costs and the marginal cost.

TABLE **10.6**

New Technology and Total Costs

Labor	Quantity (turkeys per week)	Total variable cost (TVC)	Total cost (TC)
0	0	___	___
1	120	___	___
2	360	___	___
3	540	___	___
4	672	___	___
5	756	___	___
6	792	___	___

TABLE **10.7**

New Technology and Other Costs

Quantity (turkeys per week)	Average variable cost (AVC)	Average total cost (ATC)	Marginal cost (MC)
0	XX	XX	
			___
120	___	___	
			___
360	___	___	
			___
540	___	___	
			___
672	___	___	
			___
756	___	___	
			___
792	___	___	

c. In Figure 10.9, plot the *ATC* and *MC* curves you have just entered in Table 10.7. Also draw the *ATC* and *MC* curves you have already plotted in Figure 10.8 (before the technology changed). Label the old *ATC* curve ATC_1 and the old *MC* curve MC_1; label the new *ATC* curve ATC_2 and the new *MC* curve MC_2. How do the old and new *ATC* curves compare? The old and new *MC* curves?

FIGURE **10.9**
Short Answer Problem 4 (c)

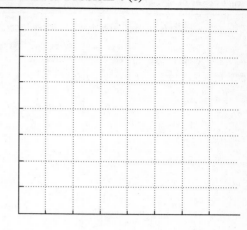

5. a. Return to the old technology for growing turkeys, which you studied and worked out in problems 2 and 3. Suppose that the cost of Al's fixed inputs remain at $4,000. Now the cost of his variable input, labor, rises. Specifically, suppose that a worker now receives $3,000 per month. Complete Table 10.8. For the two missing quantities, copy your answers from Table 10.2.

TABLE **10.8**

A Change in Variable Costs

Labor	Quantity (turkeys per week)	Total variable cost (TVC)	Total cost (TC)
0	0	___	$4,000
1	100	3,000	___
2	300	___	___
3	450	___	___
4	___	___	16,000
5	630	___	___
6	___	18,000	___

TABLE 10.9

Comparison of Costs

	Before increase		After increase	
Quantity	Average total cost (ATC)	Marginal cost (MC)	Average total cost (ATC)	Marginal cost (MC)
0	XX		XX	
		___		___
100	___		___	
		___		___
300	___		___	
		___		___
450	___		___	
		___		___
___	___		___	
		___		___
630	___		___	
		___		___
___	___		___	

b. To compare the effect of the rise in the variable cost on the average total cost and marginal cost, complete Table 10.9. (Hint: As before, copy the "before increase" *ATC* and *MC* values from Ta-ble 10.4; work out the "after increase" *ATC* and *MC* values from Table 10.8.) From Table 10.9, how did the rise in variable costs affect the average total cost? The marginal cost?

6. What is the difference between diminishing returns and diseconomies of scale?

■ **You're the Teacher**

1. "This chapter has a lot to say about firms: production, costs, and stuff like that. But I don't really see the purpose. In real life, businesses are a lot more complicated than this chapter says. Workers are different, different companies make different goods, Intel's factory sure isn't the same as what we see at Krispy Kreme and what have you. What's the use of this chapter?" This student is missing an essential point about economic theories. Can you help straighten out the student?

2. "I get the idea that marginal cost is important, but I don't know why. You have any ideas about it?" Your friend is asking you for your ideas; you have a chance to help your friend, so explain why you think marginal cost is important.

Answers

■ True/False Answers

Decision Time Frames

1. **F** In the short run, at least one input is *fixed*.
2. **T** The question presents the definition of the long run.

Short-Run Technology Constraint

3. **F** The firm has increasing *marginal* returns because only *one* input has been changed.
4. **T** The question presents the definition of diminishing returns.
5. **T** This result is a reflection of the relationship between marginals and averages.

Short-Run Cost

6. **T** Total cost is the sum of fixed cost and variable cost.
7. **F** As output increases, total cost always rises.
8. **F** The amount of variable cost and the amount of fixed cost are not necessarily related, except that in the long run all costs are variable costs.
9. **F** Marginal cost equals the *additional* total cost divided by the *additional* output.
10. **F** Marginal cost usually starts below the average total cost and then rises above it.
11. **F** The average total cost curve has a "right-side-up" U shape.
12. **F** The *MC* curve always passes through the minimum point of the *ATC* curve.

Long-Run Cost

13. **T** In the long run, all inputs can be varied so all costs are variable costs.
14. **T** The long-run average cost curve shows the least possible cost to produce any level of output.
15. **F** Economies of scale occur when an increase in *all* inputs increases output by a larger proportion.
16. **F** When the *LRAC* curve slopes upward, average cost increases when output increases, so over this range of output the firm is experiencing diseconomies of scale.

■ Multiple Choice Answers

Decision Time Frames

1. **d** This is the definition of the short run.
2. **b** The long run is the amount of time until all inputs become variable.

Short-Run Technology Constraint

3. **a** The average product of labor is total product (output) per worker.
4. **d** Answer (d) is the definition of diminishing returns.
5. **a** When $MP > AP$, the average product rises when employment increases; when $MP < AP$, the average product falls; and when $MP = AP$, the average product is at its maximum.
6. **b** This answer reflects the average/marginal relationship that when the marginal is below the average, the average falls.

Short-Run Cost

7. **c** Total cost equals fixed cost plus variable cost, so fixed cost equals total cost minus variable cost.
8. **c** The marginal cost equals the difference in total cost ($24 − $21 = $3) divided by the change in output (4 − 3 = 1), so the marginal cost is $3.
9. **a** Average total cost equals total cost divided by total output, that is, $24/4 or $6.
10. **d** Because total cost equals total fixed cost plus total variable cost, total fixed cost equals $6. Then, average fixed cost is total fixed cost divided by total output, so average fixed cost equals $6/3 = $2.
11. **c** Fixed cost remains the same regardless of the level of output, that is, whether the firm produces a million units of output or no units of output.
12. **d** Marginal cost shows the added cost from producing an added unit of output.
13. **c** The marginal cost equals the change in total cost ($52,000 − $50,000, or $2,000) divided by the change in output (51 acres of eggplant − 50 acres of eggplant, or 1 acre of eggplant). Therefore the marginal cost equals $2,000 per acre of eggplant.

FIGURE **10.10**
Multiple Choice Questions 14, 15, 16, 17

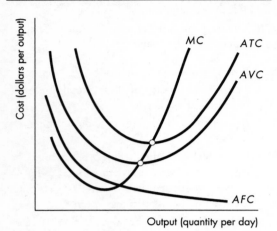

14. **c** Figure 10.10 identifies the *MC* curve. Note that it goes through the minimum points of both the *ATC* and *AVC* curves.

15. **b** Again, Figure 10.10 identifies the *ATC* curve.

16. **a** Figure 10.10 shows that the *AVC* curve is the U-shaped curve that lies below the U-shaped *ATC* curve.

17. **d** None of the curves in the original figure was the *AFC* curve, but Figure 10.10 shows the *AFC* curve.

18. **a** The *MC* curve intersects both the *ATC* and the *AVC* curves at their minimums.

19. **d** When the marginal cost is less than the average cost, the average cost falls as output expands.

20. **a** When the *MP* curve slopes upward, each additional variable input produces more additional output than the previous unit of the input. So the added cost of producing the added units falls — that is, the *MC* curve slopes downward — because each variable unit has the same additional cost as the previous unit, but each produces more additional output.

21. **a** By shifting the total product curve upward, the technological advance generally shifts the average total cost curve downward.

22. **c** Wages are a variable cost, so a rise in the wage rate shifts the average variable cost curve upward.

Long-Run Cost

23. **a** *All* inputs are subject to diminishing returns.

24. **c** The long-run average cost curve, or *LRAC* curve, shows the lowest possible average total cost for producing any level of output.

25. **b** The *LRAC* curve has a U shape: When output increases, at first the *LRAC* falls but as output increases still more, the *LRAC* rises.

26. **b** Economies of scale means that increases in output lower the firm's long-run average costs.

27. **d** This is the definition of constant returns to scale.

■ Answers to Short Answer Problems

FIGURE **10.11**
Short Answer Problem 1

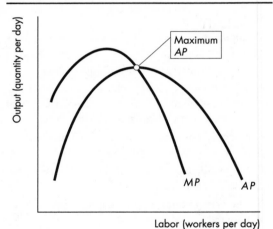

1. The marginal product curve intersects the average product curve where the average product is at its maximum. To understand why, look at Figure 10.11. To the left of the maximum point, *MP* > *AP*. That means that an additional worker produces more additional output than the average of the previously employed workers. As a result, the average product increases. So, as long as the *MP* exceeds the *AP*, the average product must be increasing. Now look to the right of the maximum point. Here *MP* < *AP*. Each new worker produces less additional output than the average of the previously employed workers, so the average product falls. As long as the *MP* is less than the *AP*, the average product must decrease. That means that whenever the marginal product exceeds the average product, which is the

case at any point left of the intersection point, the average product increases with output; whenever the marginal product is less than the average product, which is true for any point right of the intersection point, the average product falls. Hence when the marginal product equals the average product, the average product does not change. Left of this point the average product is rising and right it is falling. Therefore at this point the average product is at its maximum.

2. a. Table 10.10 completes Table 10.2. The average product of labor column is calculated by dividing the total product by the total amount of labor; that is, APL = Quantity/L. So, the AP when 2 workers are employed is 300/2, or 150. The marginal product of labor is the extra output produced by an extra worker. In terms of a formula, the MP equals the change in quantity divided by the change in labor, so that MP = $(\Delta \text{Quantity})/\Delta L$. So, between 2 and 1 workers the MP is $(300-100)/(2-1) = 200$. Because the MP equals the additional output when another unit of labor is employed, the quantity of output produced when 4 workers are employed equals the total quantity produced when 3 workers are employed (450) plus the additional amount the 4th worker produces, 110, or 560.

TABLE **10.10**

Short Answer Problem 2 (a)

Labor	Quantity (turkeys per week)	Average product of labor (AP)	Marginal product of labor (MP)
0	0	XX	
			100
1	100	100	
			200
2	300	150	
			150
3	450	150	
			110
4	560	140	
			70
5	630	126	
			30
6	660	110	

FIGURE **10.12**

Short Answer Problem 2 (b)

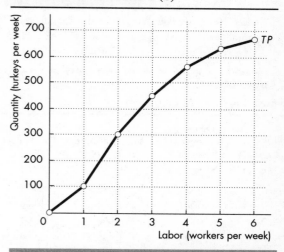

FIGURE **10.13**

Short Answer Problem 2 (c)

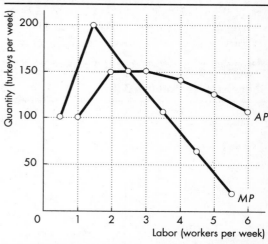

Finally, for the total quantity when 6 workers are used, multiply the average product of labor, 110, by the total number of workers employed, 6, to get the total product of 660.

b. Figure 10.12 shows the graph of the firm's total product curve.

c. Figure 10.13 shows the firm's AP and MP curves. The MP curve crosses the AP curve when the AP is at its maximum.

3. a. Table 10.11 shows the total cost for each quantity of labor. Total variable cost equals the number of workers (the variable input) multiplied by $2,000 per worker. Total cost then equals the total variable cost plus the total fixed cost, which is given in the problem as $4,000.

lated by dividing total cost by the total quantity produced. Finally, marginal cost equals the change in total cost divided by the change in quantity, that is, $MC = (\Delta TC)/\Delta q$. Hence the MC between 300 and 100 turkeys per week is ($8,000 - $6,000)/(300 - 100)$, or $10.00.

TABLE 10.11
Short Answer Problem 3 (a)

Labor	Quantity (turkeys per week)	Total variable cost (TVC)	Total cost (TC)
0	0	$0	$4,000
1	100	2,000	6,000
2	300	4,000	8,000
3	450	6,000	10,000
4	560	8,000	12,000
5	630	10,000	14,000
6	660	12,000	16,000

b. Figure 10.14 shows the firm's total cost (TC) and total variable cost (TVC) curves. The TC curve always lies $4,000 above the TVC curve.

TABLE 10.12
Short Answer Problem 3 (c)

Quantity (turkeys per week)	Average variable cost (AVC)	Average total cost (ATC)	Marginal cost (MC)
0	XX	XX	
			$20.00
100	$20.00	$60.00	
			10.00
300	13.33	26.67	
			13.33
450	13.33	22.22	
			18.18
560	14.29	21.43	
			28.57
630	15.87	22.22	
			66.67
660	18.18	24.24	

FIGURE 10.14
Short Answer Problem 3 (b)

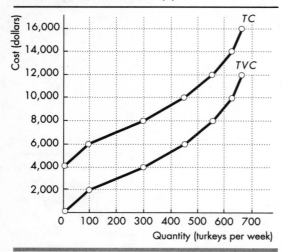

FIGURE 10.15
Short Answer Problem 3 (d)

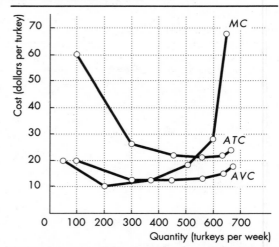

c. Table 10.12 completes Table 10.4. In Table 10.12 the average variable cost column was calculated by dividing total variable cost by the total quantity produced. So the AVC when 300 turkeys are produced is $4,000/300 = $13.33. Similarly, the average total cost column is calcu-

d. Figure 10.15 shows the ATC, AVC, and MC curves. The AVC curve lies below the ATC curve, but the vertical distance between the two (which equals AFC) shrinks as output expands. The MC curve crosses the AVC curve where the

AVC is at its minimum. (It also crosses the ATC curve where the ATC is at its minimum.)

4. a. Table 10.13 shows the new APs and MPs. These answers were calculated in the same way as the answers for short answer problem 2 (a).

TABLE 10.13
Short Answer Problem 4 (a)

Labor	Quantity (turkeys per week)	Average product of labor (AP)	Marginal product of labor (MP)
0	0	XX	
			120
1	120	120	
			240
2	360	180	
			180
3	540	180	
			132
4	672	168	
			84
5	756	151.2	
			36
6	792	132	

b. Tables 10.14 and 10.15 show the firm's new costs after the advance in technology. The answers in Table 10.16 are calculated similarly to those in Table 10.13 for short answer problem 3 (a); the answers in Table 10.17 correspond to the those in Table 10.14 for short answer problem 3 (c).

TABLE 10.14
Short Answer Problem 5 (b)

Labor	Quantity (turkeys per week)	Total variable cost (TVC)	Total cost (TC)
0	0	$0	$4,000
1	120	2,000	6,000
2	360	4,000	8,000
3	540	6,000	10,000
4	672	8,000	12,000
5	756	10,000	14,000
6	792	12,000	16,000

TABLE 10.15
Short Answer Problem 5 (b)

Quantity (turkeys per week)	Average variable cost (AVC)	Average total cost (ATC)	Marginal cost (MC)
0	XX	XX	
			$16.67
120	$16.67	$50.00	
			8.33
360	11.11	22.22	
			11.11
540	11.11	18.52	
			15.15
672	11.90	17.86	
			23.81
756	13.23	18.52	
			55.55
792	15.15	20.20	

FIGURE 10.16
Short Answer Problem 4 (c)

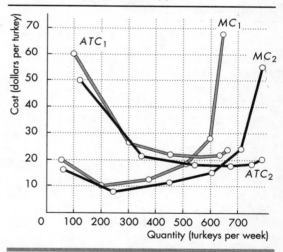

c. Figure 10.16 shows the old and new ATC and MC curves. The new ATC curve appears generally to lie beneath the old ATC curve. Actually, the new curve *always* lies below the old curve, but the large discrete changes in output that are plotted make the new ATC curve appear to lie a little above the old ATC curve at low levels of output. The new MC curve is below the old MC curve. Technological advances shift the firm's average and marginal cost curves downward.

TABLE 10.16
Short Answer Problem 5 (a)

Labor	Quantity (turkeys per week)	Total variable cost (TVC)	Total cost (TC)
0	0	$0	$4,000
1	100	3,000	7,000
2	300	6,000	10,000
3	450	9,000	13,000
4	560	12,000	16,000
5	630	15,000	19,000
6	660	18,000	22,000

5. a. Table 10.16 completes Table 10.10 and shows Al's total variable cost and total cost after the variable input, labor, and rises in cost. The rise in the cost of the variable input raises both the total variable cost and the total cost.

TABLE 10.17
Short Answer Problem 5 (b)

Quantity	Before increase Average total cost (ATC)	Before increase Marginal cost (MC)	After increase Average total cost (ATC)	After increase Marginal cost (MC)
0	XX		XX	
		$20.00		$30.00
100	$60.00		$70.00	
		10.00		15.00
300	26.67		33.33	
		13.33		20.00
450	22.22		28.88	
		18.18		27.27
560	21.43		28.57	
		28.57		42.86
630	22.22		30.16	
		66.67		100.00
660	24.24		33.33	

b. Table 10.17 shows the firm's average total cost and marginal cost after the variable cost has risen. The rise in variable cost raises both the average total cost and the marginal cost. In other words, at any level of output, both the average total cost and marginal cost are greater after the rise in variable cost than before. In a diagram, the rise in Al's variable cost would shift both the firm's *ATC* and *MC* curves upward.

6. The law of diminishing returns states that as a firm uses additional units of a variable input, while holding constant the quantity of fixed inputs, the marginal product of the variable input will eventually diminish. Diseconomies of scale occur when a firm increases all of its inputs by an equal percentage, and this increase results in a smaller percentage increase in output so that the long-run average cost rises. Diminishing (marginal) returns is a short-run concept because there is a fixed input. Diseconomies of scale is a long run concept because all inputs must be variable.

■ **You're the Teacher**

1. "Look, we've talked about this before. Economic theories are abstract on purpose; that is, they deliberately do not include all the nitty-gritty detail of the real world. Instead they focus only on the most important issues. Sure, all companies employ lots of different types of labor — skilled labor, unskilled labor, blue collar workers, white collar workers, sales representatives, and so on. So what? Including this fact in a theory would just give us a bunch more details that don't tell us anything.

"You know, consumers are different too. That didn't stop us from developing useful theories about the factors that affect their demand curves.

"The whole idea is that economic theory looks for qualities that are the same. That is what we're doing with firms. For instance, *all* firms hire labor and use capital. And these resources are different when we think about how rapidly the firm can change the amounts that it uses. So all firms have to face the difference between fixed and variable resources. I don't care if you're talking about Intel building chips or that Krispy Kreme store we both like. The point is that the theory we're learning can be applied to all types of firms, which gives the theory its power."

2. "You're lucky because I've been reading ahead in the book. Remember the discussion of marginal analysis in one of the earlier chapters? You know, where people looked at the effects from making small changes and then compared the additional costs from the change to the additional benefits? Well, that's what we'll be using marginal cost for.

When we want to know how much a firm will produce, we can ask whether it wants to increase its production. By increasing its production, the firm will incur some additional costs — its marginal cost. We'll then compare this cost to the added benefit from increasing production. So you're right: Marginal cost really is important because it's basically half the marginal analysis we'll be doing in the chapters ahead."

Chapter Quiz

1. In the short run,
   a. at least one input is fixed.
   b. all inputs are fixed.
   c. at least one input is variable.
   d. all inputs are variable.

2. In the long run,
   a. at least one input is fixed.
   b. all inputs are fixed.
   c. at least one input is variable.
   d. all inputs are variable.

3. The marginal product of labor is the
   a. inverse of the marginal product of capital when the firm is in the long run.
   b. slope of the curve showing the average product of labor.
   c. change in total product divided by the change in labor.
   d. total product divided by total labor.

4. The average product of labor curve is at its maximum when
   a. the marginal product of labor curve is below it.
   b. the marginal product of labor curve crosses it.
   c. the marginal product of labor curve is above it.
   d. the level of output is at its maximum.

5. The more shallow the total product curve,
   a. the greater is the marginal product of labor.
   b. the smaller is the marginal product of labor.
   c. the lower is the total cost curve.
   d. the lower is the variable cost curve.

6. Variable cost is sum of all
   a. the costs associated with variable inputs.
   b. the costs associated with the production of the product.
   c. the explicit costs but not all the implicit costs.
   d. the costs that do not change when the amount produced increases.

7. A firm's average variable cost is $10, its total fixed costs are $50 and the firm produces 25 units of output. Hence its average total cost is
   a. more than $50.
   b. $12.
   c. $4.
   d. $2.

8. When producing 99 units, the total cost is $595. The marginal cost of the 100th unit is $5. Hence the total cost of producing 100 units
   a. is $600.
   b. is $590.
   c. is $6.
   d. cannot be calculated without additional information.

9. The average total cost curve is lowest when
   a. the marginal cost curve is below it.
   b. the marginal cost curve crosses it.
   c. the marginal cost curve is above it.
   d. the level of output is at its maximum.

10. When long-run average costs increase when output increases, there definitely are
    a. economies of scale.
    b. diseconomies of scale.
    c. diminishing returns.
    d. constant returns to scale.

The answers for this Chapter Quiz are on page 367

11 PERFECT COMPETITION

Key Concepts

■ Competition

Perfect competition is an industry with many firms, each selling an identical good; many buyers; no restrictions on entry into the industry; no advantage for existing firms over new firms; and sellers and buyers are well informed about prices.

Perfect competition occurs when the minimum efficient scale of a firm is small relative to demand. The minimum efficient scale of a firm is the smallest quantity of output at which the long-run average total cost is at its lowest level.

♦ Each perfectly competitive firm is a **price taker,** that is, it cannot affect the price of the good.

♦ The *market* demand curve slopes downward. But each *firm* faces a horizontal — perfectly elastic — demand curve at the going price. Such a demand curve is illustrated in Figure 11.1.

Economic profit equals total revenue minus total opportunity cost. Part of the opportunity cost is a normal profit, the return the firm's entrepreneur can obtain in the in an alternative business. **Total revenue** equals the price of the output times the number sold, $TR = P \times q$, with P the price and q the amount the firm produces.

♦ **Marginal revenue,** MR, equals the change in total revenue from a one-unit increase in the quantity sold. In terms of a formula, $MR = (\Delta TR)/\Delta q$.

♦ In perfect competition $P = MR$. So, as illustrated in Figure 11.1, a perfectly competitive firm's MR curve is the same as its demand curve and both are horizontal at the market-determined price.

FIGURE **11.1**

Perfectly Competitive Firm's Demand Curve

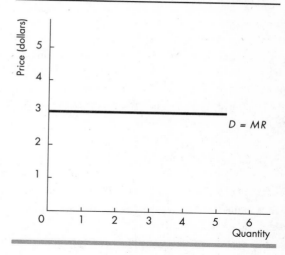

■ The Firm's Decisions in Perfect Competition

In the short run, each firm must decide:

♦ whether to produce or to shut down.

♦ if it produces, how much to produce.

In the long run, the firm must decide:

♦ whether to change its plant size.

♦ whether to enter or exit an industry.

To maximize its profit in the short run, the firm produces the quantity of output at which $MR = MC$. This result is illustrated in Figure 11.2 (on the next page), where the firm maximizes its profit by producing 4 units. In Figure 11.2, the price of the product is $3, the (given) price.

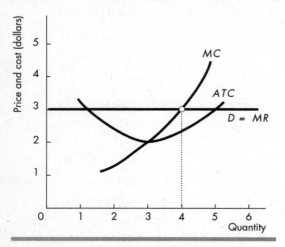

FIGURE **11.2**

A Perfectly Competitive Firm's Output

Maximizing profit by setting $MR = MC$ is an example of marginal analysis: As long as $MR > MC$, producing an extra unit of output adds to the firm's total profit.

In the short run, perfectly competitive firms can make an economic profit, a normal profit, or an economic loss:

♦ $P > ATC$ — the firm earns an economic profit. (This case is illustrated in Figure 11.2.)

♦ $P = ATC$ — the firm earns a normal profit and zero economic profit. (The firm breaks even.)

♦ $P < ATC$ — the firm incurs an economic loss.

A firm incurring economic losses must decide whether to shut down temporarily:

♦ If $P > AVC$, the firm continues to produce.

♦ If $P < AVC$, the firm shuts down temporarily. The **shutdown point** is the output and price for which total revenue just equals total variable cost and is reached when P equals the minimum AVC.

A perfectly competitive firm's supply curve is its MC curve above the minimum AVC. The **short-run industry supply curve** shows the quantity supplied by the industry at each price when the number of firms and their plant size is fixed. The short-run industry supply curve is the sum of the amounts supplied by each firm.

■ Output, Price, and Profit in Perfect Competition

The equilibrium market price and industry equilibrium level of output are determined by the industry demand and supply curves. The number of firms in the industry, and their size, is fixed in the short run. In the long run, the number of firms in the industry, and their size can adjust.

Changes in the market demand affect the price and thereby the firms' profits. The presence of an economic profit means that as time passes new firms enter the industry; the presence of an economic loss means that eventually some existing firms exit. When firms earn a normal profit, there is no incentive to enter or exit.

♦ Economic profits bring entry by new firms. The industry supply curve shifts rightward and reduces the market price. The fall in price reduces economic profit and decreases the incentive to enter the industry. New firms enter until it is no longer possible to earn an economic profit.

♦ Economic losses lead to exit by existing firms, which shifts the industry supply curve leftward. The price rises, and the higher price reduces economic losses. Firms exit until no firms incur an economic loss.

Firms change their plant size if it increases their profits.

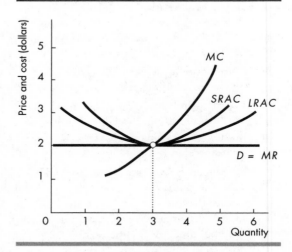

FIGURE **11.3**

Long-Run Equilibrium

Figure 11.3 illustrates a firm in long-run competitive equilibrium. Three conditions are satisfied:

♦ $MR (= P) = MC$ — the firm maximizes its profits.

♦ P = minimum short-run average cost $(SRAC)$ — the firm's economic profit is zero.

♦ P = minimum $LRAC$ — the firm's plant size cannot be changed in order to increase its profits.

■ Changing Tastes and Advancing Technology

A permanent decrease in demand leads to adjustments:

◆ The price falls. Each firm reduces its output, so the industry output decreases.

◆ Firms incur economic losses, so some exit the industry. Exit shifts the industry supply curve leftward, so the price rises and industry quantity decreases.

◆ The price eventually rises to eliminate economic losses. At this point, firms no longer exit and long-run equilibrium is established.

If there are **external economies**, factors beyond the control of an individual firm that lower its costs as the industry output expands, a decrease in demand means that the long-run equilibrium market price is higher than the initial price before the decrease in demand. If there are **external diseconomies,** factors beyond the control of an individual firm that raise its costs as industry output increases, the long-run equilibrium price is lower than the initial price. The **long-run industry supply curve** shows how the quantity supplied by an industry varies with changes in the market price after all adjustments have been made.

Technological change also creates adjustments:

◆ New technology lowers firms' costs and increases their supply. The industry supply curve shifts rightward, lowering the market price and increasing industry output.

◆ Firms that do not adopt the new technology incur economic losses and exit the industry.

◆ All firms, in the long run, use the new technology and earn only a normal profit.

■ Competition and Efficiency

Resources are used efficiently when we produce the goods and services valued most highly. When resources are used efficiently, no one can be made better off without making someone else worse off.

◆ Consumers' demands reflect their efforts to get the most value from their incomes. The demand curve is consumers' marginal benefit curve.

◆ Producers' supplies reflect the firms' efforts to maximize their profits. The supply curve is producers' marginal cost curve.

If there are no **external benefits** (benefits that accrue to people other than the buyer of the good) and no **exter-**

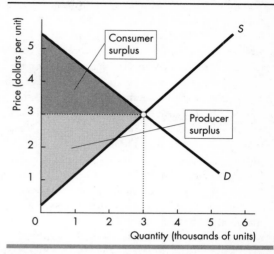

FIGURE 11.4
The Efficient Level of Output

nal costs (costs not borne by the producer of the good or service) perfect competition is efficient. Figure 11.4 shows an efficient use of resources. The production of 3,000 units sets the quantity demanded equal to the quantity supplied and so sets the marginal benefit equal to the marginal cost.

The presence of external costs or benefits, monopoly, or public goods, can lead to inefficiency.

Helpful Hints

1. **WHY STUDY PERFECT COMPETITION?** Although perfectly competitive markets are rare in the real world, there are three important reasons for developing a thorough understanding of their behavior.

   First, many markets closely *approximate* perfect competition. This chapter gives direct and useful insights into the behavior of these markets.

   Second, the theory of perfect competition allows us to isolate the effects of competitive forces that are at work in all markets, even in those that do not match the assumptions of perfect competition.

   Third, the perfectly competitive model serves as a useful benchmark for evaluating the efficiency of different market structures.

2. **THE PROFIT MAXIMIZATION RULE, MR = MC :** Profit maximization requires producing where *MR = MC*, which might seem odd. Producing where *MR > MC* might seem more reasonable be-

cause this situation apparently implies that the business is making a profit. However, this line of thought is wrong.

A firm maximizes its *total* profit. To meet this objective, the firm produces any unit of output for which the revenue from the unit exceeds the cost of producing the unit. Why? If the revenue from the unit (the marginal revenue, *MR*) is greater than the cost of producing it (the marginal cost, *MC*) the unit adds to the firm's *total* profit. Some units add more to the profit — those with *MR* much greater than *MC* — and others add less — those with *MR* only slightly larger than *MC* — but as long as producing the unit of output adds to the total profit, the firm produces it. Comparing the additional revenue from a unit to its additional costs (using marginal analysis) shows that the firm passes up profit if it produced so that *MR* > *MC*. Only by producing the quantity that sets *MR* = *MC* does the firm not forego some profit, so only at this level of output does the firm maximize its total profit.

3. **WHY OPERATE WITH ZERO ECONOMIC PROFIT?**
Why does a firm continues to operate even though its economic profit is zero? The key to this result rests in the definition of cost. Recall that the company's total costs are all its *opportunity* costs, which include both explicit and implicit costs. Among the implicit costs is the normal profit, the return the owners can earn on the average in an alternative business. When total revenue equals total cost, so that there is zero economic profit, the owners are earning the same profit they could obtain elsewhere. At this point, the firm earns a "normal profit." As the phrase implies, a normal profit is one that could normally be earned in any other industry. Even though the economic profit is zero, by earning a normal profit the firm is earning just as much profit as it could anywhere else and its owners therefore are content to continue producing in the same industry.

Questions

■ True/False and Explain

Competition

1. In a perfectly competitive industry many firms produce very similar but slightly different products.

2. The minimum efficient scale of a firm is the smallest level of output at which the long-run average total cost is at its minimum.

3. In a perfectly competitive industry, no single firm can significantly affect the price of the good.

4. The market demand curve in a perfectly competitive industry is horizontal.

5. A perfectly competitive firm must decide what price to charge for its goods.

The Firm's Decisions in Perfect Competition

6. If it does not shut down, to maximize its profit a perfectly competitive firm produces the level of output that sets *MR* = *MC*.

7. If *P* > *ATC*, the firm is incurring an economic loss.

8. If the price is below a firm's minimum *ATC*, it immediately shuts down.

9. A perfectly competitive firm's supply curve shows the quantities of output supplied at alternative prices as long as the firm earns an economic profit.

10. A perfectly competitive firm's supply curve is its *ATC* curve.

Output, Price, and Profit in Perfect Competition

11. A perfectly competitive firm can earn an economic profit, a normal profit, or incur an economic loss in the short run.

12. A perfectly competitive firm can earn an economic profit, a normal profit, or incur an economic loss in the long run.

13. Firms exit an industry whenever they cannot earn an economic profit.

14. A firm making zero economic profit makes no profit at all.

15. In the long run, a perfectly competitive firm produces at the minimum *LRAC*.

Changing Tastes and Advancing Technology

16. In the short run, a permanent increase in demand results in firms earning an economic profit.

17. In the long run, a permanent increase in demand results in firms earning an economic profit.

18. In a perfectly competitive industry with external diseconomies, a change in demand always results in a higher price.

19. New technology raises firms' costs and so causes all firms to incur an economic loss in the short run.

Competition and Efficiency

20. Efficient use of resource occurs when making someone better off must make someone else worse off.

21. The total gains from trade equal the sum of consumer surplus plus producer surplus.

22. Perfect competition always results in an efficient use of resources.

■ Multiple Choice

Competition

1. Which of the following is <u>NOT</u> a characteristic of a perfectly competitive industry?
   a. A downward-sloping market demand curve.
   b. A perfectly elastic demand for each firm.
   c. Each firm decides its quantity of output.
   d. Each firm produces a good slightly different from that of its competitors.

2. Of the following, which is a perfect competitor?
   a. AT&T, one of the three major providers of long distance telephone service in the United States.
   b. The company that provides your local cable TV service.
   c. A tomato grower living in Florida.
   d. DeBeers, the provider of more than 80 percent of the rough diamonds in the world.

Use Table 11.1 for the next question.

TABLE 11.1
Multiple Choice Question 3

Quantity	Price (dollars)
100	5.00
101	5.00

3. Using Table 11.1, what is the marginal revenue from selling 101 units of output rather than 100?
   a. $5
   b. $500
   c. $505
   d. $0

4. For a perfectly competitive firm, MR always equals
   a. ATC.
   b. P.
   c. AVC.
   d. none of the above because MR is not always equal to the same thing.

The Firm's Decisions in Perfect Competition

5. Paul runs a shop that sells printers. Paul's business is a perfect competitor and can sell each printer for a price of $500. The marginal cost of selling one printer a day is $300, the marginal cost of selling a second printer is $400, and the marginal cost of selling a third printer is $550. To maximize his profit, Paul should sell
   a. one printer a day.
   b. two printers a day.
   c. three printers a day.
   d. more than three printers a day.

6. Which of the following is necessarily true when a perfectly competitive firm is in short-run equilibrium?
   a. $MR = MC$.
   b. P = minimum $LRAC$.
   c. $P = ATC$.
   d. All of the above are true at short-run equilibrium.

7. The wage rate a firm must pay rises, so its marginal costs rise. But its demand curve does not change. As a result, the firm _____ the amount it produces and _____ its price.
   a. decreases; raises
   b. increases; lowers
   c. decreases; does not change
   d. increases; raises

8. In the short run, a perfectly competitive firm can
   a. earn an economic profit.
   b. earn a normal profit.
   c. incur an economic loss.
   d. All of the above answers are possible.

9. A perfectly competitive firm is definitely suffering an economic loss when
   a. $MR < MC$.
   b. $P > ATC$.
   c. $P < ATC$.
   d. $P > AVC$.

FIGURE 11.5
Multiple Choice Questions 10 and 11

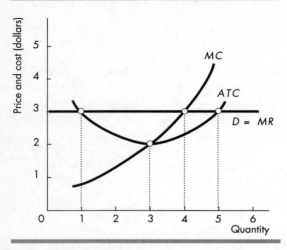

10. The firm illustrated in Figure 11.5 will produce how much output?
    a. 1 unit
    b. 3 units
    c. 4 units
    d. 5 units

11. The firm illustrated in Figure 11.5 is
    a. earning an economic profit.
    b. earning a normal profit.
    c. incurring an economic loss.
    d. in long-run equilibrium.

12. If a perfectly competitive firm is incurring an economic loss, it
    a. always shuts down immediately.
    b. continues to operate until either the price rises or its costs fall so that it no longer has an economic loss.
    c. shuts down if $P > AVC$.
    d. shuts down if $P < AVC$.

13. For prices below the minimum average variable cost, a perfectly competitive firm's supply curve is
    a. horizontal at the market price.
    b. vertical at zero output.
    c. the same as its marginal cost curve.
    d. the same as its average variable cost curve.

14. The short-run industry supply curve is
    a. the sum of the quantities supplied by all the firms.
    b. undefined because the number of firms is constant in the short run.
    c. vertical at the total level of output being produced by all firms.
    d. horizontal at the current market price.

Output, Price, and Profit in Perfect Competition

15. In the short run, which of the following is <u>FALSE</u>?
    a. Perfectly competitive firms can possibly earn an economic profit.
    b. The number of firms is fixed.
    c. To maximize its profit, a perfectly competitive firm produces enough output so that $MR = MC$.
    d. Perfectly competitive firms always produce at the minimum ATC.

16. When will new firms want to enter an industry?
    a. When $MR = MC$ for the existing firms in the industry.
    b. Any time the price of the good has risen.
    c. When the new firms can earn economic profits.
    d. When there are external economies.

17. Suppose that firms in a perfectly competitive industry are earning economic profits. Over time,
    a. other firms enter the industry so that the price rises and economic profits fall.
    b. some firms leave the industry so that both the price and economic profits rise.
    c. other firms enter the industry so that both price and economic profits fall.
    d. nothing happens because there are no incentives for change.

18. In the long run, a perfectly competitive firm can
    a. earn an economic profit.
    b. earn a normal profit.
    c. incur an economic loss.
    d. All of the above are possible.

FIGURE **11.6**
Multiple Choice Question 19

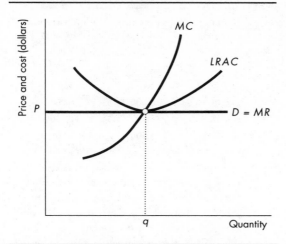

19. In Figure 11.6, the firm is producing *q*. Producing *q*
    a. cannot be the long-run equilibrium because the firm is not maximizing its profit.
    b. cannot be the long-run equilibrium because the firm is earning an economic profit.
    c. cannot be the long-run equilibrium because the firm is incurring an economic loss.
    d. is the long-run equilibrium.

20. Which of the following is true when a perfectly competitive firm is in long-run equilibrium?
    a. *MR* = *MC*.
    b. *P* = minimum *LRAC*.
    c. *P* = *ATC*.
    d. All of the above conditions are true.

Changing Tastes and Advancing Technology

21. If demand for a good decreases permanently, in the short run the price
    a. falls and each firm produces more output to make up for the lower price.
    b. falls and, as long as the price remains above the firms' average variable cost, each firm produces less output.
    c. does not change, but some firms shut down because less is demanded.
    d. does not change because each firm produces less output.

22. If firms in an industry are incurring an economic loss, then as some exit, the price _____ and the surviving firms' economic losses _____.
    a. rises; do not change
    b. rises; become smaller
    c. falls; become larger
    d. falls; become smaller

23. The term "external economies" refers to the
    a. case in which the firm's marginal cost curve slopes downward as more output is produced.
    b. situation in which the firm's average total cost curve shifts upward as more output is produced.
    c. fact that a firm's average total cost curve has a negative slope at low levels of output.
    d. situation in which an increase in an industry's output lowers the costs of the firms in the industry.

24. In a market with no external economies nor external diseconomies, following a decrease in demand, the price falls more in the _____ and the quantity decreases more in the _____.
    a. short run; short run
    b. short run; long run
    c. long run; short run
    d. long run; long run

25. If there are external diseconomies in an industry, after a permanent increase in demand, in the long run the price
    a. is higher than initially.
    b. is the same as initially.
    c. is lower than initially.
    d. might be higher or lower, depending on whether the firms are earning economic profits.

26. New technology in an industry means that
    a. all firms in the industry permanently earn economic profits regardless of whether they adopt the technology.
    b. firms that adopt the new technology permanently earn economic profits.
    c. firms that do not adopt the new technology permanently earn economic profits.
    d. firms that adopt the new technology temporarily earn economic profits.

Competition and Efficiency

27. Which of the following is <u>NOT</u> necessary for a perfectly competitive industry to be efficient?
    a. The presence of external benefits.
    b. Firms are economically efficient.
    c. The sum of consumer surplus plus producer surplus is as large as possible.
    d. All of the above answers are necessary for an industry to be efficient.

28. Resource use is efficient when
    a. the goods and services produced are those that are most highly valued.
    b. it is impossible to make someone better off without making someone else worse off.
    c. production is such that marginal benefit equals marginal cost.
    d. All of the above answers are correct.

29. Which of the following statements is true?
    a. If there are no external benefits, a competitive market is cannot use its resources efficiently.
    b. Resource use is efficient when marginal benefit exceeds marginal cost by as much as possible.
    c. In a perfectly competitive market, at the efficient level of output the price equals consumers' marginal benefit and producers' marginal cost.
    d. All of the above are all true statements.

30. Which of the following is <u>NOT</u> an obstacle to efficiency?
    a. External benefits or external costs.
    b. Monopoly.
    c. Competition.
    d. Public goods.

■ Short Answer Problems

1. Why will a firm in a perfectly competitive industry choose not to charge a price either above or below the equilibrium price?

2. Rudy runs a rutabaga farm. Rudy relishes the idea of maximizing his profit, so he must decide how many acres to farm. He receives a price of $2,000 per ton of rutabagas grown. Table 11.2 shows Rudy's total cost and total revenue for different amounts of tons grown.
    a. Based on Table 11.2, how many tons of rutabagas should Rudy farm? What is his total economic profit ?

TABLE 11.2
Rudy's Total Cost and Revenue

Quantity (tons)	Total cost (dollars)	Total revenue (dollars)
1	1,000	2,000
2	2,500	4,000
3	5,000	6,000
4	8,500	8,000
5	13,000	10,000
6	18,500	12,000

b. Complete Table 11.3, which gives Rudy's marginal cost and marginal revenue schedules. Note that both marginal costs and marginal revenues relate to changes in production, so they are located between the quantities of tons grown. That is, the first marginal cost and marginal revenue figures apply to the cost and revenue of changing from 1 ton grown to 2 tons.

TABLE 11.3
Rudy's Marginal Cost and Revenue

Quantity (tons)	Marginal cost (dollars)	Marginal revenue (dollars)
1	——	——
2	——	——
3	——	——
4	——	——
5	——	——
6		

c. Based on Table 11.3, in Figure 11.7 (on the next page), draw Rudy's marginal cost and marginal revenue curves.

d. Based on Table 11.3 and Figure 11.6, how many tons should Rudy grow? Why?

e. Are your answers to parts (a) and (d) different?

FIGURE **11.7**
Rudy's *MC* and *MR*

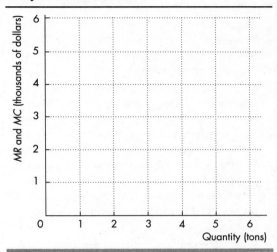

TABLE **11.4**
Samantha's Sweater Shop

Quantity (sweaters sold per day)	Total variable cost (dollars)	Total cost (dollars)
1	40	100
2	60	120
3	90	150
4	130	190
5	180	240
6	240	300

TABLE **11.5**
Samantha's Average and Marginal Costs

Quantity (sweaters sold per day)	Average variable cost (dollars)	Average total cost (dollars)	Marginal cost (dollars)
1	____	____	
2	____	____	
3	____	____	____
4	____	____	____
5	____	____	____
6	____	____	____

3. a. More people decide that they like french fried rutabagas. As a result, the revenue from growing rutabagas rises to $4,000 a ton. Rudy's costs do not change from those in Table 11.2. Draw Rudy's new *MC* and *MR* curves in Figure 11.8.

  b. How does Rudy respond to the rise in the price of a rutabaga?

  c. If all rutabaga farmers have the same cost schedule as Rudy's, does your answer in part (b) represent the long-run equilibrium? Why?

4. a. Table 11.4 presents total costs at Samantha's Sweater Shop, a perfectly competitive firm. Use these cost figures to complete Table 11.5.

  b. In Figure 11.9 draw Samantha's *MC* curve.

FIGURE **11.8**
Rudy's New *MC* and *MR*

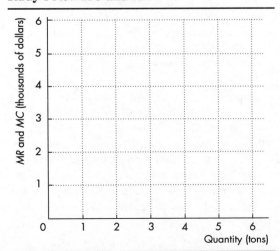

FIGURE **11.9**
Samantha's *MC* Curve and Supply Curve

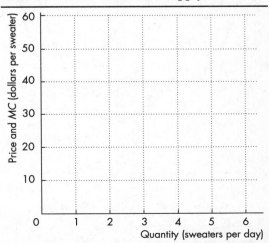

TABLE 11.6

Samantha's Supply Curve

Price (dollars per sweater)	Quantity (sweaters per day)
25	____
35	____
45	____
55	____

c. Use the costs from Table 11.5 and the graph in Figure 11.9 to determine Samantha's supply schedule in Table 11.6.

d. Draw Samantha's supply curve in Figure 11.9.

5. a. Draw a diagram illustrating the case of a perfectly competitive firm that is earning an economic profit. In the diagram, show the amount of the economic profit.

b. In a diagram, show the case of a perfectly competitive firm that is earning only a normal profit, that is, it is not incurring an economic loss nor making an economic profit.

c. Draw a diagram to illustrate the case of a perfectly competitive firm that is incurring an economic loss but is continuing to operate. Be sure to include the *AVC* curve. Show the amount of the economic loss.

FIGURE 11.10

Short Answer Problem 6

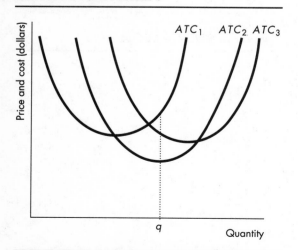

6. A firm can use three levels of capital. Figure 11.10 shows the *ATC* curves for each level; ATC_1 uses

the least amount of capital, ATC_2 the next least, and ATC_3 the most. For these three amounts of capital, carefully draw the firm's *LRAC*.

The level of output indicated by *q* can be produced by using all three levels of capital. In the long run, which amount of capital will the firm use to produce this level of output?

7. A perfectly competitive industry is at long-run equilibrium. Then there is a permanent decrease in demand for the industry's good. The industry has no external economies or diseconomies. How does the industry adjust to its new long-run equilibrium? Be sure to discuss what happens to the companies' profits and the number of firms in the industry. Also draw two diagrams showing what happens to the price and quantity during the adjustment process.

8. Why will economic profits be zero at long-run equilibrium in a perfectly competitive industry? Be sure to mention the roles played by economic profits and losses.

9. Wheat farming is a perfectly competitive industry with no external costs nor external benefits. Draw a figure showing the wheat market and identify the amount wheat that uses resources efficiently.

■ You're the Teacher

1. "I really don't get why a perfectly competitive firm wants to produce so that *MR* = *MC*. I mean, the goal of the firm is to earn the most profit possible. Why does it produce so that *MR* = *MC*? I think that it ought to want to produce so that *MR* > *MC*; that is, so that revenues exceed costs and it earns a profit." This student is making a fundamental error. Correct the student's analysis.

2. "You know, one thing that seems weird about this chapter is the claim that a business will operate even though it's losing money. I'd think that the moment a business started to incur an economic loss, unless there was some chance that the loss would be reversed in the future, the business would shut down." This student is right: A business operating even though it incurs an economic loss *does* seem weird. Can you explain why this situation happens?

Answers

■ True/False Answers

Competition

1. **F** In a perfectly competitive industry, each of the many firms produces an identical product.

2. **T** The question gives the definition of the minimum efficient scale.

3. **T** Each firm is a price taker.

4. **F** The *firm's* demand curve is horizontal, but the *market* demand curve slopes downward.

5. **F** A perfectly competitive firm is a price taker, for instance, a wheat farmer who can charge only the going price for the wheat grown.

The Firm's Decisions in Perfect Competition

6. **T** Produce the level of output so that $MR = MC$ is the rule followed to maximize profits.

7. **F** If $P < ATC$, the firm suffers an economic loss.

8. **F** If $P < ATC$, the firm suffers an economic loss but it continues to operate as long as $P > AVC$.

9. **F** The supply curve shows the amount that will be produced regardless of whether the firm earns an economic profit or not.

10. **F** The firm's supply curve is its MC curve above its AVC curve.

Output, Price, and Profit in Perfect Competition

11. **T** In the short run, depending on market demand and the firm's costs, a perfectly competitive firm can earn an economic profit, incur an economic loss, or earn a normal profit.

12. **F** In the long run, the process of entry and exit means that a perfectly competitive firm earns only a normal profit.

13. **F** Even if they do not earn an economic profit, firms remain in the industry as long as they earn a normal profit.

14. **F** A firm making zero economic profit earns a profit equal to what its owners would earn elsewhere in the best alternative business.

15. **T** In the long run, the overwhelming competition within a perfectly competitive industry forces each firm to produce as efficiently as possible.

Changing Tastes and Advancing Technology

16. **T** The increase in demand raises the price of the product, thereby allowing the firms producing it to earn an economic profit.

17. **F** The short-run economic profit from the increase in demand attracts new firms, and as the new firms produce more output, the price falls and the economic profit is eliminated.

18. **F** An increase in demand results in a higher price, but a decrease in demand results in a lower price.

19. **F** Firms that adopt the new technology lower their costs and earn a temporary economic profit.

Competition and Efficiency

20. **T** This statement conveys the general meaning of efficiency.

21. **T** Efficiency occurs when the total gains from trade are as large as possible.

22. **F** Perfect competition results in an efficient use of resources if there are no external benefits or external costs.

■ Multiple Choice

Competition

1. **d** In perfect competition, each firm produces a good identical to that of its competitors.

2. **c** The other possibilities describe industries with only a few firms, so they cannot be perfectly competitive firms.

3. **a** $MR = (\Delta TR)/\Delta q$ so in this case $MR = (\$505 - \$500)/(101 - 100) = \$5$. More directly, for a perfectly competitive firm, marginal revenue equals price.

4. **b** Because a perfectly competitive firm can always sell another unit of output at the going market price, the market price is the firm's marginal revenue.

The Firm's Decisions in Perfect Competition

5. **b** The second printer adds $100 to Paul's total profit, so it will be sold; however, the third printer would lower Paul's total profit by $50, so it will not be sold.

6. **a** The condition $MR = MC$ is necessary for the firm to be maximizing its profit.

7. **c** When the marginal costs rise, the *MC* curve shifts upward. In response, the firm decreases the amount it produces. The firm's demand curve did not change, which indicates that the (market) price is constant.

8. **d** In the short run, any type of profit or loss is possible, so that the firm might earn an economic profit, a normal profit, or incur an economic loss.

9. **c** When $P < ATC$, the firm incurs an economic loss.

10. **c** The firm produces the level of output so that $MR = MC$, 4 units of output.

11. **a** The price, $3, exceeds the average total cost of producing 4 units of output, so the firm earns an economic profit.

12. **d** As long as $P > AVC$, the firm's losses are smaller if it operates than if it shuts down.

13. **b** At prices below the minimum average variable cost, the firm shuts down and produces zero.

14. **a** At any price, the quantity supplied by the industry equals the sum of the quantities that all the firms supply.

Output, Price, and Profit in Perfect Competition

15. **d** In the long run, perfectly competitive firms produce at the minimum *ATC*, but that is not necessarily the case in the short run.

16. **c** The possibility of earning an economic profit leads to entry into the industry.

17. **c** The entry of new firms lowers the price and economic profits, thereby driving the industry toward its long-run equilibrium.

18. **b** Free entry and exit into the industry mean that only a normal profit is possible in the long run.

19. **d** Figure 11.6 illustrates the long-run equilibrium for a perfectly competitive firm.

20. **d** $MR = MC$ means that the firm is maximizing its profit; P = minimum *LRAC* occurs because competition forces firms to produce as efficiently as possible; $P = ATC$ means that the firm is earning only a normal profit.

Changing Tastes and Advancing Technology

21. **b** When the price falls, each firm moves down its *MC* curve and produces less. This response — each firm producing less — accounts for the re-

duction in the quantity supplied along the market supply curve when the price falls.

22. **b** Firms continue to leave as long as they incur an economic loss, thereby driving the price higher and reducing the survivors' economic losses.

23. **d** Answer (d) defines external economies.

24. **b** In the short run, both the price and quantity fall, and firms incur an economic loss. The economic loss means that firms leave the industry and as the supply decreases, the price rises from its initial fall, but the amount of the industry output continues to decrease.

25. **a** The diseconomies mean that, as the industry expands its output, firms' costs rise. As a result, in the long run the price, which equals the (higher) average total cost, is higher than it was initially.

26. **d** New technology creates economic profits, giving firms the incentive to adopt the technology. The increased competition from these firms ultimately eliminates the economic profit.

Competition and Efficiency

27. **a** Presence of external benefits means that a perfectly competitive industry will not be efficient.

28. **d** All the answers correctly characterize an efficient use of resources.

29. **c** Efficiency is achieved when $P = MB = MC$.

30. **c** Competition increases the likelihood that a market uses resources efficiently because, as we see in the next chapter, the lack of competition usually leads to inefficiency.

■ Answers to Short Answer Problems

1. If a firm in a perfectly competitive industry charged a price even slightly higher than the going equilibrium market price, it would lose all of its sales. So, it will not charge a price above the equilibrium price. Because it can sell all it wants at the going price, the firm would not be able to increase its sales by lowering its price. So, the firm will not charge a price below the market price because such a lower price would decrease its total revenue and thereby decrease its profits.

2. a. Table 11.2 shows that Rudy's profit-maximizing quantity of rutabagas is 2 tons. Rudy's economic profit when growing 2 tons of rutabagas is $1,500 (Rudy's total revenue of $4,000 minus

his total cost of $2,500). This amount exceeds his economic profit at any other level of production.

TABLE **11.7**

Short Answer Problem 2 (b)

Quantity (tons)	Marginal cost (dollars)	Marginal revenue (dollars)
1		
	1,500	2,000
2		
	2,500	2,000
3		
	3,500	2,000
4		
	4,500	2,000
5		
	5,500	2,000
6		

b. Table 11.7 shows the marginal cost and marginal revenue schedules. Marginal cost is defined as $(\Delta TC)/\Delta q$, with ΔTC the change in total cost and Δq the change in quantity. The marginal cost from 1 to 2 tons grown equals ($2,500 − $1,000)/(2 − 1), or $1,500. Marginal revenue can be calculated two ways. First, for a perfectly competitive firm, marginal revenue equals price. Hence marginal revenue is $2,000. Alternatively, the definition of marginal revenue is $(\Delta TR)/\Delta q$, where ΔTR is the change in total revenue. Using this formula, the marginal revenue from 1 to 2 tons is ($4,000 − $2,000)/(2 − 1) = $2,000.

c. Figure 11.11 shows the *MC* and *MR* curves.

d. Table 11.7 shows that Rudy should grow 2 tons of rutabagas. The marginal cost of increasing from 2 tons to 3 tons is $2,500, which exceeds the marginal revenue of the increase. So increasing from 2 to 3 tons would reduce Rudy's profit. Similarly, Figure 11.11 shows that the marginal revenue and marginal cost curves intersect at 2 tons, also indicating that Rudy should grow 2 tons of rutabagas.

e. The answers in parts (a) and (d) are the same: Rudy grows 2 tons of rutabagas. Note the important point that the analysis based on *marginal* revenue and cost, in part (d), gives the same answer as the analysis based on *total* revenue and cost, in part (a).

FIGURE **11.11**

Short Answer Problem 2 (c)

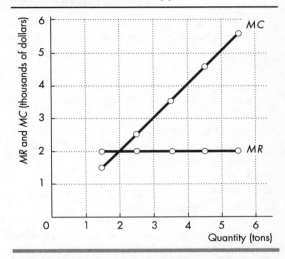

FIGURE **11.12**

Short Answer Problem 3 (a)

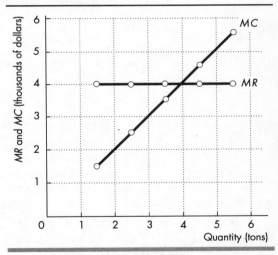

3. a. Figure 11.12 shows Rudy's new *MR* curve. The marginal cost curve does not change from before. Rudy's marginal revenue equals the price of a ton of rutabagas. The rise in the price to $4,000 shifts Rudy's *MR* curve (which is the same as Rudy's demand curve) upward to $4,000.

b. As Figure 11.12 shows, with the higher price for a ton of rutabagas, Rudy increases the quantity of rutabagas he grows to 4 tons.

c. The answer in part (b) cannot be the long-run equilibrium. When Rudy grows 4 tons of rutabagas, his total revenue is $16,000 and his total cost (from Table 11.2) is $8,500. Rudy is earning an economic profit of $7,500. The presence of an economic profit attracts new farmers to the rutabaga market. As new farmers begin to grow rutabagas, the market supply curve for these vegetables shifts rightward, lowering the price of a ton of rutabagas and eliminating some of the economic profit. New farmers continue to enter and the price of a rutabaga continues to fall as long as an economic profit exists. Only when the economic profit is entirely eliminated is the long-run equilibrium attained.

TABLE **11.8**

Short Answer Problem 4 (a)

Quantity (sweaters sold per day)	Average variable cost (dollars)	Average total cost (dollars)	Marginal cost (dollars)
1	40.00	100.00	
			20.00
2	30.00	60.00	
			30.00
3	30.00	50.00	
			40.00
4	32.50	47.50	
			50.00
5	36.00	48.00	
			60.00
6	40.00	50.00	

4. a. Table 11.8 contains Samantha's average costs and marginal cost. Average variable cost equals $(TVC)/q$, where TVC is total variable cost and q is quantity. Hence average variable cost when Samantha sells 3 sweaters a day is $90/3 or $30.

Average total cost is computed in a similar fashion, namely $(TC)/q$, with TC total cost. So for the sale of 3 sweaters per day, average total cost is $150/3 or $50.

Finally, marginal cost is $(\Delta TC)/\Delta q$. Hence the marginal cost of going from 2 to 3 sweaters sold per day is ($150-$120)/(3-2) or $30.

b. Figure 11.13 shows the MC curve.

c. Table 11.9 contains Samantha's supply schedule. The supply curve is the same as her marginal cost curve above the average variable cost curve.

FIGURE **11.13**

Short Answer Problem 4 (b)

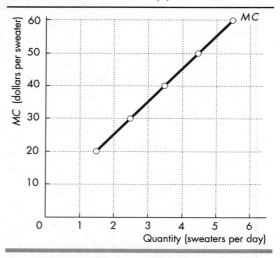

TABLE **11.9**

Short Answer Problem 4 (c)

Price (dollars per sweater)	Quantity supplied (sweaters per day)
25	0
35	3
45	4
55	5

So when the price of a sweater is $25, Figure 11.13 shows that Samantha would supply 2 sweaters except for the fact that this price is below the average variable cost. Hence when the price is $25, Samantha shuts down and does not supply any sweaters. At $35, Figure 11.13 shows that Samantha supplies 3 sweaters. Because this price is above her average variable cost, Samantha supplies 3 sweaters. The rest of Samantha's supply curve is obtained from Figure 11.13 in a similar manner.

d. Figure 11.14 (on the next page) shows Samantha's supply curve. At prices above $30, that is, at prices above the minimum average variable cost, the supply curve is identical to Samantha's marginal cost curve. For prices below $30, Samantha supplies no sweaters.

FIGURE **11.14**
Short Answer Problem 4 (d)

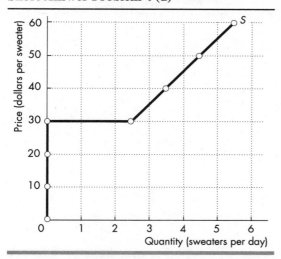

FIGURE **11.16**
Short Answer Problem 5 (b)

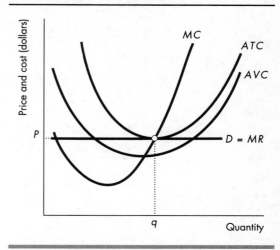

FIGURE **11.15**
Short Answer Problem 5 (a)

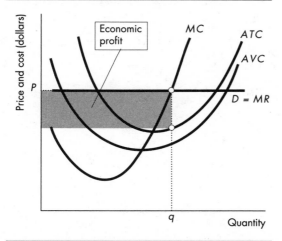

FIGURE **11.17**
Short Answer Problem 5 (c)

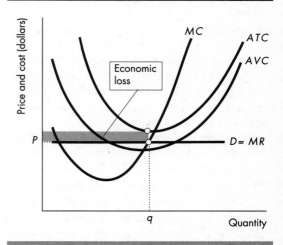

5. a. Figure 11.15 shows the case in which the firm
       earns an economic profit. To maximize its profit,
       the firm produces the level of output such that
       $MR = MC$. Because $P > ATC$, the firm is earning
       an economic profit, as shown in the figure.

    b. A perfectly competitive firm earning a normal
       profit is illustrated in Figure 11.16. To maximize
       its profit the firm produces q, the level of output
       that makes $MR = MC$. Because $P = ATC$, the
       firm is earning only a normal profit.

    c. Figure 11.17 illustrates the case of a firm that in-
       curs an economic loss but continues to operate.
       The firm suffers an economic loss because, at the
       profit-maximizing (loss-minimizing) level of
       output q, $P < ATC$. But the firm minimizes its
       loss by operating because $P > AVC$.

FIGURE **11.18**

Short Answer Problem 6

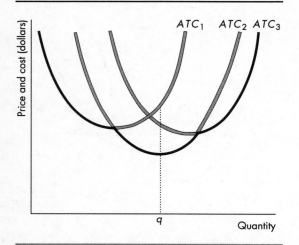

FIGURE **11.19**

Short Answer Problem 7

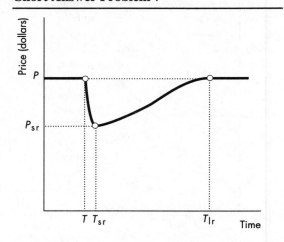

6. The dark line in Figure 11.18 is the *LRAC* curve. The dark line is constructed from the *ATC* curve that has the lowest average total cost for each level of output.

   When producing *q*, in the long run the firm will use the middle amount of capital because ATC_2 has the lowest average total cost for producing this level of output. The firm might need to adjust its capital stock to reach this amount. In the short run the firm might have, say, less than the middle amount of capital so that in the short run the business might have average total costs of ATC_1. Eventually, however, the firm will increase its capital stock to reach average total cost curve ATC_2.

7. In the short run, the decrease in demand means the price falls. In response to the fall in price, each firm produces less (some firms might even shut down if the price falls below their minimum average variable cost), so the market quantity also decreases. Figures 11.19 and 11.20 illustrate these changes: The price falls from *P* to P_{sr} and the quantity decreases from *Q* to Q_{sr} at (short-run) time T_{sr}.

   In the initial situation, each business was earning zero economic profit. The fall in price now means that firms incur economic losses. Because the decrease in demand is permanent, these losses induce some firms to leave the industry. This exit shifts the market supply curve leftward, causing a rise in the market price. The rising price reduces the economic losses for the remaining firms. Firms continue to

FIGURE **11.20**

Short Answer Problem 7

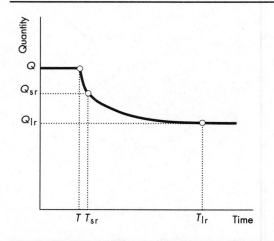

exit until the economic losses are totally eliminated. Costs have not been affected by the decrease in demand because there are no external economies or diseconomies. So the price must continue rising until, as shown in Figure 11.19, it reaches its original level in the new long-run equilibrium at time T_{lr}. At that time, each firm produces as much as it did originally. But as shown in Figure 11.20, the equilibrium quantity produced by the total industry is less than initially (*Q* versus Q_{lr}) because the number of firms in the industry has decreased.

8. In a perfectly competitive industry, the existence of positive economic profits attract the entry of newcomers. Entry of new firms shifts the market supply curve rightward, causing the price to fall and firms' profits to decline. However, entry continues as long as there are positive economic profits. Similarly, the existence of economic losses result in firms exiting the industry. Exit shifts the market supply curve leftward, causing the price to rise and (surviving) firms' losses to decline. Exit continues as long as economic losses are being incurred. So only when economic profits and losses are zero, so that a normal profit is earned, is there no tendency for firms to enter or exit the industry. The industry is in long-run equilibrium only when economic profits are zero because economic profits or losses are the signals to enter or exit an industry.

FIGURE **11.21**
Short Answer Problem 9

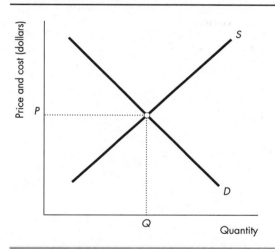

9. Figure 11.21 shows the efficient quantity of wheat as Q. In the absence of external costs or benefits, it is a remarkable result that the efficient level is also the equilibrium level!

■ You're the Teacher

1. "Look, you're making just one mistake. It's an easy mistake to make, but it's a *big* one! The idea is that a firm wants to maximize its *total* profit. That is, it wants to maximize the difference between its total revenue and its total costs. You're confusing these terms with marginal revenue and marginal cost.

Remember that the word 'marginal' means 'additional'. So, marginal revenue means additional revenue, and marginal cost means additional cost. "Now, suppose that MR is larger than MC. For instance, suppose that a wheat farmer finds that the marginal revenue from growing an additional acre of wheat is $5,000 and that the marginal cost of doing so is only $3,000. Then, growing the additional acre of wheat adds more to the farmer's revenue than it adds to the cost, so this acre will add to the farmer's total profit. In particular, this acre adds $2,000 (marginal revenue of $5,000 minus marginal cost of $3,000) to the farmer's total profit. The farmer will want to grow this additional acre of wheat.

"Next, suppose that the next acre still has a marginal revenue of $5,000, but that it has a marginal cost of $4,000. MR still is larger than MC, so this acre will continue to add to the farmer's total profit. It adds less (only $1,000), but the key point is that it adds. So the farmer will plant this acre, too.

"Now look, I know that the added profit from the second acre isn't as much as the added profit from the first acre. But who cares? As long as the acre adds to the profit, the farmer, who wants to get the maximum possible total profit, will still grow the second acre of wheat. The deal is that as long as the acre adds to total profit, the farmer will grow more wheat. In other words, as long as $MR > MC$, the additional acre adds additional profit, so the farmer will put the acreage into production. Only when $MR = MC$ does the additional acre not add to profit. So the farmer simply stops adding acres when $MR = MC$."

2. "At first thought, it does seem weird that a business would continue to produce even though it's losing money. I couldn't get the point, either, until I thought about it a bit. Here's the idea: Whenever the price of output falls below the break-even point (the minimum average total cost) but remains above the shutdown point (the minimum average variable cost), the firm continues to produce even though it's incurring an economic loss. The key here is that the firm's owner, when suffering an economic loss, wants to make the loss as small as possible.

"If the owner shuts down, the firm still must pay its fixed costs. (Recall that fixed costs are independent of output; whether the firm produces 10 million units or 0 units, fixed costs remain the same.) So if the owner shuts down, the total loss will equal the total fixed cost. The owner compares this loss to the loss incurred by operating. If the price exceeds the average variable cost, the owner loses less by operating the business. When $P > AVC$, the firm earns enough revenue to pay all its variable costs and have some revenue left over to cover part of its fixed costs. In this case, by operating the business, the owner loses less than the total amount of the fixed costs. The loss is smaller than would be incurred by shutting down, so the owner will operate the business as long as $P > AVC$. But, if $P < AVC$, the loss from running the business exceeds the total fixed cost because the business's revenue isn't sufficient to cover all of the variable costs. Hence when the average variable costs exceed the price, the owner will close the business."

Chapter Quiz

1. In perfect competition, the product of a single firm
   a. has an infinite elasticity of demand.
   b. is sold under many different brand names.
   c. is unique to that firm and cannot be copied by others.
   d. has many perfect complements.

2. A perfectly competitive firm faces a
   a. downward sloping demand curve.
   b. downward sloping marginal revenue curve.
   c. horizontal marginal revenue curve.
   d. downward sloping marginal cost curve.

3. In the case of a perfectly competitive firm, as the firm sells more output, the price of the product _____ and the marginal revenue _____.
   a falls; falls
   b. falls; does not change
   c. does not change; falls
   d. does not change; does not change

4. When a perfectly competitive firm is making zero economic profit, the owner is
   a. going to close the business in the long run.
   b. incurring an accounting loss.
   c. earning the same profit he or she could obtain elsewhere on the average.
   d. will boost output to earn a larger profit.

5. Even though it is incurring an economic loss, it pays a firm to stay open if price is
   a. above minimum average variable cost.
   b. below minimum average variable cost.
   c. above total variable cost.
   d. below total variable cost.

6. A perfectly competitive firm is producing at the point where its marginal cost equals price. If the firm decreases its output, total revenue will _____ and total profit will _____.
   a. rise; rise
   b. rise; fall
   c. fall; rise
   d. fall; fall

7. The supply curve for a perfectly competitive firm is the same as its marginal cost curve
   a. above the horizontal axis.
   b. above the minimum average variable cost.
   c. below the minimum average variable cost.
   d. below the average total cost.

8. The industry supply curve is the sum of the
   a. supply curves of all the firms.
   b. average variable cost curves of all the firms.
   c. average total cost curves of all the firms.
   d. average fixed cost curves of all the firms.

9. In a perfectly competitive industry, a permanent increase in demand creates a temporary economic _____ and _____ by some firms.
   a. profit; entry
   b. profit; exit
   c. loss; exit
   d. loss; entry

10. A perfectly competitive firm _____ earn an economic profit in the short run and _____ earn an economic profit in the long run.
    a. can; can
    b. can; cannot
    c. cannot; can
    d. cannot; cannot

The answers for this Chapter Quiz are on page 368

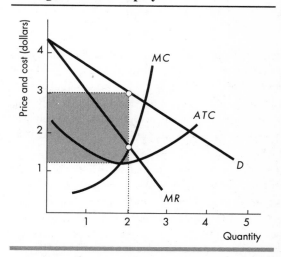

Chapter 12 MONOPOLY

Key Concepts

■ Market Power

Monopolies have **market power,** the ability to affect the market price by changing the total quantity offered for sale. A **monopoly** is an industry with one supplier of a good that has no close substitutes and the supplier is protected by a barrier to entry. Barriers to entry include:

♦ Control over a key resource.

♦ Legal barriers to entry (public franchise, government license, or patent) create **legal monopolies**.

♦ Natural barriers to entry can lead to **natural monopoly**, which occurs when economies of scale (which create a downward sloping *ATC* curve) are so large that one firm can supply the market at lower cost than two or more firms.

Monopolists can sell a larger quantity only by charging a lower price. Monopolies can price discriminate or charge a single price.

♦ **Price-discrimination** —selling different units of a good for different prices, so some customers pay a lower price than others for the good, or an individual consumer pays a lower price for larger purchases.

♦ **Single-price monopoly** — charges the same price to all its customers for every unit of output.

■ Single-Price Monopoly's Output and Price Decision

♦ The monopoly firm's demand curve is the market demand curve.

♦ At each level of output, marginal revenue for a monopoly is less than its price ($MR < P$).

In moving down the monopoly's demand curve:

♦ when demand is elastic, *MR* is positive and total revenue rises with output.

♦ when demand is unit elastic, *MR* is zero and total revenue is at its maximum.

♦ when demand is inelastic, *MR* is negative and total revenue falls with output.

A monopoly's cost curves are similar to those of a competitive firm. A profit-maximizing monopoly produces the output at which $MR = MC$. (This rule is the same used by a competitive firm.) The monopoly uses the demand curve to determine the maximum price that consumers are willing to pay for this quantity of output. Figure 12.1 shows a profit maximizing level of output, 2, and price, $3.

FIGURE 12.1
A Single-Price Monopoly

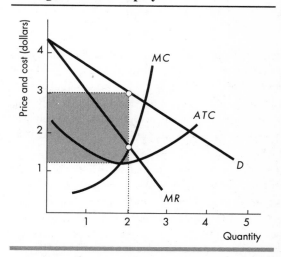

♦ As Figure 12.1 demonstrates, *P* exceeds *MC* for a monopoly.

♦ Because $P > ATC,$ the single-price monopoly in Figure 12.1 earns an economic profit equal to the area of the shaded rectangle.

♦ Barriers to entry prevent new companies from entering the market, so a monopoly's economic profit can last indefinitely.

■ Single-Price Monopoly and Competition Compared

Compared to a perfectly competitive industry, a single-price monopoly with the same costs:

♦ charges a higher price.

♦ produces less output.

FIGURE **12.2**
A Single-Price Monopoly's Deadweight Loss

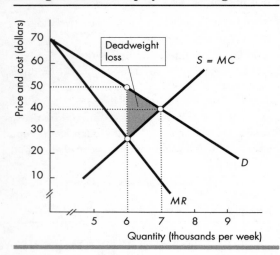

Figure 12.2 illustrates these results. If the industry was perfectly competitive, 7,000 units would be produced and the price would be $40. (The price and quantity are determined by where the demand and supply curves cross.) In comparison, as a single-price monopoly with the same costs, 6,000 units are produced and the price is $50.

By restricting its output to be less than that of a competitive industry, a single-price monopoly creates a deadweight loss. The deadweight loss is comprised of lost consumer and producer surplus. Figure 12.2 illustrates the deadweight loss from a single-price monopoly.

Rent seeking is any attempt to capture consumer surplus, producer surplus, or economic profit. Rent seekers try to buy or can create a monopoly.

Resources used in rent seeking are a cost to society. In equilibrium, rent seeking continues until the economic profit from the monopoly is eliminated.

■ Price Discrimination

Price discrimination occurs when a firm charges different prices for a good. Price discrimination transfers consumer surplus — the value a consumer receives from a good minus the price paid — away from buyers and to the firm, thereby increasing the monopoly's profit. Price discrimination can occur among units of a good, so that larger orders get a discount, or among groups of buyers, so that some buyers pay a lower price.

Price discrimination among groups requires that:

♦ groups of consumers with different willingness to pay exist;

♦ the members of each group are easily identified;

♦ and, no resales of the good are made from one group to another.

With price discrimination, the group with the high average willingness to pay pays a high price and the group with the low average willingness to pay pays a low price.

♦ **Perfect price discrimination** extracts all the consumer surplus by charging each consumer the maximum price that he or she is willing to pay for each unit of output purchased.

The more perfectly a monopoly can price discriminate, the closer its output is to the competitive level. A perfectly price-discriminating monopoly eliminates *all* the consumer surplus, but does not result in a deadweight loss, so it is efficient.

■ Monopoly Policy Issues

A monopoly might have some advantages for society:

♦ It might increase the incentive to innovate, but the empirical evidence on this possible gain is mixed.

♦ It might be able to capture *economies of scale*, when an increase in output lowers average total cost, or *economies of scope*, when an increase in the range of products produced lowers average total cost.

When economies of scale are large enough, a natural monopoly results. Natural monopolies, illustrated in Figure 12.3 (on the next page) are usually regulated by the government.

♦ Left unregulated, the firm in Figure 12.3 would maximize its profit by charging P_m and producing Q_m.

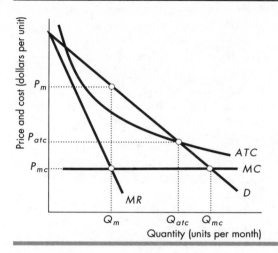

FIGURE **12.3**
A Natural Monopoly

♦ A **marginal cost pricing rule** requires the firm to set its price equal to its marginal cost. In Figure 12.3, the firm charges P_{mc} and produces Q_{mc}. The firm produces the efficient amount of output but incurs an economic loss.

♦ An **average cost pricing rule** requires the firm to set its price equal to its average cost. In Figure 12.3, the firm charges P_{atc} and produces Q_{atc}. The firm produces inefficient amount of output but earns a normal profit.

Helpful Hints

1. **WHY STUDY PERFECT COMPETITION AND MONOPOLY?** The opposite extreme from perfect competition is monopoly. In perfect competition there are many firms that can decide only the quantity they produce but not the price to be charged. In contrast, a monopoly is a single firm that sets both its quantity and price. Understanding the differences between perfect competition and monopoly is valuable because these two industry structures are the ends of the competition spectrum. If competition within an industry heats up, the industry moves closer to behaving like a perfectly competitive industry; if competition dries up, the industry's output and price approach those of a monopoly.

2. **UNDERSTANDING MARGINAL REVENUE FOR A MONOPOLY:** In a monopoly, there is only one firm, so the downward sloping market demand curve is also the firm's demand curve. If a single-price monopoly wants to sell one more unit of output, it must lower its price. Selling another unit thus has two effects on revenue:

   ♦ First, the sale of an additional unit raises revenue by the amount of the (new, lower) price. If this effect was the sole effect, the marginal revenue would equal the price. (This effect is the only one for a perfectly competitive firm, so for these firms marginal revenue equals the price.)

   ♦ Second, because the firm also lowers the price on all the units it had previously sold, revenue from these units falls. (This effect is absent from a perfectly competitive firm because it does not need to lower its price in order to sell an additional unit of output.)

   By itself, the first effect yields marginal revenue equal to the price, but the second effect subtracts from the first. Hence marginal revenue is less than the price. Therefore, for a monopoly, the marginal revenue curve lies below the demand curve.

3. **THE "*MR* = *MC*" RULE TO MAXIMIZE PROFITS:** To maximize its profit, a monopoly produces the level of output such that $MC = MR$. This rule is the same one followed by a perfectly competitive firm. Any profit-maximizing firm will produce a unit of output if $MR > MC$ because the added revenue from the unit, the marginal revenue, exceeds the added cost, the marginal cost. As a result, producing this unit adds to the firm's total profit. Similarly, any profit-maximizing firm will not produce a unit of output if $MR < MC$ because producing the unit reduces the firm's total profit. Hence regardless of whether the firm is a monopoly or perfectly competitive, it produces at the level of output that sets $MR = MC$.

Questions

■ True/False and Explain

Market Power

1. Barriers to entry are essential to a monopoly.

2. Patents grant the patent owner a legal monopoly.

3. A single-price monopoly charges each consumer the highest single price the consumer will pay.

Single-Price Monopoly's Output and Price Decisions

4. A difference between a perfectly competitive firm and a monopoly is that the monopolist's decisions about how much to product affect the good's price.

5. For a single-price monopoly, marginal revenue, *MR*, equals price, *P*.

6. To maximize their profits, both monopolies and perfectly competitive firms produce the level of output that sets $MR = MC$.

7. When a single-price monopoly is maximizing its profit, $P > MC$.

8. A monopoly can earn an economic profit indefinitely.

Single-Price Monopoly and Competition Compared

9. Monopolies decrease the deadweight loss from perfectly competitive industries.

10. In moving from perfect competition to single-price monopoly, all the surplus lost by consumers is captured by the monopoly.

11. Rent seeking is a cost to society of monopoly.

Price Discrimination

12. Price discrimination is an attempt by a monopolist to capture the producer surplus.

13. If a monopoly can successfully price discriminate, it can increase its profit.

14. Compared to a single-price monopoly, a price-discriminating monopoly reduces the amount of consumer surplus.

15. Price discrimination works only for goods that can be resold.

Monopoly Policy Issues

16. There are no possible benefits to society from a monopoly.

17. A natural monopoly is a firm that controls a vital natural resource.

18. A marginal cost pricing rule imposed on a natural monopoly creates an efficient use of resources.

■ Multiple Choice

Market Power

1. Suppose that one taxi company in your city is granted a license by the city so that it is the only cab company that may operate within the city limits. Granting this license is an example of a
   a. natural barrier to entry.
   b. case in which a single firm controls a resource necessary to produce the good.
   c. price-discriminating monopoly.
   d. legal barrier to entry.

2. Which of the following is a *natural* barrier to the entry of new firms in an industry?
   a. Licensing
   b. Economies of scale
   c. Issuing a patent
   d. Granting a public franchise

3. In order to sell more output, a single-price monopoly must _____ its price and a price-discriminating monopoly must _____ its price.
   a. raise; raise
   b. raise; lower
   c. lower; raise
   d. lower; lower

Single-Price Monopoly's Output and Price Decisions

4. Max's Christmas tree lot has a monopoly on sales of Christmas trees. To increase his sales from 100 trees to 101 trees, he must drop the price of all his trees from $28 to $27. What is Max's marginal revenue when he lowers his price and increases his sales from 100 to 101 trees?
   a. $2,800
   b. $28
   c. $27
   d. −$73

5. A monopolist finds that when it produces 20 units of output, its demand is elastic. At this level of output,
   a. its marginal revenue necessarily is positive.
   b. its marginal revenue necessarily is zero.
   c. its marginal revenue necessarily is negative.
   d. none of the above is correct because the marginal revenue does not depend upon the elasticity of demand.

6. A monopolist finds that the marginal revenue from producing another unit of output exceeds the marginal cost of the unit. Then, to increase its profit, the monopolist will
   a. produce the unit.
   b. not produce the unit, but not cut back its production at all.
   c. not produce the unit and cut back its production by at least one unit.
   d. do none of the above.

7. If a monopoly is producing a level of output such that marginal cost exceeds marginal revenue, to increase its profits the firm
   a. should raise its price and decrease its output.
   b. should lower its price and increase its output.
   c. should lower its price and decrease its output.
   d. none of the above because the firm is incurring an economic loss and it cannot alter this fact.

8. Which of the following is true for a single-price monopoly?
   a. Price always equals marginal cost, that is, $P = MC$ at all levels of output.
   b. For all levels of output, price equals marginal revenue, that is, $P = MR$.
   c. In the short run, the monopoly might earn a normal profit or incur an economic loss.
   d. None of the above because all the statements are false.

9. A single-price monopolist will maximize its profits if it produces the amount of output such that
   a. price equals marginal cost, that is, $P = MC$.
   b. price equals marginal revenue, that is, $P = MR$.
   c. marginal revenue equals marginal cost, that is, $MR = MC$.
   d. price equals average total cost, that is, $P = ATC$.

10. Because of an increase in labor costs, a monopoly finds that its MC and ATC have risen. Presuming that the monopoly does not shut down, it will _____ its price and _____ the quantity it produces.
    a. raise; increase
    b. raise; decrease
    c. lower; increase
    d. lower; decrease

FIGURE **12.4**

Multiple Choice Questions 11 and 12

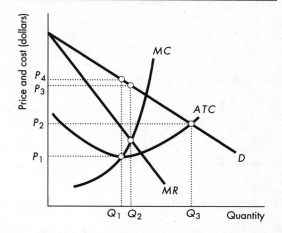

11. In Figure 12.4, a profit-maximizing single-price monopoly will produce
    a. Q_1.
    b. Q_2.
    c. Q_3.
    d. None of the above.

12. In Figure 12.4, a profit-maximizing single-price monopoly will set a price of
    a. P_1.
    b. P_2.
    c. P_3.
    d. P_4.

13. In the short run a monopoly can
    a. earn only an economic profit.
    b. earn only an economic profit or a normal profit.
    c. earn only a normal profit.
    d. earn an economic profit, or a normal profit, or incur an economic loss.

14. A monopoly might be able to earn an economic profit
    a. only in the short run.
    b. only in the long run.
    c. indefinitely, that is, in both the short run and the long run.
    d. The premise of the question is wrong because a monopoly can never earn an economic profit.

Single-Price Monopoly and Competition Compared

15. Compared to a perfectly competitive industry with the same cost, the amount of output produced by a single-price monopoly is
    a. more than the competitive industry.
    b. the same as the competitive industry.
    c. less than the competitive industry.
    d. not comparable to the competitive industry.

16. Compared to a perfectly competitive industry, the price charged by a single-price monopoly with the same costs is
    a. more than the competitive industry.
    b. the same as the competitive industry.
    c. less than the competitive industry.
    d. not comparable to the competitive industry.

Figure 12.5 illustrates a single-price monopoly. Use it for the next three questions

FIGURE 12.5
Multiple Choice Questions 17, 18, 19

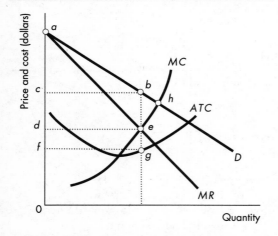

17. The deadweight loss in Figure 12.5 is the area
    a. *abc.*
    b. *bcde.*
    c. *bcfg.*
    d. *beh.*

18. The consumer surplus in Figure 12.5 is the area
    a. *abc.*
    b. *bcde.*
    c. *bcfg.*
    d. *beh.*

19. The economic profit in Figure 12.5 is the area
    a. *abc.*
    b. *bcde.*
    c. *bcfg.*
    d. *beh.*

20. If a perfectly competitive industry becomes a single-price monopoly and costs do not change, which of the following allocations of costs and benefits is correct?
    a. The producer benefits; demanders and society are harmed.
    b. The producer and society are harmed; demanders benefit.
    c. The producer, demanders, and society are harmed.
    d. The producer is harmed but demanders and society benefit.

21. If a single-price monopoly is broken up so that it becomes a perfectly competitive industry and costs do not change, which of the following statements describing the costs and benefits is correct?
    a. The producer benefits; demanders and society are harmed.
    b. The producer and society are harmed; demanders benefit.
    c. The producer, demanders, and society benefit.
    d. The producer is harmed; demanders and society benefit.

22. Activity for the purpose of creating a monopoly is
    a. not legal in the United States.
    b. called rent seeking.
    c. called price discrimination.
    d. called legal monopoly.

Price Discrimination

23. In order to successfully price discriminate, a firm must be able to
    a. reduce its *MC.*
    b. distinguish between customers who have different willingness to pay.
    c. encourage many resales of its good among its customers.
    d. exert a non-price control over the number of demanders who will buy its good.

24. Price discrimination allows a monopoly to
    a. lower its marginal cost.
    b. reduce its producer surplus.
    c. increase its total revenue.
    d. charge all customers a higher price.

25. A monopoly that is able to perfectly price discriminate
    a. charges everyone the lowest price that they want to pay for each unit purchased.
    b. produces less output than it would were it a single-price monopoly.
    c. eliminates consumer surplus.
    d. creates a larger deadweight loss than it would if it were a single-price monopoly.

26. A monopoly movie theater discovers that the average willingness to pay for watching movies is higher at 8 P.M. than at 5 P.M. As a result, if a monopoly movie theater wants to price discriminate and earn a larger profit, it charges
    a. a higher price at 8 P.M.
    b. the same price at 5 P.M. as at 8 P.M.
    c. a lower price at 8 P.M.
    d. There is not enough information given to answer the question.

27. Business travelers usually pay higher airline fares than families on a vacation. So,
    a. business travelers aren't maximizing their utility.
    b. business travelers have a higher willingness to pay than do vacation travelers.
    c. the MC of serving vacation travelers is lower than that of serving business travelers.
    d. vacation travelers have a greater demand for air travel than do business travelers.

Monopoly Policy Issues
28. Which of the following situations might be a gain to society from monopoly?
    a. Monopolies do not waste resources trying to innovate.
    b. Monopolies might be able to capture economies of scale.
    c. Monopolies might be able to price discriminate, thereby boosting consumer surplus.
    d. Monopolies might earn an economic profit in the long run.

29. A monopoly has economies of scope if
    a. average total cost declines as output decreases.
    b. average total cost declines as output increases.
    c. total profit declines as output increases.
    d. average total cost declines as the number of different goods produced increases.

30. A natural monopoly
    a. is usually regulated by the government.
    b. earns an economic profit if it must use a marginal cost pricing rule.
    c. has an average total cost curve that is positively sloped until it crosses the demand curve.
    d. has a demand curve that is positively sloped.

■ **Short Answer**

1. Why is marginal revenue less than price for a single-price monopoly?

2. In a small college town, Laura's Bookstore has a monopoly in selling textbooks. Laura's fixed costs are $100, and her total costs are shown in Table 12.1.
    a. Complete Table 12.1 by computing average total cost and marginal cost.

TABLE **12.1**

Short Answer Problem 2 (a)

Quantity (books per hour)	Total cost (dollars)	Average total cost (ATC)	Marginal cost (MC)
9	247.00	27.44	
			9.00
10	256.00	____	
			____
11	267.00	____	
			____
12	280.00	____	
			____
13	295.00	____	
			____
14	312.00	____	
			____
15	331.00	____	
			____
16	352.00	____	
			____
17	375.00	____	
			____
18	400.00	____	
			____
19	427.00	____	
			____
20	456.00	____	
			____
21	487.00	____	

b. Table 12.2 lists points on the demand curve facing Laura's Bookstore. Copy the marginal costs from Table 12.1 and complete the table.

c. What is Laura's profit-maximizing quantity of output? At what price will she sell her books? What is her total economic profit?

d. In Figure 12.6, plot the demand curve and the *MR*, *ATC*, and *MC* curves corresponding to the data in parts (a) and (b). Show the equilibrium output and price. On your diagram, illustrate the area that equals Laura's economic profit.

TABLE 12.2
Short Answer Problem 2 (b)

Quantity demanded (books per hour)	Price (dollars per book)	Total revenue (dollars)	Marginal revenue (MR)	Marginal cost (MC)
9	57.00	513.00		
			47.00	9.00
10	56.00	____		
11	55.00	____	____	____
12	54.00	____	____	____
13	53.00	____	____	____
14	52.00	____	____	____
15	51.00	____	____	____
16	50.00	____	____	____
17	49.00	____	____	____
18	48.00	____	____	____
19	47.00	____	____	____
20	46.00	____	____	____
21	45.00	____		

3. a. Laura's cost curves are unchanged from problem 2, but now consumers decrease their demand. Table 12.3 lists some points on the new demand curve. Complete the table by copying the marginal costs from Table 12.1, and by computing the new total revenue and marginal revenue.

b. What is Laura's new profit-maximizing quantity of output? At what price does she now sell her books? What is her total profit? Explain your answers.

FIGURE 12.6
Short Answer Problem 2

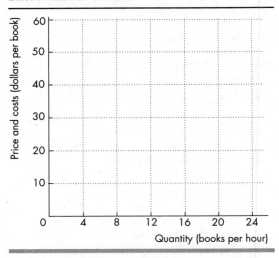

TABLE 12.3
Short Answer Problem 3 (a)

Quantity demanded (books per hour)	Price (dollars per book)	Total revenue (dollars)	Marginal revenue (MR)	Marginal cost (MC)
9	24.50	220.50		
			19.50	9.00
10	24.00	____		
11	23.50	____	____	____
12	23.00	____	____	____
13	22.50	____	____	____
14	22.00	____	____	____
15	21.50	____	____	____
16	21.00	____	____	____
17	20.50	____	____	____
18	20.00	____	____	____
19	19.50	____	____	____
20	19.00	____	____	____
21	18.50	____		

FIGURE **12.7**
Short Answer Problem 4

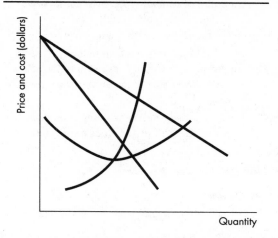

4. In Figure 12.7 label the curves. Show the amount this single-price monopolist will produce and the price it will charge. Indicate the firm's economic profit and show the deadweight loss created.

5. Why can a monopoly — but not a perfectly competitive firm — earn an economic profit in the long run?

6. Explain why the output of a perfectly competitive industry is greater than the output of the same industry if it is a single-price monopoly.

7. Derek is the owner of the only movie theater in town. By hiring several well-trained economists, Derek learns that the people watching movies after 8 P.M. have a much higher average willingness to pay than people watching at 5 P.M. The costs of showing a movie are identical at 5 P.M. and 8 P.M. To maximize his profit, what should Derek do? Give him some specific advice, including drawing him a diagram or two. (Derek can get his economists to interpret your diagrams as long as you label all the axes and all the curves.)

8. Suppose that your city grants one pizza delivery service a legal monopoly on delivering pizzas; all other pizza delivery services must close.

    a. What will happen to the price and quantity of delivered pizzas?

    b. What will happen to the profit of the owner who has been granted the monopoly?

    c. Suppose that the owner offers to sell the pizza delivery company to you. Would you be able to earn an economic profit? Be careful when you answer this question; think about the price the previous owner will charge you for the business.

9. Three industries have the same market demand and identical cost curves. Industry A is perfectly competitive, industry B is a single-price monopoly, and industry C is a monopoly able to perfectly price discriminate.

    a. Draw a figure showing the (downward sloping) market demand curve (label it D); the marginal revenue curve (label it MR); the marginal cost curve (label it MC); and the average total cost curve (label it ATC).

    b. In the figure, identify how much each industry produces by labeling the outputs as Q_A, Q_B, and Q_C for industry A, B, and C, respectively.

    c. In which industry structure or structures is consumer surplus the largest? The smallest?

    d. In the long run, in which industry structure or structures is the total economic profit the largest? The smallest?

    e. Which industry structure(s) are efficient?

10. What is rent seeking? Why does rent seeking occur in a monopoly industry, but not in a perfectly competitive industry?

■ **You're the Teacher**

1. "I don't really understand how monopoly firms decide how much to produce and what price to charge. Can you give me some help? I'd really like just a rule or two to remember." Because you have studied this material, you are in a position to help this student. Offer a couple of rules that this student can use to determine, first, how much is produced, and second, what price is charged.

2. "How does price discrimination reduce the amount of consumer surplus? I mean, by price discriminating the company charges some people a lower price, so how can this reduce consumer surplus?" These questions are short and to the point, so give a similar answer to them!

Answers

■ True/False Answers

Market Power

1. **T** Without barriers to entry, other firms will enter the industry so that it no longer is a monopoly.

2. **T** Patents legally prohibit anyone else from producing the same good.

3. **F** A single-price monopoly charges each consumer the same price.

Single-Price Monopoly's Output and Price Decisions

4. **T** The monopolist is the only producer in the market, so the monopolist's decisions about how much to produce determine the market price.

5. **F** For a single-price monopoly, $P > MR$.

6. **T** No matter its industry type, a firm producing so that $MR = MC$ earns the maximum profit.

7. **T** A single-price monopoly produces at $MR = MC$. Because $P > MR$, the equality between MR and MC means that $P > MC$.

8. **T** Barriers to entry limit the competition faced by the monopoly, so it is able to earn an economic profit indefinitely.

Single-Price Monopoly and Competition Compared

9. **F** A monopoly creates deadweight loss; it does not reduce it.

10. **F** Single-price monopolists capture only part of the consumer surplus. They create deadweight loss, part of which is the consumer surplus lost to everyone in society.

11. **T** Rent seeking refers to the use of resources to establish a monopoly.

Price Discrimination

12. **F** Price discrimination captures consumer surplus, not producer surplus.

13. **T** This motivation lies behind price discrimination.

14. **T** Effectively, the price-discriminating monopolist converts consumer surplus into additional economic profit for itself.

15. **F** Price discrimination requires goods that cannot be resold.

Monopoly Policy Issues

16. **F** Monopolies might be able to capture more economies of scale or scope than competitive firms. And, monopolies might have a greater incentive to innovate than competitive firms.

17. **F** A natural monopoly is a firm that enjoys such economies of scale that it can supply the entire market at lower cost than could two (or more) firms.

18. **T** However, a marginal cost pricing rule might mean that the firm incurs an economic loss.

■ Multiple Choice Answers

Market Power

1. **d** The taxi company has been granted a legal monopoly.

2. **b** The other possibilities are legal barriers to entry.

3. **d** *All* monopolies must lower their price in order to sell more output.

Single-Price Monopoly's Output and Price Decisions

4. **d** Total revenue when 100 trees are sold is $2,800; when 101 trees are sold, it is $2,727. Hence the marginal revenue from the 101st tree is −$73.

5. **a** When demand is elastic, MR is positive; when demand is inelastic, MR is negative.

6. **a** As long as MR exceeds MC, producing the unit adds to the firm's total profit because it adds more to revenue than to cost.

7. **a** Output should be decreased because the last units produced lower the firm's profit and, by reducing output, the firm can raise its price.

8. **c** Like any firm, if demand for its good declines or its costs rise, in the short run a monopoly might earn a normal profit or incur an economic loss.

9. **c** *All* firms maximize their profit by producing the amount of output so that $MR = MC$.

10. **b** The rise in marginal costs shifts the MC curve leftward. The firm thus decreases the quantity it produces and raises the price it charges.

11. **b** The firm produces the level of output that sets $MR = MC$.

12. **c** The firm produces Q_2 of output. The highest price the firm can charge and sell this amount of output is P_3.

13. **d** In the short run, depending on demand and cost, any firm can earn an economic profit, a normal profit, or incur an economic loss.

14. **c** A monopoly might be able to earn an economic profit and, because of the barriers to entry, the economic profit can last indefinitely.

Single-Price Monopoly and Competition Compared

15. **c** A single-price monopoly creates a deadweight loss because it produces less than a competitive industry.

16. **a** Because it produces less output, the monopoly is able to boost the price it charges.

17. **d** The deadweight loss is created because a single-price monopoly produces less than a perfectly competitive industry.

18. **a** The consumer surplus is the area between the demand curve and the price.

19. **c** The economic profit is the area of the rectangle with its height the difference between P and ATC and with its length the quantity produced.

20. **a** The producer benefits because the monopoly can earn an economic profit; consumers lose because of the reduction in consumer surplus; and society loses due to the deadweight loss.

21. **d** This answer is the reverse of the previous answer and shows that society benefits from breaking up a monopoly.

22. **b** The question defines rent seeking.

Price Discrimination

23. **b** The firm must be able to distinguish between high and low willingness to pay customers in order to determine who should be charged a high price and who a low price.

24. **c** The monopoly raises its total revenue by capturing some consumer surplus.

25. **c** Any price discrimination eliminates some consumer surplus and perfect price discrimination eliminates it all.

26. **a** Customers with a high average willingness to pay are charged a higher price.

27. **b** Airlines price discriminate and charge business travelers, who have a high average willingness to pay, more than vacation travelers, who have a low average willingness to pay.

Monopoly Policy Issues

28. **b** If economies of scale are large enough, a monopoly might produce more than a competitive industry.

29. **d** The answer defines economies of scope.

30. **a** Natural monopolies, such as electric power distributors and local telephone companies, are usually regulated by the government.

■ Answers to Short Answer Problems

1. To sell an additional unit of output, a monopoly must lower its price. The additional unit sold at the lower price adds to the firm's revenue an amount equal to the price. But a single-price monopoly also lowers the price to previous customers who had been paying more. Marginal revenue equals the new revenue, the new price, minus the loss of revenue from lowering the price to previous customers, so marginal revenue is less than the price.

TABLE **12.4**

Short Answer Problem 2 (a)

Quantity (books per hour)	Total cost (dollars)	Average total cost (ATC)	Marginal cost (MC)
9	247.00	27.44	
			9.00
10	256.00	25.60	
			11.00
11	267.00	24.27	
			13.00
12	280.00	23.33	
			15.00
13	295.00	22.69	
			17.00
14	312.00	22.29	
			19.00
15	331.00	22.07	
			21.00
16	352.00	22.00	
			23.00
17	375.00	22.06	
			25.00
18	400.00	22.22	
			27.00
19	427.00	22.47	
			29.00
20	456.00	22.80	
			31.00
21	487.00	23.19	

2. a. Table 12.4 shows the average total costs and marginal costs. The average total costs are cal-

culated by dividing the total costs by the total outputs. For instance, the average total cost when 10 books are sold is $256/10 or $25.60. The rest of the *ATC*s are calculated similarly. Marginal cost equals the change in the total cost divided by the change in output. For example, the marginal cost going from 10 to 11 units of output is ($267 – $256)/(11 – 10), which equals $11.00. The remainder of the *MC*s are calculated in the same way.

TABLE 12.5
Short Answer Problem 2 (b)

Quantity demanded (books per hour)	Price (dollars per book)	Total revenue (dollars)	Marginal revenue (MR)	Marginal cost (MC)
9	57.00	513.00		
			47.00	9.00
10	56.00	560.00		
			45.00	11.00
11	55.00	605.00		
			43.00	13.00
12	54.00	648.00		
			41.00	15.00
13	53.00	689.00		
			39.00	17.00
14	52.00	728.00		
			37.00	19.00
15	51.00	765.00		
			35.00	21.00
16	50.00	800.00		
			33.00	23.00
17	49.00	833.00		
			31.00	25.00
18	48.00	864.00		
			29.00	27.00
19	47.00	893.00		
			27.00	29.00
20	46.00	920.00		
			25.00	31.00
21	45.00	945.00		

b. Table 12.5 gives the total revenue and marginal revenue. Total revenue equals (Quantity)(Price). By way of example, the total revenue at the quantity of 10 books is (10)($56) = $560. After finishing with the total revenue, the marginal revenue can be calculated as the change in total revenue divided by the change in output. Take the marginal revenue going from 10 to 11 books sold per hour as an example. This marginal

revenue equals ($605 – $560)/(11 – 10) or $45. The rest of the marginal revenues are computed the same way.

c. To maximize her profit, Laura produces at *MR* = *MC*. Between 18 and 19 books the marginal revenue is $29 and between 19 and 20, it is $27. So, at 19 books the marginal revenue is $28. Similarly, the marginal cost is $27 between 18 and 19 books and $29 between 19 and 20 books, which indicates that at 19 books the marginal cost is $28. Marginal revenue equals marginal cost at an output of 19 books, so this quantity is the profit-maximizing level of output. The data for the demand curve show that Laura can sell 19 books at a price per book of $47, so the monopoly price is $47 per book. (Note that the price, $47, is greater than the marginal cost, $28.) Laura's economic profit equals her total revenue minus her total cost. From Table 12.5, the total revenue when selling 19 books is $893, and, from Table 12.4, the total cost of selling 19 books is $427. Laura's total economic profit is $893 – $427 = $466.

d. Figure 12.8 shows the demand, *MR*, and cost curves. The area of the darkened rectangle equals Laura's economic profit.

FIGURE 12.8
Short Answer Problem 2 (d)

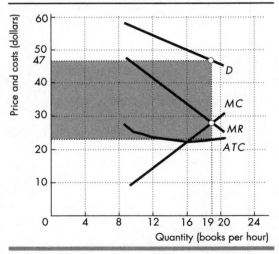

3. a. Table 12.6 (on the next page) shows the total revenue, marginal revenue, and marginal cost after the decrease in demand. The total and

TABLE 12.6
Short Answer Problem 3 (a)

Quantity (books per hour)	Price (dollars per book)	Total Revenue (dollars)	Marginal Revenue (MR)	Marginal Cost (MC)
9	24.50	220.50		
			19.50	9.00
10	24.00	240.00		
			18.50	11.00
11	23.50	258.50		
			17.50	13.00
12	23.00	276.00		
			16.50	15.00
13	22.50	292.50		
			15.50	17.00
14	22.00	308.00		
			14.50	19.00
15	21.50	322.50		
			13.50	21.00
16	21.00	336.00		
			12.50	23.00
17	20.50	348.50		
			11.50	25.00
18	20.00	360.00		
			10.50	27.00
19	19.50	370.50		
			9.50	29.00
20	19.00	380.00		
			8.50	31.00
21	18.50	388.50		

marginal revenue schedules are calculated similarly to those in Table 12.5.

b. After the decrease in demand, Laura finds that *MR* = *MC* when she sells 13 books per hour. (The *MR* equals $16, the same as the *MC*.) So, 13 books is the profit-maximizing level of sales. When Laura sells 13 books per hour, the (new) demand schedule shows that she can charge $22.50 per book and sell all 13. Hence the new profit-maximizing price is $22.50 per book. Laura's economic profit equals her total revenue of $292.50 minus her total cost of $295.00. Hence her "profit" is –$2.50; that is, with the decrease in demand, Laura actually incurs an economic loss of $2.50. Table 12.6 indicates that this loss is the minimum possible loss. Laura will continue to operate in the short run because this loss is less than her shut-down loss, which would be $100, the amount of the business's fixed cost. In the long run, however, if matters do not improve, Laura will close down as soon as at least $97.51 of her (current) fixed cost becomes a variable cost.

FIGURE 12.9
Short Answer Problem 4

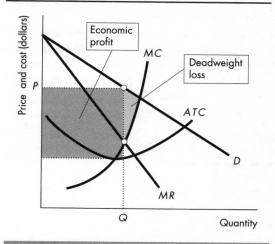

4. All the curves are labeled in Figure 12.9. Also illustrated in the figure is the economic profit (the darker rectangle) the monopoly earns and the deadweight loss (the lighter triangular area) the monopoly creates.

5. The fundamental reason that monopolies are able to earn an economic profit in the long run is that they are protected from competition by barriers to entry. Essentially when the monopolist is earning an economic profit, other firms would like to enter that market. However, they are precluded from doing so by the existence of barriers to entry — some feature of the market, be it economies of scale or perhaps a patent, that prevents new firms from entering the industry. Perfectly competitive firms are not protected by barriers to entry. If they are earning an economic profit, new competitors *will* enter the market and, by so doing, compete away the economic profit. Hence it is the barriers to entry that allow a monopoly to indefinitely earn an economic profit.

6. A perfectly competitive industry produces the level of output at which the industry's marginal cost curve (which is the same as the industry's supply curve) intersects the industry's demand curve. A single-price monopoly produces the level of output at which the industry's (the firm's) marginal cost curve intersects the monopoly's marginal revenue curve. Because the marginal revenue curve lies below the demand curve, the monopoly industry pro-

duces less. More intuitively, compared to a perfectly competitive industry, a single-price monopoly restricts its output in order to raise its price and generate an economic profit.

7. In order to maximize his profits, Derek should charge a lower price for his 5 o'clock movies and a higher price for his 8 o'clock movies. In other words, Derek should price discriminate because by so doing, Derek increases his profit.

Price discrimination is possible because this situation easily fulfills its requirements. First, Derek can readily distinguish between customers with a high average willingness to pay and those with a low average willingness to pay by noting when they want to see the movie: those who want to view at 8 P.M. have a higher average willingness to pay than those who want to view at 5 P.M. Second, to resell the good is impossible; that is, people attending at 5 P.M. are not going to be able to resell viewing the movie to those who want to attend at 8 P.M. Thus Derek can "separate" his market into two groups and charge the 5 P.M. group a low price and the 8 P.M. group a higher price.

Why does price discrimination increase Derek's profit? Figures 12.10 and 12.11 shed light on this question. The marginal cost of showing a movie at 5 P.M. or at 8 P.M. is assumed to be constant. In order to maximize his profit in the 5 o'clock market, Derek equates MR to MC and sells Q_L ("L" for "low willingness to pay") tickets by charging P_L. In the high willingness to pay, 8 P.M. market, Derek sells Q_H ("H" for "high willingness to pay") tickets by charging P_H per ticket. By charging a lower price at 5 P.M. and a higher price at 8 P.M., Derek is able to convert into economic profit some of the consumer surplus that would result if he charged both classes of customers the same price. Price discrimination raises Derek's economic profit.

8. a. When the one firm is granted a monopoly on pizza delivery, it boosts its price and thereby reduces its output. The price of a pizza will rise, the quantity of pizzas delivered will decrease, and so the quantity of pizzas consumed decreases as fewer pizzas are delivered.

    b. The owner of the (new) monopoly pizza delivery service will earn an economic profit.

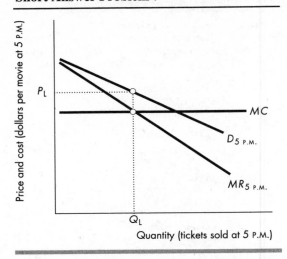

FIGURE 12.10
Short Answer Problem 7

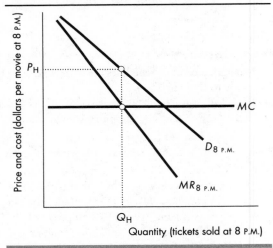

FIGURE 12.11
Short Answer Problem 7

c. Perhaps surprisingly, though you might be rent seeking by offering to buy the delivery service, you will not be able to earn an economic profit. Why not? Think of the selling price the pizza owner will charge to buy the pizza delivery company and its monopoly. The selling price must compensate the owner for all the economic profit that he or she will lose in the future by not owning the business. Hence the price of the business will rise with the economic profit that it is earning, both now and in the future. The fact that the price of the business rises means that you will be able to earn only a normal profit on the funds that you use to buy the business. So, if you want to earn an economic profit, you must be in on the ground floor: Buying into a business after it is already earning an economic profit will not work because the higher price of buying-in eliminates the economic profit.

9. a. Figure 12.12 shows the demand, marginal revenue, average total cost, and marginal cost curves for the three industries.

b. Figure 12.13 shows the level of output for each industry structure. The single-price monopoly produces the least. Both the perfectly competitive industry and the monopoly able to perfectly price discriminate produce the same amount, which is more than that produced by the single-price monopolist.

c. The consumer surplus is largest in the perfectly competitive industry; it is smallest (zero) with the perfectly price-discriminating monopoly.

d. The total economic profit is largest for the monopoly able to perfectly price discriminate because this monopoly converts all the potential consumer surplus to economic profit. It is smallest for the perfectly competitive industry because in the long run firms in this industry cannot earn economic profits.

e. Both the perfectly competitive industry and the perfectly price-discriminating monopoly produce the efficient amount.

10. Rent seeking refers to the attempt to create a monopoly. People rent seek because, if they can create a monopoly, they stand to earn an economic profit for an indefinite period of time. Rent seeking occurs in a monopoly industry precisely because monopolies can earn economic profits. It does not occur in perfectly competitive industries because firms in these industries cannot earn a long-lasting economic profit. Hence the incentive to rent seek is much less in a perfectly competitive industry.

■ You're the Teacher

1. "A couple of mechanical rules might be helpful when we're studying how a monopoly selects its output and determines its price. First, decide how much the firm produces. Second, determine the price charged.

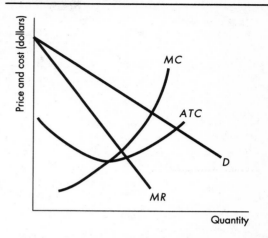

FIGURE 12.12

Short Answer Problem 9

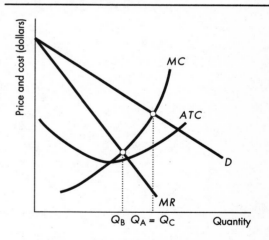

FIGURE 12.13

Short Answer Problem 9

"To find the profit-maximizing quantity, use the *MR* and *MC* curves. The equilibrium quantity is where these curves cross: Draw a vertical line down to the horizontal axis and read the quantity. Then, to find the profit-maximizing price, continue this vertical line up to the demand curve. From the intersection of the demand curve and your vertical quantity line, draw a horizontal line over to the price axis. Where this line meets the price axis is the profit-maximizing price. Use these rules and you'll be okay."

2. "Look, the whole idea of price discrimination is that a monopoly wants to charge you a price for the good that more closely reflects how much you value it. If you value it a lot, the monopoly wants to stick you with a really high price; if you don't value it too much, the monopoly will let you buy it for a lower price. Now, the idea behind consumer surplus is that it measures the difference between how much you value a good and how much you have to pay for it. By price discriminating, the monopoly can reduce this difference: Customers who value it a lot, pay a lot, and customers who don't value it as much don't pay as much. So, a price-discriminating monopoly moves the price closer to how much the good is valued, and so the monopoly reduces consumer surplus."

Chapter Quiz

1. Which of the following is a feature of a monopoly?
   a. Monopoly has no barriers to entry.
   b. Monopolies produce a product with a very close substitute.
   c. A monopoly is the only supplier of the product.
   d. A monopoly faces a perfectly elastic demand for its product.

2. A patent is a _____ barrier to entry and a public franchise is a _____ barrier to entry.
   a. natural; natural
   b. natural; legal
   c. legal; natural
   d. legal; legal

3. In a monopoly, the marginal revenue curve lies
   a. above the demand curve.
   b. on top of the demand curve.
   c. below the demand curve.
   d. sometimes above, sometimes on top of, and sometimes below the demand curve depending on the marginal cost curve.

4. The more perfectly a monopoly can price discriminate, the _____ its output and the _____ its profit.
   a. higher; higher
   b. higher; lower
   c. lower; higher
   d. lower; lower

5. A price discriminating monopoly charges higher prices to customers with
   a. lower quantities demanded.
   b. higher quantities demanded.
   c. higher average willingness to pay.
   d. lower average willingness to pay.

6. Which of the following occurs with *both* a perfectly competitive industry and a perfectly price discriminating monopoly?
   a. The amount of output is inefficient.
   b. The amount of output is efficient.
   c. Deadweight loss is created.
   d. All consumer surplus is lost to the firm(s).

7. A single-price monopolist will shut down if price is
   a. less than average fixed cost.
   b. less than the minimum average variable cost.
   c. greater than the minimum average total cost.
   d. greater than minimum average variable cost but less than minimum average total cost.

8. The reason that a perfectly competitive industry is more efficient than a single-price monopoly is because the perfectly competitive industry
   a. has higher total costs.
   b. produces more output.
   c. has a market demand that is more elastic.
   d. None of the above.

9. Compared to a perfectly competitive industry, a monopoly transfers
   a. deadweight loss to consumers.
   b. deadweight loss to producers.
   c. producer surplus to consumers.
   d. consumer surplus to the producer.

10. Economies of scope arise when
    a. an increase in output leads to a fall in average total cost.
    b. an increase in the range of goods produced causes average total cost to fall.
    c. doubling the monopoly firm's inputs more than doubles its output.
    d. high profit allows the company to undertake more research and development.

The answers for this Chapter Quiz are on page 368

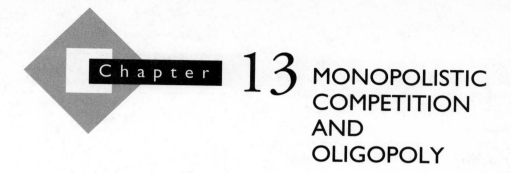

Chapter 13 MONOPOLISTIC COMPETITION AND OLIGOPOLY

■ Monopolistic Competition

The market structure of most industries lies between the extremes of perfect competition and monopoly. Monopolistic competition is one such "intermediate" industry structure. **Monopolistic competition** is a market structure in which:

♦ A large number of firms compete.

♦ Each firm produces a differentiated product (**product differentiation** is when a firm makes a good that is slightly different from the products of competing firms).

♦ Firms compete on product quality, price, and marketing. Brand-name products advertise their superiority to generics and generics advertise their low price.

♦ Firms are free to enter or exit the industry.

A monopolistically competitive firm faces a downward sloping demand curve because it produces a differentiated product. As a result, a monopolistically competitive firm's marginal revenue curve lies below its demand curve.

■ Output and Price in Monopolistic Competition

In the short run:

♦ The firm maximizes its profit by producing the level of output such that $MR = MC$.

♦ The firm might earn an economic profit. If it does, free entry means that competitors eventually enter the industry. Alternatively, the firm might incur an economic loss. If it does, it (or other firms) eventually exit the industry.

In the long run:

♦ The firm maximizes its profit by producing the amount of output that sets $MR = MC$.

♦ The firm does not earn an economic profit or incur an economic loss, so $P = ATC$.

Figure 13.1 shows the long-run equilibrium for a monopolistically competitive firm.

FIGURE **13.1**

The Long Run in Monopolistic Competition

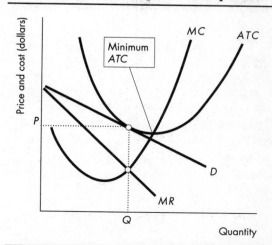

Capacity output is the output at which average total cost is at its minimum. A monopolistically competitive firm has *excess capacity* because, as Figure 13.1 shows, in the long run it does not produce at the minimum *ATC*. From a social standpoint, monopolistically competitive firms are not efficient. However monopolistically competitive firms produce a large variety of differentiated products and consumers value variety.

■ Product Development and Marketing

Monopolistically competitive firms constantly strive to differentiate their products and (temporarily) earn an economic profit. The extent of innovation and product development is determined by the marginal cost and marginal revenue of innovation and development.

Monopolistically competitive firms spend huge amounts on marketing. Such selling costs are fixed costs, which shift the firm's *ATC* curve upward. Because all firms advertise, the effect of advertising on the demand for any particular firm's product is ambiguous. The efficiency of monopolistic competition is unclear:

♦   On the plus side, consumers value variety and advertising might provide valuable information.

♦   On the minus side, advertising is costly and monopolistically competitive firms have higher costs because of their excess capacity.

■ Oligopoly

Oligopoly is a market structure in which a few firms compete. Each firm considers the effects of its actions on the behavior of the others and the actions of the others on its own profit.

The kinked demand curve model:

♦   The firm believes that, if it raises its price, no competitors will follow but that, if it lowers its price, all its competitors will follow. The firm faces a kinked demand curve, with the kink at the current price and quantity, as illustrated in Figure 13.2.

♦   The kink causes a break in the *MR* curve. As long as the *MC* curve remains within this break, the firm's price and quantity do not vary.

♦   The model fails to tell what happens if firms discover that their beliefs are incorrect.

The dominant firm oligopoly model:

♦   One large firm has a substantial cost advantage over its many small competitors.

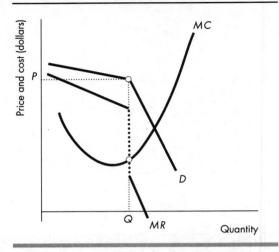

FIGURE 13.2
The Kinked Demand Curve Oligopoly

♦   The large firm acts like a monopoly and sets its profit-maximizing price. The small firms take this price as given and act like perfect competitors.

■ Oligopoly Games

Game theory is a tool for studying strategic behavior. Games have rules, strategies, payoffs, and an outcome:

♦   *Rules* specify permissible actions by players.

♦   *Strategies* are actions, such as raising or lowering price, output, advertising, or product quality.

♦   *Payoffs* are the profits and losses of the players. A **payoff matrix** is a table that shows the payoffs for every possible action by each player.

♦   The *outcome* is determined by the players' choices. In a **Nash equilibrium**, Player A takes the best possible action given the action of Player B, and B takes the best possible action given the action of A.

A "prisoners' dilemma" is a two-person game. In a one-time prisoners' dilemma game, each player has a dominant strategy of cheating, that is, confessing. A dominant strategy occurs when each player has a unique best strategy independent of the other player's action. The outcome is not the best equilibrium for the prisoners.

♦   **Duopoly** is a market with two competitors.

In a duopoly, the firm's might have a **collusive agreement** to decrease output and raise price. A **cartel** is a group of firms that have engaged in a collusive agreement. In this game, each firm can comply with the agreement or can cheat by lowering its price and increasing its output. In a one-time game, a prisoners' dilemma Nash equilibrium emerges, in which each firm has the dominant strategy of cheating. Each firm earns zero economic profit.

Other decisions of a firm — how much to spend in research and development, how much to spend on advertising, and so on — can often be analyzed using game theory.

■ Repeated Games and Sequential Games

In a repeated game, other strategies can create a **cooperative equilibrium,** an equilibrium in which the players make and share the monopoly profit.

♦ A "tit-for-tat" strategy consists of taking the same action (cheating or not cheating) the other player took last period.

♦ A trigger strategy cooperates until the other player cheats and then plays the Nash strategy (cheating) forever after.

In a repeated game the players might be able to attain the cooperative equilibrium because the long-run profit from colluding is greater than the short-run profit from cheating. But price wars can occur when new firms enter an industry, and the industry finds itself in a prisoners' dilemma game.

A game tree, which shows the decisions made at the first stage and second stage of a game, can be used to analyze a sequential game, such as a contestable market. A **contestable market** is a market in which one firm (or a small number operate) but in which entry and exit are free, so the existing firm(s) face competition from potential entrants. The company (or companies) in the market can play an entry-deterrence game:

♦ In an entry-deterrence game the firm in the market sets a competitive price (rather than a monopoly price) and earns a normal profit to order to keep potential competitors from entering the market.

♦ **Limit pricing** refers to the situation in which a firm charges a price lower than the monopoly price (and earns less than the monopoly profit) to keep potential competitors out of the market.

Helpful Hints

1. **MARGINAL ANALYSIS IN DIFFERENT INDUSTRY STRUCTURES :** Firms in any type of market struc-

ture follow the same rule to maximize profit: Produce the level of output that sets $MC = MR$. This rule applies in perfect competition, monopoly, monopolistic competition, and kinked demand curve and dominant firm oligopolies. The essential reason for its widespread applicability is that the rule does not depend on industry structure. The framework of the $MR = MC$ rule is marginal analysis: As long as another unit of output adds more to the firm's revenue than to its cost ($MR > MC$), producing more output adds its total profit. The fact that $MR = MC$ applies to all industry structures reflects the importance of marginal analysis. (More pragmatically, it also means that you do not have to remember a separate profit-maximizing rule for each type of industry structure!)

2. **BARRIERS TO ENTRY AND LONG-RUN ECONOMIC PROFIT :** Free entry leads to zero long-run economic profits both in perfect competition and monopolistic competition. If a monopoly is earning an economic profit, other firms would like to enter the monopoly's industry, but barriers to entry keep them out. Whether a business can earn an economic profit in the long run revolves around the presence or absence of barriers to entry.

3. **HOW TO DETERMINE THE EQUILIBRIUM IN A PRISONERS' DILEMMA GAME :** Learning how to find the equilibrium of a prisoners' dilemma-type game is important. Take the example of Chris and Loren in a prisoner's dilemma. Each player has to choose between two strategies, confess or deny. First, set up the payoff matrix. Then look at the payoff matrix from Chris's point of view. Chris does not know whether Loren is going to confess or deny, so Chris asks two questions: (1) Assuming that Loren confesses, do I get a better payoff if I confess or deny? (2) Assuming that Loren denies, do I get a better payoff if I confess or deny? If Chris's best strategy is to confess, regardless of whether Loren confesses or denies, confessing is Chris's dominant strategy.

Next, look at the payoff matrix from Loren's point of view. Let Loren ask the equivalent two questions, and determine whether Loren has a dominant strategy. The combination of Chris's strategy and Loren's strategy comprises the equilibrium outcome of the game.

4. **THE PRISONERS' DILEMMA GAME AND THE REAL WORLD :** The key insight of the prisoners' di-

lemma game is the tension between the equilibrium outcome (in which both players' best strategy is to confess because they can't trust each other) and the fact that both players could make themselves better off if only they would cooperate. This tension helps explain complex events in the real world.

The Organization of Petroleum Exporting Countries (OPEC) provides a classic example of this tension. OPEC is a cartel that controls a large fraction of the world's oil. Looking at OPEC as a whole, restricting the supply of petroleum and keeping the price of petroleum high is in OPEC's interest. Keeping the price of petroleum high, perhaps near $40 a barrel, which was the price about 20 years ago, would maximize the total revenues and profits of the OPEC nations. But when the price is this high, the *individual* interest of each nation lies in pumping more oil than the amount allocated to it under the OPEC agreement. Each nation figures that if it — and it alone — cheats on the output restriction imposed by the cartel agreement, the effect on the world price of oil would be small but the positive impact on its profit from selling more oil would be large. So each nation is tempted to cheat on the cartel.

Questions

■ True/False and Explain

Monopolistic Competition

1. Product differentiation gives each monopolistically competitive firm a downward sloping demand curve.

2. Monopolistically competitive firms compete only on price.

3. Similar to a monopoly, a monopolistically competitive industry has large barriers to entry.

Output and Price in Monopolistic Competition

4. In the short run, to maximize its profit, a monopolistically competitive firm produces the level of output that sets $P = ATC$.

5. Monopolistically competitive firms can earn an economic profit in the long run.

6. Free entry is the basic reason that monopolistically competitive firms have excess capacity.

7. Monopolistically competitive firms have excess capacity in the long run.

Product Development and Marketing

8. A monopolistically competitive firm can earn an economic profit if it develops new products.

9. Monopolistically competitive firms have large marketing and selling costs.

Oligopoly

10. An oligopolist will consider the reactions of other firms before it decides to cut its price.

11. The kinked demand curve model of oligopoly predicts that the firm will change its price only infrequently.

Oligopoly Games

12. Game theory is used to analyze the behavior of monopolistically competitive firms.

13. In a one-time only prisoners' dilemma game, the best strategy for a prisoner is to confess only if the prisoner believes that the other player will confess.

14. If oligopolistic firms are able to sustain an output-restricting, price-increasing collusive agreement, they will produce the efficient level of output.

Repeated Games and Sequential Games

15. Repeated games are more likely to have a cooperative equilibrium than one-time only games.

16. Price wars can break out when a small number of new firms enter an industry.

17. A single firm in a contestable market might be unable to earn an economic profit.

18. Limit pricing refers to attempts by firms to set their price at the highest possible limit.

■ Multiple Choice

Monopolistic Competition

1. A monopolistically competitive firm is like a *monopoly* firm insofar as
   a. both face perfectly elastic demand.
   b. both earn an economic profit in the long run.
   c. both have *MR* curves that lie below their demand curves.
   d. neither is protected by high barriers to entry.

2. A monopolistically competitive firm is like a *perfectly competitive* firm insofar as
   a. both face perfectly elastic demand.
   b. both earn an economic profit in the long run.
   c. both have *MR* curves that lie below their demand curves.
   d. neither is protected by high barriers to entry.

3. Product differentiation
   a. means that monopolistically competitive firms can compete on quality and marketing.
   b. occurs when a firm makes a product that is slightly different from that of its competitors.
   c. makes the firm's demand curve downward sloping.
   d. All of the above answers are correct.

Output and Price in Monopolistic Competition

Figure 13.3 represents a monopolistically competitive firm in the short run. Use it for the next four questions.

FIGURE **13.3**

Multiple Choice Questions 10, 11, 12, 13

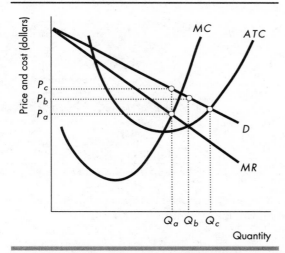

4. How much output does the firm produce?
   a. Q_a
   b. Q_b
   c. Q_c
   d. None of the above

5. What price does the firm charge?
   a. P_a
   b. P_b
   c. P_c
   d. None of the above

6. What type of profit or loss is the firm earning?
   a. An economic profit
   b. A normal profit
   c. An economic loss
   d. An accounting loss

7. In the long run,
   a. new firms will enter, and each existing firm's demand decreases.
   b. new firms will enter, and each existing firm's demand increases.
   c. existing firms will leave, and each remaining firm's demand decreases.
   d. existing firms will leave, and each remaining firm's demand increases.

8. A monopolistically competitive firm has excess capacity because in the
   a. short run $MR = MC$.
   b. short run the firm's average total cost does not equal the minimum average total cost.
   c. long run the firm's average total cost does not equal the minimum average total cost.
   d. long run the firm earns an economic profit.

9. In the long run, a monopolistically competitive firm's economic profits are zero because of
   a. product differentiation.
   b. the lack of barriers to entry.
   c. excess capacity.
   d. the downward-sloping demand curve of each firm.

Product Development and Marketing

10. Monopolistically competitive firms constantly develop new products in an effort to
    a. make the demand for their product more elastic.
    b. increase the demand for their product.
    c. increase the marginal cost of their product.
    d. None of the above answers is correct.

11. When deciding upon how much to spend on product development, a firm will consider
    a. only the marginal revenue from product development.
    b. only the marginal cost of product development.
    c. both the marginal revenue and marginal cost of product development.
    d. the price and average total cost of product development.

12. Which of the following statements about monopolistically competitive firms is correct?
    a. They produce more than the capacity amount of output.
    b. They have high selling costs.
    c. They produce the efficient amount of output.
    d. They rarely advertise.

Oligopoly

13. A firm that has a kinked demand curve assumes that, if it raises its price, _____ of its competitors will raise their prices and that, if it lowers its price, _____ of its competitors will lower their prices.
    a. all; all
    b. none; all
    c. all; none
    d. none; none

14. In the dominant firm model of oligopoly, the large firm acts like
    a. an oligopolist.
    b. a monopolist.
    c. a monopolistic competitor.
    d. a perfect competitor.

15. In the dominant firm model of oligopoly, the smaller firms act like
    a. oligopolists.
    b. monopolists.
    c. monopolistic competitors.
    d. perfect competitors.

Oligopoly Games

16. A game always contains all of the following EXCEPT
    a. rules.
    b. a dominant strategy.
    c. strategies.
    d. payoffs.

17. In the prisoners' dilemma game with a Nash equilibrium,
    a. only one prisoner confesses.
    b. neither prisoner confesses.
    c. both prisoners confess.
    d. any confession is thrown out of court.

18. If a collusive agreement in a duopoly maximizes the industry's profit,
    a. each firm must produce the same amount.
    b. the industry level of output is efficient.
    c. industry marginal revenue must equal industry marginal cost at the level of total output.
    d. total output will be greater than without collusion.

Firms A and B are in a duopoly game, so they can either comply with a cartel agreement or cheat on the agreement. The cartel agreement calls for each firm to boost its price and restrict the amount it produces. For the next 5 questions, use the following payoff matrix that shows the firms' economic profits.

19. If firm A cheats on the cartel and firm B complies with the agreement, firm A's profit is
    a. $3 million.
    b. $2 million.
    c. zero.
    d. −$1 million.

20. If firm A cheats on the cartel and firm B complies with the agreement, firm B's profit is
    a. $3 million.
    b. $2 million.
    c. zero.
    d. −$1 million

21. If this game is played only once,
    a. both firms A and B will cheat.
    b. firm A will cheat and firm B will not cheat.
    c. firm A will not cheat and firm B will cheat.
    d. neither firm A nor firm B will cheat.

22. The equilibrium in question 21 is called a
    a. credible strategy equilibrium.
    b. Nash equilibrium.
    c. duopoly equilibrium.
    d. cooperative equilibrium.

23. If this game is played repeatedly and both firms adopt trigger strategies so that the cooperative equilibrium emerges,
    a. both firms A and B will cheat.
    b. firm A will cheat and firm B will not cheat.
    c. firm A will not cheat and firm B will cheat.
    d. neither firm A nor firm B will cheat.

24. In a duopoly with a collusive agreement, when is the *industry-wide* profit as large as possible?
    a. When both firms comply with the collusive agreement.
    b. When one firm cheats on the cartel and the other firm does not.
    c. When both firms cheat on the collusive agreement.
    d. The answer is indeterminate because it depends on the industry's *MR* curve.

25. In a duopoly with a collusive agreement, when can *one firm* have the maximum possible profit?
    a. When both firms comply with the collusive agreement.
    b. When one firm cheats on the agreement and the other firm does not cheat.
    c. When both firms cheat on the agreement.
    d. The answer is indeterminate because it depends on the firm's *MR* curve.

26. A prisoners' dilemma equilibrium is most likely to emerge when
    a. a monopolistically competitive industry is dominated by a dominant firm.
    b. an oligopolistic industry faces a repeated game.
    c. a monopoly is forced to compete repeatedly with an oligopolistic industry.
    d. an oligopolistic industry plays a game once.

Repeated Games and Sequential Games

27. A strategy in which a firm takes the same action that the other firm did in the last period is a
    a. dominant strategy.
    b. trigger strategy.
    c. tit-for-tat strategy.
    d. wimp's strategy.

28. Price wars can be the result of
    a. a cooperative equilibrium.
    b. a firm playing a tit-for-tat strategy in which last period the competitors complied with a collusive agreement.
    c. new firms entering the industry and immediately agreeing to abide by a collusive agreement.
    d. new firms entering an industry and all firms then finding themselves in a prisoners' dilemma.

29. In a contestable market,
    a. the HHI is usually quite low.
    b. the firm in the market usually earns a large economic profit.
    c. the firm in the market might play an entry-deterrence game.
    d. two of the above answers are correct.

30. Limit pricing refers to
    a. the fact that a monopoly firm always sets the highest price possible.
    b. a situation in which a firm might lower its price to keep potential competitors from entering its market.
    c. how the price is determined in a kinked demand curve model of oligopoly.
    d. none of the above.

■ Short Answer Problems

1. In Figure 13.4 (on the next page) draw a diagram illustrating a monopolistically competitive firm that is earning an economic profit in the short run. Identify the area that equals the economic profit.

2. In Figure 13.5 (on the next page) draw the long-run equilibrium for a monopolistically competitive firm. What conditions must be satisfied for long-run equilibrium?

FIGURE **13.4**
Short Answer Problem 1

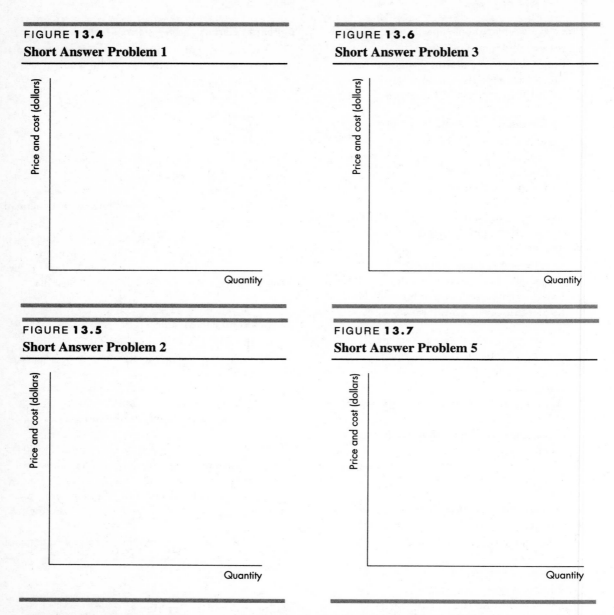

FIGURE **13.6**
Short Answer Problem 3

FIGURE **13.5**
Short Answer Problem 2

FIGURE **13.7**
Short Answer Problem 5

3. Suppose that a monopolistically competitive firm is initially in long-run equilibrium and it succeeds in further differentiating its product. As a result, the demand for its product increases. In Figure 13.6 show what happens to this firm in the short run. Without drawing a diagram, describe what happens in the long run.

4. Compare the advantages and disadvantages of perfect competition and monopolistic competition in terms of how they benefit society.

5. In Figure 13.7 draw a diagram showing a kinked demand curve oligopoly. Indicate the range between which the marginal cost can vary and still leave the firm's output and price the same.

6. How can a price war that eliminates profits be explained with game theory?

7. Two firms — Tom's Taxis and Chet's Cabs — are the only two taxicab companies in a small college town. These firms are engaged in a duopoly game. If they both adhere to a collusive cartel agreement to restrict the number of their cabs and raise their

Payoff Matrix for Short Answer Problem 7

Tom's strategies

	Cheat	Comply
Chet's strategies — Cheat		
Chet's strategies — Comply		

Payoff Matrix for Short Answer Problem 8

Tom's strategies

	Cheat	Comply
Chet's strategies — Cheat		
Chet's strategies — Comply		

price, each can earn an economic profit of $2 million. However, if one company cheats on the agreement — by shading its price a bit and perhaps quietly acquiring some more taxis — and the other complies with the agreement, the cheater earns an economic profit of $2.5 million and the compiler suffers an economic loss of $1 million. If both cheat, both earn $0 economic profit; that is, both earn a normal profit.

a. Use the description of the situation to complete the payoff matrix above. Put Tom's payoffs in the darker triangles and Chet's in the other triangles.

b. If this game is played only once, what is Tom's best strategy? What is Chet's best strategy? What will be the equilibrium outcome?

c. When is the *joint* total profit the largest? When is Tom's profit the largest? Chet's profit?

8. Suppose that the taxi firm duopoly game played in problem 7 changes: The payoffs are the same as before except when one player cheats and the other does not. Now the cheating player earns an economic profit of $2.5 million, and the player complying with the agreement earns an economic profit of $0.5 million.

a. Complete the second payoff matrix above for the new taxi firm duopoly game.

b. Does Tom have a clear-cut best strategy? Does Chet? Is there a clear equilibrium outcome in this game?

9. The taxi market changes again so that the payoff matrix is as shown in the matrix for problem 9 below. Chet and Tom now see that they will be playing a repeated game. Chet knows that Tom has adopted a tit-for-tat strategy. Last period Chet did not cheat on the cartel agreement.

a. If Chet cheats this period, what is his profit? If he cheats this period, what is the maximum profit he can earn next period? What is his maximum two-period profit if he cheats?

b. If Chet complies with the agreement, what is the maximum profit he earns this period? If he complies next period, what will be his profit? If he does not cheat in either period, what is the two-period total profit he earns?

c. Is Chet likely to cheat this period? Why?

Payoff Matrix for Short Answer Problem 9

Tom's strategies

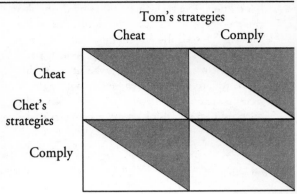

	Cheat	Comply
Chet's strategies — Cheat	$0 / $0	−$2 million / $2.5 million
Chet's strategies — Comply	$2.5 million / −$2 million	$2 million / $2 million

■ You're the Teacher

1. "You know, I've really been studying the book and this study guide and now a lot of this stuff is making sense. I liked the helpful hint that pointed out that firms in all types of industries actually had only one profit-maximization rule, what it called the $MR = MC$ rule. It sure makes it easy if we don't have to memorize different rules for different industries! Can you think of any other rules that are the same across all industries?" This student is correct: Common rules ease your work. Perhaps more importantly, common rules also show you that there are factors in common to all firms regardless of their industry structure. There is another rule that is common across all types of industries; it deals with when a firm earns an economic profit. With this hint, explain the other rule to the eager student.

Answers

■ True/False Answers

Monopolistic Competition

1. **T** By making its product different from those of its competitors, each monopolistically competitive firm has a unique product and hence a downward-sloping demand curve.

2. **F** Because its product is differentiated, monopolistically competitive firms compete on product quality and marketing, as well as on price.

3. **F** Similar to a perfectly competitive industry, a monopolistically competitive industry has many firms in it because there are no barriers to entry.

Output and Price in Monopolistic Competition

4. **F** Monopolistically competitive firms use the same rule as all firms: to maximize their profit, produce so that MR equals MC.

5. **F** The firms cannot earn an economic profit in the long run because of the absence of barriers to entry.

6. **F** Monopolistically competitive firms have excess capacity because they produce differentiated goods.

7. **T** Because they do not produce at the minimum ATC, monopolistically competitive firms have excess capacity, that is, if they boosted their production, their average total costs would fall.

Product Development and Marketing

8. **T** Monopolistically competitive firms constantly try to further differentiate their products, and developing new products is one method they use.

9. **T** Marketing and advertising play key roles in monopolistically competitive firms' efforts to differentiate their products.

Oligopoly

10. **T** This mutual interdependence makes oligopoly a difficult industry structure to analyze.

11. **T** Shifts in the MC curve that do not move it beyond the vertical section of the MR curve have no effect on the price that the firm charges nor on the quantity it produces.

Oligopoly Games

12. **F** Game theory is used to analyze the behavior of oligopolistic firms.

13. **F** In a prisoners' dilemma game, the dominant strategy is to confess; that is, regardless of the other players' action, each player will confess.

14. **F** The collusive agreement described in the problem decreases output below its efficient level.

Repeated Games and Sequential Games

15. **T** Repeated games have strategies absent from games played only once, such as the tit-for-tat strategy, that can support the cooperative equilibrium. So, repeated games are more likely to have a cooperative equilibrium.

16. **T** When a small number of new firms enter a market, the firms might find themselves in a prisoners' dilemma in which competition forces the price of the product down.

17. **T** In a contestable market, if the firm sets its price so that it earns an economic profit, competitors enter the market.

18. **F** Limit pricing refers to the situation in which an established firm sets a low price in order to keep new competitors out of the market.

■ Multiple Choice Answers

Monopolistic Competition

1. **c** Both have downward-sloping demand curves, so both have MR curves that lie below their demand curves.

2. **d** The absence of high barriers to entry accounts for the large number of firms in each industry.

3. **d** Answer b is the definition of product differentiation and answers a and c are results of product differentiation.

Output and Price in Monopolistic Competition

4. **a** The monopolistically competitive firm maximizes its profit by producing so that $MR = MC$.

5. **c** With the firm producing Q_a output, the demand curve shows that a price of P_c is the highest price that can be charged and still sell all that is produced.

6. **a** The firm earns an economic profit because, at output of Q_a, $P > ATC$.

7. **a** New firms enter because they, too, want to earn an economic profit. As these firms enter, they decrease the demand for the existing firms' products, which reduces the economic profit.

8. **c** The firm produces less output than that which minimizes its long-run *ATC*.

9. **b** If firms in the industry are earning an economic profit, the absence of barriers to entry means that new firms enter the industry and compete away the economic profit.

Product Development and Marketing

10. **b** If the firm can increase the demand for its product, it can temporarily earn an economic profit.

11. **c** For virtually all business decisions, a firm compares the marginal revenue and marginal cost resulting from the decision.

12. **b** Monopolistically competitive firms incur large selling costs trying to differentiate their products.

Oligopoly

13. **b** With this set of assumptions, the business believes that it will lose a large amount of sales if raises its price, but pick up only a small amount if it lowers its price.

14. **b** When setting its price and quantity, the dominant firm acts as if it were a monopoly.

15. **d** The smaller firms are unable to affect the price charged by the large firm.

Oligopoly Games

16. **b** A game might or might not have a dominant strategy.

17. **c** Both players confess even though it is in their joint interest for neither to confess.

18. **c** To maximize its profit, the industry behaves as a monopoly, which means that it produces the level of output needed for *MR* = *MC*.

19. **a** Firm A's profits are in the darkened triangle in the square at the lower left.

20. **d** Firm B's profits are in the white triangle in the square at the lower left.

21. **a** Both firms adopt the strategy of cheating.

22. **b** A Nash equilibrium occurs when each player takes the best action possible, given the action of the other player.

23. **d** The cooperative equilibrium maximizes each firm's profit over the long haul.

24. **a** The interest of the industry as a whole is to maintain the cartel.

25. **b** Each firm's individual interest is to be the lone cheater on the cartel agreement. Compare this answer to the previous answer.

26. **d** In one-time only games, a dominant strategy for each firm likely is to cheat, so this strategy emerges as the Nash equilibrium.

Repeated Games and Sequential Games

27. **c** Tit-for-tat implies that "I'll do to you what you did to me."

28. **d** Neither the new firms nor the old ones want a price war, but a prisoners' dilemma game might make a price war inevitable.

29. **c** By playing an entry-deterrence game, the firm in the market sets a low price to keep competitors from entering the market.

30. **b** Limit pricing can occur in contestable markets when the firm plays an entry deterrence game.

■ Answers to Short Answer Problems

FIGURE **13.8**

Short Answer Problem 1

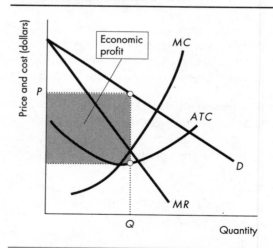

1. Figure 13.8 shows the short-run equilibrium of a monopolistically competitive firm. To maximize its profit, the firm produces so that *MR* = *MC*. At this level of output, *P* > *ATC*, so the firm earns an economic profit, as illustrated by the darkened rectangle. This diagram is identical to that of a monopoly firm earning an economic profit. Both monopoly

and monopolistically competitive firms face down-ward-sloping demand curves, both produce so that $MR = MC$, and, as long as $P > ATC$, both firms earn an economic profit.

FIGURE **13.9**
Short Answer Problem 2

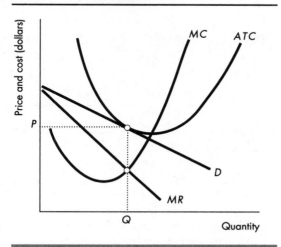

2. Figure 13.9 shows the long-run equilibrium for a monopolistically competitive firm. Two conditions must be satisfied for this diagram to show the long-run equilibrium. Think of these requirements as a *firm condition* and a *market condition*. For the firm to be satisfied, it must maximize its profit, which requires that it be producing the amount of output so that $MR = MC$. Then, for there to be long-run equilibrium in the market, firms must have no incentive either to enter or exit the industry. As a result, there can be no economic profit, so $P = ATC$. (This second condition is not a choice of the firm; the firm would rather earn an economic profit. But for the market to be in long-run equilibrium, it is required.) Both conditions — production at $MR = MC$ and $P = ATC$ — are met in Figure 13.9 so Figure 13.9 illustrates the long-run equilibrium.

3. Figure 13.10 shows the effect when a monopolistically competitive firm succeeds in further differentiating its product. The demand for the firm's good increases, thereby shifting the demand curve and the MR curve rightward. As a result, the firm increases its output from Q_1 to Q_2 and raises its price from P_1 to P_2. The firm earns an economic profit.

In the long run, other firms copy its product. As they copy, the demand for the initial firm's good

FIGURE **13.10**
Short Answer Problem 3

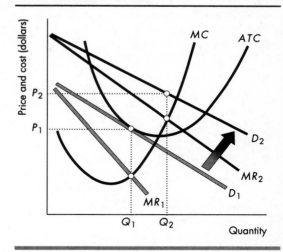

decreases; that is, the demand curve and MR curve shift leftward. Ultimately, demand decreases enough that the pioneering firm — and all other "copier" firms — no longer earn an economic profit. At this point, other firms do not have an incentive to copy the good and the market is in long-run equilibrium.

4. An advantage of perfect competition is that it produces at minimum average total cost, whereas monopolistic competition produces at a higher average total cost because of its excess capacity. Another advantage is that a perfectly competitive industry is efficient; it produces the level of output that sets the marginal social benefit equal to the marginal social cost. A monopolistically competitive industry, however, is not efficient because the price of the product (which equals the marginal social benefit) exceeds the marginal social cost (which equals the marginal cost).

The advantage of monopolistic competition is that product differentiation leads to greater product variety, which consumers value. In addition, monopolistically competitive firms have a greater incentive to innovate new and improved products and methods of production. Monopolistically competitive firms must do more advertising and sales promotion than perfectly competitive firms. To the extent that these activities provide valued services to consumers, they benefit society.

So, the loss in efficiency and the higher ATC that occurs in monopolistic competition must be weighed against the gain of greater product variety, greater incentives to innovate, and potentially valuable promotional activity.

FIGURE 13.11
Short Answer Problem 5

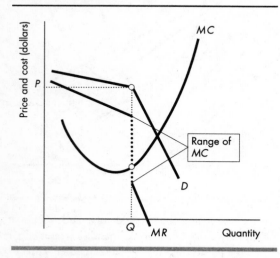

5. Figure 13.11 illustrates a kinked demand curve oligopoly and the range over which the *MC* can change and not affect the price, *P*, or quantity, *Q*.

6. Game theory explains price wars as the consequence of firms in a colluding industry responding to the cheating of a firm or as the response to new firms entering the industry. If one firm cheats by cutting its price, all other firms will cut their prices, and a price war ensues. After the price has fallen sufficiently (perhaps so the firms earn zero economic profit), they have an incentive to rebuild their collusion. Alternatively, if new firms (or even just one) enter an industry, the old and new players might find themselves playing a prisoners' dilemma game. Neither set of firms wants the price to fall and profits to shrink, but they might be unable to collude successfully to keep the price and profit high.

7. a. The payoff matrix is given above.
   b. Tom's best strategy is to cheat without regard to what Chet does. If Chet adheres to the agreement and does not cheat, Tom will cheat because his profit when cheating ($2.5 million) exceeds his profit when he does not cheat ($2 million). And, if Chet cheats, Tom also will cheat because his profit ($0) is higher than the

Short Answer Problem 7 (a)

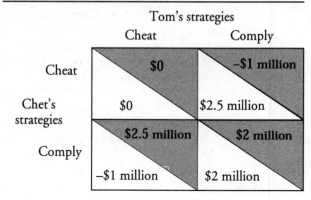

loss he would incur by not cheating (–$1 million). Tom has a dominant strategy: cheat.

In exactly the same way, Chet's profits are higher if he cheats regardless of what Tom does. So, Chet also has a dominant strategy of cheating. The equilibrium outcome is for both Tom and Chet to cheat on the cartel agreement.

c. The industry's total profits are highest ($4 million) when neither Tom nor Chet cheat. Tom's profit is largest if he cheats and Chet does not. Similarly, Chet's profit is greatest if he alone cheats. Though each player's *individual* interest is to cheat, their *joint* interest is to comply.

Short Answer Problem 8 (a)

	Tom's strategies	
	Cheat	**Comply**
Chet's strategies — Cheat	$0 / $0	$.5 million / $2.5 million
Comply	$2.5 million / $0.5 million	$2 million / $2 million

8. a. The new payoff matrix is given above.
   b. Tom and Chet no longer have a dominant strategy. In particular, if Chet complies with the agreement, Tom wants to cheat because in this

case his profit by cheating ($2.5 million) exceeds his profit by complying ($2 million). But, if Chet cheats on the agreement, Tom will want to comply. If Chet is cheating, Tom earns a profit of $0.5 million by complying but $0 by cheating. Hence Tom's best strategy depends on what Chet does. Chet is in the same situation: His best strategy depends on what Tom does. Unlike the situation in problem 7, the outcome is not clear-cut. The equilibrium depends on which strategy Chet and Tom decide to pursue.

9. a. Last period Chet did not cheat, so Tom's tit-for-tat strategy means that Tom will not cheat this period. Because Tom will comply with the cartel agreement, Chet's profit this period by cheating is $2.5 million. Next period Tom will cheat because Chet cheated this period. Therefore next period the most profit that Chet can earn is $0 by also cheating. (If Chet complied with agreement and Tom cheated, Chet loses –$2 million.) Over the two periods, Chet's total profit if he cheats in the first period is $2.5 million.

   b. If Chet does not cheat this period, this period he will earn $2 million. Because Chet complied with the agreement this period, Tom's tit-for-tat strategy means that next period Tom will comply with the agreement. Then, if Chet also complies next period, he will earn $2 million. By complying each period Chet earns a total of $4 million over the two periods.

   c. Chet is not likely to cheat. If he does, his total profits over the two periods are significantly less than if he complies over the two periods. So players in a repeated game are more likely to reach the cooperative equilibrium than players in a one-time game.

■ You're the Teacher

1. "One other rule works for a firm in any type of industry structure. In particular, if $P > ATC$, the firm earns an economic profit; if $P = ATC$, the firm earns a normal profit; and if $P < ATC$, the firm suffers an economic loss. Let's take the case of $P > ATC$ and find out why it means that the firm earns an economic profit. If we multiply both sides of the inequality by q, the amount of output the firm produces, we get $Pq > (ATC)q$. Now, Pq (the price times the amount produced) equals the firm's total revenue. And $ATC = TC/q$, so multiplying ATC times q gives TC, the firm's total cost. Hence when $P > ATC$, total revenue exceeds total cost. Because the firm's normal profit is already included in its total cost, the fact that the firm's total revenue exceeds its total cost means that the 'extra' profit is an economic profit.

"But look, the main point of what I am saying is that we do have it easy: Here's another case where we don't have to memorize a bunch of different rules. If *any* firm finds that P exceeds ATC, it's earning an economic profit."

Chapter Quiz

1. In a duopoly game that is repeated many times, each player tries to
   a. maximize the industry's total profit.
   b. minimize the other player's profit.
   c. maximize its market share.
   d. maximize its profit.

2. If *P > MR* for each firm in an industry, the industry is <u>NOT</u>
   a. perfectly competitive.
   b. monopolistically competitive.
   c. an oligopoly.
   d. a monopoly.

3. An industry with one large firm with a large cost advantage over its many smaller competitors is called
   a. a dominant firm oligopoly.
   b. a kinked demand curve oligopoly.
   c. a monopolistically competitive market.
   d. a near-monopoly oligopoly.

4. The major distinction between a monopolistically competitive industry and a perfectly competitive industry is that firms in a monopolistically competitive industry
   a. produce identical products.
   b. are protected by high barriers to entry.
   c. produce at the minimum *ATC* in the long run.
   d. produce a product that is different from those produced by its competitors.

5. If firms in a monopolistically competitive industry earn an economic profit,
   a. other firms will enter the industry.
   b. some firms will leave the industry.
   c. firms will neither enter nor exit.
   d. The premise of the question is wrong because monopolistically competitive firms cannot earn an economic profit.

6. A firm in which type of industry always has excess capacity in the long run?
   a. Perfect competition
   b. Monopolistic competition
   c. Oligopoly
   d. Monopoly

7. According to the kinked demand curve theory of oligopoly, each firm believes that if it lowers its price
   a. its competitors will not lower their prices.
   b. its competitors will lower their prices.
   c. its profit will rise.
   d. its marginal revenue will exceed its marginal cost.

8. In the long run, a monopolistically competitive firm ____ earn an economic profit and a monopoly ____ earn an economic profit.
   a. can; can
   b. can; cannot
   c. cannot; can
   d. cannot; cannot

9. When each player selects his or her best strategy taking as given what the other player will do, the resulting equilibrium is called a
   a. cooperative equilibrium.
   b. tit-for-tat equilibrium.
   c. Nash equilibrium.
   d. trigger strategy equilibrium.

10. A strategy in which a player cooperates in the current period if the other player cooperated in the previous period, but cheats in the current period if the other player cheated in the previous period is called a
   a. tit-for-tat strategy.
   b. trigger strategy.
   c. duopoly strategy.
   d. dominant firm strategy.

The answers for this Chapter Quiz are on page 368

Reading Between the Lines

SONY CORP. HAS CUT THE U.S. PRICE OF ITS PLAYSTATION 2

On May 14, 2002 Sony announced it was cutting the cost of its PlayStation 2 by 33 percent, from $299 to $199. PlayStation 2 competes with Microsoft's X-box and Nintendo's Game Cube as the latest generation game consoles. After keeping its price at $299 since it introduced the PlayStation 2 in 2000, Sony lowered the price in May a few days before Microsoft was expected to announce that it was lowering the price of its X-Box from $299 to $199. Both the X-Box and the Game Cube were introduced in 2001.

For details, go to The Economics Place web site, the Economics in the News archive, www.economicsplace.com/econ5e/einarchives.html

■ Analyze It

Sony's PlayStation 2 has by far the largest market share in the latest generation game consoles. Between the X-Box and the Game Cube, Sony likely believes that the X-Box is a closer substitute because its power and features are more similar to those of the PlayStation than is the case for the Game Cube. After Sony announced it was lowering its price, Microsoft made the expected announcement that it, too, was lowering its price.

1. In what type of market is the Sony PlayStation 2 sold?
2. Assume that Microsoft is Sony's only competitor and describe the prisoners' dilemma game Sony and Microsoft are playing.
3. Sony kept the price of the PlayStation 2 at $299 in the months preceding and the months following the introduction of the X-Box. What might Sony have done instead to try to keep Microsoft from entering the market?

Mid-Term Examination

■ **Chapter 9**

1. Partners of a partnership have
    a. limited liability. So do shareholders in a corporation.
    b. limited liability. Shareholders in a corporation have unlimited liability.
    c. unlimited liability. So do shareholders in a corporation.
    d. unlimited liability. Shareholders in a corporation have limited liability.

2. An economically efficient method of production
    a. is always technologically efficient.
    b. lies below the production function.
    c. lies below the supply curve.
    d. may not always be technologically efficient.

3. An electrician quits her current job, which pays $30,000 per year. She can take a job with another firm for $40,000 per year or work for herself. The opportunity cost of working for herself is
    a. $10,000.
    b. $30,000.
    c. $40,000.
    d. $70.000.

4. In their relation to a firm's managers, shareholders act
    a. as agents.
    b. as principals.
    c. in loco parentis.
    d. as a cabinet for advice.

■ **Chapter 10**

5. If a firm's marginal product of labor is greater than its average product of labor, then an increase in its use of labor necessarily will
    a. reduce its total product.
    b. raise its average product of labor.
    c. raise its marginal product of labor.
    d. not change its average product of labor.

6. The additional cost of producing an additional unit of output is the firm's
    a. *MC.*
    b. *ATC.*
    c. *AVC.*
    d. *AFC.*

7. In general, diseconomies of scale occur
    a. as output expands at low levels of production.
    b. through the entire range of production.
    c. as output expands at high levels of production.
    d. whenever the slope of the total product curve is positive.

8. The intersection of the *MC* and *ATC* curves is the point at which
   a. average total cost is minimized.
   b. average variable cost is minimized.
   c. average fixed cost is minimized.
   d. total product is maximized.

■ **Chapter 11**

9. In perfect competition, which is the case?
   a. A firm can influence the price of the good.
   b. There are many sellers.
   c. There are restrictions on entry.
   d. All firms sell a slightly different product.

10. A firm should decrease its output as long as its
    a. average total revenue exceeds its average total cost.
    b. average total revenue exceeds its average variable cost.
    c. marginal cost exceeds its marginal revenue.
    d. marginal revenue exceeds its marginal cost.

11. At a firm's shutdown point, its average variable cost equals its
    a. average total cost.
    b. average fixed cost.
    c. price.
    d. None of the above.

12. A perfectly competitive firm finds that at its current output, *MR* = *MC* and *P* > *ATC*. Then this firm will
    a. expand its output and lower its price.
    b. reduce its output and raise its price.
    c. shut down.
    d. not change its production nor its price.

■ **Chapter 12**

13. Public franchises are
    a. legal barriers to entry. So are patents.
    b. legal barriers to entry. Patents are natural barriers to entry.
    c. natural barriers to entry. So are patents.
    d. natural barriers to entry. Patents are legal barriers to entry.

14. The demand curve for a monopoly
    a. lies above its marginal revenue curve.
    b. lies on its marginal revenue curve.
    c. lies below its marginal revenue curve.
    d. is horizontal.

15. When a single-price monopoly is maximizing its profit, then the level of output it produces is
    a. efficient because profit is maximized.
    b. inefficient.
    c. efficient because $MR = MC$.
    d. efficient because costs are minimized.

16. Which of the following occurs with <u>BOTH</u> a perfect price discriminating monopoly and a single-price monopoly?
    a. The level of output is inefficient.
    b. All consumer surplus goes to the monopoly.
    c. Both create deadweight loss.
    d. There is a redistribution of surplus to the monopoly.

■ **Chapter 13**

17. An industry with many firms, each making a differentiated product is a(n) _____ industry.
    a. perfectly competitive
    b. monopolistically competitive
    c. oligopoly
    d. monopoly

18. When firms in an industry that is monopolistically competitive incur an economic loss, firms will
    a. enter the industry, and demand will increase for the original firms.
    b. exit the industry, and demand will increase for the remaining firms.
    c. exit the industry, and demand will decrease for the remaining firms.
    d. enter the industry, and demand will decrease for the original firms.

19. In the dominant firm model of oligopoly, the dominant firm acts as if it was a
    a. perfect competitor.
    b. monopolistic competitor.
    c. oligopoly.
    d. monopoly

20. The cooperative strategy in the prisoners' dilemma game would cause
    a. both players to win.
    b. both players to lose.
    c. the first player to take an action to win.
    d. the last player to take an action to win.

Answers

■ Reading Between the Lines

1. The only manufacturers of the latest video game players are Sony, Microsoft, and Nintendo. Because this market has only a few firms, it is an oligopoly.

2. In setting the prices of their products, Sony and Microsoft are competing in a prisoners' dilemma game. Both firms' profits would be substantially higher if both kept the price at $299 rather than lowering it to $199. And, both firms' profits would be lower if they both set a price of $199. However, if *only* one firm dropped its price to $199 while the other kept its price high, the firm lowering its price would gain a substantial increase in its market share and with it a huge profit. However, the firm with the higher price would make a much smaller profit; indeed, it likely would incur an economic loss. In this sort of prisoners' dilemma game, the Nash equilibrium is for both firms to charge the lower price and earn the lower profit. The Nash equilibrium, with its lower price and lower profit, is exactly what happened in this case!

3. Sony, faced with potential competition from Microsoft, might have played a sequential game in which it set a limit price. In particular, Sony was in the market supplying video game players well before Microsoft entered. In order to deter Microsoft from entering, Sony could have set a lower price than otherwise. For instance, Sony might have set a limit price, which is a price set at the highest level that would inflict a loss on Microsoft. By setting the highest price that inflicts a loss on Microsoft, Sony's profit would have been as high as possible while also keeping Microsoft from entering. And by inflicting a loss on Microsoft, Sony could hope to keep Microsoft from entering the market. It seems likely that Sonly was not playing this sort of game for two reasons. First, Microsoft indeed did enter the market. (So if Sony was playing this game, Sony misjudged the price it should set.) Second, even immediately before Microsoft entered, Sony kept the price of its PlayStation 2 at a relatively high level, $299.

■ Mid-Term Exam Answers

1. d;   2. a;   3. c;   4. b   5. b;   6. a;   7. c;   8. a;   9. b;   10. c;   11. c;   12. d;
13. a;   14. a;   15. b;   16. d;   17. b;   18. b;   19. d;   20. a.

DEMAND AND SUPPLY IN FACTOR MARKETS

Key Concepts

Prices and Incomes in Competitive Factor Markets

Factors of production (*labor*, *capital*, *land*, and *entrepreneurship*) are used to produce output. As illustrated in Figure 14.1, demand and supply in factor markets determine the prices for factors. The income earned by a factor equals the factor price times the quantity employed.

◆ An increase in the demand for a factor raises the factor's price and income while a decrease in the demand lowers the price and income.

◆ An increase in the supply of a factor lowers the factor's price while a decrease in supply raises the price. The effect on the factor's income depends if the demand is elastic or inelastic.

Labor Markets

Firms' demand for labor is a **derived demand**, stemming from the demand for the goods and services produced by the factor. The derived demand is driven by the firm's goal of maximizing its profit.

◆ **Marginal revenue product** (*MRP*) is the change in total revenue from employing one more unit of labor. *MRP* equals the marginal product times the marginal revenue, $MP \times MR$. As more workers are hired, the *MRP* diminishes.

A firm hires an additional worker if the wage paid the worker is less than the worker's *MRP*. To maximize its profit, a firm hires the quantity of workers such that the wage equals the marginal revenue product.

FIGURE 14.1

Equilibrium in a Resource Market

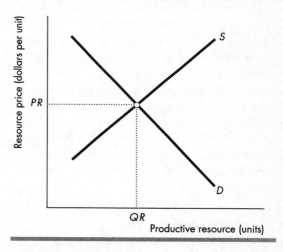

◆ When the firm hires the profit-maximizing number of workers, it produces the profit-maximizing amount of output. And when the firm produces the profit-maximizing amount of output, it employs the profit-maximizing number of workers.

A firm's demand for labor increases when:

◆ the price of output rises.

◆ the prices of other productive factors rise.

◆ technological change increases the marginal product of labor.

The market demand curve for labor is the sum of the quantities of labor demanded by all the firms at each wage rate.

The market demand for labor is the total demand by all firms. The demand for labor is less elastic in the short run than in the long run. The elasticity of demand for labor depends on the:

♦ *Labor intensity* — the greater the proportion of the total cost accounted for by wages, the more elastic is the demand for labor.

♦ *Elasticity of demand for the product* — the greater the elasticity of demand for the product, the more elastic is the demand for labor.

♦ *Substitutability of capital for labor* — the more easily capital can be substituted for labor, the more elastic the demand for labor.

The supply of labor is determined by decisions made by households. Households allocate time between labor supply and leisure.

♦ At wage rates above a household's *reservation wage*, the household supplies labor.

♦ The *substitution effect* from a higher wage rate increases the quantity of labor supplied.

♦ The *income effect* from a higher wage rate decreases the quantity of labor supplied and increases the amount of time spent at leisure.

♦ An individual household labor supply curve bends backward, as Figure 14.2 shows. The curve bends backward when the income effect from a higher wage rate outweighs the substitution effect.

The market supply of labor curve is the sum of all household supply curves and slopes upward over the normal range of wage rates.

The supply of labor increases when:

♦ the adult population increases.

♦ technological change so that less time needs to be spent in the home.

♦ more capital is used in home production.

Over the years, both the wage rate and employment have increased. The demand for labor has increased because of technological change and the accumulation of capital. The supply of labor has increased because of population growth and the use of more technologically advanced capital in the home. For most workers, the demand for labor has increased more than the supply of labor, so the wage rate and quantity of employment have both increased. For low-skilled workers, the demand for labor has decreased a bit and so their wage rates have not risen.

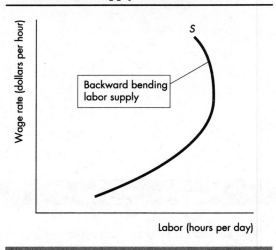

FIGURE **14.2**
A Household's Supply of Labor Curve

■ Capital Markets

Capital markets link the savings decisions of households and the investment decisions of businesses. The price of capital is the interest rate. Over the years, real interest rates have fluctuated while the quantity of capital has steadily increased.

The demand for capital is determined by firms' profit-maximizing choices. They calculate the present value of the future marginal revenue products of capital. **Discounting** is converting a future amount of money to a present value. The **present value** of a future amount of money is the amount of money that, if invested today, will grow with earned interest to be as large as the future amount. (Calculating a present value means that the value of money to be received in the future must be decreased ("discounted") to express it in terms of today's money.)

In a formula, the present value of an amount of money to be received one year in the future is:

$$\text{Present Value} = \frac{\text{Future Amount}}{(1+r)}$$

The present value of money to be received n years in the future is:

$$\text{Present Value} = \frac{\text{Future Amount}}{(1+r)^n}$$

In both formulas, r is the interest rate.

The **net present value** (*NPV*) of a piece of capital equipment is the present value of its marginal revenue products minus the cost of the capital.

♦ Firms buy additional capital when its net present value is positive.

♦ A rise in the interest rate lowers the *NPV* from buying capital and thereby decreases the quantity of capital that firms demand.

The *demand curve for capital* shows how the interest rate and quantity of capital demanded are inversely related. Factors that changes in the demand for capital are:

♦ *population growth* — an increase in the population increases the demand for capital.

♦ *technological change* — Technological change increases the demand for some types of capital and decreases it for other types.

The supply of capital is determined by households' saving decisions. The more that is saved, the greater is the amount of capital. A household's savings depends on three factors:

♦ *income* — the higher the household's income, the more it saves.

♦ *expected future income* — the higher the household's expected future income, the less it saves today.

♦ *interest rate* — the higher the interest rate, the more people save.

A *supply curve of capital* shows a positive relationship between the interest rate and the quantity of capital supplied. This supply of capital increases with:

♦ increases in income or population.

♦ increases in the fraction of the population that is middle-aged.

The equilibrium interest rate is determined by equality between the quantity of capital demanded and supplied.

■ Natural Resource Markets

♦ **Renewable natural resources** — natural resources that can be used repeatedly and not be depleted.

♦ **Nonrenewable natural resources** — resources that can be used only once and cannot be replaced.

The *aggregate* quantity of land (and other renewable natural resources) is fixed, so its supply is perfectly inelastic. Because the aggregate supply of land is perfectly inelastic, the demand for land determines the price.

♦ The supply of land to an individual perfectly competitive firm is perfectly elastic.

For a nonrenewable natural resource, the *stock* supply of a natural resource is the total amount that exists. The stock supply is perfectly inelastic. The *known stock* supply is the amount currently discovered. The known stock supply increases with technology and new discoveries of the resource. While both the stock supply and the known stock supply affect the resource's price, the *flow* supply has a more immediate impact on the price.

♦ The *flow* supply is the amount offered during a given time period. The flow supply is perfectly elastic at the price equal to the present value of next period's expected price.

Because the flow supply is perfectly elastic, the current period's price equals the present value of next period's expected price.

♦ If the present value of next year's expected price exceeds this year's price, it is more profitable to sell the resource next year.

♦ If the present value of next year's expected price is less than this year's price, it is more profitable to sell the resource this year.

Hotelling Principle — the price of a natural resource is expected to grow at a rate equal to the interest rate. But the actual price might not equal the expected price because of unexpected new technology.

■ Income, Economic Rent, and Opportunity Cost

Economic rent is income received by a factor owner above the amount required to induce the quantity supplied of the factor. Income required to induce the quantity supplied is the factor's opportunity cost. Figure 14.3 (on the next page) illustrates economic rent and opportunity cost.

♦ A factor's total income is the sum of economic rent and opportunity cost.

♦ The more inelastic the supply of a factor, the larger the fraction of its income that is economic rent.

It is possible for all factors (for instance, labor, capital, or entrepreneurship as well as land) to earn an economic rent.

FIGURE **14.3**
Economic Rent and Opportunity Cost

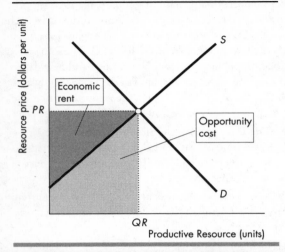

Helpful Hints

1. **PROFIT MAXIMIZATION AND FIRMS' DEMANDS FOR FACTORS :** This chapter discusses characteristics that are common to the markets for all factors. In particular, firms hire each factor up to the point at which the marginal revenue product equals the cost of the factor. This result holds regardless of whether the factor is labor, land, or capital. Why? When deciding whether to hire another unit of a factor, profit-maximizing firms compare the added revenue the factor would generate (the *MRP*) to the cost of hiring the factor. As long as the additional revenue from hiring the factor exceeds the additional cost, hiring the factor is profitable. However, if the added revenue falls short of the added cost, hiring the factor reduces the firm's profit. The maximum profit is reached by hiring the amount of the factor necessary to equalize the marginal revenue product and the factor's cost.

2. **THE LABOR DEMAND CURVE :** The most important graph in this chapter demonstrates that a firm's demand curve for labor is the same as its marginal revenue product curve of labor.

   Why is the *MRP* curve the same as a firm's demand curve for labor? We construct the demand curve for labor by asking the question: "How much labor is a firm willing to hire at alternative wage rates?" Because firms are profit maximizers, they will want to

hire labor up to the point at which the marginal revenue product of labor equals the wage rate. For example, if the wage rate is $10 per hour and the marginal revenue product is $10 when three workers are hired, the firm will hire three workers. Other points on the labor demand curve can be obtained in similar fashion. The result is that the demand curve for labor is the same as the *MRP* curve.

Questions

■ True/False and Explain

Prices and Incomes in Competitive Factor Markets

1. An increase in the supply of a factor always lowers the factor's price.

2. An increase in the supply of a factor always lowers the factor's total income.

Labor Markets

3. The marginal revenue product of labor is the same as the marginal product of labor.

4. A firm's labor demand curve is the same as its marginal revenue product of labor curve.

5. The greater the labor intensity of a production process, the smaller is the elasticity of demand for labor.

6. A household supplies no labor when the wage rate is above its reservation wage rate.

7. An individual's labor supply curve bends backward when the substitution effect is larger than the income effect.

Capital Markets

8. Money to be received in the future is worth less than the same amount of money received today.

9. If the interest rate is 10 percent a year, the present value of $100 received in one year is $110.

10. If the net present value of investing in a unit of capital is positive, a profit-maximizing firm invests in the unit.

11. The higher the interest rate, the greater the quantity of capital demanded.

12. By itself, an increase in the demand for capital raises the interest rate.

Natural Resource Markets

13. All natural resources can be used only once and cannot be replaced.

14. Rivers are an example of a renewable natural resource.

15. The aggregate supply of land is perfectly elastic.

16. For a nonrenewable natural resource, if the present value of next year's expected price exceeds this year's price, it pays to sell the resource next year rather than this year.

Income, Economic Rent, and Opportunity Cost

17. Only land earns economic rent.

18. If Pearl Jam's opportunity cost of playing a concert is $25,000 — but instead they receive $125,000 — they earn an economic rent of $100,000.

■ Multiple Choice

Prices and Incomes in Competitive Factor Markets

1. Increasing the supply of a factor decreases the income received by the factor when the elasticity of ____.
   a. demand is greater than 1.
   b. demand is less than 1.
   c. supply is greater than 1.
   d. supply is less than 1.

2. You notice that a factor's price and total income rise. This set of events can be the result of the
   a. demand for the factor decreasing and the supply of factor being elastic.
   b. demand for the factor increasing and the supply of the factor being elastic.
   c. demand for the factor decreasing and the supply of the factor being inelastic.
   d. None of the above is correct because higher factor prices decrease the quantity of the factor firms demand and hence must decrease the factor's income.

Labor Markets

3. An example of derived demand is the demand for
   a. sweaters derived by an economics student.
   b. sweaters produced by labor and capital.
   c. labor used in the production of sweaters.
   d. sweater brushes.

4. The change in total revenue resulting from employing an additional worker is the
   a. marginal product of labor.
   b. marginal revenue of labor.
   c. marginal revenue cost of labor.
   d. marginal revenue product of labor.

5. A company finds that, when it hires the next worker, the worker's marginal revenue product exceeds the cost of hiring the worker. In this case the company should
   a. definitely hire the worker.
   b. perhaps hire the worker, depending on the relationship between the company's marginal cost and its marginal revenue.
   c. definitely not hire the worker.
   d. perhaps not hire the worker, depending on the relationship between the company's marginal cost and its marginal revenue.

6. A firm's marginal revenue product of labor curve is the same as its
   a. labor supply curve.
   b. labor demand curve.
   c. marginal cost curve.
   d. marginal revenue curve.

7. The price of the good produced by a perfectly competitive firm falls. As a result, the labor
   a. supplied to the firm decreases.
   b. supplied to the firm increases.
   c. demanded by the firm increases.
   d. demanded by the firm decreases.

8. A technological change that increases the marginal revenue product of labor shifts the
   a. demand curve for labor rightward.
   b. demand curve for labor leftward.
   c. supply curve of labor leftward.
   d. supply curve of labor rightward.

9. A worker's reservation wage is the
   a. highest wage rate before the income effect starts to dominate the substitution effect.
   b. lowest wage rate before the income effect starts to dominate the substitution effect.
   c. the lowest wage rate for which the worker will supply labor.
   d. wage rate paid to head waiters, who are involved in taking reservations at fine restaurants.

10. If the wage rate rises, the substitution effect gives a household the incentive to
    a. raise its reservation wage.
    b. increase its time spent at leisure and decrease its time spent supplying labor.
    c. increase its time spent supplying labor and decrease its time spent at leisure.
    d. increase both the time spent at leisure and at supplying labor.

11. If the wage rate rises, the income effect gives a household the incentive to
    a. raise its reservation wage.
    b. increase its time spent at leisure and decrease its time spent supplying labor.
    c. increase its time spent supplying labor and decrease its time spent at leisure.
    d. increase both the time spent at leisure and at supplying labor.

12. The supply of airline pilots is elastic. An increase in demand for airline pilots leads to a _____ increase in employment and a _____ rise in the wage rate.
    a. large; small
    b. large; large
    c. small; small
    d. small; large

Capital Markets

13. The present value of $100 to be received in a year is
    a. less the lower the interest rate.
    b. less the higher the interest rate.
    c. not at all related to the interest rate.
    d. related, though in no consistent manner, to the interest rate.

14. If the interest rate is 5 percent, the present value of $100 to be received in one year is
    a. $105.00.
    b. $100.00.
    c. $95.24.
    d. $95.00.

15. If the interest rate is 10 percent, the present value of $100 to be received in one year is
    a. $110.00.
    b. $100.00.
    c. $90.91.
    d. $90.00.

16. If the interest rate is 10 percent, the present value of $100 to be received in two years is
    a. $121.00.
    b. $120.00.
    c. $100.00.
    d. $82.64.

17. The net present value of an investment
    a. is always positive as long as the MRP from the increased capital stock is positive.
    b. equals the present value of the cost of the capital minus the interest rate.
    c. is negative for a profitable investment.
    d. falls when the interest rate rises.

18. The higher the interest rate, the
    a. higher is the net present value of a firm's investment.
    b. lower is the present value of the marginal revenue products of an investment.
    c. greater is the quantity of capital demanded.
    d. lower is the marginal revenue product of capital.

19. Which of the following shifts the supply curve of capital rightward?
    a. An increase in the proportion of young households in the population.
    b. A rise in the interest rate.
    c. An increase in average household income.
    d. An increase in the marginal revenue product of capital.

20. Technological change increases both the supply of capital and the demand for capital by the same amount. As a result, the interest rate _____ and the quantity of capital _____.
    a. rises; increases
    b. does not change; increases
    c. falls; increases
    d. falls; decreases

Natural Resource Markets

21. A nonrenewable natural resource is
    a. coal.
    b. land.
    c. water.
    d. a river.

22. The supply curve of land facing an individual *firm* in a perfectly competitive land market
    a. only slopes upward.
    b. first slopes upward and then bends backward as the land rental rate rises.
    c. is vertical.
    d. is horizontal.

23. For a nonrenewable natural resource, which of the following is perfectly elastic?
    a. Stock supply
    b. Known stock supply
    c. Flow supply
    d. Demand

Income, Economic Rent, and Opportunity Cost

24. Economic rent is the ʹ
    a. price paid for the use of an acre of land.
    b. price paid for the use of a unit of capital.
    c. income required to induce the supply of a given quantity of a factor.
    d. income received above the amount required to induce the supply of a given quantity of a factor.

25. Jennifer will supply 40 hours of labor as a lawyer for $2,000. She actually receives $2,400 for her 40 hours at work. The opportunity cost of Jennifer's labor is
    a. $2,400.
    b. $2,000.
    c. $400.
    d. undefined.

26. Jennifer will supply 40 hours of labor as a lawyer for $2,000. She actually receives $2,400 for her 40 hours at work. Jennifer's economic rent is
    a. $2,400.
    b. $2,000.
    c. $400.
    d. undefined.

27. Which of the following statements about the aggregate supply of land is correct?
    a. The aggregate supply of land is perfectly elastic, so all income earned by land is transfer income.
    b. The aggregate supply of land is perfectly inelastic, so all income earned by land is economic rent.
    c. The aggregate supply of land is perfectly inelastic in the short run and perfectly elastic in the long run.
    d. Land has no supply.

■ Short Answer Problems

TABLE **14.1**

Christopher's Cookies

Quantity of labor (L)	Quantity of cookies per hour (Q)	Marginal product of labor (MP)
3	550	
		30
4	580	
		10
5	590	
		5
6	595	
		2
7	597	

1. Table 14.1 shows the marginal product of labor schedule for Christopher's Cookies, a perfectly competitive store that, unsurprisingly, sells cookies.
    a. Based on Table 14.1, if Christopher can sell a cookie for $1.00, complete the first *MRP* column of Table 14.2 (on the next page).
    b. If Christopher must pay workers $6 an hour, how many workers does Christopher hire? If the wage rate rises to $11 an hour, how many workers will Christopher employ?
    c. The price of a cookie rises to $1.50. Complete the second *MRP* column in Table 14.2.
    d. If Christopher must pay workers $6 an hour, how many workers does Christopher hire now?

TABLE 14.2

Christopher's Marginal Revenue Product

Quantity of labor (L)	Cookies @ $1.00 Marginal revenue product (MRP)	Cookies @ $1.50 Marginal revenue product (MRP)
3	___	___
4	___	___
5	___	___
6	___	___
7		

If the wage rate rises to $11 an hour, how many workers does he hire?

e. In Figure 14.4, draw Christopher's demand for labor curve when the price of a cookie is $1.00 and when the price is $1.50. How does the rise in the price of a cookie affect Christopher's demand for labor?

FIGURE 14.4

Short Answer Problem 1 (e)

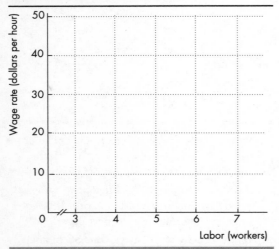

2. Why does the labor supply curve bend backward? In your answer, be sure to discuss the role played by the substitution and income effects.

3. In the short run, what effect does a lower price have on the quantity of output that a perfectly competitive firm produces? What effect does it have on the quantity of employment? (In both cases, assume that the firm does not shut down.) How do these two effects correspond?

4. Explain present value by discussing why $110 received one year from now has a present value of $100 if the interest rate is 10 percent per year.

TABLE 14.3

Larry's Lawn Care

Number of lawn mowers	MRP in first year (dollars)	MRP in second year (dollars)
1	100	80
2	80	64
3	72	62

TABLE 14.4

Short Answer Problem 5 (a)

Number of lawnmowers	NPV (r = 0.05)	NPV (r = 0.10)	NPV (r = 0.15)
1	___	___	___
2	___	___	___
3	___	___	___

5. Larry, the owner of Larry's Lawn Care Company, is considering the purchase of up to three additional lawn mowers. These lawn mowers have a life of two years and cost $120 each. The marginal revenue products for both years are given in Table 14.3.

   a. Complete Table 14.4 by computing the net present values (NPVs) if the interest rate is 5 percent (0.05); 10 percent (0.10); or 15 percent (0.15) per year.

   b. How many lawn mowers will Larry's Lawn Care purchase if the interest rate is 15 percent? or 10 percent? or 5 percent?

   c. Construct Larry's demand for capital curve in Figure 14.5 (on the next page) by plotting the three points identified in part (b) and drawing a line through them.

6. Why does the quantity of capital demanded increase when the interest rate falls? Why does the quantity of capital supplied decrease when the interest rate falls? In your answer, be sure to distinguish between and explicitly mention the economic agents that demand capital and those that supply it.

FIGURE **14.5**

Short Answer Problem 5 (c)

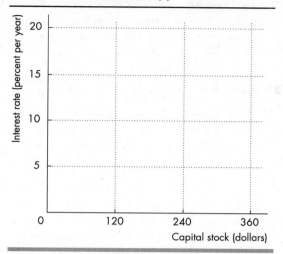

FIGURE **14.6**

Short Answer Problem 7

7. In Figure 14.6 show what happens to the interest rate and quantity of capital if people's incomes generally increase.

FIGURE **14.7**

Short Answer Problem 8

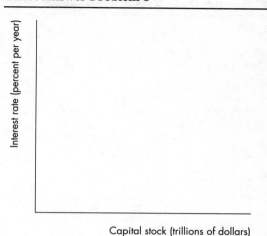

8. In Figure 14.7 show what happens to the interest rate and capital stock if there are general technological advances that boost the *MRP* from most types of capital.

TABLE **14.5**

Labor Demand and Supply

Wage rate (dollars per hour)	Quantity of labor demanded (millions of hours)	Quantity of labor supplied (millions of hours)
$0	4.5	0.0
I	4.0	I.0
2	3.5	2.0
3	3.0	3.0
4	2.5	4.0
5	2.0	5.0
6	1.5	6.0

9. The demand and supply schedules for labor in a developing nation are given in Table 14.5.

   a. Draw the demand and supply curves in Figure 14.8 (on the next page). What is the equilibrium wage? Quantity of employment?

FIGURE **14.8**
Short Answer Problem 9

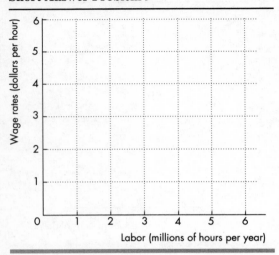

b. What is the total income earned by these workers? Show the total income in your figure. How much of the total income is opportunity cost? How much is economic rent?

10. Suppose that a new shopping center on the outskirts of town raises the *MRP* of the surrounding land. What happens to the rental rate for this land? Does the land's *economic* rent rise or fall? Does its opportunity cost rise or fall? Draw a diagram to help explain your answers.

■ **You're the Teacher**

1. "I really don't get the whole idea about the supply of labor. People don't have a choice about how much labor to supply: Once you get out of school, you either work 40 hours a week or you don't work. But the book talks like people have got a choice about how many hours to work. That really seems silly." While your friend is laughing over this point, take a moment to explain why the idea of a "supply of labor" is perhaps not as funny as it seems to your friend... Indeed, explain to your friend why it's not a laughing matter at all!

Answers

■ True/False Answers

Prices and Incomes in Competitive Factor Markets

1. **T** When the supply curve shifts rightward, the factor's price falls.

2. **F** The effect on the income depends on the elasticity of demand: If demand is elastic, total income rises but, if demand is inelastic, total income falls.

Labor Markets

3. **F** The marginal revenue product of labor equals the marginal product of labor times the marginal revenue.

4. **T** The firm's demand curve for any factor is the same as the factor's *MRP* curve.

5. **F** The greater the labor intensity, the larger the proportion of the costs accounted for by labor, the more elastic the demand for labor.

6. **F** The household supplies labor whenever the wage rate exceeds its reservation wage.

7. **F** The supply curve bends backward when the income effect — which encourages an increase in leisure and hence a reduction in the quantity of labor supplied — is larger than the substitution effect.

Capital Markets

8. **T** Money received in the present can be *immediately* saved and earn additional interest, an opportunity not available with money received in the future.

9. **F** The present value equals $100/(1.10) = \$90.91$.

10. **T** As long as the net present value is positive, investing in the unit of capital is profitable.

11. **F** As the interest rate rises, the quantity of capital demanded decreases because fewer investments have positive net present value.

12. **T** An increase in demand shifts the demand curve rightward, which raises the interest rate.

Natural Resource Markets

13. **F** Nonrenewable resources can be used only once, but renewable resources can be used any number of times or else can be replaced.

14. **T** Rivers can be used repeatedly, so they are renewable natural resources.

15. **F** The aggregate supply of land is perfectly inelastic, not perfectly elastic.

16. **T** If the present value of next year's expected price exceeds this year's price, it is more profitable to sell the resource next year, and so none of the resource would be sold this year.

Income, Economic Rent, and Opportunity Cost

17. **F** Any factor earns economic rent as long as its supply is not perfectly elastic.

18. **T** Economic rent is the difference between how much a factor (Pearl Jam) receives minus the opportunity cost of having the factor supplied.

■ Multiple Choice Answers

Prices and Incomes in Competitive Factor Markets

1. **b** The increase in supply lowers the factor's price. If demand is inelastic, the quantity employed increases by proportionally less than the price falls, so the total income paid to the factor decreases.

2. **b** Regardless of whether the supply is elastic or inelastic, an increase in demand raises both the factor's price and its total income.

Labor Markets

3. **c** The demand for a factor is derived from the demand for the final goods and services that the factor produces.

4. **d** The question gives the definition of the marginal revenue product of labor.

5. **a** The worker will add to the firm's total profit (because the additional revenue, the *MRP*, exceeds the additional cost) and should be hired.

6. **b** The *MRP* of labor curve shows how many workers a firm hires for any wage rate, so it is the same as the firm's demand for labor curve.

7. **d** The demand for labor decreases when the price falls because the fall in price means that the firm will produce less output.

8. **a** By raising the marginal revenue product from hiring workers, firms respond by increasing their demand for workers.

9. **c** The answer is the definition of the reservation wage.

10. **c** By increasing the opportunity cost of leisure, the substitution effect of a higher wage rate encourages households to substitute away from leisure and toward labor supply.

11. **b** By raising a household's income, the income effect of a higher wage rate encourages a household to "buy" more normal goods, such as leisure, and thereby decrease its labor supply.

12. **a** When the supply is elastic, an increase in demand leads to a small rise in the factor price and a large increase in the quantity, as illustrated in Figure 14.9.

FIGURE **14.9**

Multiple Choice Question 12

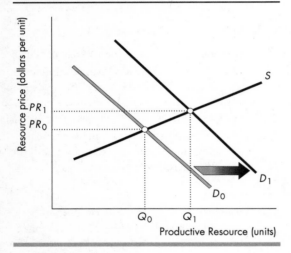

Capital Markets

13. **b** The present value is $\$100/(1+r)$, so the higher is r, the lower is the present value.

14. **c** The present value equals $\$100/(1+r)$, with r the interest rate, which equals $\$100/(1+0.05) = \$95.24$.

15. **c** Comparing this answer with the previous answer shows that the higher the interest rate, the lower the present value of funds to be received in the future.

16. **d** The present value is $\$100/(1+r)^2$, or $\$100/(1.10)^2$. Comparing this answer and the previous answer shows that the longer the time until a sum of money is received, the lower is its present value.

17. **d** The net present value of a unit of capital equals the present value of the current and future $MRPs$ minus the cost of the unit of capital. If the interest rate rises, the present value of the $MRPs$ falls, which reduces the net present value.

18. **b** As the interest rate rises, the present value of future revenues falls.

19. **c** An increase in income increases saving.

20. **b** When both the demand and supply increase by the same amount, the price — in this case, the interest rate — does not change and the quantity — the capital stock — increases.

Natural Resource Markets

21. **a** Once used, coal is gone forever.

22. **d** A firm in a perfectly competitive land market can buy or rent whatever amount of land it wants at the going rate.

23. **c** The flow supply is perfectly elastic at a price equal to the present value of next period's expected price.

Income, Economic Rent, and Opportunity Cost

24. **d** This is the definition of economic rent. It says nothing specifically about land; any resource can receive economic rent.

25. **b** The opportunity cost is the amount necessary to have the resource supplied, namely, $2,000.

26. **c** Economic rent is the difference between the resource's total income ($2,400) and its opportunity cost ($2,000).

27. **b** If any factor has a perfectly inelastic supply, all its income is economic rent.

■ **Answers to Short Answer Problems**

1. **a.** Table 14.6 (on the next page) has the completed marginal revenue products. To calculate these answers, recall that the marginal revenue product equals marginal product times the marginal revenue and for a perfectly competitive firm, the marginal revenue equals the price. The price is $1.00, so using this value, the MRP between 3 and 4 workers is ($1.00)(30), or $30. The rest of the marginal revenue product schedule is computed in the same way.

   b. If the wage rate is $6 an hour, Christopher will hire 5 workers. Hiring a sixth worker is not

TABLE 14.6

Short Answer Problem 1

Quantity of labor (L)	Cookies $1.00 Marginal revenue product (MRP)	Cookies $1.50 Marginal revenue product (MRP)
3		
	$30.00	$45.00
4		
	10.00	15.00
5		
	5.00	7.50
6		
	2.00	3.00
7		

profitable because that worker costs $6 an hour but contributes only $5 an hour in revenue. If the wage rate rises to $11 an hour, Christopher will hire 4 workers.

c. The *MRPs* are calculated the same way as outlined for part (a), using a price of $1.50 per cookie rather than $1.00.

d. At a wage rate of $6 an hour, Christopher will now hire 6 workers. If the wage rate rises to $11 an hour, Christopher will hire 5 workers.

FIGURE 14.10

Short Answer Problem 1 (e)

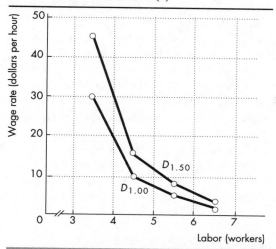

e. The labor demand curves are the same as the marginal revenue product schedules. Figure 14.10 shows both demand curves. The demand

curve when cookies are $1.00 is labeled $D_{1.00}$ and when cookies are $1.50 is labeled $D_{1.50}$. The rise in the price of a cookie shifts Christopher's demand for labor curve rightward.

FIGURE 14.11

Short Answer Problem 2

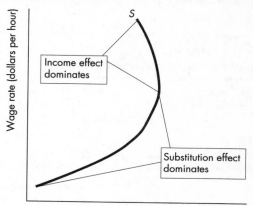

2. Suppose that the wage rate rises. As a result, the opportunity cost of leisure increases so households have a tendency to shift from leisure to work. This change is the substitution effect, which leads to an increase in the quantity of labor supplied. The higher wage rate also increases the household's income and so the household increases its demand for leisure (and other normal goods). This result is the income effect, which leads to a decrease in the quantity of labor supplied. As Figure 14.11 illustrates, at low wage rates, the substitution effect dominates the income effect, so the labor supply curve slopes upward. At high wage rates, the income effect is larger and the labor supply curve bends backward.

3. A perfectly competitive firm produces the level of output so that $P = MC$. When the price falls, the firm decreases the amount it produces. On the input side, a perfectly competitive firm hires the level of labor so that $W = MRP$, with W the wage rate and MRP the marginal revenue product, which equals $P \times MP$. (Recall that for a perfectly competitive firm, $P = MR$.) The fall in the price lowers the MRP and so the firm decreases its level of employment These two effects — reducing output and reducing employment — correspond. If the firm produces

less output, it needs less employment, and if the firm has less employment, it can produce less output.

4. The present value of $110 received one year from now is the amount that, if saved today at the market interest rate, would grow to be $110 in one year. The interest rate is 10 percent, so $100 saved grows to $110 in one year. So, $100 is the present value of $110 in one year.

TABLE **14.7**

Short Answer Problem 5 (a)

Number of lawnmowers	NPV (r = 0.05)	NPV (r = 0.10)	NPV (r = 0.15)
1	$47.80	$37.02	$27.45
2	14.24	5.62	−2.04
3	4.81	−3.31	−10.51

5. a. Table 14.7 shows the *NPVs*. The *NPV* is the present value of the stream of marginal revenue products resulting from an investment minus the cost of the investment. For lawn mowers with a two-year life, the *NPV* is calculated using the following equation:

$$NPV = \frac{MRP_1}{(1+r)} + \frac{MRP_2}{(1+r)^2} - P_m$$

In this formula, MRP_1 and MRP_2 are the marginal revenue products in the first and second years, respectively, and P_m is the price of a lawn mower. The values of MRP_1 and MRP_2 are given in Table 14.3 for the first, second, and third lawn mowers and P_m is $120. The answers for the *NPVs* given in Table 14.7 are obtained by substituting these values into the net present value formula and then evaluating the expression for the alternative interest rates, r.

b. If the interest rate is 15 percent, only one additional lawn mower will be purchased because the second lawn mower has a negative net present value. If the interest rate is 10 percent, two lawn mowers will be purchased; if the interest rate is 5 percent, three lawn mowers will be purchased.

c. The demand curve for capital is illustrated in Figure 14.12.

FIGURE **14.12**

Short Answer Problem 5 (c)

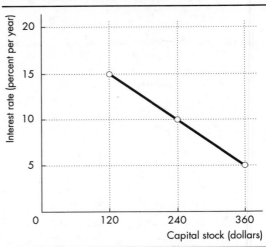

6. Firms demand capital as long as the present value of the stream of the future marginal revenue products from the new capital exceeds the price of the new capital; in other words, as long as the net present value is positive. Because a lower interest rate means that the present value of any given future stream of marginal revenue products is higher, the net present value is positive for a larger number of additional capital goods. So, the quantity of capital demanded increases as the interest rate falls.

The supply of capital is determined by households' saving. Consider the effect on saving from a fall in the interest rate. Essentially, the lower interest rate reduces the reward from saving because, with a lower interest rate, any amount of saving is able to buy fewer goods in the future. Hence a fall in the interest rate decreases the quantity of saving.

7. The increase in income boosts people's saving. As a result, the supply curve of capital shifts rightward. This situation is illustrated in Figure 14.13 (on the next page) in which the supply curve shifts from S_0 to S_1. The shift lowers the equilibrium interest rate from R_0 to R_1 and increases the capital stock from K_0 to K_1.

FIGURE **14.13**

Short Answer Problem 7

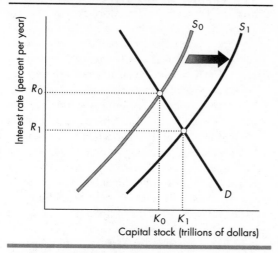

FIGURE **14.15**

Short Answer Problem 9

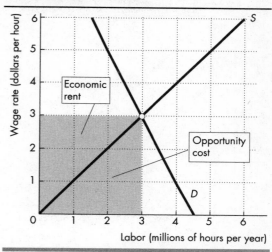

FIGURE **14.14**

Short Answer Problem 8

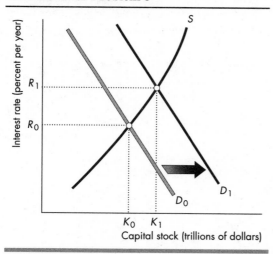

b. Workers are paid a wage rate, W, of $3 an hour. Employment, L, in aggregate is 3.0 million hours. The total income earned by all the workers is the wage rate times the hours employed, $W \times L$, or $9.0 million. In Figure 14.15, the total income is the area of the shaded rectangle.

The opportunity costs are the area of the shaded triangle below the labor supply curve, and the economic rent is the area of the shaded triangle above the labor supply curve. To calculate the amount of opportunity cost, calculate the area of its triangle, or ½ times the base times the height. The base is 3.0 million hours and the height is $3. Thus, the area is (½)(3.0 million hours)($3) so that the opportunity cost of these workers equals $4.5 million. Economic rent can be calculated similarly, and it (coincidentally) also equals $4.5 million.

8. When the *MRP* from capital increases, the demand curve for capital shifts rightward (in Figure 14.14 the shift from D_0 to D_1). As a result of this shift, the interest rate rises (from R_0 to R_1) and the capital stock increases (from K_0 to K_1).

9. a. Figure 14.15 plots the demand and supply schedules. The equilibrium wage rate is $3 an hour, and the equilibrium quantity of employment is 3.0 million hours.

10. Figure 14.16 (on the next page) illustrates how the increase in the marginal revenue product affects the rental rate on this land. The supply of this land is perfectly inelastic, so the supply curve is vertical. Then, the increase in the marginal revenue product of the land increases the demand for the land, thereby shifting the demand curve from D_0 to D_1.

As a result, the rent rises from R_0 to R_1. Because the supply is perfectly inelastic, *all* of the income

FIGURE **14.16**

Short Answer Problem 10

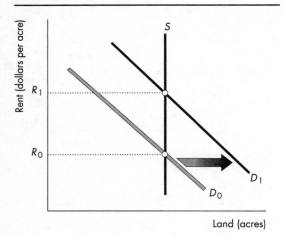

paid to this land is economic rent. Therefore all the rise in income represents an increase in economic rent. There is no opportunity cost, so none of the increase is opportunity cost.

■ **You're the Teacher**

1. "You're missing the point, so quit laughing and listen up. First, a lot of jobs don't require 40 hours of work per week; think about my part-time job at JCPenney, where I'm working 20 hours a week. Then there are other jobs, like when I've graduated from law school and I'm an attorney, where you have to work a whole lot more than 40 hours a week. I understand that attorneys working for large firms often put in 60 or 70 hours a week! There are also jobs like in construction where you might work 40 hours a week some weeks but not at all in others. Some jobs have 2 weeks of vacation, others 4 or 5 weeks. Still other jobs offer a lot of overtime at various times in the year. So the whole idea that you either work 40 hours or not at all is nonsense. In fact, I was talking with our economics teacher and I found out that nowadays the average person in the United States works about 34 hours a week! So, it makes sense to think about a supply of labor because people can decide what sort of jobs they want to look for and can decide how many hours they will be putting in at work."

Chapter Quiz

1. A decrease in the demand for a factor normally _____ the factor's price and _____ the quantity employed of the factor.
   a. raises; increases
   b. raises; decreases
   c. lowers; increases
   d. lowers; decreases

2. Which supply curve can "bend-backwards"?
   a. The supply curve of capital.
   b. The supply curve of land.
   c. The supply curve of labor.
   d. None of the above.

3. The marginal revenue product of a factor is the
   a. additional output produced by using an additional unit of the factor.
   b. total revenue divided by the total amount of the factor used.
   c. revenue gained by employing an additional unit of the factor.
   d. revenue gained by selling one more unit of output.

4. A firm's marginal revenue product of labor curve is
   a. upward sloping.
   b. the same as the firm's supply of labor curve.
   c. the same as the firm's demand for labor curve.
   d. the same as the firm's marginal cost curve.

5. If a new technology increases the marginal product of capital, the firm's demand for capital curve
   a. shifts rightward.
   b. does not shift.
   c. shifts leftward.
   d. becomes steeper.

6. The demand for labor *always* increases (shifts rightward) when
   a. the price of capital falls.
   b. technology increases the productivity of capital.
   c. the price and marginal revenue of the firm's output rise.
   d. the wage rate falls.

7. The demand for the services of labor _____ a derived demand and the demand for the services of capital _____ a derived demand.
   a. is; is
   b. is; is not
   c. is not; is
   d. is not; is not

8. The less sensitive a firm's demand for capital is to interest rates, the
   a. flatter its demand curve for capital.
   b. steeper its demand curve for capital.
   c. less its demand curve for capital shifts when the interest rate changes.
   d. more its demand curve for capital shifts when the interest rate changes.

9. For a nonrenewable natural resource, which supply is perfectly elastic?
   a. The stock supply only.
   b. The known stock supply only.
   c. The flow supply only.
   d. Both the stock supply and the flow supply.

10. In a factor market in which the supply is perfectly elastic, an increase in demand for the factor will _____ its opportunity cost and _____ its economic rent.
    a. increase; increase
    b. not change; increase
    c. increase; not change
    d. not change; not change

The answers for this Chapter Quiz are on page 368

Appendix

LABOR UNIONS

Key Concepts

Market Power in the Labor Market

A **labor union** is an organized group of workers that aims to increase wages and influence other job conditions.

- *Craft union* — a group of workers with similar skills working for different companies.
- *Industrial union* — a group of employees with different skills working in the same industry or firm.

Unions negotiate with employers using *collective bargaining*. Unions' objectives for their members include increasing compensation, improving working conditions, and expanding job opportunities. Methods of achieving these objectives include:

- restricting the supply of labor.
- increasing the demand for union labor and/or making it more inelastic.

Unions work to increase the demand for their members' labor by raising the marginal product of their members, encouraging import restrictions, supporting minimum wage laws, supporting immigration restrictions, and increasing the demand for the product produced by their members.

In competitive labor markets, unions have the following effects:

- In unionized labor markets, the increased demand and decreased supply raise union members' wages and incomes. If the supply decreases more than the demand increases, the quantity of employment falls.

After allowing for differences in skills, the union-nonunion wage differential is between 10 and 25 percent.

Monopsony

A **monopsony** is a market in which there is a single buyer. A firm that is the only employer in town is a monopsonist in the labor market.

- A monopsony determines what wage it will pay and pays the lowest wage that lets it hire the number of workers it wants to employ.

FIGURE A14.1

A Monopsony Labor Market

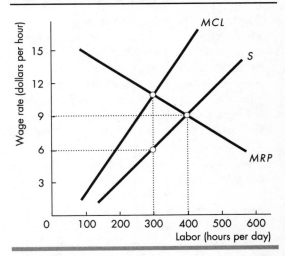

To hire more labor, a monopsony must pay a higher wage to *all* its workers. Because it raises the wage it pays all workers, for a monopoly the marginal cost of labor exceeds the wage paid the new worker. As illustrated in Figure A14.1, the marginal cost of labor curve (*MCL*) for the monopsony slopes upward and lies above the supply curve (*S*) of labor.

The profit-maximizing rule for a monopsony is to (1) hire the quantity of labor indicated by the intersection of the *MCL* curve and the *MRP* curve, and (2) then use the labor supply curve to offer the lowest wage rate possible that allows it to hire the quantity of labor it wants. In Figure A14.1, the monopsony hires 300 hours of labor and pays $6 per hour.

♦ With a monopsony, employment and the wage rate are lower than in a competitive labor market. In Figure A14.1 a competitive labor market would result in employment of 400 hours of labor and a wage rate of $9 per hour.

♦ If the monopsonist faces a union, the labor market is characterized as a **bilateral monopoly**. In this case the wage rate is determined by the relative bargaining strengths of the firm and the union.

♦ A minimum wage law can affect the outcome in a monopsony market. The minimum wage makes labor supply perfectly elastic at the minimum wage so that the *MCL* falls to equal the minimum wage. In response, the monopsonist hires more labor and pays a higher wage rate.

Helpful Hints

1. **SIMILARITIES BETWEEN MONOPSONY AND MONOPOLY:** There is a close parallel between (a) the relationship between the labor supply curve and the *MCL* curve for a monopsony, and (b) the relationship between the demand curve and the marginal revenue curve, *MR*, for a monopoly discussed in Chapter 12. Both relationships stem from market power: a monopsony sets the wage it pays and a monopoly sets the price it charges.

The monopoly, as the only seller in an output market, faces a downward-sloping demand curve. The marginal revenue from the sale of an additional unit of output is less than the price because the monopolist must lower the price on *all* the units it sells, not only the one new unit but also all previous units sold as well. So the *MR* curve lies below the demand curve for the single-price monopoly.

The monopsony in a labor market faces an upward sloping labor supply curve. The marginal cost of hiring an additional unit of labor is higher than the wage because the monopsony must raise the wage for *all* the workers it hires, not only the one new worker but also all previous workers hired. So the *MCL* curve lies above the labor supply curve for the monopsony.

Questions

■ True/False and Explain

Market Power in the Labor Market

1. Unions try to improve their members' working conditions.

2. A closed shop refers to a firm that is not operating because its workers are on strike.

3. Unions support minimum wage laws in part because they raise the cost of low-skilled labor, a substitute for high-skilled union labor.

4. Most union members earn about 50 percent more than nonunion workers in comparable jobs.

Monopsony

5. For a monopsony, the marginal cost of hiring another worker is less than the wage it must pay.

6. A monopsony determines the amount of labor it hires by where the *MCL* curve crosses the labor supply curve.

7. A monopsony pays a higher wage rate than would be paid in a perfectly competitive labor market.

■ Multiple Choice

Market Power in the Labor Market

1. An arrangement in which workers can be employed without joining a union is a (an)
   a. non-union shop.
   b. union shop.
   c. closed shop.
   d. open shop.

2. Unions attempt to do all of the following EXCEPT
   a. increase the demand for their members' labor.
   b. decrease the supply of labor in their market.
   c. lower the price of labor.
   d. raise the wage paid their members.

3. Which of the following would unions be most likely to support?
   a. Decreasing the legal minimum wage.
   b. Encouraging immigration.
   c. Restricting imports.
   d. Decreasing demand for the goods that their workers produce.

4. With competitive labor markets, in a unionized labor market, unions _____ the wage rate and _____ employment.
   a. lower; decrease
   b. lower; increase
   c. raise; decrease
   d. raise; increase

Monopsony

5. In order to hire an additional worker, a monopsony must pay
   a. a higher wage rate than it paid before.
   b. the same wage rate it paid before.
   c. a lower wage rate than it paid before.
   d. a wage rate that is sometimes higher, sometimes lower, and sometimes the same as before, depending on its labor supply curve.

6. For a monopsony, the *MCL* curve
   a. lies above the labor supply curve.
   b. is the same as the labor supply curve.
   c. lies below the labor supply curve.
   d. is the same as the labor demand curve.

Use Figure A14.2 for the next four questions.

FIGURE A14.2
Multiple Choice Questions 7, 8, 9, 10

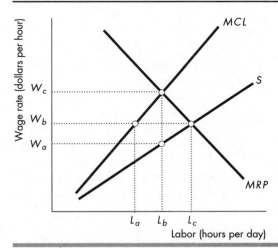

7. If Figure A14.2 illustrates a monopsony, the level of employment is
   a. L_a.
   b. L_b.
   c. L_c.
   d. none of the above.

8. If Figure A14.2 illustrates a monopsony, the wage rate is
   a. W_a.
   b. W_b.
   c. W_c.
   d. none of the above.

9. If Figure A14.2 illustrates a perfectly competitive labor market, the level of employment is
   a. L_a.
   b. L_b.
   c. L_c.
   d. none of the above.

10. If Figure A14.2 illustrates a perfectly competitive labor market, the wage rate is
    a. W_a.
    b. W_b.
    c. W_c.
    d. none of the above.

11. A bilateral monopoly occurs when a
    a. group of unorganized firms bargain with a group of unorganized workers.
    b. single monopsony firm bargains with a group of unorganized workers.
    c. group of unorganized firms bargains with a union representing the workers.
    d. monopsony bargains with a union representing the workers.

12. If a strike or lockout occurs in a bilateral monopoly situation, it usually is because the
    a. demand for labor is relatively inelastic.
    b. supply of labor is relatively inelastic.
    c. firm is not maximizing its profit.
    d. union or firm has misjudged the bargaining situation.

13. A minimum wage can lead a monopsony to
    a. lower its wage rate and lower its level of employment.
    b. increase employment.
    c. lower its wage rate and increase its level of employment.
    d. none of the above.

■ Short Answer Problems

FIGURE **A14.3**
Short Answer Problems 1 and 2

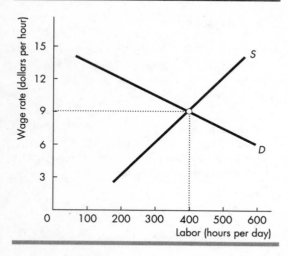

1. Figure A14.3 shows a competitive labor market. The initial equilibrium wage rate is $9 an hour, and the level of employment is 400 hours. Suppose that a union organizes and raises the wage rate to $12 an hour. In the figure, illustrate what happens to the level of employment. Is there any unemployment? What happens in the long run?

2. Suppose that the union in problem 1 manages to make the demand for its members more inelastic. The wage rate stays at $12 an hour. What effect does making the demand more inelastic have on the amount of employment? The amount of unemployment?

3. Table A14.1 shows the demand and supply of labor for one industry in the economy. (For simplicity, the supply is assumed to be perfectly inelastic.)

   a. What is the equilibrium quantity of labor employed? The equilibrium wage rate?

   b. A union organizes in this industry and negotiates a raise in the wage rate to $8 an hour. Now what is the level of employment? Is there any unemployment?

4. Continuing with the situation in Problem 3, suppose that after the union negotiates the higher wage rate, all the workers who cannot find employment leave the first industry and switch to a second.

   a. The initial labor demand and supply schedules for the second industry are shown in Table

TABLE **A14.1**
Unionized Industry

Wage rate (dollars per hour)	Quantity demanded (thousands of workers)	Quantity supplied (thousands of workers)
$4	150	140
5	145	140
6	140	140
7	135	140
8	130	140
9	125	140
10	120	140

TABLE **A14.2**
Nonunionized Industry

Wage rate (dollars per hour)	Quantity demanded (thousands of workers)	Initial quantity supplied (thousands of workers)	New quantity supplied (thousands of workers)
$4	150	140	____
5	145	140	____
6	140	140	____
7	135	140	____
8	130	140	____
9	125	140	____
10	120	140	____

   A14.2. Complete the table showing the new quantity of labor supplied.

   b. Based on Table A14.2, before the first industry became unionized, what was the equilibrium wage rate in the second industry? After the first industry was unionized, what is the equilibrium wage rate in the second industry?

   c. After the first industry is unionized, what is the wage differential between the two industries?

5. Most members of labor unions earn wages well above the minimum wage. Why, then, do unions support raising the legal minimum wage?

6. Table A14.3 (on the next page) shows the supply of nurses facing North Towne Hospital, the only employer of nurses in a small town.

   a. Calculate the values for the *MCL* column and complete the table.

TABLE **A14.3**

North Towne Hospital

Wage rate (dollars per day)	Labor demand (workers)	Labor supply (workers)	Marginal cost of labor, MCL (dollars per hour)
$20	10	2	
30	9	3	____
40	8	4	____
50	7	5	____
60	6	6	____
70	5	7	____
80	4	8	____
90	3	9	____

FIGURE **A14.4**

Short Answer Problem 6 (b)

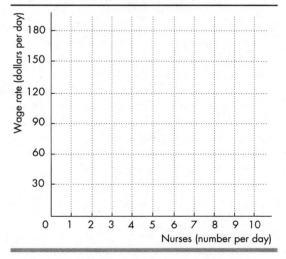

b. Plot the labor demand, labor supply, and *MCL* schedules in Figure A14.4.

c. How many nurses does North Towne hire? What wage rate does North Towne pay?

d. Suppose there were many hospitals so that the market for nurses was perfectly competitive rather than a monopsony. In this case, how many nurses would be hired and what wage rate would they be paid?

e. How does the wage rate that North Towne pays when it is a monopsony compare with the wage rate paid if the market was perfectly competitive? How does the number of nurses hired compare in the two cases?

■ **You're the Teacher**

1. "Unions ought to be banned. After all, they're just monopolies operating in a labor market! And my bet is that they somehow cause inefficiency!" React to the student's statement and then explain how unions do, indeed, result in inefficiency.

Answers

■ True/False Answers

Market Power in the Labor Market

1. **T** Improving their members' working conditions is one of the union's goals.

2. **F** A closed shop is a factory or business in which a worker must be a union member in order to work at a particular job.

3. **T** By raising the cost of substitute inputs, such as low-skilled workers, unions increase the demand for their members' labor.

4. **F** Union members earn about 10 to 25 percent more than nonunion workers with comparable jobs.

Monopsony

5. **F** The marginal cost of hiring another worker *exceeds* the wage rate that must be paid.

6. **F** The level of employment is determined where the *MCL* curve crosses the *MRP* curve.

7. **F** A monopsony exploits its market power by paying a lower wage rate.

■ Multiple Choice Answers

Market Power in the Labor Market

1. **d** The question defines an open shop.

2. **c** Unions strive to *raise* the price of labor, the wage rate.

3. **c** Imports are produced by foreign labor, which is a substitute for domestic, union labor. Hence unions try to restrict imports.

4. **c** By raising the wage rate that must be paid their members, unions decrease employment in the unionized industry.

Monopsony

5. **a** The monopsony must pay the higher wage to *all* the workers it employs, so the marginal cost of hiring another worker exceeds the wage rate.

6. **a** As Figure A14.5 shows, the *MCL* curve is above the labor supply curve.

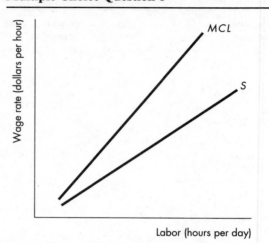

FIGURE **A14.5**
Multiple Choice Question 6

7. **b** A monopsony determines the level of employment by setting the marginal cost of labor (the *MCL*) equal to the marginal revenue product of labor (the *MRP*) so it hires L_b labor.

8. **a** The monopsony hires L_b labor. The supply curve indicates that the lowest wage rate it can pay and still hire this amount of labor is W_a.

9. **c** In a perfectly competitive labor market, the equilibrium quantity of labor is determined by the intersection of the supply curve and demand curve, which is the same as the *MRP* curve.

10. **b** The last four answers show that a monopsony pays a lower wage rate and hires fewer workers then in a perfectly competitive labor market.

11. **d** Bilateral monopoly occurs when both the demand side and supply side of a market are monopolies.

12. **d** By misjudging the situation, either the union or firm might make an offer that it does not realize will drive the other to close the company through a lockout or strike.

13. **b** In a competitive labor market, a minimum wage decreases employment, but it might increase employment in a monopsony labor market.

■ Answers to Short Answer Problems

FIGURE **A14.6**
Short Answer Problem 1

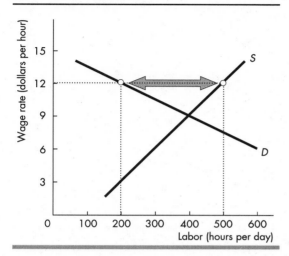

1. Figure A14.6 shows the union's effect on this labor market. After the rise in the wage to $12 an hour firms in the industry hire only 200 hours of labor per week. Employment falls from 400 hours to 200 hours. Unemployment results. The amount of unemployment will depend on how many workers believe that they will find work at the wage rate of $12 an hour. The supply curve of labor shows that at this wage rate, 500 hours of labor are supplied. Therefore there can be unemployment up to 300 hours of labor a week (500 hours − 200 hours), the length of the gray arrow.

2. If the union is able to make demand for its labor more inelastic, the demand curve changes as illustrated in Figure A14.7. Demand D_1 is more inelastic than the initial demand, D_0, because the percentage reduction in the quantity of labor demanded as a result of the higher wage rate is less along D_1 than along D_0. When demand is more inelastic, the decrease in employment from the higher wage is smaller, with employment falling only to 300 hours rather than all the way to 200 hours per week. (The accompanying increase in unemployment from the higher wage also is smaller.) This answer shows why unions strive to make the demand for their members' labor less elastic: It partly offsets the adverse employment effect from the higher union wage rate.

FIGURE **A14.7**
Short Answer Problem 2

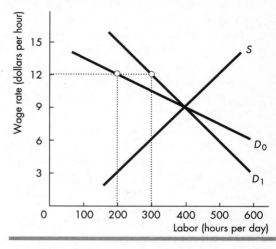

3. a. The equilibrium quantity of labor employed is 140,000 workers and the equilibrium wage rate is $6 an hour.

 b. Once the union negotiates a wage of $8, firms decrease the quantity of employment they demand to 130,000. Hence employment now equals 130,000. Unemployment equals the number of workers willing to work at $8 an hour (140,000) minus the number actually employed (130,000), so unemployment is 10,000.

TABLE **A14.4**
Nonunionized Industry

Wage rate (dollars per hour)	Quantity demanded (thousands of workers)	Initial quantity supplied (thousands of workers)	New quantity supplied (thousands of workers)
$4	150	140	150
5	145	140	150
6	140	140	150
7	135	140	150
8	130	140	150
9	125	140	150
10	120	140	150

4. a. Table A14.4 shows the new situation in the nonunionized industry. The 10,000 unemployed workers who could no longer find work in the unionized industry have switched to the nonun-

ionized industry, thereby increasing the supply of labor in this industry.

b. Before the first industry was unionized, the equilibrium wage rate in the second industry was $6 an hour because this wage rate equated the quantity of labor demanded to the (old) quantity of labor supplied. After the first industry became unionized, the wage rate in the second industry falls to $4 an hour because this wage rate equates the quantity demanded of labor to the (new) quantity supplied.

c. The union-nonunion wage differential is $4. This differential equals the $2 rise in the wage rate in the unionized industry and the $2 drop in the wage rate in the nonunionized industry.

5. A rise in the minimum wage boosts the cost of hiring low-skilled labor. Low-skilled labor can substitute — to an extent — for high-skilled union labor. Hence the rise in the cost of low-skilled labor increases the demand for high-skilled labor and makes sustaining its higher wage easier for the union.

TABLE **A14.5**
Short Answer Problem 6 (a)

Wage rate (dollars per day)	Labor demand (workers)	Labor supply (workers)	Marginal cost of labor, MCL (dollars per hour)
$20	10	2	
			$50
30	9	3	
			70
40	8	4	
			90
50	7	5	
			110
60	6	6	
			130
70	5	7	
			150
80	4	8	
			170
90	3	9	

6. a. Table A14.5 shows the marginal cost of labor, the *MCL*. To calculate these values, consider the *MCL* between 2 and 3 workers. The marginal cost of labor is $(\Delta \text{total wages})/\Delta L$. Total wages equals the number of workers employed times the wage rate, so for 2 nurses it is $20 times 2 workers, or $40 and for 3 nurses it is $90. So the *MCL* between 2 and 3 workers is equal to

FIGURE **A14.8**
Short Answer Problem 6 (b)

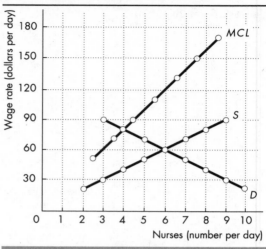

($90 − $40)/(3 − 2) = $50. The rest of the *MCLs* in the table are calculated similarly.

b. Figure A14.8 contains plots of the labor demand, labor supply, and *MCL* schedules.

c. As Figure A14.8 illustrates, North Towne hires 4 nurses because employing this number of nurses sets the marginal cost of labor equal to the marginal revenue product of labor, given by the demand curve. This number of workers is the amount determined by the intersection of North Towne's *MCL* curve and its labor demand curve. The labor supply curve shows that 4 nurses will work for $40 a day, so North Towne pays a wage rate of $40 a day.

d. If the labor market was perfectly competitive, the intersection of the demand curve for labor and the supply curve of labor shows the quantity of labor employed. Figure A14.8 indicates that 6 nurses would be the equilibrium level of employment and that the equilibrium wage rate would be $60 a day.

e. North Towne hires fewer workers and pays them a lower wage when it is a monopsony.

■ You're the Teacher

1. "Well, it's your view that unions ought to be banned. This is your normative judgment, and I might agree or disagree with it. But I will agree with your positive — not normative — guess that unions

create inefficiency. The way to see this result is fairly straightforward. Perfectly competitive firms produce the efficient level of output. To do so, they have to hire the efficient level of employment. But unions restrict the level of employment in order to boost their members' wage rates. Hence firms can't hire the 'right' number of workers, and thus they can't produce the 'right' level of output. Therefore unions, like monopolies, create inefficiency and deadweight losses."

Chapter Quiz

1. The type of union an autoworker belongs to is
   a. an open shop union.
   b. a craft union.
   c. an industrial union.
   d. a closed union.

2. Why do unions try to increase the demand for their members' labor?
   a. Because if the demand for their members' labor increases, the wage rate paid their members as well as the level of employment both increase.
   b. Because unions are unable to decrease the supply of labor, so in order to raise their members' wage rates, they must increase the demand for labor.
   c. The premise of the question is incorrect because unions do *not* try to increase the demand for their members' labor.
   d. None of the above answers is correct.

3. A union that only manages to restrict the supply of labor in its market _____ its member's wage rates and _____ their employment.
   a. raises; increases
   b. raises; decreases
   c. lowers; increases
   d. lowers; decreases

4. A shop that hires only union members is
   a. an open shop.
   b. a closed shop.
   c. a union shop.
   d. None of the above.

5. Unions support
   a. repealing minimum wage laws.
   b. encouraging immigration.
   c. import restrictions.
   d. All of the above.

6. A market with a single buyer is
   a. a monopoly.
   b. a union market.
   c. a monopsony.
   d. illegal.

7. An economy has two sectors, industry and services. Labor markets in both are initially competitive. If a union forms in the industrial labor market, wage rates in the industrial sector _____ and wages rates in the service sector _____.
   a. rise; rise
   b. rise; fall
   c. fall; rise
   d. fall; fall

8. Compared to a perfectly competitive market, a monopsony firm pays a _____ wage rate and hires _____ labor.
   a. higher; more
   b. high; less
   c. lower; more
   d. lower; less

9. If a minimum wage above the existing wage rate is imposed in a monopsony labor market, then
   a. it is possible for both the wage rate and level of employment to increase.
   b. employment definitely decreases, but the effect on the wage rate is ambiguous.
   c. employment definitely decreases and the wage rate definitely increases.
   d. None of the above answers is correct.

10. The Taft-Hartley Act in 1947 made illegal
    a. all labor unions.
    b. craft unions.
    c. professional associations.
    d. closed shops.

The answers for this Chapter Quiz are on page 368

Chapter 15 ECONOMIC INEQUALITY

Key Concepts

■ Measuring Economic Inequality

Money income equals market income plus cash payments to households by the government. **Market income** equals wages, interest, rent, and profit before paying income taxes. In 2000,

- the mode (most common) household income in 2000 was near $12,500;
- the median (the income for which 50 percent of families have higher incomes and 50 percent have lower) household income was $42,148, and
- the mean (or average) household income was $57,045.

The distribution of income is positively skewed, so that a relatively few people make very high incomes.

- The poorest 20 percent of families received 3.6 percent of the total income; the richest 20 percent received 49.6 percent of the total income.

Inequality in income and wealth is illustrated by a Lorenz curve. A **Lorenz curve** for income (wealth) graphs the cumulative percentage of income (wealth) against the cumulative percentage of households. Figure 15.1 illustrates a Lorenz curve.

- The "line of equality" shows the (hypothetical) distribution of income (wealth) if everyone had the same income (wealth).
- The farther the Lorenz curve is from the line of equality, the more unequal is the distribution.

Income is the amount of earnings received by an individual over a period of time while wealth is the value of things the individual owns at a point in time. Measured wealth is more unequally distributed than income.

FIGURE 15.1
The Lorenz Curve

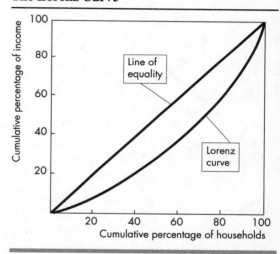

- The data used to construct the wealth distribution do not include human capital and therefore overstate wealth inequalities.
- The distributions of *annual* income are more unequal than distributions of *lifetime* income.

Since 1970, the distribution of income in the United States has become more unequal. On the average, married families, families with more education, middle-aged families and white families have higher incomes than the average.

Poverty exists when a household cannot buy the quantities of food, shelter, and clothing that are deemed necessary. In 2000, 31.1 million individuals had incomes below the official poverty level, $17,761 for a four-person household. A disproportionate number of these households were of Hispanic origin or were black.

■ The Sources of Economic Inequality

Differences in wages and earnings are partly a result of skill differentials, that is, differences in human capital. High-skilled labor has higher wages because:

♦ Demand — the demand for high-skilled labor exceeds the demand for low-skilled labor.

♦ Supply — skills are costly to acquire, so the supply of high-skilled labor is less than that of low-skilled labor.

FIGURE 15.2
High-skilled and Low-skilled Labor

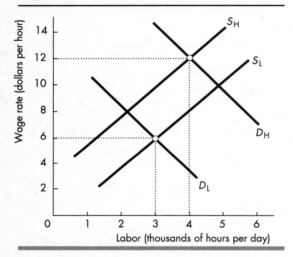

Figure 15.2 illustrates the demand and supply for high-skilled and low-skilled labor. As the figure shows, high-skilled labor receives higher wages than low-skilled labor both because the demand for skilled labor is greater and also because the supply is smaller.

Human capital is the skills and knowledge of human beings. Workers with more human capital (more skills) receive higher wages. Less schooling, less work experience, and more career interruptions reduce human capital. Between races, differences in schooling have almost disappeared; between sexes, differences in work interruptions still exist though they have diminished.

♦ Over the past years, technological changes have increased the demand for demand for high-skilled workers and decreased it for low-skilled workers, thereby increasing the differences in wages.

♦ *Discrimination* can lead to differences in income. Those discriminated against receive lower wages and less employment than others. Economists point out

that the higher wages paid more favored workers boosts firms' costs and thereby makes it hard for firms to sustain this discrimination.

♦ *Differences in degree of specialization* can affect income differences. Specializing in market production increases productivity and hence wages. Social conventions have led men to specialize in market activities and women to divide their time between market activities and nonmarket activities, such as household production.

♦ *Unequal ownership of capital* contributes to differences in incomes. Inequalities can be passed to future generations through bequests (gifts to the next generation) and assortative mating (marrying within one's socioeconomic class).

■ Income Redistribution

Income is redistributed by governments through income taxes, income maintenance programs, and provision of goods and services below cost.

An income tax can be a:

♦ **Progressive income tax** — the average tax rate increases when income increases.

♦ **Regressive income tax** — the average tax rate decreases when income increases.

♦ **Proportional income tax** — the average tax rate does not change when income increases. (This type of tax is also known as a *flat-rate income tax.*)

Income maintenance programs include social security, unemployment compensation, and welfare. Taxes and income maintenance programs reduce the degree of inequality in the United States. The poorest 20 percent of household receive only 1.1 percent of market income but 4.6 percent of income *after* taxes and benefits.

The **big trade-off** indicates that a more equal income distribution creates less efficiency. Redistribution weakens the incentive to work.

Young women who have not completed high school, have at least one child, and live without a partner are a major welfare challenge. More education and job training are the long-term solutions to removing these people from poverty. In the short run, welfare is the solution. The current welfare program for this group is the Temporary Assistance for Needy Families (TANF) program, which requires an adult member of the family work or perform community service and generally has a 5-year limit for receiving assistance.

Helpful Hints

1. **HOW TO CALCULATE A LORENZ CURVE :** If you are ever called upon to construct a Lorenz curve, the crucial point to recall is that it measures *cumulative* percentages. In other words, along the horizontal axis is the cumulative percentage of households and along the vertical axis is, say, the cumulative percentage of income. *Cumulate* is just a fancy word for *sum* or *add,* so the cumulative percentage of income means the total (the "added up") income received by *all* households up to the point under consideration in the income distribution.

   To construct a Lorenz curve, obtain a summary of the incomes of all the households. Calculate the income of the 20 percent having the lowest incomes, which in recent years is 3.6 percent of the nation's total income. Plot this point. Then determine the income for the next 20 percent, which in recent years is 8.9 percent of the nation's total income. Add these two to obtain the cumulative percentage, in this case 12.5 percent. Then plot another point representing the cumulative percentage of households, 40 percent, and the cumulative percentage of income, 12.5 percent. Continue until you reach 100 percent of the households. Connect the points that you have plotted to get the Lorenz curve.

Questions

■ True/False and Explain

Measuring Economic Inequality

1. Income in the United States is distributed normally; that is, it has the common bell shape.

2. The line of equality in a Lorenz curve shows what the income distribution would be if everyone received the same income.

3. The poorest 20 percent of American families receive about 15 percent of the nation's total income; the richest 20 percent receive about 25 percent of the nation's total income.

4. Measured income is less equally distributed than measured wealth.

5. The farther the Lorenz curve is from the line of equality, the more equal is the distribution of income.

6. Income is a flow of earnings; wealth is a stock of assets.

7. The lifetime distribution of income is more equal than the annual distribution of income.

The Sources of Economic Inequality

8. Human capital refers to capital equipment that has been constructed by human workers.

9. The demand for low-skilled workers is less than that for high-skilled workers.

10. More years of schooling and more years of work experience both will increase human capital.

11. If males on average earn more than females, there must be discrimination in the labor market.

12. Bequests generally make the income distribution more equal.

Income Redistribution

13. A progressive income tax is one whose average tax rate falls as income increases.

14. Government redistribution makes the income distribution more equal.

15. The big trade-off is the idea that equalizing the distribution of income reduces economic efficiency.

■ Multiple Choice Questions

Measuring Economic Inequality

1. The mean (average) U.S. family income in 2000 was approximately
   a. $12,000.
   b. $57,000.
   c. $93,000.
   d. $150,000.

2. In a Lorenz diagram for income, the line of equality shows
   a. the most equitable income distribution.
   b. how unequally incomes are distributed.
   c. how much redistribution occurs.
   d. the income distribution if everyone received the same income.

Use Figure 15.3 for the next two questions.

FIGURE 15.3
Multiple Choice Questions 3 and 4

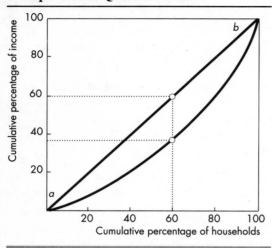

3. In Figure 15.3 the straight line labeled *ab* is the
   a. Lorenz curve.
   b. line of equality.
   c. line of poverty.
   d. line of distribution.

4. In Figure 15.3 the poorest 60 percent of households have what percent of the nation's total income.
   a. About 37 percent
   b. About 60 percent
   c. About 63 percent
   d. Precisely 100 percent

5. The farther away a Lorenz curve for income is from the line of equality, the
   a. more equally wealth is distributed.
   b. more equally income is distributed.
   c. less equally income is distributed.
   d. None of the above.

6. The measured annual distribution of wealth
   a. understates inequality because it does not take into account the family's stage in its life cycle.
   b. understates inequality because it does not take into account the distribution of human capital.
   c. overstates inequality because it takes into account the family's stage in its life cycle.
   d. overstates inequality because it does not take into account the distribution of human capital.

7. Which of the following would show the <u>LEAST</u> amount of inequality?
   a. Measured annual income
   b. Measured annual wealth
   c. Lifetime income
   d. Measured annual income and annual wealth are equally distributed and are more equally distributed than lifetime income.

8. On average, which families have the highest incomes?
   a. Black households
   b. Households of Hispanic origin
   c. White households
   d. Households of Hispanic origin and white households are tied for the highest income

9. Of the approximate total population of 280 million people in America, about how many have incomes below the official poverty level?
   a. Approximately 13 million.
   b. Approximately 31 million.
   c. Approximately 59 million.
   d. Approximately 94 million.

The Sources of Income Inequality

10. The higher the cost of acquiring skills, the _____ are the high-skilled and low-skilled labor _____ curves.
    a. closer together; demand
    b. farther apart; demand
    c. closer together; supply
    d. farther apart; supply

11. Which of the following is a reason why the wage rate of high-skilled workers exceeds the wage rate of low-skilled workers?
    a. The market for high-skilled workers is more competitive than the market for low-skilled labor.
    b. The demand for high-skilled workers exceeds the demand for low-skilled workers.
    c. The number of high-skilled workers exceeds the number of low-skilled workers.
    d. Low-skilled workers often are in the process of acquiring more human capital.

12. Which of the following is <u>NOT</u> a potential reason for wage differences by race or sex?
    a. Discrimination
    b. Differences in human capital
    c. Differences in the degree of specialization
    d. All of the above are potential reasons for wage differences by race or sex

13. Which of the following will <u>NOT</u> increase a worker's human capital?
    a. More work experience
    b. More training
    c. More schooling
    d. A higher wage rate

14. Comparing the wage rates between never-married men and women with the same amount of human capital, researchers have found that the wage rates are
    a. farther apart than the wage rates of other men and women in the labor force generally.
    b. the same as wage rates of other men and women in the labor force generally.
    c. equal.
    d. not comparable because men and women work at different jobs.

15. An example of a bequest is
    a. a pair of rich individuals marrying each other.
    b. money given by the government to a person living below the poverty level.
    c. a guaranteed annual income under a negative income tax.
    d. an inheritance left to a child.

16. An example of assortative mating is
    a. a poor woman marrying a rich man.
    b. a rich man marrying a rich woman.
    c. a rich woman marrying a poor man.
    d. something that cannot be expressed in polite society.

Income Redistribution

17. Which of the following reduces the inequality of income?
    a. Government payments to the poor.
    b. A regressive income tax.
    c. Large bequests.
    d. Assortative mating.

18. Government tax and redistribution programs
    a. generally redistribute income away from the poor and give it to the rich.
    b. have no net redistributive effects.
    c. generally redistribute income away from the rich and give it to the poor.
    d. are dwarfed by the scale of government programs designed to give away goods and services below cost.

19. The idea that increasing the equality of the income distribution reduces economic efficiency is called the
    a. negative tax trap.
    b. progressive tax problem.
    c. big trade-off.
    d. problem of poverty.

■ Short Answer Problems

TABLE **15.1**

Market Income

Households grouped by income	Group income (dollars)	Percentage of total national income	Cumulative percentage
Lowest 20%	$200,000	5%	5%
Second lowest 20%	300,000	____	____
Middle 20%	500,000	____	____
Second highest 20%	1,000,000	____	____
Highest 20%	2,000,000	____	____

1. Table 15.1 gives information regarding the distribution of market income in Microland, a small nation with 100 residents.
   a. Complete the table.
   b. Based on Table 15.1, plot the Lorenz curve for this nation in Figure 15.4 (on the next page).

2. The government of Microland imposes a progressive income tax. Only those in the highest 20 percent income bracket pay the tax, and they must pay 30 percent of their income. From the tax receipts, the government gives 1/3 to the lowest 20 percent group, 1/3 to the next lowest, and 1/3 to the next lowest (the middle 20 percent group).
   a. If none of the groups in the economy alter their behavior — so that their market incomes remain the same as those in Table 15.1 — finish

FIGURE **15.4**

Short Answer Problems 1 and 2

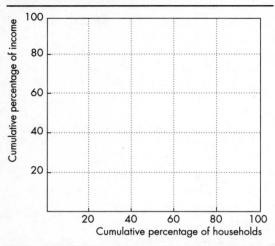

TABLE **15.2**

Group Income After Redistribution

Households grouped by income	Group income (dollars)	Percentage of total national income	Cumulative percentage
Lowest 20%	____	____	____
Second lowest 20%	____	____	____
Middle 20%	____	____	____
Second highest 20%	____	____	____
Highest 20%	____	____	____

FIGURE **15.5**

Short Answer Problem 6

Table 15.2 for the post-tax, post-transfer income distribution.

b. In Figure 15.4 draw the new Lorenz curve showing the distribution of income *after* the government redistribution program.

c. When is income distributed more equally: before or after the government program?

3. With the redistribution policy discussed in problem 2, what are the likely reactions of the recipients of the tax money? Of the taxpayers? How do these reactions affect your answer to part (c) of problem 2?

4. What is the difference between wealth and income? If you know one of these for an individual, can you calculate the other?

5. Jake has human capital worth $100,000 and tangible capital worth $100,000. James has only human capital worth $200,000. The return on both types of capital is 15 percent.

a. What is Jake's income? James's income? Who has more income?

b. Suppose that human capital is not measured. What is Jake's capital? James's capital? According to this measure, who has more capital?

c. If income can be measured correctly, will Jake's and James's income or capital appear to be less equally distributed?

6. Suppose that new technology is developed that increases the demand for high-skilled workers.

In Figure 15.5 illustrate the effect the increase in demand has on the wage rate paid to high-skilled workers. If the new technology does not affect the demand for low-skilled workers, how is the relative wage rates paid high-skilled and low-skilled workers affected?

■ **You're the Teacher**

1. "No citizen of the United States should be forced to live in poverty!" Comment on this assertion. Do you think attaining this goal is likely? Why or why not?

Answers

■ True/False Answers

Measuring Economic Inequality

1. **F** Income in the United States is skewed, with relatively few people earning above-average incomes and many people earning below-average incomes.

2. **T** The question gives the definition of the line of equality.

3. **F** Income is less equally distributed than the question suggests: The poorest 20 percent receive less than 5 percent of the nation's income, and the richest 20 percent receive more than 45 percent of the nation's income.

4. **F** Measured wealth, because it excludes human capital, is distributed much less equally than measured income.

5. **F** The *closer* the Lorenz curve to the line of equality, the more equal the income distribution.

6. **T** Income is received over a period of time and so is a flow; wealth is an amount at a point in time and so is a stock.

7. **T** Over people's lifetimes, income is distributed more equally than annual income.

The Sources of Economic Inequality

8. **F** Human capital is people's skills and talents.

9. **T** The labor demand curve is the *MRP* curve. Because the *MRP* of low-skilled workers is less than high-skilled workers, the demand for low-skilled workers is less than that for high-skilled workers.

10. **T** In general, people with more human capital have higher wages, so more schooling and more work experience generally lead to higher wages.

11. **F** There might be discrimination, but there are other possibilities, such as specialization, that can account for wage differentials.

12. **F** Bequests make the income distribution less equal.

Income Redistribution

13. **F** A progressive income tax is one whose average tax rate *increases* with income.

14. **T** Government redistribution programs increase the income of poorer households and decrease the income of richer households.

15. **T** The trade-off results because more redistribution, and hence more equal incomes, lessens incentives to work, thereby creating inefficiency.

■ Multiple Choice Answers

Measuring Economic Inequality

1. **d** Measured wealth is distributed much less equally than income.

2. **d** This answer defines the line of equality.

3. **b** The line of equality shows the income distribution if everyone received the same income.

4. **a** Follow the dotted line up from 60 percent of the households to the Lorenz curve and then left to determine that these households have about 37 percent of the nation's total income.

5. **c** The farther away the Lorenz curve is from the line of equality, the less equally income is distributed.

6. **d** If human capital were included in the measured wealth distribution, the distribution would be more equal.

7. **c** Over people's lifetimes, the degree of inequality is less than in any given year.

8. **c** White households have the highest average income.

9. **b** According to the government's measure of poverty, 35.6 million people lived in poverty.

The Sources of Economic Inequality

10. **d** The vertical distance between the supply curve of high-skilled labor and of low-skilled labor equals the cost of acquiring the skill.

11. **b** Because the demand for high-skilled workers exceeds the demand for low-skilled, high-skilled workers have a higher wage rate.

12. **d** All of these factors potentially can account for wage differentials.

13. **d** A higher wage rate is the result of an increase in human capital, not a cause.

14. **c** Never-married men and never-married women have the same degree of specialization in market work and their wage rates are the same.

15. **d** Bequests generally make the income distribution less equal.

16. **b** *Assortative mating* refers to like marrying like.

Income Redistribution

17. **a** Government payments to the poor raise their income and reduce income inequality.

18. **c** These government programs result in income after redistribution being distributed more equally than market income.

19. **c** The big trade-off points out a cost of increasing income equality: decreasing economic efficiency.

■ Answers to Short Answer Problems

TABLE **15.3**
Short Answer Question 1

Households grouped by income	Group income (dollars)	Percentage of total national income	Cumulative percentage
Lowest 20%	$ 200,000	5.0%	5.0%
Second lowest 20%	300,000	7.5	12.5
Middle 20%	500,000	12.5	25.0
Second highest 20%	1,000,000	25.0	50.0
Highest 20%	2,000,000	50.0	100.0

1. a. The answers are in Table 15.3. To calculate the answers, first obtain the total income in the nation, $4,000,000, the sum of all the groups' incomes. The percentage earned by the second lowest 20 percent is $300,000/$4,000,000, or 7.5 percent. The cumulative percentage for the second group equals the percentage earned by it and all lower groups, which in this case is only the bottom 20 percent group. So, the cumulative percentage is 5 percent + 7.5 percent = 12.5 percent. The rest of the answers in the table are calculated similarly.

    b. Figure 15.6 shows the Lorenz curve for Microland.

2. a. Table 15.4 shows the income distribution after the government redistribution. The richest 20 percent of households are taxed 30 percent of their income, which equals $600,000. Their after-tax income therefore equals $1,400,000. Then, $200,000 (1/3 of the total $600,000) is given to the lowest 20 percent, so their income rises to $400,000; another 1/3 is given to the next lowest group, so their income rises to

FIGURE **15.6**
Short Answer Problem 1

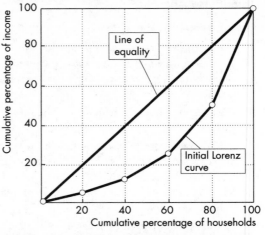

TABLE **15.4**
Short Answer Problem 2

Households grouped by income	Group income (dollars)	Percentage of total national income	Cumulative percentage
Lowest 20%	$ 400,000	10.0%	10.0%
Second lowest 20%	500,000	12.5	22.5
Middle 20%	700,000	17.5	40.0
Second highest 20%	1,000,000	25.0	65.0
Highest 20%	1,400,000	35.0	100.0

$500,000; and the final 1/3 is given to the middle group, so their income rises to $700,000. The percentages are calculated in the same way as in problem 1.

    b. Figure 15.7 (on the next page) shows both Lorenz curves.

    c. Income is distributed more equally after the government programs. The Lorenz curve for income after the government redistribution is closer to the line of equality than the Lorenz curve showing market income before the redistribution.

3. The recipients of the tax money likely will work less. If they were to work more, they might earn enough to move into a higher income bracket and lose the money the government is giving to them. The taxpayers also will tend to work less. The government

FIGURE 15.7

Short Answer Problem 2

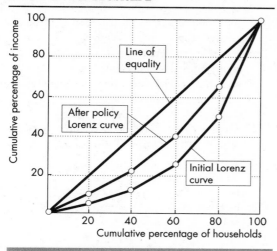

is taxing them so that they must pay 30 percent of their income as taxes. As a result, they will tend to cut back on their work because the income they get to keep for themselves from working, their after-tax income, has fallen. On both counts, people work less and so the nation's total income decreases.

Both of these effects illustrate the force of the big trade-off. By making incomes more equal, the government program has blunted people's incentives to work and thereby lessened economic efficiency and decreased the overall size of the nation's income. These big trade-off effects indicate the cost to redistributing income and should play at least a minor role in your decision whether you think the income distribution before or after the redistribution is best.

4. Wealth is the stock of assets owned by an individual, whereas income is the flow of earnings received by an individual. These concepts are connected because an individual's income is the earnings that flow from the person's stock of wealth. If we know the person's stock of wealth and rate of return, we can calculate his or her income flow. If we know the person's income flow and the rate of return, we can calculate his or her stock of wealth.

5. a. Jake's income equals the return on capital, 15 percent, times the amount of capital. Hence Jake's income equals $30,000. James's income equals $30,000, so the incomes are the same.

   b. Jake's capital is measured as $100,000. James's capital is measured as $0 because human capital

is not included when capital is measured. Jake seems to have more capital.

   c. Capital *appears* to be less equally distributed. The two measured incomes are equal but the two measured capitals are different. This line of reasoning helps explain the difference between the measured income distribution and the measured wealth distribution in the United States.

FIGURE 15.8

Short Answer Problem 7

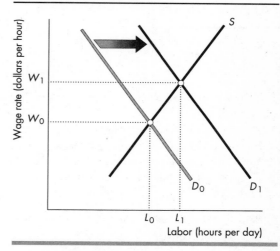

6. The increase in the demand for high-skilled workers shifts the demand curve rightward as shown in Figure 15.8, where the shift is from D_0 to D_1. As a result, the wage rate rises from W_0 to W_1. The wage rates of low-skilled workers are not directly affected by this change, so the relative wage rate of high-skilled to low-skilled workers rises.

■ You're the Teacher

1. "Oh come on, you can't really be serious about this statement, can you? Think of the amount of redistribution it would take to insure that no one has less than the poverty-level income and then think about the idea of the big trade-off that we studied. The opportunity cost of this policy would be immense because it would really blunt people's incentives to work — both the high-income people who would have to pay heavy taxes and the low-income people who would lose a lot of transfer payments if they earned more income. I think the big trade-off points out that this suggestion, appealing in concept, simply isn't practical in reality."

Chapter Quiz

1. In 2000, mean (average) household income in the United States was closest to
   a. $17,000.
   b. $29,000.
   c. $57,000.
   d. $102,000.

2. In the United States, the 20 percent of families with the highest incomes receive about _____ of total income.
   a. 20 percent
   b. 35 percent
   c. 50 percent
   d. 66 percent

3. The closer the Lorenz curve for income is to the line of equality,
   a. the larger is the nation's total income.
   b. the smaller is the nation's total income.
   c. the more equally are incomes distributed.
   d. the larger the fraction of the nation's income received by the richest families.

4. Which of the following makes the distribution of income more equal?
   a. Bequests
   b. Progressive income taxes
   c. Assortative mating
   d. The fact that people paid higher wage rates work more hours

5. Government tax and transfer payments generally
   a. shift the Lorenz curve toward the line of equality.
   b. shift the Lorenz curve away from the line of equality.
   c. have no effect on the Lorenz curve.
   d. shift the Lorenz curve away from the line of equality at low incomes and toward it at high incomes.

6. The big trade-off
   a. would not exist if income taxes were proportional.
   b. points out that the redistribution of income increases people's incentives to work.
   c. says that economic efficiency is decreased as more redistribution is undertaken.
   d. says that richer families trade off more hours at work for more income.

7. The supply curve of high-skilled workers lies _____ the supply curve of low-skilled workers.
   a. above
   b. on top of
   c. below
   d. below at low wage rates and above at high wage rates

8. Over the last decade, technological change has _____ the demand for high-skilled workers and _____ the demand for low skilled workers.
   a. increased; increased
   b. increased; decreased
   c. decreased; increased
   d. decreased; decreased

9. Income is measured _____ and wealth is measured _____.
   a. at a point in time; at a point in time
   b. at a point in time; over a period of time
   c. over a period of time; at a point in time
   d. over a period of time; over a period of time

10. Because the measured distribution of wealth does not consider the role of human capital, the measured wealth distribution
    a. is more equal than measured income distributions.
    b. is less equal than measured income distributions.
    c. is more equal than actual wealth distributions.
    d. cannot be compared to the actual wealth distribution.

The answers for this Chapter Quiz are on page 368

Part Review 5 FACTOR MARKETS

Reading Between the Lines

WRESTLING STILL HAS HOLD ON THE ROCK

On April 21, when his movie "The Scorpion King" was newly released, Dwayne Johnson (perhaps better known as "The Rock") was interviewed by Larry King. Mr. Johnson, star of "The Scorpion King" and also a premier wrestler for the WWF, said that he loved both acting and wrestling and did not know how he would be able to balance both careers. In acting, he has been compared to Arnold Schwarzenegger and it has been suggested that he might be the "next Arnold." In wrestling, although he started his career as a good guy, he changed his persona to become a villain and is currently one of hottest performers on the wrestling circuit.

For details, go to The Economics Place web site, the Economics in the News archive, www.economicsplace.com/econ5e/einarchives.html

■ **Analyze It**

Dwayne Johnson, aka "The Rock," is in an enviable position of becoming a major player in both acting and wrestling. He had an important supporting role in the hit movie "The Mummy II" and now has been the star in another hit movie, "The Scorpion King." At the same time, he is an important star in the World Wrestling Federation's stable of wrestlers. It will be difficult and likely impossible to devote himself full-time to both careers, so at some time Mr. Johnson probably will need to make a decision about which career to pursue.

1. Suppose that Mr. Johnson will supply a maximum of 200 hours a month of work. Further, say the WWF pays him $5,000 per hour. Now, consider his labor supply curve for movies. If a movie studio offers him a wage rate below $5,000 per hour, he will supply no labor for movies because he can work for the WWF at $5,000 per hour. At a wage rate of $5,000 per hour for a movie, he will supply any quantity of labor demanded, up to his maximum of 200 hours per month. And, for any wage rate that exceeds $5,000 per hour for a movie, he will supply his maximum, 200 hours per month. Draw Mr. Johnson's labor supply curve.

2. If Mr. Johnson is paid $6,000 per hour for his next movie, what is his total income per month, his opportunity cost per month, and his economic rent per month?

283

Mid-Term Examination

■ **Chapter 14**

1. An increase in the demand for a factor
   a. decreases both its price and its income.
   b. increases both its price and its income.
   c. decreases its price and increases its income.
   d. increases its price and decreases its income.

2. As the quantity employed of a factor decreases, total product
   a. falls and the factor's marginal product falls.
   b. falls and the factor's marginal product rises.
   c. rises and the factor's marginal product falls.
   d. rises and the factor's marginal product rises.

3. A decrease in the interest rate results from a shift of the supply curve of capital
   a. leftward or a shift of the demand curve for capital leftward.
   b. leftward or a shift of the demand curve for capital rightward.
   c. rightward or a shift of the demand curve for capital leftward.
   d. rightward or a shift of the demand curve for capital rightward.

4. The labor supply curve bends backward if the
   a. substitution effect outweighs the income effect.
   b. income effect outweighs the substitution effect.
   c. demand for labor is elastic.
   d. demand for labor is inelastic.

■ **Chapter 15**

5. Distributions of wealth that include human capital
   a. are more equal than distributions of wealth that exclude human capital.
   b. overstate the degree of income inequality.
   c. understate the degree of income inequality.
   d. None of the above.

6. The high-skilled labor demand curve lies _____ the low-skilled labor demand curve and the high-skilled labor supply curve lies _____ the low-skilled labor supply curve.
   a. above; above
   b. above; below
   c. below; above
   d. below; below

7. On average, compared to women, men are _____ specialized in earning an income in the market and receive _____ pay as a result.
    a. less; lower
    b. less; higher
    c. more; lower
    d. more; higher

8. If the average tax rate rises with income, the tax is
    a. a sales tax.
    b. an excise tax.
    c. a regressive tax.
    d. a progressive tax.

Answers

■ Reading Between the Lines

1. Mr. Johnson's labor supply curve for movies is in Figure 1. For any wage rate less than $5,000 per hour, he supplies no labor to making movies, so his labor supply is perfectly inelastic along the vertical axis. At the wage rate of $5,000 per hour, he is willing to supply whatever quantity of hours is demanded, up to his maximum of 200 hours per month. At this wage rate, his labor supply is perfectly elastic and so his labor supply curve is horizontal. Finally, at wage rates above $5,000 per hour he is willing to supply his maximum of 200 hours per month. For wage rates above $5,000 per hour his labor supply is perfectly inelastic at 200 hours per month and so is labor supply curve is vertical.

2. If Mr. Johnson is paid $6,000 per hour, his total income in a month is ($6,000 per hour) × (200 hours) or $1.2 million. Of the $6,000 per hour, $5,000 per hour is his opportunity cost because that is what the WWF will pay him. As a result, his total opportunity cost is $1.0 million per month. Mr. Johnson obtains an economic rent of $1,000 per hour, the difference between his wage rate and his opportunity cost. So, Mr. Johnson's economic rent is $0.2 million per month.

FIGURE 1

Mr. Johnson's Labor Supply Curve

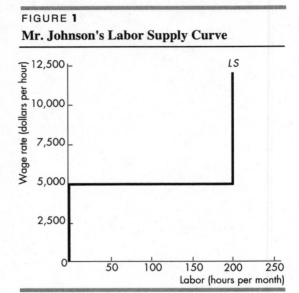

■ Mid-Term Exam Answers

1. b;   2. b;   3. c;   4. b;   5. a;   6. a;   7. d;   8. d.

16 PUBLIC GOODS AND TAXES

■ The Economic Theory of Government

Government economic action often results in response to four problems:

♦ *Public goods* — goods or services that can be consumed by everyone and from which no one can be excluded (discussed in this chapter).

♦ *Taxes and redistribution* — government actions modify the distribution of income (see Chapter 15).

♦ *Monopoly* — monopolies and cartels restrict the amount of output produced (see Chapter 17).

♦ *Externalities* — when the production or consumption of goods and services create a cost or benefit that falls on someone who did not participate in the transaction (discussed in Chapter 18).

Public goods, monopoly, and externalities can create **market failure**, when an unregulated market results in inefficiency.

Public choice theory treats the government sector as a political marketplace, analogous to the economic marketplace. Participants in the political marketplace are:

♦ Voters — the consumers of the outcomes of the political process. They express their demand by voting, lobbying, and making campaign contributions.

♦ Politicians — the officials elected by voters. Their objective is to get elected and reelected.

♦ Bureaucrats — the hired officials who work in the government and are appointed by politicians.

A **political equilibrium** occurs when the choices of voters, politicians, and bureaucrats are compatible and no group can make itself better off with a different choice.

■ Public Goods and the Free-Rider Problem

A **public good** can be consumed simultaneously by everyone and no one can be excluded. The two features of a public good are that it is:

♦ *Nonrival* — one person's consumption does not reduce the amount available for anyone else.

♦ *Nonexcludable* — no one can be excluded from consuming the good.

Nonexcludability means that public goods are subject to free riding:

♦ **A free rider** is someone who consumes a good without paying for it.

Free riding creates the *free-rider problem*, which is the tendency for too little of a public good to be provided if it is produced and sold privately.

The *total benefit* of a public good is the total dollar value placed on it by all citizens, while the *marginal benefit* from a public good is the change in the total benefit from a unit change in its quantity. The *net benefit* is the total benefit minus the total cost.

The *efficient quantity* of a public good is the amount that maximizes net benefit, which occurs when the marginal benefit of another unit equals the marginal cost of supplying it.

♦ With private provision, free riding limits the amount produced and results in an inefficiently low level of output.

♦ Government provision can attain efficiency because free riding is prevented by imposing taxes to finance payment for the good.

The amount of the good that is provided by the government depends on the political marketplace and the actions of politicians, bureaucrats, and voters.

Politicians often follow the principle of minimum differentiation:

♦ **Principle of minimum differentiation** — the tendency for competitors (political parties) to be identical in order to appeal to the maximum number of clients or voters.

Bureaucrats try to maximize the budgets of their agencies.

♦ If voters are well informed, politicians won't allow bureaucrats to expand expenditure beyond the level that maximizes net benefit.

♦ Voters might be **rationally ignorant**; that is, they decide *not* to acquire information because the personal cost of acquisition is larger than the personal benefit from having the information.

If voters are rationally ignorant, politicians, influenced by bureaucrats and lobbyists representing special interests, might allow inefficient overprovision of the public good. If the government is inefficiently providing too many public goods, a voter backlash might occur when voters act to shrink the size of the government.

Two theories of government action are:

♦ *Public interest theory* — predicts that governments act to eliminate waste and achieve economic efficiency.

♦ *Public choice theory* — predicts that government can create inefficiency.

■ **Taxes**

Most of the federal government's revenue comes from income taxes.

♦ The **marginal tax rate** is the percentage of an additional dollar paid as taxes.

♦ The **average tax rate** is the percentage of total income paid as taxes.

Taxes can be *progressive* — when the average tax rate rises when income increases — or *proportional* — when the average tax rate is the same at all levels of income — or *regressive* — when the average tax rate falls as income increases.

Income taxes decrease employment and create deadweight losses. With a progressive income tax, the decrease in employment and deadweight loss are greater for high-wage workers than for low-wage workers.

High-income citizens want to pay lower tax rates; low-income individuals want them to pay higher tax rates. Politicians balance these desires according to the median voter theorem:

♦ *Median voter theorem* — political parties pursue policies maximizing the net benefit of the median voter.

Because the median voter is a low-income voter, income taxes are progressive.

The corporate profits tax is imposed on corporations' profits. This tax decreases the quantity of capital, thereby decreasing productivity and workers' incomes.

Social security taxes are levied on wages. The proportion of the tax really paid by workers and employers depends on the elasticity of labor demand and labor supply, not on the fractions specified in the law.

Property taxes, collected by local governments, finance **local public goods**, public goods consumed by local residents. Elementary, middle, and high schools are examples of local public goods.

An **excise tax** is a tax on the sale of particular good.

♦ An excise tax decreases the supply of the good being taxed. An excise tax is illustrated in Figures 16.1 and 16.2 (both on the next page). The amount of tax is the same in both figures and equals the length of the double-headed arrow.

♦ The tax raises the equilibrium price and decreases the equilibrium quantity. In Figures 16.1 and 16.2, the price including the tax rises the price from P_c to P_t and the quantity decreases from Q_c to Q_t.

♦ The tax creates a deadweight loss, also shown in Figures 16.1 and 16.2.

♦ Comparing of Figure 16.1 and Figure 16.2 shows that taxes imposed on goods with more elastic demand create larger deadweight losses. Hence the government more commonly taxes goods with inelastic demands.

FIGURE **16.1**

The Effect of an Excise Tax

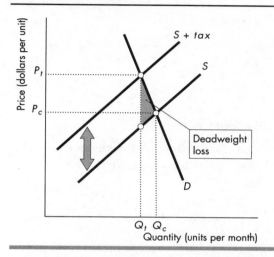

FIGURE **16.2**

Deadweight Loss with an Elastic Demand

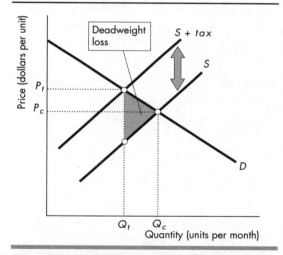

Helpful Hints

1. **PUBLIC GOODS AND GOVERNMENT PROVIDED GOODS :** Not all goods provided by the government are public goods. A public good is defined by the characteristics of nonrivalry and nonexcludability, not by whether it is publicly provided. For example, some cities and communities provide swimming pools; others provide utility services such as electricity. None of these are public goods even though they are provided by the government. Indeed, in many communities, the same services are provided by the private sector.

2. **THE MARGINAL BENEFIT FROM A PUBLIC GOOD :** The properties of nonrivalry and nonexcludability associated with pure public goods imply that the marginal benefit curve for the economy as a whole is different from that for private goods.

   A private good is rival in consumption. Therefore, to obtain the marginal benefit curve for the entire economy, we sum the individual marginal benefit curves horizontally. For instance, at a price of $8 you demand 5 units and I demand 5 units. Because the goods are rival in consumption, none of the 5 units you will consume at this price can be the same as any of the 5 units I will consume. So, we sum the *quantities* so that at $8, in total we demand 10 units.

   However, for the economy's marginal benefit curve for a public good, we sum the individual marginal benefit curves vertically. For instance, for 5 units you are willing to pay $8 and I am willing to pay $8. If 5 units are provided, because the public good is nonrival, the 5 units that you consume are precisely the same as the 5 units that I consume. So, we sum the *prices* so that for 5 units, in total we are willing to pay $16.

   The key difference — that for a public good we consume the same units but for a private good we must consume different units — is the reason that the marginal benefit curve for a public good is derived differently from that for a private good.

3. **POLITICAL MARKETS AND PRODUCT MARKETS :** Public choice theory provides a theory of the political marketplace that parallels the economic theory of markets for goods and services. Drawing analogies between the operation of political markets and ordinary markets is a good way to grasp their similarities.

   In political markets the demanders are voters, whereas in ordinary markets, the demanders are consumers. In both cases, demanders are concerned about their costs and benefits.

   The suppliers in political markets are politicians and bureaucrats, and in ordinary markets, the suppliers of goods and services are firms.

   In political markets, voters express their demands by means of votes, political contributions, and lobbying because the suppliers (politicians) in this market desire to retain political office. In ordinary markets, consumers express their demands by means of dollars because suppliers are motivated by a desire to maximize profit.

In both markets, in equilibrium there is no tendency to change because participants cannot become better off by making a different choice or by engaging in an additional transaction.

Questions

■ True/False and Explain

The Economic Theory of Government

1. Market failure refers to the situation in which the private market fails to produce the efficient amount of output.

2. Political equilibrium occurs only in the absence of market failure.

Public Goods and the Free-Rider Problem

3. Any product supplied by government is a public good.

4. A movie shown in an uncrowded movie theater is both nonexcludable and nonrival in consumption.

5. Public goods — but not private goods — face the free-rider problem.

6. The marginal benefit curve for a public good is obtained the same way as the marginal benefit curve for a private good.

7. A private, unregulated market produces less than the efficient quantity of pure public goods.

8. Rational ignorance is the situation wherein politicians are uninformed about certain voters' desires.

9. The public choice theory predicts that the government makes choices that achieve efficiency.

Taxes

10. The U.S. income tax is a progressive tax.

11. An income tax decreases employment.

12. To be elected, politicians choose platforms that appeal to the median voter.

13. If the demand for labor is perfectly inelastic, workers pay the entire amount of the social security tax.

14. Provision of local public goods usually is financed with excise taxes.

15. The more inelastic the demand for a good, the larger is the deadweight loss created by an excise tax levied on it.

■ Multiple Choice

The Economic Theory of Government

1. Which of the following is NOT a source of market failure?
   a. The existence of public goods
   b. The presence of externalities
   c. The fact that some goods are rival in consumption
   d. The existence of monopolies

2. Market failure refers to the situation when
   a. a market does not create a deadweight loss.
   b. a market uses resources inefficiently.
   c. the government prohibits free riding.
   d. None of the above.

Public Goods and the Free-Rider Problem

3. Which of the following is nonrival and excludable?
   a. The defense services provided by a new stealth bomber
   b. A pair of pants
   c. A beautiful sunset
   d. An uncrowded theme park such as Walt Disney World

4. To two fishermen, a codfish swimming in the middle of the ocean is a good that is
   a. nonrival and nonexcludable.
   b. nonrival and excludable.
   c. rival and nonexcludable.
   d. rival and excludable.

5. To two farmers, a steer (owned by one of the farmers) grazing in the middle of the farmer's pasture is
   a. nonrival and nonexcludable.
   b. nonrival and excludable.
   c. rival and nonexcludable.
   d. rival and excludable

6. A free rider is someone who
   a. does not pay taxes.
   b. cannot be excluded from consuming a public good even though he or she did not pay for the good.
   c. paid more than his or her fair share for the provision of a public good.
   d. cannot be forced to pay for his or her consumption of a private good.

7. Governments provide pure public goods such as national defense because
   a. governments know how to produce these goods.
   b. of the free-rider problems that result in underproduction by private markets.
   c. people do not value national defense very highly.
   d. of the potential that private firms will make excess profits.

8. The economy's marginal benefit curve for a public good is obtained by
   a. summing the individual marginal cost curves horizontally.
   b. summing the individual marginal cost curves vertically.
   c. summing the individual marginal benefit curves horizontally.
   d. summing the individual marginal benefit curves vertically.

9. The efficient amount of a public good
   a. is as much as the public demands.
   b. cannot be provided unless the problem of nonexcludability is overcome.
   c. equates total benefit and total cost.
   d. is such that the marginal benefit equals the marginal cost.

10. Suppose that the marginal benefit from another unit of a public good exceeds the marginal cost of producing it. Then
    a. the net benefit from the product is at its maximum, and its provision is at the efficient level.
    b. the net benefit from the product is at its maximum, but the provision of the product is not at its efficient level.
    c. less of the product should be produced because its provision exceeds the efficient level.
    d. more of the product should be produced because its provision is less than the efficient level.

11. The idea that political parties will have similar policy proposals reflects
    a. free riding.
    b. rational ignorance.
    c. government failure.
    d. the principle of minimum differentiation.

12. Amy realizes that her personal benefit from becoming an expert on welfare reform is limited, so she does not learn about this issue. Amy's decision best reflects
    a. free riding.
    b. the nonexcludability principle.
    c. the median voter theorem.
    d. rational ignorance.

13. The amount of a public good that maximizes the net benefit to the economy is likely to be provided if
    a. voters are well informed.
    b. rational ignorance is combined with special interest lobbying.
    c. politicians are well informed.
    d bureaucrats are rationally ignorant.

14. Public choice theory predicts that
    a. the government conducts policies that move the economy toward an efficient use of resources.
    b. politicians and bureaucrats tend to be more concerned about the public interest than individuals in the private sector.
    c. the choices of government maximize net benefits.
    d. the choices of government can create inefficiency.

Taxes

15. Income taxes _____ employment and _____ a deadweight loss
    a. increase; do not create
    b. increase; create
    c. decrease; do not create
    d. decrease; create

16. Voters are asked to vote for either proposition A or proposition B. Proposition A will win if it
    a. is closer to efficiency.
    b. is supported by bureaucrats.
    c. is preferred by the median voter.
    d. generates greater total social benefits than total social costs.

17. When income increases, a regressive tax's average tax rate ____ and an example of a regressive tax is ____.
    a. increases; the income tax
    b. decreases; the income tax
    c. decreases; a sales tax
    d. increases; a sales tax

Figure 16.3 illustrates the effects from an excise tax that has been imposed on compact discs. Use this figure for the next four questions.

FIGURE **16.3**
Multiple Choice Questions 18, 19, 20, 21

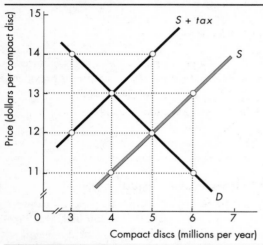

18. The amount of the tax per CD is
    a. $14.
    b. $13.
    c. $12.
    d. $2.

19. The equilibrium price, including the tax, after the tax has been imposed is
    a. $14.
    b. $13.
    c. $12.
    d. $11.

20. The amount of tax revenue the government collects is
    a. $70 million.
    b. $52 million.
    c. $44 million
    d. $8 million.

21. The amount of deadweight loss created is
    a. $12 million.
    b. $8 million.
    c. $6 million.
    d. $1 million.

22. The deadweight loss triangle from an excise tax is the loss of
    a. only consumer surplus.
    b. only producer surplus.
    c. consumer surplus plus the loss of producer surplus.
    d. consumer surplus plus the loss of producer surplus minus the tax revenue collected.

23. Suppose that the demand for wine is not perfectly inelastic and that initially 5 million bottles of wine are produced and consumed in the United States. If the government imposes an excise tax of $1 per bottle of wine, the government will collect
    a. more than $5 million in tax revenues.
    b. $5 million in tax revenues.
    c. less than $5 million in tax revenues.
    d. An amount that might be more than, equal to, or less than $5 million in tax revenues, depending on the elasticity of demand.

24. Products with elastic demands often are lightly taxed because
    a. they usually are goods consumed largely by the poor.
    b. the amount of the deadweight loss created is large.
    c. free riders ensure that the government's tax revenue is small.
    d. The premise of the question is wrong because products with elastic demands usually are taxed heavily.

■ **Short Answer Problems**

1. Explain the nonrivalry and nonexcludability features of a pure public good. Why are both necessary for the good to be a pure public good?

2. What is the free-rider problem? For what type of goods is the free-rider problem particularly acute? Why does free riding hinder private firms from producing the efficient amount (or any amount!) of a public good?

TABLE 16.1

Security at Parkin Springs Apartments

Number of guards	Total cost of guards (dollars)	Marginal benefit per resident (dollars)	Marginal benefit to all residents (dollars)
1	$300	$10	$____
2	600	4	____
3	900	2	____
4	1,200	1	____

3. Parkin Springs Apartments has 100 residents who all are concerned about security. Table 16.1 gives the total cost per day of hiring a 24-hour security guard service and the marginal benefit per day to each of the residents.

   a. Why is a security guard a public good for the residents of Parkin Springs Apartments?

   b. Why will no guards be hired if each of the residents must act individually?

   c. Complete the last column of Table 16.1 by computing the marginal benefit of security guards to all the residents combined.

4. Now suppose that the residents form an Apartment Council that acts as a governing body to address the security issue.

   a. What is the efficient number of guards? What is the net benefit of this amount?

   b. Show that net benefit is less for either one less guard or for one more guard than the net benefit for the efficient number of guards.

   c. How might the Apartment Council pay for the guards it will hire?

5. The ships of 10 companies must navigate a treacherous section of coastline. Each year each shipping line incurs $200,000 in shipping costs from ships running aground there. If a lighthouse was built, these costs would fall to zero. Building and maintaining the lighthouse would cost $1,900,000 a year. If it was constructed, all the ships that pass that way would benefit from the lighthouse and none would run aground.

   a. From society's point of view, is building the lighthouse efficient?

   b. From a company's point of view, if each company pays ¹/₁₀ the total cost of building a lighthouse, is building it profitable?

   c. Suppose that the lighthouse was constructed but that one company did not help pay for it. What is this company's profit from the lighthouse?

   d. Based on your answers to parts (b) and (c), what incentive does each company have?

   e. If one company decides not to pay for the lighthouse, will it be constructed?

   f. What might the government do in this case?

6. Explain why voter ignorance might be rational.

TABLE 16.2

Income Tax Rates

Person	Desired income tax rate
April	80%
Brian	40
Christopher	25
Diane	30
Eric	10

7. Table 16.2 shows the citizens in a (small!) democratic nation and their desired income tax rates. The political parties are trying to decide what income tax rate to propose.

   a. Who is the median voter? What income tax rate will be proposed by the parties? Why?

   b. Before the next election, April changes her mind and decides that she wants an income tax rate of 50 percent. What income tax rate will now be proposed? How does this tax rate compare with that in part (a)? If it is different, why is it different; if it is the same, why is it the same?

   c. April continues to change her mind and before the third election she decides that she wants an income tax rate of 20 percent. Now what income tax rate will be proposed? How does this tax rate compare with those in parts (a) and (b)? If it is different, why is it different; if it is the same, why is it the same?

8. Suppose the demand for labor is perfectly *elastic*. What is the effect on the wage rate of a social security tax that workers must send to the government? How is the tax divided? Use a diagram to illustrate your answer.

9. Suppose the demand for labor is perfectly *inelastic*. What is the effect on the wage rate of a social security tax that workers must send to the government? Who pays the tax? Use a diagram in your answer.

TABLE 16.3

The Initial Market for Shoes

Price (dollars per pair of shoes)	Quantity of shoes supplied (millions)	Quantity of shoes demanded (millions)
$55	70	90
60	75	85
65	80	80
70	85	75
75	90	70
80	95	65

TABLE 16.4

The Market for Shoes After the Tax

Price, including tax (dollars per pair of shoes)	Quantity of shoes supplied (millions)	Quantity of shoes demanded (millions)
$55	60	____
60	65	____
65	____	____
70	____	____
75	____	____
80	____	____

10. Table 16.3 shows the initial demand and supply schedules for shoes.

   a. Based on Table 16.3, what is the initial equilibrium price of a pair of shoes? The equilibrium quantity?

   b. Suppose that the government imposes a tax of $10 per pair of shoes that the supplier must pay. Complete Table 16.4, showing the demand and supply schedules after the tax has been levied.

   c. In Figure 16.4, illustrate the effect of the tax on the market for shoes by drawing the pre-tax and post-tax supply and demand curves.

FIGURE 16.4

Short Answer Problem 10 (c)

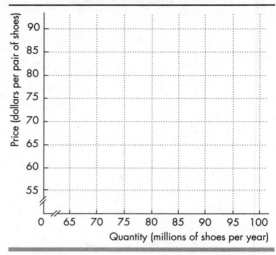

   d. After the tax is imposed, what is the equilibrium price (including the tax) for a pair of shoes? The equilibrium quantity?

   e. How much of the tax do suppliers pay? Demanders?

   f. What is the amount of deadweight loss from this tax? (Hint: Figure 16.4 should be helpful when answering this question.)

■ You're the Teacher

1. "I don't see why the government would ever do anything that leads to inefficiency. Inefficiency hurts the nation and I thought that the government would try to help us." Comment on this student's views and give an example of how the government might take actions that create inefficiency.

Answers

■ True/False Answers

The Economic Theory of Government

1. **T** This is the definition of market failure.

2. **F** Political equilibrium occurs when neither voters, politicians, nor bureaucrats have an incentive to change their actions.

Public Goods and the Free-Rider Problem

3. **F** Public goods are characterized by nonrivalry and nonexcludability.

4. **F** The movie is nonrival but not nonexcludable because a theater can easily exclude people who do not pay to see the movie.

5. **T** Public goods are nonexcludable and so they face a severe free-rider problem.

6. **F** The marginal benefit curve for a public good is derived by adding *vertically* each individual's marginal benefit curve; the marginal benefit curve for a private good is derived by adding *horizontally* each person's marginal benefit curve.

7. **T** Because of the free-rider problem, a private un-regulated market might produces less than the efficient amount of a public good.

8. **F** Rational ignorance occurs when a voter is uninformed about an issue because the benefit to the voter of becoming informed is less than the cost to the voter.

9. **F** The public interest theory predicts that the government makes choices to achieve efficiency; the public choice theory says that government choices can result in inefficiency.

Taxes

10. **T** Because the income tax's marginal tax rates increase with income, the average tax rate also rises with income.

11. **T** An income tax decreases employment and creates a deadweight loss.

12. **T** By appealing to the median voter, the politician will attract more than half the votes and so win the election.

13. **F** If the demand for labor is perfectly inelastic, employers pay the entire amount of the social security tax.

14. **F** Local public goods are usually financed with property taxes.

15. **F** The more elastic the demand, the larger is the deadweight loss from a tax.

■ Multiple Choice Answers

The Economic Theory of Government

1. **c** Nonrivalry, not rivalry, can create market failure.

2. **b** Government action can sometimes help overcome the problem of market failure.

Public Goods and the Free-Rider Problem

3. **d** The uncrowded theme park is nonrival because your enjoyment does not limit my enjoyment of it, but it is excludable as anyone who ever tried to sneak into Walt Disney World can testify.

4. **c** If one fisherman catches the fish, the other cannot, so the codfish is rival; but in the middle of the ocean no fisherman can exclude another from trying to catch the fish, so the codfish is nonexcludable.

5. **d** The farmer who owns the steer can use it but the other farmer cannot, so the steer is rival; in the middle of a pasture, the first farmer can exclude the other farmer from trying to catch the steer. Note the fundamental difference between the steer, which is owned and therefore is both rival and excludable, and the codfish, which is not owned and therefore is rival but nonexcludable.

6. **b** This answer is the definition of a free rider.

7. **b** The free-rider problem limits the private market's ability to produce the efficient amount of public goods.

8. **d** Vertical summation shows the price everyone in total is willing to pay for any particular quantity.

9. **d** If the marginal benefit from *any* good equals the marginal cost, the efficient amount is produced.

10. **d** If one more unit is produced, the gain to society (the marginal benefit) exceeds the cost to society (the marginal cost), so the additional net benefit from the unit is positive.

11. **d** Both parties want to appeal to the median voter. Hence both parties present similar proposals and so follow the principle of minimum differentiation.

12. **d** Amy is pursuing her own self-interest and rationally decides not to become an expert on welfare reform.

13. **a** If voters are well informed, they can ensure that politicians force bureaucrats to provide the efficient amount of the public good.

14. **d** Public choice theory says that rational ignorance might lead to inefficient outcomes.

Taxes

15. **d** By decreasing employment, income taxes create a deadweight loss.

16. **c** If the median voter supports proposition A, proposition A will receive a majority of votes and will win.

17. **c** The sales tax is a regressive tax because wealthy people pay a lower fraction of their income on the sales tax than do poor people.

18. **d** The vertical distance between the supply curve with the tax and the supply curve without the tax equals the amount of the tax, $2 in this case.

19. **b** After the tax, the quantity supplied equals the quantity demanded at $13.

20. **d** The equilibrium quantity is 4 million CDs, and the government imposes a tax of $2 on each CD. So the total tax revenue is $8 million.

21. **d** The deadweight loss is shown as triangle *abc* in Figure 16.5. The triangle's area is (½)(1 million CDs)($2 per CD), so the deadweight loss is $1 million.

22. **c** Both producers and consumers suffer a loss from an excise tax.

23. **c** The new equilibrium quantity of wine is less than 5 million bottles, so the government collects less than $5 million in tax revenue.

24. **b** The more elastic the demand for a product, the more a tax decreases the quantity produced and the greater is the deadweight loss.

■ Answers to Short Answer Problems

1. A good has the nonrivalry feature if its consumption by one person does not reduce the amount available for others. The nonexcludability feature means that if the good is produced and consumed by one person, others cannot be excluded from consuming it. Both characteristics are necessary for the good to be a pure public good. The nonrivalry feature of a

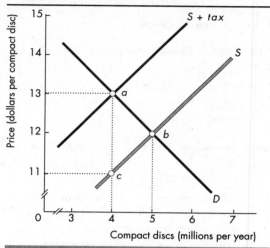

FIGURE 16.5
Multiple Choice Question 21

public good means that everyone can consume the good simultaneously. Limiting the consumption to one person at a time would be inefficient because others can consume the product without denying it to anyone else. In addition, private goods are sold by firms so that the firms' owners can earn an income and thereby purchase goods and services for themselves. Public goods are nonexcludable, which means that anyone can consume the product regardless of the amount paid. This fact gives people the incentive to free ride. Free riding makes the provision of such goods by private companies unlikely because the firm will not be able to collect any revenue from selling the product.

2. The free-rider problem is that people will try to avoid paying for a public good. In unregulated markets the free-rider problem results in the production of too little of a pure public good because there is little incentive for individuals to pay for it. The free rider will not pay because that payment will likely have no perceptible effect on the amount the person will be able to consume. Hence avoiding payment is rational. This incentive creates a problem for the private sector when it attempts to provide the product. In particular, suppliers — firms — produce goods in exchange for payments because the suppliers want to use their income to buy goods and services for themselves. If people do not pay for the goods, suppliers receive no income and hence have no incentive to produce the goods.

TABLE **16.5**

Short Answer Problem 3

Number of guards	Total cost of guards (dollars)	Marginal benefit per resident (dollars)	Marginal benefit to all residents (dollars)
1	$300	$10	$1,000
2	600	4	400
3	900	2	200
4	1200	1	100

3. a. A security guard is a public good in this case. Because the guard has the features of nonrivalry and nonexcludability. Employment of the guard involves nonrivalry because one resident's consumption of the security provided does not reduce anyone else's security. Nonexcludability is involved because, once a security guard is in place, all residents enjoy the increased security and none can be excluded.

   b. If each resident must act individually to hire a security guard none will be hired because each resident receives only $10 in benefit from the first guard, who costs $300 per day.

   c. The entries in the last column of Table 16.5 show the total marginal benefit. These answers are obtained by multiplying the marginal benefit per resident by the number of residents, 100. This multiplication is the numerical equivalent of summing the individual marginal benefit curves vertically for each quantity of guards.

4. a. If the apartment council hires each guard for whom the marginal benefit exceeds the marginal cost, they will hire the efficient number of guards. The marginal cost of each additional guard is $300. The marginal benefit of the first guard is $1,000, so this guard is hired. Similarly, the marginal benefit of the second guard is $400, and this guard also is hired.

      However, the marginal benefit of the third guard is only $200, which is less than marginal cost. Therefore the efficient number of guards is 2. For 2 guards, the net benefit is $800, the total benefit ($1,400) minus the total cost ($600).

   b. For one guard, the net benefit is $700, the total benefit ($1,000) minus the total cost ($300). For three guards, the net benefit also is $700, the total benefit ($1,600) minus the total cost

($900). So the net benefit of $800 is greatest for two guards.

   c. The apartment council might pay for the guards by collecting a security fee of $6 per day from each of the 100 residents in order to hire two security guards.

5. a. Yes, building the lighthouse is efficient. The marginal benefit to society from the lighthouse is the saving in shipping costs because of its existence. Each firm would save $200,000 annually, so society as a whole would save $2,000,000 annually. The marginal cost of building and running the lighthouse is $1,900,000 annually, so, on balance, society would be better off by $100,000 a year if the lighthouse was constructed.

   b. Yes, building the lighthouse would be profitable. The company would incur a cost of $190,000, its $1/10$ share of the cost. But the company would save $200,000 in shipping costs. So, on balance, each company comes out $10,000 ahead.

   c. After the lighthouse is built, the company would save $200,000 in shipping costs. If the company did not help pay for the lighthouse, its profit would increase by $200,000.

   d. Each company has the incentive to free ride, that is, to not pay for the lighthouse. If the company can avoid payment, its profit increases by $200,000, but if it must pay its $1/10$ share of the cost, its profit increases by only $10,000.

   e. If one company decides not to help pay for the lighthouse, the lighthouse will not be constructed. In this case, each of the other companies would have to pay $1/9$ the cost of the lighthouse, or $211,111.11 annually. But the lighthouse saves them only $200,000 in shipping costs, so building the lighthouse would not be a profitable venture for the 9 firms that would jointly pay the cost.

   f. Free riding might prevent the lighthouse from being built. Because providing the lighthouse would be efficient, the government might use its taxing powers to tax each company $190,000 and then use the funds to construct and operate the lighthouse.

6. Most issues have only a small and indirect effect on most voters. So for a voter to spend much time and effort to become well informed about such issues would be irrational because the additional cost in-

curred *by the voter* would exceed any additional benefit enjoyed *by the voter*. Only if the voter is significantly and directly affected by an issue does becoming well informed pay. As a result, most voters will be rationally ignorant about any specific issue.

7. a. Diane is the median voter: April and Brian want higher tax rates; Christopher and Eric want lower tax rates. The parties will propose the income tax rate that appeals to the median voter, so they will propose an income tax rate of 30 percent. If a party proposed a lower tax rate, it would gain the votes of Eric and Christopher, but the competing party would win votes from April, Brian, and Diane by proposing a 30 percent tax rate. Analogously, if a party proposed a tax rate higher than 30 percent, only April and Brian would vote for it, and the party would lose the election when its competitor proposed a tax rate of 30 percent.

   b. The income tax rate will be 30 percent. This tax rate is the same as in part (a) because Diane is still the median voter. Even with April's change, two voters (April and Brian) still want higher tax rates than Diane, and two voters (Christopher and Eric) want lower tax rates. Note that there is no response to April's switch in this case.

   c. The proposed tax rate will be 25 percent. This tax rate is lower than those in parts (a) and (b). The tax rate is different because the median voter has changed. With April's desire for a lower tax rate, Christopher has become the median voter (April and Eric want lower tax rates, whereas Brian and Diane want higher tax rates), which results in a change in the proposed tax rate. The answers to parts (b) and (c) make the point that the policy proposal is insensitive to changes that do not affect the median voter. However, a change that affects the median voter will alter the policies that are proposed.

8. Figure 16.6 shows the effect of the social security tax when the demand for labor is perfectly elastic. The wage rate does not rise; that is, the wage rate that includes the tax, W_t, equals the initial wage rate, W. When the demand is perfectly elastic, the wage rate does not rise, and so in this case workers are forced to pay the entire tax.

9. Figure 16.7 shows the impact of the social security tax when the demand for labor is perfectly inelastic. The wage rate rises by the entire amount of the tax,

FIGURE 16.6
Short Answer Problem 8

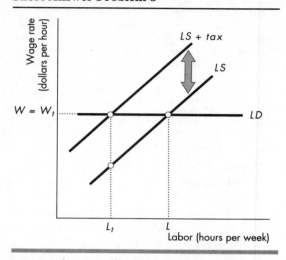

FIGURE 16.7
Short Answer Problem 9

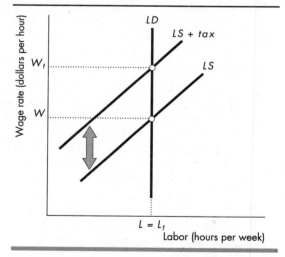

from W to W_t. In this case, firms pay the entire tax in the form of a higher wage rate.

Comparing the answers to problems 8 and 9 demonstrates that firms pay a greater share of a tax imposed on labor the less elastic is their demand for labor. Conversely, the more elastic the demand for labor, the greater the share of a tax paid by workers.

10. a. The initial equilibrium price of a pair of shoes is $65, and the initial equilibrium quantity is 80 million pairs of shoes.

TABLE 16.6
Short Answer Problem 10 (b)

Price, including tax (dollars per pair of shoes)	Quantity of shoes supplied (millions)	Quantity of shoes demanded (millions)
$55	60	90
60	65	85
65	70	80
70	75	75
75	80	70
80	85	65

b. Table 16.6 shows the demand and supply schedules after the tax. The tax does not change the demand schedule. Consumers demand, say, 80 million pairs of shoes if the price is $65 regardless of whether suppliers receive all $65 or if suppliers receive only $55 and $10 is sent to the government as taxes. However the supply schedule does change. If the price including the tax is $65, suppliers receive only $55, because they must send $10 to the government. The initial supply schedule indicates that, when suppliers receive $55, they produce 70 million pairs of shoes. Hence, when the after-tax price is $65, suppliers — who receive only $55 for themselves — produce 70 million pairs of shoes. The rest of the answers are calculated similarly.

c. Figure 16.8 shows the effect of the tax. Note that the supply curve with the tax lies above the supply curve without the tax by $10, the amount of the tax.

d. From either Figure 16.8 or Table 16.6, the new equilibrium price is $70 and the equilibrium quantity is 75 million pairs of shoes.

e. The price rose from $65 to $70, so demanders pay $5 of the tax in the form of a higher price. Suppliers initially received $65 per pair; after the tax they receive only $60, so they pay $5 of the tax in the form of lower receipts per shoe.

f. The deadweight loss is the area of the darkened triangle *abc* in Figure 16.8. The height of this triangle is $10 per pair, the amount of the tax. The base of the triangle is 5 million shoes, the decrease in the quantity. Hence the area equals one-half the base times the height, or (½)(5 million shoes)($10 per pair) = $25 million.

FIGURE 16.8
Short Answer Problem 10 (c)

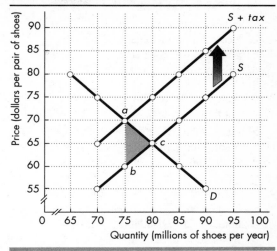

■ You're the Teacher

1. "The idea that the government won't create inefficiency is called the 'public interest' theory of government. It's based on the assumption that government actions lead to efficiency. However, 'public choice' theories of government suggest that at times government actions can result in inefficiency, that is, can cause government failure. Public choice theories assert that well-informed special interest groups are able to induce the government to undertake programs that do not maximize net benefits because most voters are rationally ignorant. For most voters, being well informed about any particular issue does not pay. As a result, a small, well-informed interest group has an influence on government programs that greatly exceeds its size relative to all voters.

"Suppose there are three large producers of copper in the United States. If they can convince the government to tax foreign copper $1 per ton, each U.S. copper producer may benefit by $80 million dollars. Meanwhile, this tax might cost each consumer in the United States 80¢. It seems clear to me that the copper producers are going to lobby like crazy for this policy and contribute a lot of dough to candidates' campaigns. But you and I aren't going to care much. It sure isn't in our personal interest to study this issue because we can gain, at most 80¢! So we'll stay rationally ignorant, but the copper producers will lobby hard, so this policy might be enacted."

Chapter Quiz

1. An externality can be
   a. either a cost or a benefit.
   b. a cost, but not a benefit.
   c. a benefit, but not a cost.
   d. neither a cost nor a benefit.

2. "Government failure" is predicted by
   a. public interest theory.
   b. rational ignorance theory.
   c. public choice theory.
   d. market failure theory.

3. A pure public good is necessarily
   a. nonrival and nonexcludable.
   b. nonrival and excludable.
   b. rival and nonexcludable.
   d. rival and excludable.

4. The best example of a pure public good is
   a. a rock concert in a large stadium.
   b. a radio broadcast of news.
   c. building a large apartment for low-income families.
   d. producing paper for use in newspapers.

5. Which theory of government says that the government acts to eliminate inefficiency?
   a. Public good theory.
   b. Public choice theory.
   c. Public interest theory.
   d. Political marketplace theory.

6. What characteristic of a public good makes free riding possible?
   a. The nonrival characteristic.
   b. The rival characteristic.
   c. The nonexcludable characteristic.
   d. The excludable characteristic.

7. In the public choice theory of government, the objective of politicians is to
   a. remove all inefficiency.
   b. eliminate market failure.
   c. decrease rational ignorance.
   d. get elected and reelected.

8. Who might opt to be rationally ignorant?
   a. Special interest groups.
   b. Voters.
   c. Politicians.
   d. Bureaucrats.

9. If the average tax rate increases with income, the tax is _____ and the U.S. income tax is a _____ tax.
   a. progressive; progressive
   b. progressive; regressive
   c. regressive; progressive
   d. regressive; regressive

10. The deadweight loss from an excise tax is largest when taxing goods with
    a. elastic demands.
    b. inelastic demands.
    c. unit elastic demand.
    d. rationally ignorant consumers.

The answers for this Chapter Quiz are on page 368

17 REGULATION AND ANTITRUST LAW

Chapter

Key Concepts

■ Market Intervention

- ◆ **Regulation** consists of rules administered by a government agency to that determine prices, product standards and types, and conditions for entry into the market.
- ◆ **Antitrust law** regulates and prohibits certain kinds of market behavior.

■ Economic Theory of Regulation

Both consumers and producers demand regulation that will be in their interest.

- ◆ Consumers' demand for regulation increases when consumer surplus per buyer increases and the number of buyers increases.
- ◆ Producers' demand for regulation increases when producer surplus per seller increases and the number of firms increases.

Regulation is supplied by politicians and bureaucrats. The supply increases in the consumer or producer surplus from the regulation increases and when the number of voters who benefit and know that they have benefited from the regulation increases.

In political equilibrium, no interest group presses for changes in existing regulations. There are two theories of the political equilibrium:

- ◆ **Public interest theory** — predicts that regulation maximizes total surplus, that is, attains efficiency.
- ◆ **Capture theory** — predicts that regulation maximizes producer surplus.

■ Regulation and Deregulation

From 1887, when the first federal regulatory agency was formed until 1977, regulation expanded until about one-quarter of the economy was regulated. Since then, there has been gradual deregulation.

Both natural monopolies and cartels are regulated.

- ◆ *Natural monopoly* — when one firm can supply the market at lower cost than two or more firms. As illustrated in Figure 17.1, this definition means that the firm's *ATC* curve slopes downward until it is beyond the demand curve.

FIGURE 17.1
A Natural Monopoly

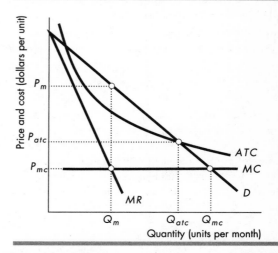

If unregulated, the firm produces Q_m and charges P_m. Two methods of regulating a natural monopoly are:

- ◆ **Marginal cost pricing rule** — sets the price equal

to marginal cost. In Figure 17.1 the price would be P_{mc} and the quantity produced Q_{mc}. This policy maximizes total surplus, but the firm incurs an economic loss.

♦ **Average cost pricing rule** — sets the price equal to average total cost. In Figure 17.1, the price would be P_{atc} and the quantity produced Q_{atc}. A deadweight loss is created, but the firm does not suffer an economic loss.

Methods used to regulate natural monopolies include rate of return and incentive regulation:

♦ **Rate of return regulation** — sets the price at a level that lets the company earn a specified target rate of return on its capital. The firm has an incentive to inflate its costs as well as use more capital because higher costs are passed along to the consumers by the regulator in the form of a higher price and using more capital means the firm's profit is larger.

♦ **Price cap regulation** — sets a price ceiling. This type of regulation gives the firm an incentive to operate efficiently. It lowers the price and increases output. **Earnings sharing regulation** is a type of price cap regulation under which the firm is required to share its profits with its customers if the profit rises above a target level.

The evidence about whether natural monopoly regulation is best characterized by the public interest theory or the capture theory is mixed.

Cartel — a collusive agreement among firms designed to boost the price and increase their profit.

Public interest theory predicts that oligopolies are regulated to ensure a competitive outcome; the capture theory predicts that regulation will help the producer. Although the evidence is mixed, it tends to favor the capture theory.

Deregulation began in the 1970s. The transportation industry was deregulated in response to higher energy prices. The communications industry was deregulated because of improvements in technology that ended some natural monopolies by reducing the cost of telecommunications so that two or more firms could compete.

■ Antitrust Law

♦ *Sherman Act* — the first federal antitrust law, passed in 1890, prohibited restrictions of trade and monopolization.

♦ *Clayton Act* — passed in 1914, prohibited certain business practices only if they substantially lessen competition or create a monopoly.

The courts have ruled that price fixing is *per se* illegal.

The *rule of reason* was the U.S. Supreme Court's initial interpretation that only unreasonable acts violated the Sherman Act; eventually this rule was replaced by a view that some acts are illegal even if they are "reasonable."

Merger guidelines used by the Federal Trade Commission include:

♦ If the initial Herfindahl-Hirschman Index (HHI) is less than 1,000, a merger will be unopposed.

♦ If the initial HHI is between 1,000 and 1,800, a merger that raises the HHI by 100 or more will be contested.

♦ If the initial HHI is larger than 1,800, a merger that increases the HHI by 50 or more will be challenged.

In general, antitrust law seems to have moved the economy toward the goal of efficiency.

Helpful Hints

1. **WHICH MARKETS SHOULD BE REGULATED ?** According to the public interest theory, regulations and antitrust laws will be designed to make markets behave more competitively. The ultimate goal is a perfectly competitive market because it maximizes the total surplus (the sum of consumer surplus plus producer surplus) enjoyed by society. Markets that behave like monopolies lead to economic inefficiency by creating deadweight losses. However, there are fewer reasons to regulate markets that are already competitive.

2. **DEFINITION AND DISCUSSION OF NATURAL MONOPOLY:** The defining characteristic of a natural monopoly in a diagram is that its *ATC* curve slopes downward until it crosses the demand curve. That condition implies that one firm can serve the market with lower costs than two or more firms.

   When the *ATC* curve falls until it crosses the demand curve, why can one company supply the market at a lower cost than two or more? Suppose that the *ATC* crosses the demand curve at 100 units of output, that the *ATC* of 50 units of output is $15, and that the *ATC* of producing 100 units is

$10. If one firm produced 100 units of output, the total cost is (100)($10) = $1,000. To have two firms produce 100 units, say each produces 50 units. Then, each firm's total cost is (50)($15) = $750. The total cost of having 100 units produced by these two firms is $750 + $750, or $1,500. So, the total cost of having two firms produce 100 units of output — $1,500 — exceeds the total cost of having only one firm produce 100 units.

Because one company can supply the market at a lower cost than two or more firms, a tension is created from society's point of view. Having one firm in the industry and thereby reducing costs is good; the lower the cost of producing a product, the more resources available to produce other goods and services. However, monopolies restrict the level of their output in order to raise their prices and earn economic profits. The restriction of output creates economic inefficiency and harms society.

The result from these countervailing forces is regulation: The government grants the right to one firm to have a monopoly, but in exchange the government regulates it. In this way, society attempts to gain the advantage of lower costs and side step the disadvantage of monopoly behavior. The capture theory of regulation, however, reminds us that this effort might not be successful.

Questions

■ True/False Questions

Market Intervention

1. Currently, about one-half of the nation's output is produced by regulated industries.

2. Antitrust law is aimed at competitive industries.

Economic Theory of Regulation

3. The more producer surplus per seller, the greater are producers' demands for regulation.

4. The public interest theory of regulation holds that regulations aim to attain efficiency.

5. According to the capture theory, government regulatory agencies eventually capture the profits of the industries they regulate.

6. According to the public interest theory of regulation, government regulation moves the economy closer to efficiency.

Regulation and Deregulation

7. For a natural monopoly, the *ATC* curve slopes upward when it crosses the demand curve.

8. A natural monopoly regulated using a marginal cost pricing rule might need to be subsidized in order to avoid an economic loss.

9. A natural monopoly regulated according to an average cost pricing rule produces an inefficient level of output.

10. Rate of return regulation gives producers a strong incentive to minimize their costs.

11. Evidence about cartel deregulation strongly supports the public interest theory of regulation.

Antitrust Law

12. The Sherman Act prohibits conspiracies that restrict interstate trade.

13. The rule of reason was a U.S. Supreme Court interpretation of the Sherman Act that said only "unreasonable" restraints of trade or other actions violated the Sherman Act.

14. The only situation in which price fixing is legal is if it is necessary to prevent a firm from going bankrupt.

15. The larger the initial Herfindahl-Hirschman Index, the more likely the Federal Trade Commission is to allow a merger to take place.

■ Multiple Choice Questions

Market Intervention

1. The main thrust of antitrust law is to
   a. prohibit monopoly practices that raise the price of a good and restrict the amount that firms produce.
   b. ensure that producers can earn the maximum possible profit.
   c. foster the role of deregulation.
   d. help firms overcome the constraints on their behavior imposed by regulations.

Economic Theory of Regulation

2. Economic regulation is supplied by

   a. monopolists.

   b. labor unions.

   c. voters.

   d. politicians and bureaucrats.

3. A large demand for regulation by consumers will result when there is a

   a. small consumer surplus per buyer.

   b. large consumer surplus per buyer.

   c. small number of buyers.

   d. large producer surplus per firm.

4. The public interest theory of regulation predicts that the political process seeks to maximize

   a. producer surplus.

   b. consumer surplus.

   c. deadweight loss.

   d. total surplus.

5. The capture theory of intervention predicts that government regulation will maximize

   a. producer surplus.

   b. consumer surplus.

   c. deadweight loss.

   d. total surplus.

Regulation and Deregulation

6. The history of regulation in the economy shows that from 1880 the extent of regulation generally

   a. increased until about 1977 and since then deregulation has occurred.

   b. increased steadily.

   c. decreased until about 1977 and since then has increased.

   d. none of the above.

7. An industry in which one firm can serve the market at a lower total cost than two or more firms is known as a(n)

   a. duopoly.

   b. oligopoly.

   c. deadweight loss industry.

   d. natural monopoly.

8. In a large city, which of the following is most likely to be a natural monopoly?

   a. Burger King, a seller of hamburgers

   b. Cox Cable, the only company supplying cable TV

   c. Nike, a maker of shoes sold in the city

   d. JCPenney, a large department store

Use Figure 17.2 for the next four questions.

FIGURE 17.2
Multiple Choice Questions 9, 10, 11, 12

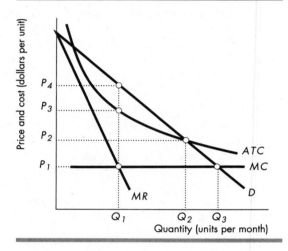

9. In Figure 17.2 total surplus is at its maximum when the quantity is

   a. Q_1 and the price is P_4.

   b. Q_1 and the price is P_3.

   c. Q_2 and the price is P_2.

   d. Q_3 and the price is P_1.

10. In Figure 17.2 profit is at its maximum when the quantity is

   a. Q_1 and the price is P_4.

   b. Q_1 and the price is P_3.

   c. Q_2 and the price is P_2.

   d. Q_3 and the price is P_1.

11. If the natural monopoly in Figure 17.2 is unregulated and operates as a private profit-maximizer, what output will it produce?

    a. 0, because the firm suffers an economic loss when $MR = MC$.

    b. Q_1

    c. Q_2

    d. Q_3

12. If a regulatory agency sets a price just sufficient for the firm to earn a normal profit, what output will it produce?

    a. 0, because the firm suffers an economic loss when $MR = MC$.

    b. Q_1

    c. Q_2

    d. Q_3

13. If a natural monopoly is required to set its price equal to its marginal cost,

    a. the company earns an economic profit.

    b. the company incurs an economic loss.

    c. competitors will enter the market.

    d. the company will produce more than the efficient level of output.

14. When will the price charged by a natural monopoly be the lowest?

    a. When the monopoly is left unregulated.

    b. When the monopoly is regulated according to an average cost pricing rule.

    c. When the monopoly is regulated according to a marginal cost pricing rule.

    d. When the monopoly is regulated according to a deadweight loss pricing rule.

15. When will the output produced by a natural monopoly be the largest?

    a. When the monopoly is left unregulated.

    b. When the monopoly is regulated according to an average cost pricing rule.

    c. When the monopoly is regulated according to a marginal cost pricing rule.

    d. When the monopoly is regulated according to a deadweight loss pricing rule.

16. A natural monopoly under rate of return regulation has an incentive to

    a. inflate its costs.

    b. produce more than the efficient quantity of output.

    c. charge a price equal to marginal cost.

    d. maximize consumer surplus.

17. Price cap regulation give a natural monopoly the incentive to

    a. behave more like an unregulated monopoly by raising its price to maximize its profit.

    b. raise its price to the maximum amount consumers will pay.

    c. inflate its costs.

    d. reduce its costs.

18. Regulation that sets a price cap and then requires that the regulated firm share with its customers any profit above a target level is called

    a. rate of return regulation.

    b. average cost pricing regulation.

    c. marginal cost pricing regulation.

    d. earnings sharing regulation.

19. When airlines and trucking were deregulated, the evidence shows that consumer surplus _____ and total surplus _____.

    a. rose; rose

    b. rose; fell

    c. fell; rose

    d. fell; fell

Antitrust Law

20. Which of the following statements about the Sherman Act is correct?

    a. The Sherman Act was the second federal antitrust law.

    b. The Sherman act legalized monopolization if the company behaved "reasonably" once it became a monopoly.

    c. The Sherman Act outlawed natural monopolies.

    d. The Sherman Act made restriction of interstate trade illegal.

21. Which of the following statements about the "rule of reason" is FALSE?
    a. The U.S. Supreme Court announced the rule of reason as a ruling.
    b. The rule of reason states that only unreasonable restraints of trade violate the Sherman Act.
    c. The rule of reason remains in effect today.
    d. None of the above because they are all true statements.

22. All of the following are prohibited only if they substantially lessen competition EXCEPT
    a. price discrimination.
    b. price fixing.
    c. contracts that prevent a firm from selling competing items (exclusive dealing).
    d. acquiring a competitor's shares or assets.

23. Microsoft
    a. was found guilty of violating antitrust laws and was forced to give up some of its businesses.
    b. was allowed to merge even though the HHI in the industry exceeded 1,800.
    c. admitted it was a monopoly and was split into two companies.
    d. None of the above.

24. The Herfindahl-Hirschman index (HHI) in an industry is 900. A merger is proposed that will raise the HHI to 980. In this case, the
    a. Sherman Act will prohibit the merger.
    b. Federal Trade Commission will challenge the merger.
    c. Federal Trade Commission will not challenge the merger.
    d. rule of reason will prevent the merger if it is a merger among competitors.

■ **Short Answer Questions**

1. a. Describe the demand for and the supply of regulation.
   b. What is a political equilibrium? How is it similar to the equilibrium that occurs in the market for a good?
   c. What are two possible political equilibriums?

2. Suppose that two electric companies, Watts Up and Power to the People, can serve a residential block. The block has 10 houses on it. To serve the houses

a main cable needs to be strung down the street; a main cable costs $100 to maintain. Then small feeder cables need to be extended to each house; these cost $10 to maintain per house.
   a. Suppose that Watts Up and Power to the People split the market so that each services 5 houses on the street. If both companies string their own main cables and then each extends feeder wires to its customers, what is Watts Up's total cost of supplying power to its 5 customers? Watts Up's average total cost? What are Power to the People's total and average total costs?
   b. When Watts Up and Power to the People split the market evenly, as in part (a), what is the total cost to society of serving these 10 families?
   c. Suppose that only one company — say, Watts Up — supplies power to all the residents of the street. So there is one main cable and 10 feeder wires. Now, what is Watts Up's total cost of supplying power to the street's residents? What is its average total cost?
   d. If Watts Up has the monopoly in serving the customers on this street, what are the total costs incurred by society to serve these 10 families?
   e. Is this industry a natural monopoly? Explain your answer.

3. The last question reflected a social perspective when exploring the situation of a natural monopoly supplying power to 10 residents on a street. Let's now explore the situation from the industry's vantage point.
   a. If both companies string their own main cables and then extend feeder wires to 5 houses each, what is each company's average total cost of servicing a house?
   b. Suppose that Watts Up gains a customer on the street so that it now serves 6 houses and Power to the People serves only 4. What is Watts Up's average total cost? Power to the People's average total cost?
   c. After Watts Up gains its customer, if Watts Up charges its customers a price between $26.67 and $35, does Watts Up earn an economic profit? What is the minimum price that Power to the People can charge and not incur an economic loss? Presuming that the residents on the street can switch power companies, what is likely to happen?

FIGURE **17.3**
Short Answer Problem 4

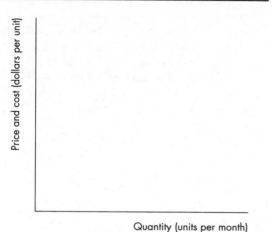

Quantity (units per month)

FIGURE **17.4**
Short Answer Problem 7 (a)

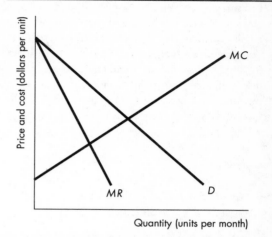

Quantity (units per month)

FIGURE **17.5**
Short Answer Problem 7 (b)

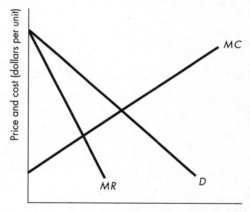

Quantity (units per month)

4. In Figure 17.3 draw a diagram illustrating a natural monopoly. If the company is regulated under an average cost pricing rule, show the level of production, the price, and the deadweight loss.

5. a. How is rate of return regulation of a natural monopoly implemented? What incentive do companies have to reduce their costs?

    b. What is price cap regulation? With this type of regulation, what incentive do companies have to reduce their costs?

6. We've met Igor in some past chapters. Igor has quit his job with his old master and now works for a new master: the Federal Trade Commission. Igor is overseeing a merger in the snake market. Currently, the snake market comprises 5 firms of equal size; that is, each firm has a 20 percent market share. Two firms are considering a merger so that after the merger the market will have 4 firms, one with a 40 percent share and 3 with 20 percent shares. Will Igor challenge the merger? Why or why not?

7. Igor's new masters were pleased with his work in the snake market, so they put him to work regulating the bat industry. The bat industry has three firms in it. Figures 17.4 and 17.5 are identical: Both show the market demand for bats, the associated marginal revenue curve for the market demand, and the horizontal sum of the marginal cost curves for the three firms in the bat industry.

    a. Suppose that Igor regulates the bat industry in the public interest. In Figure 17.4 indicate the

equilibrium quantity and price of a bat. Show the consumer surplus, the producer surplus, and the total surplus.

b. Now suppose that the bat industry is able to capture Igor. After being captured, Igor regulates the industry so that the bat producers can earn the maximum possible industrywide profit. In Figure 17.5 show the equilibrium number of bats and their price. Also show the consumer surplus, the producer surplus, and indicate the area that is the deadweight loss.

■ **You're the Teacher**

1. "I just don't get how a natural monopoly happens. I mean, why are some firms natural monopolies and not others? Is it because the government is regulating them that they are natural monopolies?" Your friend is struggling and is confused. Although it would be nice if your friend could sometimes help you, save your friend's grade once again by explaining the origins of a natural monopoly. Be sure to address the (erroneous) idea that it is govern- ment regulation that makes an industry a natural monopoly.

2. "I think our teacher sometimes says that efficiency means that helping someone without hurting someone else is impossible. I seem to remember this comment from our book. But does this mean that when there is inefficiency, we can take actions that help everyone?" This student is close to seeing an important point. If you already see it, explain it; if you don't, sneak a look at the answer...

Answers

■ True/False Answers

Market Intervention

1. **F** At its maximum in 1977, about one fourth of the nation's output was produced by regulated industries. Since 1977, that fraction has fallen substantially.

2. **F** Antitrust law is aimed at monopolistic and oligopolistic industries.

Economic Theory of Regulation

3. **T** The more producer surplus per seller, the greater the payoff to an individual producer if regulation is shaped to benefit producers' interests.

4. **T** The public interest theory stands in contrast to the capture theory.

5. **F** The capture theory is that the industry captures the regulator, so the regulator allows the industry to charge (near) the monopoly price and produce (near) the monopoly level of output.

6. **T** If regulation follows the public interest theory, it will increase economic efficiency, but if the industry captures its regulator, regulation can create inefficiency.

Regulation and Deregulation

7. **F** The *ATC* curve slopes downward until it crosses the demand curve.

8. **T** The price set under a marginal cost pricing rule is less than the *ATC*, so the firm incurs an economic loss.

9. **T** The natural monopoly produces the efficient level of output when it is regulated to produce so that its price equals its marginal cost.

10. **F** If the costs rise, the producer knows that the regulators will allow the company to hike its price to offset the higher costs.

11. **F** The evidence is mixed, but it tends to support the capture theory of regulation.

Antitrust Law

12. **T** Conspiracies that restrain trade are outlawed in the first section of the Sherman Act.

13. **T** This question essentially presents the definition of the rule of reason.

14. **F** Price fixing is automatically and always — *per se* — illegal.

15. **F** The *lower* the initial HHI, the more likely the Federal Trade Commission will not challenge a merger.

■ Multiple Choice Answers

Market Intervention

1. **a** Antitrust laws generally try to make the economy more competitive and closer to the efficient level of production.

Economic Theory of Regulation

2. **d** Consumers and producers demand regulation; politicians and bureaucrats supply it.

3. **b** Large consumer surplus per buyer increases the potential payoff if buyers can sway regulators to produce regulations in their favor.

4. **d** Total surplus is the sum of consumer surplus plus producer surplus; when total surplus is as large as possible, efficiency is achieved.

5. **a** By capturing the regulators, producers are able to promote their own interests.

Regulation and Deregulation

6. **a** Deregulation started in 1977 and has continued in recent years.

7. **d** The question presents the defining characteristic of an industry that is a natural monopoly.

8. **b** Most locales have only one cable TV supplier because cable TV is currently close to being a natural monopoly.

9. **d** Total surplus is maximized at the level of output where the *MC* curve crosses the demand curve because at that point there is no deadweight loss.

10. **a** This is the monopoly level of output and price, which is the combination of output and price that maximizes economic profit.

11. **b** Left alone, it will operate as a monopoly and maximize its profit.

12. **c** Earning a normal profit means that the company produces so that $P = ATC$, which means it produces Q_2 and charges P_2. This price–output combination is exactly what the company would do under an average cost pricing rule.

13. **b** Because the company suffers an economic loss, it will need to be subsidized, or be allowed to price discriminate in order to earn a normal profit.

14. **c** A marginal cost pricing rule results in the largest level of output. To induce demanders to buy the largest amount of output, the price must be the lowest.

15. **c** When regulated according to a marginal cost pricing rule, the natural monopoly produces the efficient amount of output.

16. **a** This incentive accounts for the recent adoption of incentive regulation methods in many telecommunications markets.

17. **d** By reducing its costs, regulators hope to make the firm more efficient.

18. **d** Price cap regulations and earning sharing regulations attempt to sharpen regulated firms' incentives to cut costs and have become more common in the telecommunications industry.

19. **a** Because the total surplus increased, economic efficiency increased when these industries were deregulated.

Antitrust Law

20. **d** The Sherman Act was the first federal antitrust law and part of it outlawed restriction of interstate trade.

21. **c** The U.S. Supreme Court backed away from the rule of reason in its decision in the Alcoa case. There Alcoa was found guilty simply because it was "too big."

22. **b** Price fixing is *always* illegal. If proved, there is no acceptable defense.

23. **d** In past years, the Justice Department has imposed some sanctions on Microsoft and might impose more in the future.

24. **c** Whenever the initial HHI is below 1,000, the U.S. Department of Justice will not contest a merger in the industry.

■ Answers to Short Answer Problems

1. a. The demand for regulation comes from consumers and producers, who both demand regulation that will be in their interest. Further, the demand for regulation on the part of consumers increases with the amount of consumer surplus per buyer and with the number of buyers. The demand for regulation from producers is affected by similar factors: It increases with the amount of producer surplus per producer and the number of producers.

    The supply of regulation comes from politicians and bureaucrats. The supply increases when the amount of consumer or producer surplus increases and when the number of people who know they benefit from the regulation increases.

    b. A political equilibrium occurs when no one finds it worthwhile to change his or her behavior. The political equilibrium is analogous to the equilibrium in a market insofar as once the economy reaches the equilibrium, unless something else changes, the equilibrium situation will persist. In a market equilibrium, there is a market price and quantity. So, too, in a political equilibrium there is a quantity of regulation.

    c. The public interest theory and the capture theory describe the two possible equilibriums. In the public interest theory, the equilibrium is one that aims the economy toward efficiency by maximizing the total surplus (the sum of consumer surplus plus producer surplus) in the market. In the capture theory, the regulation supports the interests of producers. In this case, the demand for specific types of regulations by producers exceeds the demand for other types from consumers and so the supply of regulation goes to meet producers' desires. This type of regulation can result in an inefficient level of production of the product.

2. a. Watts Up strings a main cable, which costs $100, and provides 5 feeder wires, at a cost of $10 each. So Watts Up's total cost is $150. It supplies 5 families, so its average total cost is $150 divided by 5 customers, or $30. Power to the People's total cost and average total cost are the same.

    b. Watts Up incurs a total cost of $150; Power to the People has the same total cost. Hence the total cost to society is $300.

    c. If only Watts Up supplies power, it strings a main cable ($100) and 10 feeder wires ($10 each) for a total cost of $200. Watts Up's average total cost is $20 per customer.

    d. With only one company supplying power, the total cost incurred by society is $200, the company's total cost.

e. Yes, this industry is a natural monopoly because the total cost of having one firm supply the market is less than the total cost of two (or more) firms. Another way to see that this industry is a natural monopoly is by noting that the average total cost with 10 customers is less than that with 5 customers. The average total cost declines until the entire market is served, which means that this industry is a natural monopoly.

3. a. As worked out in part (a) of question 2, the average total cost when 5 houses are served is $30.

   b. After Watts Up gains a customer, its total cost is $160: $100 for the main cable and $60 for 6 feeder wires. Its average total cost is $160/6, or $26.67 per customer. Power to the People's total cost is now $140, or $100 for the main cable and $40 for the 4 feeder wires. Hence Power to the People's average total cost is $140/4, or $35 per customer.

   c. For any price greater than $26.67, Watts Up will earn an economic profit because its price will exceed its average total cost. Hence for prices between $26.67 and $35, Watts Up earns an economic profit. Power to the People must charge a price no less than $35 (so that its price is not less than its average total cost) to avoid an economic loss. So Watts Up can charge a lower price than Power to the People and still earn an economic profit. Customers are likely to switch from Power to the People, where they pay a higher price, to Watts Up, where they pay a lower price. As this switching occurs, Watts Up's ATC continues to fall and Power to the People's ATC rises. The ultimate result is likely to be that Watts Up becomes the monopoly supplier of electricity on this street. A key point is how the industry (naturally) evolves into a monopoly.

4. Figure 17.6 shows a natural monopoly. The distinguishing characteristic of a natural monopoly is that its ATC curve falls until after it crosses the demand curve. Under an average cost pricing rule, the company must set its price equal to its average cost, which means that the price that will be charged is P_{atc} and the level of output is Q_{atc}. (To buy Q_{atc}, consumers are willing to pay P_{atc}, and this price equals the average cost of producing output Q_{atc}.) The deadweight loss equals the loss of consumer and producer surplus on the difference between the efficient level of output Q_{eff} — where

the demand (the marginal social benefit) and the marginal cost (the marginal social cost) curves cross — and the amount of output actually produced, Q_{atc}. It is illustrated by the shaded triangle.

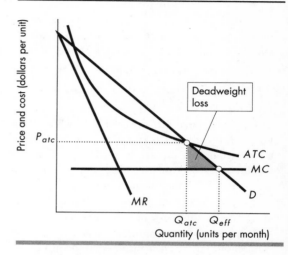

FIGURE **17.6**
Short Answer Problem 4

5. a. Rate of return regulation is related to an average total cost price rule. Regulators determine a fair rate of return on the company's capital. This rate of return is then multiplied by the total amount of the firm's capital to determine the total "profit" that the regulators consider fair. (If the company has, say, $10 million in capital and the rate of return is 15 percent, the total amount of "profit" is $1.5 million, $10 million times 15 percent.) This total profit is added to the firm's other costs and the amount becomes the regulators' "target" for the firm's total revenue. Then, the regulators determine a price that will enable the firm to earn this amount of revenue. Companies have very little incentive to reduce their costs; if costs rise, the regulators will raise the price that the company can charge, thus allowing the company to recoup the increased costs. Similarly, companies have an incentive to use more capital than necessary because the regulators will allow increase the company's total return when its capital increases.

   b. Price cap regulation sets a price ceiling and then allows the company to charge whatever price it wishes as long as the price remains under the ceiling. Typically there is an earnings sharing provision so that if the company's profits rise above a certain level, they must be shared with consumers by reducing the price the company charges. These methods give the company more incentive to control its costs because, if the business can lower its costs and hence increase its profit, the company will be allowed to keep (at least part of) the higher profit.

6. Igor's decision whether to challenge the merger depends on the initial Herfindahl–Hirschman index (HHI) and the effect of the merger on the HHI. Before the merger, HHI = 2,000, from $20^2 + 20^2 + 20^2 + 20^2 + 20^2$. If the merger occurs, the HHI = 2,800, or $40^2 + 20^2 + 20^2 + 20^2$. This merger would increase the HHI by 800. If the initial HHI exceeds 1,800, any merger that raises it by 50 or more is contested by the Federal Trade Commission. So, Igor will challenge this merger.

7. a. Figure 17.7 shows the industry output as Q and the price as P when this industry is regulated in the public interest. The consumer and producer surpluses also are shown; the total surplus is the sum of the consumer surplus and the producer surplus.

   b. Once Igor is captured by the industry, the industry will operate as a monopoly. That is, it will operate at the level where the industry MC equals the market MR, so, as shown in Figure 17.8, it produces Q_m and is allowed to charge P_m. The consumer and producer surpluses also are shown. The total surplus is, as always, the sum of the consumer surplus and the producer surplus. Comparing Figure 17.7 with Figure 17.8 shows that although producer surplus increases, the total surplus is less when the industry is able to capture its regulator. The amount by which it is less is the deadweight loss, also illustrated in Figure 17.8. As usual, the deadweight loss is made of lost consumer surplus plus lost producer surplus.

FIGURE 17.7
Short Answer Problem 7 (a)

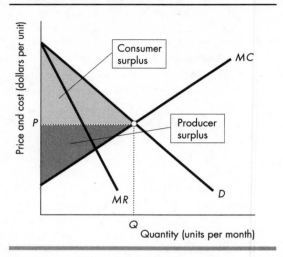

FIGURE 17.8
Short Answer Problem 7 (b)

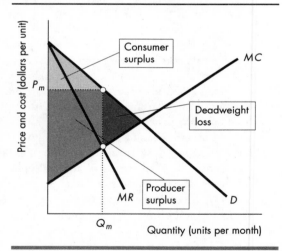

■ You're the Teacher

1. "If you're confused about the origin of a natural monopoly, you might be trying to make it too hard. But I finally figured it out. Here's the deal: A natural monopoly occurs when the technology within an industry allows one firm to serve the market at lower cost than more than one firm can. In other words, a natural monopoly just happens; if the technology makes it possible for one firm to serve the market at lower total cost than a lot of firms, this industry is a natural monopoly. I used to confuse regulation with the formation of natural monopolies. Natural monopolies are *not* the result of regulation. It's just the opposite: The industries are regulated *because* they are natural monopolies. You see, it's the type of technology that has been developed determines whether the industry is a natural monopoly."

2. "Yeah, you're right: When there is inefficiency, we can take actions that help everyone! The idea is that inefficiency means a deadweight loss. When we remove the inefficiency, we eliminate the deadweight loss. That serves as a bonus — something that we can spread around and make everyone better off.

   "Look, a numerical example will make this point a lot clearer. Take some industry. Suppose that consumer surplus would be $200 and producer surplus would be $100, for a total surplus of $300 if this industry is perfectly competitive. However, suppose that this industry is a monopoly. Then consumer surplus is, say, $80 and producer surplus is $150. In this case, the total surplus is $230 and the deadweight loss (the difference between the two total surpluses) is $70.

   "Now, if we broke up the monopoly and made the industry perfectly competitive, we'd get a total surplus of $300. It would include a consumer surplus of $200 (so that consumers would gain $120, the new consumer surplus of $200 minus the current consumer surplus of $80) and a producer surplus of $100 (so that producers would lose $50, the difference between the current producer surplus of $150 minus the new producer surplus of $100). But suppose that we took away, say, $75 of the gain from consumers and gave it to producers. Then consumers would still be better off because their new consumer surplus would be $125, as compared to only $80 when the industry was a monopoly. And producers would also be better off because their producer surplus would be $175 versus only $150 as a monopoly. You see, with this redistribution, *both* consumers and producers can be better off when the industry is perfectly competitive!

   "Okay, I'll agree that this outcome is unrealistic because we've assumed that we can redistribute the gain as we want. If we didn't do any redistribution and just broke up the monopoly, consumers would gain ($120) and producers would lose ($50). But what this story shows is important anyway: Whenever there is inefficiency, it can be eliminated and *everyone* made better off. You know, now that I think about it, it's my guess that this is why our teacher likes the idea of efficiency so much!"

Chapter Quiz

1. In recent years,
   a. an increasing number of industries have been regulated and none deregulated.
   b. there has been little change in the total amount of regulation.
   c. many new industries have been regulated and few industries have been deregulated.
   d. several industries have been deregulated.

2. Firms' demand for regulation will increase when _____ rise.
   a. consumer surplus per buyer and the number of buyers
   b. total revenue per firm and the number of firms
   c. the number of buyers and the number of firms
   d. the producer surplus per firm and the number of firms

3. The public interest theory of regulation predicts that _____ will be maximized and the capture theory predicts that _____ will be maximized.
   a. total surplus; deadweight loss
   b. consumer surplus; producer surplus
   c. total surplus; producer surplus
   d. deadweight loss; total surplus

4. Today, a regulated natural monopoly includes
   a. sellers of clothing.
   b. colleges.
   c. electrical generating companies.
   d. producers of personal computers.

5. For a regulated natural monopoly, setting an average cost pricing rule
   a. maximizes total surplus.
   b. maximizes consumer surplus.
   c. maximizes producer surplus.
   d. causes the firm to earn a normal profit.

6. Rate of return regulation is often imposed on
   a. a monopolistically competitive firm.
   b. a perfectly competitive firm.
   c. an oligopoly.
   d. a natural monopoly.

7. A cartel usually is designed to _____ and it also _____.
   a. increase consumer surplus; increases producer surplus
   b. increase producer surplus; creates a deadweight loss
   c. eliminate deadweight losses; increases total surplus
   d. increase producer surplus; increases total surplus

8. The Sherman Act
   a. made the rule of reason illegal.
   b. was the nation's first antitrust law and was passed in 1945.
   c. prohibited restrictions of trade and attempts to monopolize.
   d. None of the above.

9. Which of the following business practices, if proven to exist, will *always* be held to be illegal under U.S. antitrust law?
   a. Contracts that require other goods be bought from the same firm (tying arrangements).
   b. Price fixing among three or fewer firms.
   c. Contracts that prevent a firm from selling competing items (exclusive dealing).
   d. All of the above.

10. The larger the initial HHI,
   a. the more likely the government will challenge a merger in the industry.
   b. the less likely the government will challenge a merger in the industry.
   c. the more competitive the industry.
   d. None of the above.

The answers for this Chapter Quiz are on page 368

Key Concepts

Externalities in Our Lives

An **externality** is a cost or benefit that arises from production and falls on someone other than the producer or a cost or benefit that arises from consumption and falls on someone other than the consumer. S

♦ **Negative externality** — an externality that imposes an external cost.

♦ **Positive externality** — an externality that provides an external benefit.

There can be negative production externalities (pollution) and positive production externalities (bees making honey fertilizing an orchard). There also can be negative consumption externalities (a noisy party) and positive consumption externalities (flu vaccination).

Negative Externalities: Pollution

Environmental problems can be divided into air pollution, water pollution, and land pollution. The trends in air pollution show generally decreasing pollution.

♦ **Marginal private cost** (*MC*) — the cost of producing an additional unit of a good or service that is paid by the producer of the good or service.

♦ **Marginal external cost** — the cost of producing an additional unit of a good or service that falls on people other than the producer.

♦ **Marginal social cost** (*MSC*) — the marginal cost incurred by the entire society, by the producer and by everyone else on whom the cost falls. In an equation, *MSC* = *MC* + Marginal external cost.

Figure 18.1 shows the marginal cost curve, which is the private supply curve, labeled *MC* = *S,* and the marginal social cost curve, labeled *MSC*. The marginal external

FIGURE 18.1
A Product With an External Cost

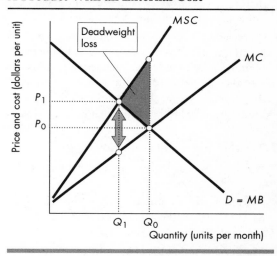

cost is the vertical distance between the two curves, which is equal at Q_1 to the length of the double headed arrow. The demand curve is the same as the marginal benefit curve and is labeled *D* = *MB*. The efficient quantity is Q_1, where the *MSC* and *MB* curves intersect and the equilibrium quantity is Q_0, where the *D* and *S* curves intersect. A deadweight loss is created because more than the efficient amount is produced.

The inefficiency can sometimes be reduced by establishing a property right.

♦ **Property rights** — legally established titles to the ownership, use, and disposal of factors of production and goods and services.

♦ **Coase theorem** — the proposition that if property rights exist, if only a small number of parties are involved, and transactions costs are low, then private transactions are efficient. **Transactions costs** are the opportunity costs of conducting a transaction. The Coase theorem implies that, regardless to whom the property right is given (the polluter or the victim), as long as a property right is granted, the efficient level of pollution results.

The government has three main methods it can use to cope with external costs:

♦ Taxes — the government can levy a tax equal to the marginal external cost. Such a tax is called a **Pigovian tax.** Imposing a tax equal to the marginal external cost shifts the private supply curve so that it is the same as the marginal social cost curve, *MSC.*

♦ Emission charges — a price per unit of pollution that the government sets and the polluter pays. It is difficult to determine the correct price.

♦ Marketable permits — each polluter is given a pollution limit. If it reduces its pollution below this limit, it can sell the "excess" reduction to other firms who then do not need to reduce their pollution by this amount. Marketable permits provide a sharp incentive to find technologies that reduce pollution.

■ Positive Externalities: Knowledge

Knowledge as well as research and development can create external benefits.

♦ **Marginal private benefit** (*MB*) — the benefit from an additional unit of a good or service that the consumer of that good or service receives.

♦ **Marginal external benefit** — the benefit from an additional unit of a good or service that people other than the consumer enjoy.

♦ **Marginal social benefit** (*MSB*) — the marginal benefit enjoyed by the entire society, both by the consumer and by everyone else. In an equation, *MSB = MB* + Marginal external benefit.

Figure 18.2 shows the marginal benefit curve, which is the private demand curve and is labeled *MB = D*. The marginal social benefit curve is labeled *MSB*. The marginal external benefit is the vertical distance between the two curves, equal at Q_1 to the length of the double headed arrow. The supply curve is the same as the marginal cost curve and is labeled *S = MC*. The efficient quantity is Q_1, where the *MC* and *MSB* curves intersect. The equilibrium quantity is Q_0, where the *D* and *S* curves intersect. A deadweight loss is created because less than the efficient quantity is produced.

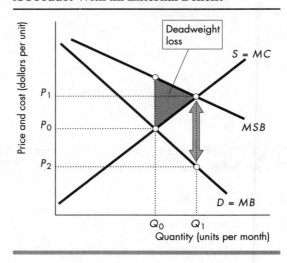

FIGURE 18.2

A Product With an External Benefit

The government has four methods it can use to attain a more efficient outcome when external benefits exist:

♦ **Public provision** — a public authority that receives its revenue from the government can produce the good or service. In Figure 18.2, the government would produce the efficient quantity, Q_1. It would then set the price equal to P_2 to insure that demanders buy Q_1.

♦ Private subsidies — a **subsidy** is a payment from the government to the private producers of the good or service. A subsidy increases the supply of the good and thereby increases the quantity produced.

♦ Voucher — A **voucher** is a token that the government provides to households, which they can use when they buy specified goods or services. In Figure 18.2, a voucher equal to the length of the double headed arrow would shift the demand curve so that the quantity would be Q_1, the efficient amount, and the price, including the voucher, would be P_1.

♦ Patents and copyrights — **Patents** and **copyrights** are government-sanctioned exclusive rights granted to the inventor of a good, service, or new production technique for a given number of years. Patents and copyrights help ensure that the inventor will personally profit from the invention and so increase the incentive to innovate, which benefits society. But, once the invention is made, patents and copyrights give the developer a monopoly, which harms society.

Helpful Hints

1. **THE EQUILIBRIUM QUANTITY COMPARED TO THE EFFICIENT QUANTITY :** The *equilibrium* quantity in a competitive market is the amount at which the marginal private cost equals the marginal private benefit. The *efficient* quantity is the amount at which the marginal social cost equals the marginal social benefit. If the marginal private cost equals the marginal social cost and the marginal private benefit equals the marginal social benefit, the two quantities are the same.

   In most transactions, there are no external costs or benefits. In other words, private and social costs coincide as do private and social benefits and so competitive markets are efficient. But when external costs or benefits arise, competitive markets are not be efficient. With external benefits, the marginal private benefit is less than the marginal social benefit. With external costs, the marginal private cost is less than the marginal social cost. In both instances, the amount produced in an unregulated market, the amount at which the marginal private benefit and private cost curves intersect, is not the efficient amount.

Questions

■ True/False and Explain

Externalities in Our Lives

1. Externalities can arise from both production and consumption.

2. Flu vaccination is a good example of a negative production externality.

Negative Externalities: Pollution

3. Because pollution reflects an external cost, there can be no demand for a pollution-free environment.

4. If the production of a good involves an external cost, the marginal social cost exceeds the marginal private cost.

5. When external costs are present, the private market produces less than the efficient level of output.

6. The Coase theorem states that if property rights exist, the number of parties is small, and transac-

tions costs are low, there will be no externalities regardless of who owns the property rights.

7. The inefficiency created by a negative production externality can be overcome if the government subsidizes production of the good.

8. Emission charges and marketable permits can be used to cope with the problem of a negative production externality.

Positive Externalities: Knowledge

9. Knowledge is an example of a product with external benefits.

10. The private market produces more than the efficient amount of a good having an external benefit.

11. A subsidy can be the appropriate policy for a good or service with an external benefit.

12. Taxing *private* producers of education can help overcome the externality problem of education.

13. Patents increase the incentive to discover new products and new production techniques.

■ Multiple Choice

Externalities in Our Lives

1. An externality can be a cost or benefit arising from the production of a good that falls upon
   a. consumers but not producers.
   b. producers but not consumers.
   c. the consumer and the producer both.
   d. someone other than the consumer or producer.

2. A noisy party that keeps neighbors awake is an example of a
   a. negative production externality.
   b. positive production externality.
   c. negative consumption externality.
   d. positive consumption externality.

3. Which of the following illustrates the concept of external cost?
   a. Bad weather decreases the size of the wheat crop.
   b. An increase in the demand for cheese raises the price paid by consumers of pizza, thereby harming these consumers.
   c. Smoking harms the health of the smoker.
   d. Smoking harms the health of nearby nonsmokers.

Negative Externalities: Pollution

4. Which of the following statements is correct?

 a. Most air pollution arises from generating electric power.

 b. Air pollution in the United States is becoming less severe for most substances.

 c. Lead from gasoline remains a major air pollution problem.

 d. All of the above statements are correct.

Use Figure 18.3 for the next five questions.

FIGURE **18.3**
Multiple Choice Questions 5, 6, 7, 8, 9

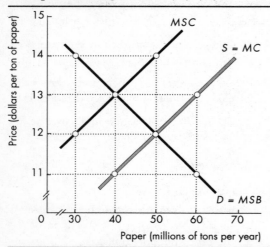

5. As illustrated in Figure 18.3, the production of paper creates

 a. only an external benefit.

 b. only an external cost.

 c. both external benefits and costs.

 d. no externalities.

6. The amount of the externality illustrated in Figure 18.3 is

 a. $14 per ton.

 b. $12 per ton.

 c. $2 per ton.

 d. $0 per ton because no externality is produced.

7. In the absence of any government intervention, how many tons of paper are produced in a year?

 a. 60 million tons.

 b. 50 million tons.

 c. 40 million tons.

 d. 30 million tons.

8. The efficient amount of paper produced in a year is

 a. 60 million tons.

 b. 50 million tons.

 c. 40 million tons.

 d. 30 million tons.

9. What amount of tax is necessary to lead to production of the efficient amount of paper?

 a. $14 a ton

 b. $12 per ton

 c. $2 per ton

 d. zero because the efficient amount is produced without any government intervention.

10. A copper ore refiner pollutes the water upstream from a brewery. The transactions costs of reaching an agreement between the two are low. When will the amount of copper refining be at its efficient level?

 a. If the property right to the stream is assigned to the ore refiner but not if it is assigned to the brewery.

 b. If the property right to the stream is assigned to the brewery but not if it is assigned to the ore refiner.

 c. Whenever the property right to the stream is assigned to *either* the refiner or the brewer.

 d. None of the above because there is no such thing as the efficient level of copper refining since refining copper creates pollution.

11. Suppose that the government allows firms to emit sulfur dioxide and pollute the air as long as the firms pay the government $70 per ton of sulfur dioxide emitted. This approach to handling pollution is an example of

 a. the Coase theorem.

 b. an emission charge.

 c. a marketable permit.

 d. None of the above answers are correct.

12. Production of rubber for sneakers creates an external cost of $2 per ton of rubber, but no external benefits. What government tax or subsidy program will lead to the efficient amount of rubber being produced?

 a. A subsidy of more than $2 per ton of rubber.

 b. A subsidy of $2 per ton of rubber.

 c. A tax of more than $2 per ton of rubber.

 d. A tax of $2 per ton of rubber.

Positive Externalities: Knowledge
Use Table 18.1 for the next four questions.

TABLE **18.1**

Multiple Choice Questions 13, 14, 15, 16

Quantity	Marginal private cost (dollars)	Marginal private benefit (dollars)	Marginal social benefit (dollars)
500	$5	$9	$11
550	6	8	10
600	7	7	9
650	8	6	8
700	9	5	7

13. Table 18.1 represents the market for a good with
    a. only an external cost.
    b. only an external benefit.
    c. both external costs and benefits.
    d. no externalities.

14. Left unregulated, the equilibrium quantity is
    a. 550.
    b. 600.
    c. 650.
    d. 700.

15. The efficient level of output is
    a. 550.
    b. 600.
    c. 650.
    d. 700.

16. What can the government do so that the efficient amount is produced?
    a. Subsidize suppliers $8 per unit.
    b. Subsidize suppliers $2 per unit.
    c. Tax suppliers $2 per unit.
    d. Tax suppliers $8 per unit.

17. An unregulated market produces too ___ of a good with an external cost and too ___ of a good with an external benefit.
    a. much; much
    b. much; little
    c. little; much
    d. little; little

18. Which of the following is a possible government solution to the problem posed by a good with an external benefit?
    a. Subsidize the production of the good.
    b. Tax the production of the good.
    c. Tax the consumption of the good.
    d. All of the above are possible solutions.

19. Which of the following statements about knowledge is FALSE?
    a. Knowledge can have an external benefit.
    b. As a productive resource, knowledge might not be subject to diminishing productivity.
    c. Intellectual property rights can help create incentives for accumulation of more knowledge.
    d. Patents help create incentives for creating knowledge and do so without any cost.

20. Patents are a solution to the external
    a. benefit from attending college.
    b. benefit from discovering new knowledge.
    c. cost from attending college.
    d. cost from discovering new knowledge.

■ Short Answer Problems

FIGURE **18.4**
Short Answer Problem 1

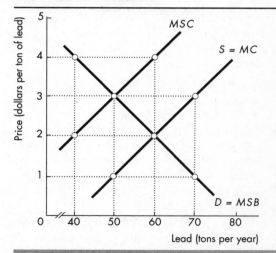

1. The figure above shows the market for lead. The production of lead creates pollution. What is the efficient quantity? If the market is left unregulated, what is the equilibrium quantity? How much is the deadweight loss and illustrate it in the figure.

2. Farmer Dave's and farmer Mark's farms are next to each other. They get along well so transactions costs are low. The only problem in their existence is Dave's pig, Justin, who occasionally gets into Mark's corn field and eats the corn. If Justin did not get into the corn, he would eat valueless garbage, not the corn. A fence can keep Justin out of the corn. Suppose that Justin eats $350 of corn per year and that to erect a fence to keep Justin off Mark's farm costs $250 per year. Either Dave or Mark can erect the fence and, once the fence is in place, Justin eats none of the corn.

    Property rights that allow Justin to roam, or that keep Mark's farm free from Dave's pig, have yet to be assigned

    a. Suppose that the property right is given to Dave, so that Justin can roam free any time he desires. Will Mark erect a fence?

    b. Now suppose that the property right is given to Mark, so that he can charge Dave whenever Justin shows up on Mark's farm and eats the corn. Will Dave erect a fence?

    c. What general proposition is illustrated in this question?

3. Explain how a tax can be used to achieve efficiency in the face of external costs.

4. In a small town two factories — factory A and factory B — each produce 10 units of pollution so that the total pollution is 20 units. Factory A can decrease its pollution at a constant marginal cost of $50 per unit; factory B can reduce its pollution at a constant marginal cost of $100 per unit.

    a. If both factories A and B decrease their pollution by 5 units, what is the total amount of pollution in the town and what is the total cost of reaching this level of pollution?

    b. If factory A decreases its level of pollution by 10 units and factory B does not decrease its pollution, what is the total amount of pollution in the town and what is the total cost of achieving this level of pollution?

    c. From a social standpoint, to reach a total of 10 units of pollution, which is more desirable: both factories cutting back by 5 units each or A cutting back by 10 units and B not cutting back? Why?

    d. Suppose that the EPA determines that the efficient level of pollution is 10 units. The EPA introduces marketable permits and grants each

firm 5 permits. Each permit allows the firm to produce 1 unit of pollution. What is likely to occur? In particular, will factory A or B want to sell its permits to the other factory and is the other factory willing to buy them? If there is a potential buyer and seller of the permits, what is the price range in which the permits will trade?

    e. From a social standpoint, what have marketable permits accomplished?

5. At public colleges and universities, governments provide education at a price (tuition) less than cost. What economic argument supports the policy of charging students at public universities less than the full cost of their education?

FIGURE **18.5**
The Market for Chicken Pox Vaccine

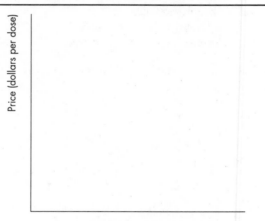

Vaccine (million of doses per year)

6. Vaccination creates an external benefit and has no external costs. Use Figure 18.5 to illustrate the market for chicken pox vaccination. Label the doses that will be taken in the absence of any government intervention as Q_0 and label the efficient number of doses Q_1. How can the government move this market toward efficiency?

7. The first two columns of Table 18.2 (on the next page) give the demand schedule for education in Transylvania, and the third column gives the marginal private cost. Because education generates external benefits, the marginal social benefit shown in the last column is greater than marginal private benefit. Education creates no external costs.

    a. What equilibrium price and quantity would result if the market for education is unregulated?

TABLE 18.2

Education in Transylvania

Quantity (number of students)	Marginal private benefit (dollars)	Marginal private cost (dollars)	Marginal social benefit (dollars)
1	$500	$200	$800
2	400	250	700
3	300	300	600
4	200	350	500
5	100	400	400
6	0	450	300

b. What is the efficient quantity of students in Transylvania?

c. In an attempt to address the inefficient level of education in his nation, Igor — the newly appointed minister of education — has decided to provide a low-cost public university, Igor Omphesus (Igor's middle name is Omphesus) University. To attain the efficient level of schooling, what must tuition be at the new university, I.O.U.?

d. What is the marginal cost of schooling the last student at this university?

■ You're the Teacher

1. "I just don't understand some of this stuff. I mean, even after the government taxes a product with pollution, there's still an external cost. I mean, that's got to mean that there's some pollution, right? I mean, come on, pollution is bad; we don't want any of it. I mean, the best level of pollution has to be zero, right?" Aside from having a severe "I mean" problem, this student also has a severe problem understanding that the efficient level of pollution is not zero. You probably can't do anything about the "I mean" problem, but you should be able to help the student grasp why zero pollution is not desirable.

Answers

■ True/False Answers

Externalities in Our Lives

1. **T** Externalities can arise from both production and consumption and can be either positive or negative.

2. **F** Flu vaccination is a good example of a positive consumption externality.

Negative Externalities: Pollution

3. **F** The existence of negative production externality, such as pollution, means that the private marginal cost differs from the social marginal cost but has no effect on the demand. The demand for a clean environment continues to exist.

4. **T** The marginal social cost equals the marginal private cost plus the marginal external cost. So, if there is a marginal external cost then the marginal social cost is greater than the marginal private cost.

5. **F** The existence of external costs means that the private market produces *more* than the efficient amount of the good.

6. **T** The question essentially is the definition of the Coase theorem.

7. **F** If production of a good creates an external cost, to attain efficiency its production needs to be taxed, not subsidized.

8. **T** Both emission charges and marketable permits are methods the government can use to overcome the inefficiency from a negative production externality such as pollution.

Positive Externalities: Knowledge

9. **T** Knowledge has benefits that spill over to others, so knowledge has external benefits.

10. **F** The private market produces *less* than the efficient amount of a good with an external benefit.

11. **T** Left alone, the private market would produce less than the efficient amount of the good. A subsidy will increase the amount produced.

12. **F** Education has an external benefit, so the right policy is to subsidize, not tax, education.

13. **T** Patents are one method the government uses to overcome the problem of knowledge's external benefit.

■ Multiple Choice Answers

Externalities in Our Lives

1. **d** Answer (d) is correct because an externality falls upon someone who is neither the producer nor consumer of the good or service.

2. **c** The party-goers are "consuming" the services of the party and they are inflicting an external cost on the neighbors.

3. **d** The bystanders are not the consumers of the cigarettes, so the harm that befalls them is an external cost.

Negative Externalities: Pollution

4. **b** Not widely recognized is the fact that for most substances, air pollution is becoming less of a problem.

5. **b** Because the *MSC* curve is above the *MC* curve, the figure indicates that paper production creates an external cost.

6. **c** The vertical distance between the *MSC* curve and the *MC* curve is the marginal external cost, which in this case is $2 per ton.

7. **b** In the absence of any intervention, the private market produces where the private demand curve (which is the same as the private marginal benefit curve) intersects the private supply curve (which is the same as the private marginal cost curve).

8. **c** Efficiency requires that production be the amount for which marginal social cost, *MSC*, equals marginal social benefit, *MSB*.

9. **c** The tax must shift the private *MC* curve until it is the same as the *MSC* curve. Imposing a $2 tax shifts the *MC* curve by the amount of the tax, $2, which is the amount desired. More generally, by imposing a tax equal to the marginal external cost, the new marginal private cost, which includes the tax, is the same as the marginal social cost.

10. **c** The Coase theorem shows that when transactions costs are low and the number of parties involved is small, to whom a property right is assigned makes no difference: The externality will be eliminated and the efficient level of production will result.

11. **b** Emission charges allow firms to pollute as long as they pay the fee for the pollution. Emission

charges are common in Europe, but are less common in the United States.

12. **d** Imposing a tax equal to the marginal external cost sets the marginal private cost — which includes the tax — equal to the marginal social cost, thereby ensuring that the efficient amount of rubber will be produced.

Positive Externalities: Knowledge

13. **b** At any level of output, the marginal social benefit exceeds the marginal private benefit, which indicates that there must be an external benefit.

14. **b** The private market produces the level of output that equalizes the marginal private cost (the private supply curve) and the marginal private benefit (the private demand curve).

15. **c** Efficiency requires that the amount of the good produced equalize the marginal social cost and the marginal social benefit. In this case, efficiency requires that output be 650.

16. **b** If suppliers are granted a $2 per unit subsidy, the marginal private cost schedule drops by $2 at every unit of output. Hence to produce 650 units of output, the new marginal private cost becomes $6. This equals the marginal private benefit of 650 units, so the (new) equilibrium price is $6 and the quantity produced is the efficient amount, or 650 units.

17. **b** This answer summarizes the "bottom line" results about how externalities affect efficiency.

18. **a** Subsidies are a solution to the problem posed by an external benefit.

19. **d** Once a patent is granted, the holder becomes the monopoly owner of the resource. Monopolies create inefficiency by setting the price higher than the competitive level and this inefficiency is a cost of issuing a patent.

20. **b** New discoveries often may be used by many people, which is an externality from the point of view of the discoverer.

■ **Answers to Short Answer Problems**

1. The equilibrium quantity is 60 tons of lead, determined by the intersection of the demand and supply curves. The efficient quantity is 50 tons of lead, determined by the intersection of the marginal social benefit and marginal social cost curves. The deadweight loss is the triangle illustrated in Figure 18.6.

FIGURE 18.6
Short Answer Problem 1

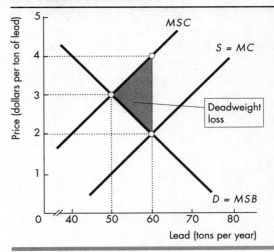

The area of the triangle is (½)(base)(height). The base is 10 tons of lead. The height is $2 per ton of lead, the difference between the marginal social cost of another ton of lead and the marginal benefit from another ton. So the deadweight loss is equal to (½)(10 tons)($2 per ton) = $10 million.

2. a. Farmer Mark will erect the fence. Doing so costs him $250 a year, but it saves him the $350 Justin would otherwise eat.

   b. Farmer Dave will erect the fence. If he did not do so, Justin would eat $350 worth of corn, and Mark would bill Dave for the corn. Thus erecting the fence costs Dave $250 a year, but saves him $350.

   c. These answers illustrate the Coase theorem. Erecting the fence is efficient because the cost to society of the fence, $250, is less than the benefit to society of the fence, $350 saved by preventing the pig from eating the corn. As the Coase theorem points out, regardless of whether Dave or Mark is given the property right, the fence is erected and Justin dines on valueless garbage rather than valuable corn.

3. The existence of external costs means that producers do not take into account all costs when deciding how much to produce. If a tax is levied that is exactly the amount of the external cost, the cost is no longer external. As a result, the producer takes it into account and so is induced to produce the efficient quantity.

4. a. The total amount of pollution is 10 units, 5
       remaining units from factory A and 5 remaining
       units from factory B. The total cost of achieving
       this level of pollution is $750, the cost of $250
       incurred by factory A plus the cost of $500 in-
       curred by factory B.

    b. The total amount of pollution (again) is 10
       units, comprising no pollution from factory A
       and 10 units from factory B. The total cost of
       attaining this level of pollution is $500, all in-
       curred by factory A.

    c. From a social standpoint, having factory A de-
       crease its pollution by 10 units and factory B do
       nothing is the most efficient because it has the
       lowest total social cost, $500 versus $750 for an
       equal reduction at each factory. Eliminating the
       10 units of pollution by having only A cut back
       has inflicted the lowest possible total cost on so-
       ciety, which is a desirable outcome.

    d. Factory A will sell its permits to factory B. This
       transaction will occur because decreasing its
       pollution is less expensive for factory A than it is
       for factory B. In particular, the price of a permit
       for a unit of pollution will range between $50
       and $100. For any price greater than $50, fac-
       tory A is willing to sell its permits and reduce its
       pollution because this transaction is profitable:
       The cost to A is $50 per unit of pollution elimi-
       nated but, as long as the price exceeds $50, fac-
       tory A profits. Factory B is willing to buy
       permits for any price less than $100 because
       buying permits at this price reduces B's costs.
       For each permit that B can buy, it saves $100 by
       not having to decrease its pollution. As long as
       the price of a permit is less than $100, buying
       the permits reduces B's costs.

    e. With marketable permits only factory A de-
       creases its pollution. Factory B does not lower its
       pollution but instead buys permits from factory
       A. With marketable permits we obtain, as in part
       (c), the socially desirable outcome: Factory A de-
       creases its pollution and factory B does not.

5. The economic argument is that education generates
    external benefits. In particular, when individuals are
    educated, society at large receives benefits beyond
    the private benefits that accrue to those choosing
    how much education to obtain. The presence of the
    external benefit means that in the absence of gov-
    ernment intervention, the private sector would pro-

vide too little education for efficiency. Hence to
attain efficiency in the market for education, the
government provides below-cost education at public
colleges and universities.

FIGURE 18.7
Short Answer Problem 6

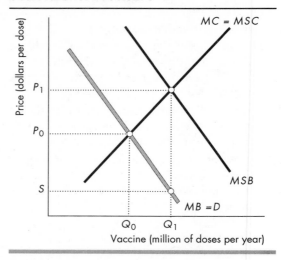

6. Figure 18.7 shows the market for chicken pox vac-
    cine. Because there are no external costs, the mar-
    ginal social cost curve equals the marginal private
    cost. This curve is labeled $MC = MSC$ in the figure.
    It also is the private supply curve. However, the
    presence of the external benefit means that the mar-
    ginal social benefit (MSB) curve lies right of the
    marginal private benefit curve, which is the same as
    the private demand curve (labeled $MB = D$). The
    vertical distance between the curves equals the mar-
    ginal externality; that is, it is the additional (exter-
    nal) benefit to society over and above the benefit to
    the consumer. In the absence of government inter-
    vention, Q_0 is produced but the efficient amount
    is Q_1. To move this market closer to the efficient
    level of output, the government might subsidize
    production. This policy could take the form of
    paying producers to produce more vaccine. The aim
    is to shift the private supply curve rightward so that
    it intersects the private demand at output Q_1, the
    efficient amount, and price S. Alternatively, the
    government might buy Q_1 worth of doses and then
    resell them to consumers below cost at price S, the
    price necessary to induce consumers to buy Q_1
    doses.

7. a. In an unregulated market, the equilibrium price and quantity are determined by the intersection of the marginal private benefit and cost curves because these are the market's demand and supply curves, respectively. Thus the equilibrium price is $300, and the equilibrium quantity is 3 students.

    b. Because there are no external costs, the efficient quantity is determined by the intersection of the marginal private cost and marginal *social* benefit curves. This result implies that efficiency is attained at a quantity of 5 students attending college.

    c. Igor wants 5 students to attend his new university, I.O.U. Five students will attend only when the tuition is $100.

    d. When 5 students attend the university, the marginal cost of the 5th student is $400. By charging the student only $100 in tuition, Igor apparently is losing money on this student. However, the loss is only apparent: Five students are the efficient level of education because the *total* marginal social benefit from the 5th student

is $400, which equals the marginal cost of educating this student.

■ **You're the Teacher**

1. "I agree with you that pollution is bad, but clearly to totally eliminate it isn't optimal because it would cost way too much. Think about it this way: Society could get rid of all air pollution by outlawing all cars, all trains, all planes, shutting down all factories, and eliminating all cows. (Cows produce methane you know.) But, come on, you know we won't do this and we don't want to do it. The reason is immediate: It's just too expensive.

    "Sure, we'd like less pollution, but the cost to get to zero pollution is prohibitive — a whole lot more than the benefit! So, anyone that says 'Zero pollution is best' hasn't thought through the issue. In fact, some pollution is good. We get to drive rather than walk, we get to have pizza delivered rather than doing without, we get to air condition our homes rather than perspire, and we get to heat our homes rather than freeze."

Chapter Quiz

1. An example of an activity with an external cost is
   a. planting flowers around a house.
   b. playing a CD very loud in an apartment.
   c. watching a movie in a theater.
   d. reading a textbook.

2. If a good has an external benefit, a market left unregulated will produce
   a. more than the efficient amount.
   b. the efficient amount.
   c. less than the efficient amount.
   d. an amount that may be more than, less than, or equal to the efficient amount depending on how large the external benefit is relative to the private benefit.

3. The relationship between marginal private cost (MC), marginal external cost, and marginal social cost (MSC) is
   a. $MC = MSC$ + marginal external cost.
   b. marginal external cost = $MC + MSC$.
   c. $MSC = MC$ + marginal external cost.
   d. None of the above answers is correct.

4. If production of a good creates an external cost, to move the economy closer to efficiency the government might
   a. subsidize production of the good.
   b. tax consumption of the good.
   c. remove the offending property right.
   d. None of the above actions move the economy closer to efficiency.

5. Resource use definitely is efficient when production is at the level such that marginal
   a. external cost equals marginal external benefit.
   b. private cost equals marginal private benefit.
   c. social cost equals marginal social benefit.
   d. external cost is zero and marginal external benefit is as large as possible.

6. Potential solutions to the negative production externality created by pollution include
   a. subsidizing the production of the good or using emissions charges.
   b. taxing the production of the good or using marketable permits.
   c. using marketable permits or issuing patents or copyrights.
   d. public provision by the government or using vouchers.

7. When a student makes a decision about how much schooling to acquire, the student considers only the
   a. private marginal benefits and private marginal costs.
   b. social marginal benefits and social marginal costs.
   c. marginal external benefits and marginal external costs.
   d. private marginal benefits and social marginal costs.

8. The private marginal benefit from a good is less than the social marginal benefit but the private marginal cost of the good equals the social marginal cost. As a result, the good _____ external benefits and _____ external costs.
   a. has; has
   b. has; has no
   c. has no; has
   d. has no; has no

9. To offset the externality from knowledge, governments use all of the following EXCEPT
   a. patents.
   b. copyrights.
   c. below-cost provision.
   d. taxes.

10. An external cost of a good is
    a. its total cost minus its consumer surplus.
    b. its total cost minus producer surplus.
    c. its total cost minus total surplus.
    d. any cost it imposes on people who do not buy it.

The answers for this Chapter Quiz are on page 368

6 MARKET FAILURE AND PUBLIC CHOICE

Reading Between the Lines

COLLEGE COSTS OUTPACE FAMILY INCOME

On May 2, 2002 data were released confirming what many college students already knew: the cost of college rose faster than did the average family income over the two decades between 1980 and 2000. Nowadays 64 percent of college seniors graduate with debt and the average amount of debt doubled between 1990 and 2000. Government aid for education has remained roughly constant, while tuition has risen twice as rapidly as inflation over the last decade. As a result, a federal Pell grant typically covered 98 percent of tuition at a four-year public college in 1986 but in 1998 it covered only 57 percent.

For details, go to The Economics Place web site, the Economics in the News archive, www.economicsplace.com/econ5e/einarchives.html

■ Analyze It

Everyone reading this book is familiar with college tuition! On the average, tuition has been skyrocketing while government aid for higher education has been stagnating. As a result, more college students and their families are borrowing to pay for college and they are borrowing more than before.

1. Although college tuition is an important cost of attending college, there are other costs. List some of these (opportunity) costs.

2. Is it good public policy to allow college to become so expensive that fewer students can afford it? In your answer, be sure to mention the role played by externalities.

Mid-Term Examination

■ **Chapter 16**

1. The public choice theory of government argues that politicians try to
   a. maximize the likelihood of their election and re-election.
   b. maximize the amount of their campaign contributions.
   c. promote an efficient allocation of resources.
   d. None of the above.

2. Nonrivalry is a feature of
   a. external goods.
   b. nonexcludable goods.
   c. private goods.
   d. public goods.

3. In general, an excise tax reduces
   a. only consumer surplus.
   b. only producer surplus.
   c. both consumer and producer surplus.
   d. neither consumer nor producer surplus.

4. A radio station is a
   a. private good, as is access to its broadcast signal.
   b. private good, but access to its broadcast signal is a public good.
   c. public good, as is access to its broadcast signal.
   d. public good, but access to its broadcast signal is a private good.

■ **Chapter 17**

5. The goal of regulators is to maximize producer surplus according to the
   a. capture theory of regulation.
   b. public interest theory of regulation.
   c. consumer surplus theory of regulation.
   d. producer surplus theory of regulation.

6. The supply of economic regulation will be smaller whenever
   a. consumer surplus per buyer increases.
   b. the number of buyers decreases.
   c. producer surplus per supplier increases.
   d. the total surplus decreases.

7. Price cap regulation _____ the incentive to inflate their costs and rate of return regulation _____ the incentive to inflate their costs.
   a. gives regulated firms; gives regulated firms
   b. gives regulated firms; removes from regulated firms
   c. removes from regulated firms; gives regulated firms
   d. removes from regulated firms; removes from regulated firms

8. Average cost pricing for a natural monopoly is equivalent to
   a. marginal cost pricing.
   b. maximizing consumer surplus.
   c. maximizing producer surplus.
   d. rate of return regulation.

■ **Chapter 18**

9. An example of an activity that generates external benefits is
   a. dumping soap suds into a trout stream.
   b. planting flowers along an interstate highway.
   c. eating an apple.
   d. None of the above.

10. Unregulated perfectly competitive markets are efficient when there are
   a. external benefits and external costs.
   b. external benefits but no external costs.
   c. external costs but no external benefits.
   d. no external benefits nor external costs.

11. The Coase theorem applies when transactions costs are
   a. low and property rights have been assigned.
   b. low and property rights do not exist.
   c. high and property rights have been assigned.
   d. high and property rights do not exist.

12. When individuals make decisions about the amount of education to acquire,
   a. they undervalue the private benefits that it creates.
   b. they undervalue the external benefits that it creates.
   a. they overvalue the private benefits that it creates.
   a. they overvalue the external benefits that it creates.

Answers

■ Reading Between the Lines

1. When thinking of the costs of attending college, be sure that you think of *all* the *opportunity* costs. For instance, the tuition you pay is an opportunity cost because if you were not attending college, you would not pay the tuition. So, too, is the cost of the textbooks that you buy. The interest on student loans is yet another cost. However, keep in mind that the cost of food and housing is *not* an opportunity cost of attending college because you would be paying for these even if you were not attending college. An important and often overlooked cost of college is the income given up by attending college. In particular, if you were not attending college, likely you would have a full-time job and be earning more than whatever you are presently earning. A point to keep in mind, however, is that even with all these costs, college remains a tremendous financial investment because the payoff in higher lifetime income is, on the average, substantial.

2. A college education generates external benefits. As a result, the rest of society, and not just the college graduate, benefits when someone receives a college education. When a good or service has external benefits, a competitive market will produce less than the efficient quantity, leading to a deadweight loss. An appropriate government policy in this case is to subsidize the production or consumption of the good. Government aid plays this role because it lessens the price paid to attend college. In recent years, the relative amount of government aid has been reduced. Reducing the amount of aid is the correct public policy only if the external benefits from a college education have decreased. There is no evidence that this has occurred and, indeed, given the high-tech nature of our world, some evidence that the external benefits have increased. So, decreasing the amount of public aid given to college students seems an incorrect public policy.

■ Mid-Term Exam Answers

1. a;   2. d;   3. c;   4. b;   5. a;   6. b;   7. c;   8. d;   9. b;   10. d;   11. a;   12. b.

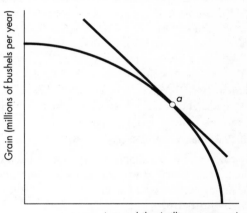

FIGURE **19.1**

Slope of the *PPF* is the Opportunity Cost

Grain (millions of bushels per year)

a

Automobiles (millions per year)

Chapter 19 TRADING WITH THE WORLD*

Key Concepts

■ Patterns and Trends in International Trade

The goods and services we buy from producers in other nations are our **imports**; the goods and services we sell to people in other nations are our **exports**. Most U.S. exports and imports are manufactured goods. Trade in goods accounts for most of U.S. international trade; trade in services (travel and transportation) accounts for the rest.

Trade has accounted for an increasingly large fraction of total output in the United States. **Net exports** is the value of exports minus the value of imports. In 2000, the value of U.S. imports exceeded that of U.S. exports.

■ The Gains from International Trade

Comparative advantage is the factor that drives international trade. Countries can produce anywhere on their production possibility frontier (*PPF*) curve. Figure 19.1 shows a *PPF* for a nation producing at point *a*.

◆ The *PPF's* slope is (Δ bushels of grain)/(Δ cars), with Δ meaning "change in." The slope equals the opportunity cost of one more car at point *a*.

◆ A country has a **comparative advantage** in the production of a good if the country can produce it at a lower opportunity cost than any other country.

A country can gain by buying the goods from other nations that the nations produce at the lowest opportu-

nity cost and selling the goods it produces at the lowest opportunity cost to the other countries.

◆ A nation gains from trade by specializing in production of goods for which it has a comparative advantage and trading for other goods.

◆ With international trade, a nation receives a higher relative price for the goods it exports and pays a lower relative price for the goods it imports. The **terms of trade** is the price of a nation's imports.

◆ International trade allows all nations to consume *outside* their *PPFs*. The added consumption is the gains from trade.

---

*This is Chapter 32 in *Economics*.

Some trade involves similar goods. There are two reasons for trade in similar goods:

♦ Diversified tastes — people demand many similar but slightly different products.

♦ Economies of scale — average total cost declines with output.

A nation can specialize in the production of one of the similar goods and capture economies of scale by trading the good throughout the world.

■ International Trade Restrictions

Governments restrict trade to protect domestic industries. The main methods used to restrict trade are:

♦ **Tariffs** — taxes on imported goods.

♦ **Nontariff barrier** — any action other than a tariff that restricts international trade.

Today, U.S. tariffs are low compared to their historical levels. The **General Agreement on Tariffs and Trade** (GATT) is an international agreement designed to reduce tariffs and increase international trade. The **World Trade Organization**, to which the United States belongs, requires that nations more closely obey GATT rules. The **North American Free Trade Agreement** (NAFTA) is a 1994 agreement between the U.S., Canada, and Mexico that will remove most tariffs between these nations over a 15-year period.

Figure 19.2 illustrates the effects of a tariff.

♦ A tariff decreases the supply of the imported good. The new supply curve with the tariff lies above the old supply curve by the amount of the tariff (the length of the arrow).

♦ The price rises from P_0 to P_1 and the quantity decreases from Q_0 to Q_1. The government gains revenue as indicated in the figure. The tariff reduces the gains from trade and creates inefficiency.

♦ By decreasing imports to the domestic economy, foreigners can buy less from the domestic economy. Therefore the value of domestic exports decreases by an amount equal to the drop in the value of domestic imports.

Nontariff barriers include quotas and voluntary export restraints.

♦ **Quota** — a quantitative restriction on the maximum amount of a good that can be imported.

♦ **Voluntary export restraint** — an agreement between governments in which the exporting nation agrees to limit the volume of its exports.

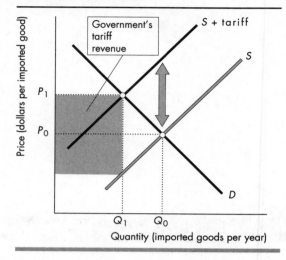

FIGURE **19.2**
The Effect of a Tariff

Similar to tariffs, nontariff barriers raise the prices of imported goods and decrease the quantities imported. Unlike a tariff, the government gets no revenue from a nontariff barrier; the revenue from the higher price goes to importers in the case of quotas and to foreign exporters in the case of voluntary export restraints.

■ The Case Against Protection

Arguments in favor of protection are flawed. The arguments and their errors are:

♦ *National security* — the nation should protect industries that are necessary for its defense.
Error: Virtually every industry may be considered "vital" for defense; direct subsidies to targeted industries are more efficient than protection from international competition.

♦ **Infant-industry argument** — the nation should protect a young industry that will reap learning-by-doing gains in productivity and eventually be able to compete successfully in the world market.
Error: If the learning-by-doing benefits accrue only to the firms in the industry, this argument fails because these firms can finance their own start-ups; direct subsidies are more efficient.

♦ **Dumping** — the nation should protect an industry from foreign competitors who sell goods below cost.
Error: Determining when a firm sells below cost is very difficult; only global natural monopolies are able to sustain a monopoly; if the firm is a natural

monopoly, regulation is the more efficient way to restrain it.

♦ *Protection saves jobs* — imports cost U.S. jobs.
Error: Free trade costs jobs in importing industries, but it creates them in exporting industries; tariffs that protect jobs in import-competing industries do so at an exceedingly high cost.

♦ *Cheap foreign labor* — tariffs are necessary to compete with cheap foreign labor.
Error: U.S. labor is more productive than cheap foreign labor; U.S. firms can compete successfully in industries in which they have a comparative advantage because of their productivity relative to other nations.

♦ *Diversity and stability* — nations specialized in the production of one good might be subject to economic fluctuations.
Error: The United States is not specialized; nations that are specialized can gain by such specialization and then diversify by investing abroad.

♦ *Lax environmental standards* — protection is needed to compete against nations with weak environmental standards.
Error: Not all poor nations have weak standards; poor nations' concerns about the environment will increase when they grow richer through trade; currently poor nations might have a comparative advantage in pollution-intensive goods.

♦ *National culture* — protection is necessary to protect the nation's national culture.
Error: Those clamoring for protection are simply "rent-seekers" involved in the country's national media outlets; many "American" producers of media are from other nations.

♦ *Rich nations exploit developing countries* — protection prevents developed nations from forcing people in poor nations to work for slave wages.
Error: By allowing poor nations to trade with rich ones, wages in poor nations rise because of the increased demand for labor.

■ Why Is International Trade Restricted?

♦ The government collects revenue from tariffs. This revenue source is important in developing nations.

♦ Some people are harmed by international trade and so they lobby politicians to limit free trade.

Helpful Hints

1. **DOES PROTECTION SAVE JOBS?** This argument is popular but incorrect. Imposing a tariff on imports costs jobs in export industries. We lose jobs because foreigners, unable to sell as much to us, are thus unable to buy as much from us. Hence our export industries shrink, or fail to grow as much as otherwise.

   Moreover, saving the jobs in the import-competing industry comes at a very high cost. For example, protection in the textile industry annually costs American residents $221,000 per job; in the automobile industry, $105,000 per job; in dairy products, $220,000 per job; and in steel, $750,000 per job. These costs greatly exceed the wages in these jobs. Just as it would be foolish to spend $221,000 to obtain $45,000, so, too, is it foolish for the nation to protect jobs when the cost of the protection exceeds the wages paid for the jobs!

2. **WHY DOES PROTECTION PERSIST?** Gains from free trade can be considerable, so why do countries impose trade restrictions? The key is that, although free trade creates overall benefits to the economy as a whole, there are both winners and losers. The winners gain more in total than the losers lose, but the latter tend to be concentrated in a few industries. In other words, the gains from free trade are spread amongst many people — so the gain per person is small — while the costs are concentrated amongst only a few people— so the costs per person are large.

   Because of this concentration, free trade is resisted. Even though trade restrictions benefit only a small minority while the overwhelming majority are harmed, implementation of trade barriers is not surprising. The cost of a particular trade restriction to each of the majority individually is quite small, but the benefit to each of the few individually large. So the minority has a strong incentive to have a restriction imposed, whereas the majority has little incentive to expend time and energy in resisting a trade barrier. The net result is that governments frequently wind up restricting free trade, even though the restrictions cost their nations more than they benefit it.

Questions

True/False and Explain

Patterns and Trends In International Trade

1. Nations can trade goods but not services.

2. The United States is a large importer and exporter of manufactured goods.

3. In 2000, the value of American imports exceeded the value of American exports.

The Gains from International Trade

4. Each nation's opportunity cost of producing any good or service is the same.

5. A nation has a comparative advantage in a good if it can produce the good at a lower opportunity cost than other nations.

6. Trade allows a nation to consume combinations of products that lie beyond its *PPF*.

7. Only the nation exporting a good gains from trade.

8. Nations do not trade similar goods.

9. Firms can capture economies of scale with international trade.

International Trade Restrictions

10. Tariffs in the United States are at an all-time high.

11. Economists generally agree that high tariffs improve a nation's standard of living.

12. When governments impose tariffs, they increase their consumers' welfare.

13. A quota and a voluntary export restraint on an imported good both raise its price.

The Case Against Protection

14. The only argument for protection without any error is the infant-industry argument.

15. U.S. workers can compete with lower paid foreign workers in industries in which the U.S. has a comparative advantage.

16. International trade lowers wages in poor nations.

Why Is International Trade Restricted?

17. Free international trade benefits some citizens and harms others.

Multiple Choice Questions

Patterns and Trends In International Trade

1. Which of the following is a U.S. service export?
   a. A U.S. citizen buys dinner while traveling in Switzerland.
   b. A Canadian buys a dinner while traveling in Canada.
   c. A Swiss citizen buys a computer made in the United States.
   d. A Mexican citizen spends the night in a motel while visiting the United States.

2. In 2000
   a. trade in services accounted for about 50 percent of total U.S. exports.
   b. agricultural products accounted for over 50 percent of total U.S. exports.
   c. the U.S. government rejected the NAFTA treaty.
   d. U.S. imports were greater in value than U.S. exports.

The Gains from International Trade

3. Musicland and Videoland produce two goods, CDs and DVDs. Musicland has a comparative advantage in the production of CDs if in Musicland
   a. fewer DVDs must be given up to produce 1 CD than in Videoland.
   b. less labor is required to produce 1 CD than in Videoland.
   c. less capital is required to produce 1 CD than in Videoland.
   d. less labor and capital are required to produce 1 CD than in Videoland.

4. International trade allows a nation to
   a. produce and consume at a point beyond its *PPF*.
   b. produce at a point beyond its *PPF* but not consume at a point beyond its *PPF*.
   c. consume at a point beyond its *PPF* but not produce at a point beyond its *PPF*.
   d. neither produce nor consume at a point beyond its *PPF*.

5. The maximum gains from trade occur when
   a. there is no international trade.
   b. each nation produces according to its comparative advantage and trades with other nations.
   c. each nation uses tariffs rather than quotas.
   d. each nation uses quotas rather than tariffs.

Figures 19.3 and 19.4 show production in two nations, Solaris and Chaff. Production is taking place at point *a* in Solaris and at point *b* in Chaff. Use these figures for the next four questions.

FIGURE **19.3**
Production in Solaris

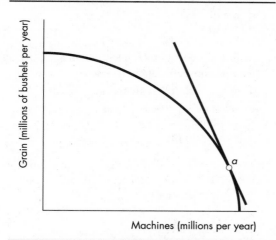

FIGURE **19.4**
Production in Chaff

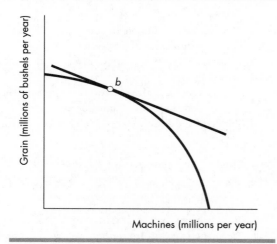

6. The slope of the *PPF* at point *a* in Solaris is 200 bushels of grain per machine; the slope of the *PPF* at point *b* in Chaff is 15 bushels of grain per machine. Without trade between the nations, what is the opportunity cost of a machine in Solaris?
   a. The cost is 200 bushels of grain.
   b. The cost is $1/200$ bushels of grain.
   c. The cost is 15 bushels of grain.
   d. The cost is $1/15$ bushel of grain.

7. Without trade between the nations, what is the opportunity cost of a machine in Chaff?
   a. The cost is 200 bushels of grain.
   b. The cost is $1/200$ bushels of grain.
   c. The cost is 15 bushels of grain.
   d. The cost is $1/15$ bushel of grain.

8. Solaris has a comparative advantage in _____, and Chaff has a comparative advantage in _____.
   a. machines; grain
   b. grain; machines
   c. machines and grain; neither good
   d. neither good; machines and grain.

9. Once Solaris and Chaff begin to trade, Solaris exports _____ to Chaff and Chaff exports _____ to Solaris.
   a. machines; grain
   b. grain; machines
   c. machines and grain; neither good
   d. neither good; machines and grain

10. International trade based on comparative advantage can allow each country to consume
   a. more of the goods it exports, but always less of the goods it imports.
   b. more of the goods it imports, but always less of the goods it exports.
   c. more of the goods it exports and imports.
   d. less of the goods it exports and imports.

11. The combination of diversified tastes and economies of scale can account for

    a. a nation importing and exporting similar products.
    b. why tariffs create inefficiency.
    c. specialization according to comparative advantage.
    d. the result that free trade allows nations to consume at points beyond their *PPF* even though they cannot produce at points beyond their *PPF*.

International Trade Restrictions

12. A tariff is

    a. a government imposed limit on the amount of a good that can be exported from a nation.
    b. a government imposed barrier that sets a fixed limit on the amount of a good that can be imported into a nation.
    c. a tax on a good imported into a nation.
    d. an agreement between governments to limit exports from a nation.

13. Who benefits from a tariff on a good?

    a. Domestic consumers of the good
    b. Domestic producers of the good
    c. Foreign governments
    d. Foreign producers of the good

14. Suppose that the United States imports only textiles from Mexico and exports only computers to Mexico. If the United States imposes a tariff on Mexican textiles, the U.S. textile industry _____ and the U.S. computer industry _____.

    a. expands; expands
    b. expands; does not change
    c. expands; contracts
    d. contracts; expands

15. When does the government gain the most revenue?

    a. When it imposes a tariff.
    b. When it imposes a quota.
    c. When it negotiates a voluntary export restraint.
    d. The amount of revenue it gains is the same with a tariff and a voluntary export restraint.

The Case Against Protection

16. The (false) idea that an industry should be protected because of learning-by-doing until it is large enough to compete successfully in world markets is the _____ argument for protection.

    a. absolute advantage
    b. infant industry
    c. dumping
    d. diversity

17. Selling a product in a foreign nation at a price less than its cost of production is called

    a. infant industry exploitation.
    b. absolute advantage.
    c. dumping.
    d. net exporting.

18. When a rich nation buys a product made in a poor nation, in the poor nation the demand for labor _____ and the wage rate _____.

    a. increases; rises
    b. increases; falls
    c. decreases; rises
    d. decreases; falls

19. Which of the following is a valid reason for protecting an industry?

    a. The industry is unable to compete with low-wage foreign competitors.
    b. The industry is necessary to diversify the nation's production.
    c. Protection keeps richer nations from exploiting the workers of poorer countries.
    d. None of the above reasons is a valid reason for protection.

Why Is International Trade Restricted?

20. Which of the following statements about the gains from international trade is correct?

    a. Everyone gains from international trade.
    b. Some people gain from international trade and some lose, though overall the gains exceed the losses.
    c. Some people gain and some people lose from international trade; overall the losses exceed the gains.
    d. Everyone loses from international trade.

■ Short Answer Problems

FIGURE 19.5
Short Answer Problem 1

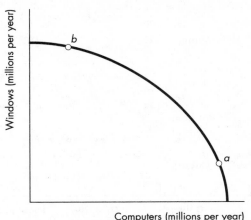

Windows (millions per year) — *Computers (millions per year)*

1. Two nations, Disc and Chip, have the same *PPF*. Both nations produce only two goods, windows and computers. Figure 19.5 shows their current production points: Disc at point *a* and Chip at point *b*.
   a. In which nation is the opportunity cost of a window lowest? In which is the opportunity cost of a computer lowest? Explain how you arrived at your answer.
   b. Which nation has a comparative advantage in producing windows? In producing computers? Why?
   c. If Disc and Chip trade, which nation would export windows? Which would export computers? Why?
2. A nation produces only wheat and computer chips. It has a comparative advantage in chips. Draw a production possibility frontier and use it to show how the nation specializes and the gains from trade.
3. How does a tariff on an imported good affect the domestic price of the good? The quantity of the good imported? The quantity of the good produced domestically?
4. How does a quota on an imported good affect the domestic price of the good, the quantity imported, and the quantity produced domestically?

5. How does a tariff on imports affect the exports of the country?

TABLE 19.1
Market for Watches in Norolex

Price (dollars per watch)	Quantity demanded (millions of watches)	Quantity supplied (millions of watches)
$20	65	15
25	60	20
30	55	25
35	50	30
40	45	35
45	40	40
50	35	45

6. Table 19.1 gives the domestic supply and demand schedules for watches for the nation of Norolex.
   a. Draw the supply and demand schedules in Figure 19.6.
   b. What is the equilibrium price?
   c. How many watches are produced in Norolex? How many are purchased by consumers in Norolex?

FIGURE 19.6
Short Answer Problems 6 and 7

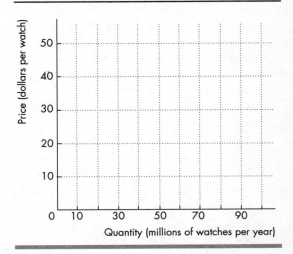

Price (dollars per watch) — *Quantity (millions of watches per year)*

TABLE 19.2

Supply Schedule of Watches with Trade

Price (dollars per watch)	Quantity supplied in Norolex (millions of watches)	Quantity supplied by Switch (millions of watches)	Total quantity supplied (millions of watches)
$20	15	20	___
25	20	25	___
30	25	30	___
35	30	35	___
40	35	40	___
45	40	45	___
50	45	50	___

TABLE 19.3

Short Answer Problem 8 (a)

Price (dollars per watch)	Pre-tariff quantity supplied by Switch (millions of watches)	Post-tariff quantity supplied by Switch (millions of watches)
$20	20	5
25	25	10
30	30	15
35	35	___
40	40	___
45	45	___
50	50	___

TABLE 19.4

Short Answer Problem 8 (b)

Price (dollars per watch)	Quantity supplied in Norolex (millions of watches)	Quantity supplied by Switch (millions of watches)	Total quantity supplied (millions of watches)
$20	15	5	___
25	20	10	___
30	25	15	___
35	30	___	___
40	35	___	___
45	40	___	___
50	45	___	___

7. Norolex now trades with another nation, Switch. Switch exports watches to Norolex. Switch's export supply schedule is in Table 19.2 along with Norolex's domestic supply schedule.

   a. Complete Table 19.2 by determining the total supply schedule of watches.

   b. Graph the total supply schedule in Figure 19.6, which already contains the domestic supply and demand schedules you graphed from the previous question.

   c. What is the new equilibrium price of a watch?

   d. How many watches are produced in Norolex? How many are purchased by consumers in Norolex? How many are imported?

8. The watch industry in Norolex is unhappy with the situation after trade with Switch has occurred. The watch industry lobbies the government to impose a $15 per watch tariff on imports from Switch.

   a. Complete Table 19.3, which shows how the tariff affects imports from Switch.

   b. Using your answers from Table 19.3, complete Table 19.4, which shows the new total supply schedule after the tariff has been imposed.

   c. After the tariff is imposed, what is the equilibrium price of a watch in Norolex?

   d. How many watches are produced in Norolex? How many watches are purchased by consumers in Norolex? How many watches are imported?

   e. Relative to the situation in problem 6, explain who has gained from the tariff and who has lost. Explain why the gainers have gained and the losers have lost.

■ You're the Teacher

1. "I understand the stuff about comparative advantage. But I can't see how the United States can compete with nations like Mexico, where the wages are so low. We have to protect our high wages by keeping Mexican products out of our markets." Your friend thinks he understands comparative advantage, but he does not. Help him understand comparative advantage. Explain how American firms can compete with Mexican companies.

2. After you explain the error in question 1, your friend makes another mistake: "OK, now I see how U.S. firms can compete. But, still, international trade can't be good. After all, if this trade helps Mexico, we must lose. So I still think that international trade should be banned." Explain to your friend how international trade benefits both America and Mexico.

Answers

■ True/False Answers

Patterns and Trends In International Trade

1. **F** Services, such as travel abroad, transportation, and insurance, can be traded internationally.

2. **T** About 60 percent of U.S. imports and about 50 percent of U.S. exports are manufactured goods.

3. **T** In 2000, as throughout the 1980s and 1990s, the value of imports exceeded that of American exports.

The Gains from International Trade

4. **F** Because nations have different opportunity costs, international trade can raise the welfare of *each* nation.

5. **T** The question presents the definition of comparative advantage.

6. **T** By allowing consumption to occur beyond the limits expressed by the *PPF*, the nation gains from trade.

7. **F** All nations engaged in international trade gain from the trade.

8. **F** Diversity of tastes and economies of scale account for the considerable international trade that takes place in similar goods.

9. **T** Long production runs, which create economies of scale, can be sold internationally.

International Trade Restrictions

10. **F** Tariffs in the United States are near an all-time low.

11. **F** Economists agree that tariffs reduce a nation's standard of living.

12. **F** By raising the price of imported goods, tariffs harm consumers.

13. **T** Tariffs, quotas, and voluntary export restraints all limit the quantity of imports and thus all raise the price of imports.

The Case Against Protection

14. **F** All arguments for protection are flawed.

15. **T** In industries with a comparative advantage, higher productivity more than offsets higher wages, so American firms can successfully compete.

16. **F** International trade *raises* wages in poor nations.

Why Is International Trade Restricted?

17. **T** Free trade benefits consumers and workers (and firms) in exporting industries. It harms workers (and firms) in import-competing industries.

■ Multiple Choice Answers

Patterns and Trends In International Trade

1. **d** The Mexican resident has purchased a service, lodging, from an American firm.

2. **d** The value of U.S. imports exceeded the value of U.S. exports in 2000 and in most recent years.

The Gains from International Trade

3. **a** The opportunity cost of a good is the number of other goods that must be foregone to increase production of the good.

4. **c** With or without international trade, producing at points beyond the *PPF* is impossible, but international trade allows consumption to occur at points beyond the *PPF*.

5. **b** Free trade with production taking place according to comparative advantage creates the maximum gains from trade.

6. **a** The opportunity cost equals the slope of the *PPF* because the slope is the opportunity cost, in terms of grain, of producing 1 more machine.

7. **c** For the reason outlined in the answer to question 6, the opportunity cost of a machine in Chaff is 15 bushels of grain.

8. **b** The opportunity cost of grain is less in Solaris, and the opportunity cost of a machine is less in Chaff.

9. **b** Each nation exports the good in which it has a comparative advantage.

10. **c** By specializing in the products with a comparative advantage and trading with other nations, the nation can consume more of both the goods it imports and the goods it exports.

11. **a** By specializing in the production of one good that is similar to another and then exporting the good, a firm can capture economies of scale and satisfy people's desires for its particular variation of the good.

International Trade Restrictions

12. **c** Answer (c) is the definition of a tariff.

13. **b** Domestic producers gain because the price of the product rises.

14. **c** The textile industry gains from the tariff, and the computer industry loses.

15. **a** Unlike tariffs, the government gets no revenue from quotas and voluntary export restraints.

The Case Against Protection

16. **b** The description in the problem is the definition of the infant industry argument for protection.

17. **c** Although often alleged, dumping is difficult to prove because it is difficult to determine whether a firm is selling below its cost.

18. **a** By increasing the demand for the goods produced in the poor nation, the demand for labor increases, thereby raising the wage rate in that nation.

19. **d** All of the reasons offered for protection are faulty.

Why Is International Trade Restricted?

20. **b** Because the overall gains exceed the overall loses, in principle the losers from international trade can be compensated so that, on balance, everyone gains from the trade.

■ **Answers to Short Answer Problems**

1. a. The opportunity cost of a window is lowest in Disc. The opportunity cost of a computer is lowest in Chip.

    Figure 19.7 demonstrates these result. The opportunity cost of a computer equals the magnitude of the slope of the line tangent to the *PPF*. In Figure 19.7, the magnitude of the slope of the line tangent at point *b* is less than the magnitude of the line tangent at point *a*. Hence the opportunity cost of a computer is less at point *b*, which is where Chip produces. The opportunity cost of a window equals the inverse of the slopes of these lines, so the opportunity cost of a window is less at point *a*, which is Disc's production point.

FIGURE **19.7**
Short Answer Problem 1

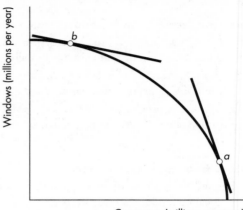

b. Disc has a comparative advantage in producing windows because its opportunity cost of producing a window is less than Chip's opportunity cost. Similarly, Chip has a comparative advantage in producing computers.

c. Disc would export windows and Chip would export computers because these are the goods for which each nation has a comparative advantage. Alternatively, windows are relatively cheaper in Disc, so Disc will export Windows. Computers are relatively less expensive in Chip, so Chip will export computers.

2. Figure 19.8 (on the next page) shows the situation in the nation. In the figure, before trade the nation initially produces and consumes *W* bushels of wheat and *C* chips. Without trade, the amount of wheat consumed equals the amount produced and the number of chips consumed equals the number produced. Once the nation trades, it changes its production of wheat and chips. With trade, the nation increases its production of computer chips and decreases its production of wheat. This change is illustrated in Figure 19.8, where the nation produces C_p chips and W_p bushels of wheat. However, the nation does not consume these amounts of chips and wheat. Instead, it exports chips and imports

FIGURE **19.8**

Short Answer Problem 2

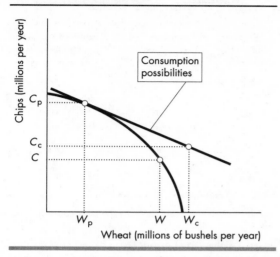

wheat so that it consumes (along its consumption possibilities line) C_c computer chips and W_c bushels of wheat. Note that the nation consumes fewer chips than it produces and more wheat than it grows.

The gains from trade are illustrated in Figure 19.8 because with trade the nation consumes more chips *and* more wheat than it consumed without trade. (Compare the initial consumption bundle of C chips and W bushels of wheat to the post-trade bundle of C_c chips and W_c bushels of wheat.) International trade has allowed this nation to increase its consumption of *all* goods, which makes its inhabitants better off.

3. A tariff on an imported good raises its price to domestic consumers because the foreign export supply decreases. As the domestic price of the good climbs, the quantity of the good demanded decreases, so the quantity imported decreases. The rise in the domestic price leads to an increase in the quantity of the good produced domestically.

4. The effect of a quota on the domestic price of the good, the quantity imported, and the quantity of the good produced domestically are exactly the same as the effects of a tariff discussed in the answer to short answer problem 3. The difference is that with a tariff the rise in the domestic price occurs because foreigners decrease their supply of the good at all prices (that is, the foreign supply curve with the tariff lies above the initial supply curve without the

tariff). A quota, however, forces the export supply curve to become vertical at the quota amount.

5. When a country imposes a tariff on its imports, the volume of its imports shrink, and the volume of its exports to other countries shrinks by the same amount. A tariff limits the amount of goods that other nations can sell to the first country and also lowers the price the other nations receive for their products. So when a nation limits its imports, foreign nations cannot afford to buy as many exports from the first country, so the tariff decreases the nation's exports.

FIGURE **19.9**

Short Answer Problem 6

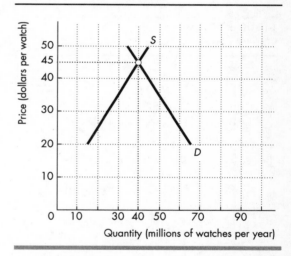

6. a. Figure 19.9 shows the demand and supply schedules.

   b. Either from Figure 19.9 or from the demand and supply schedules, the equilibrium price with no international trade is $45 because at this price the quantity demanded equals the quantity supplied.

   c. With no trade, forty million watches per year are produced domestically, and so 40 million watches per year are purchased by consumers in Norolex.

7. a. Table 19.5 (on the next page) shows the total supply schedule. At any price, the total quantity supplied in Norolex equals the sum of the quantity produced in Norolex plus the quantity supplied by Switch.

TABLE **19.5**

Short Answer Problem 7 (a)

Price (dollars per watch)	Quantity supplied in Norolex (millions of watches)	Quantity supplied by Switch (millions of watches)	Total quantity supplied (millions of watches)
$20	15	20	35
25	20	25	45
30	25	30	55
35	30	35	65
40	35	40	75
45	40	45	85
50	45	50	95

FIGURE **19.10**

Short Answer Problem 7

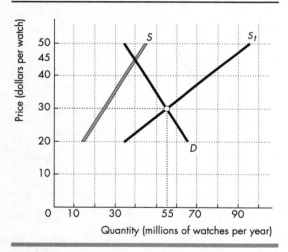

b. Figure 19.10 shows the total supply curve, S_t, the initial supply curve, and the demand curve.

c. The new equilibrium price of a watch is $30.

d. At the equilibrium price of $30, consumers in Norolex buy 55 million watches per year. At this price, watch firms in Norolex produce 25 million watches. The difference between the total quantity of watches purchased and the total quantity produced, 30 million watches per year, is imported from Switch.

8. a. Table 19.6 shows how the tariff affects the supply schedule of imports from Switch. A $15 per watch tariff lowers the receipts of the firms in Switch by $15 per watch. Hence when the price,

TABLE **19.6**

Short Answer Problem 8 (a)

Price (dollars per watch)	Pre-tariff quantity supplied by Switch (millions of watches)	Post-tariff quantity supplied by Switch (millions of watches)
$20	20	5
25	25	10
30	30	15
35	35	20
40	40	25
45	45	30
50	50	35

TABLE **19.7**

Short Answer Problem 8 (b)

Price (dollars per watch)	Quantity supplied in Norolex (millions of watches)	Quantity supplied by Switch (millions of watches)	Total quantity supplied (millions of watches)
$20	15	5	20
25	20	10	30
30	25	15	40
35	30	20	50
40	35	25	60
45	40	30	70
50	45	35	80

including the tariff, is $35 a watch, the watch companies receive only $20 per watch. As the initial supply schedule shows, when the Switch watch companies receive $20 per watch, they supply 20 million watches. The remainder of the supply schedule is calculated similarly.

b. The new total supply schedule equals the sum of the Norolex supply schedule plus the new, post-tariff Switch supply schedule. Table 19.7 shows the new total supply schedule.

c. The equilibrium price of a watch is $35.

d. At the price of $35, consumers buy 50 million watches per year. Firms in Norolex produce 30 million watches per year. Imports from Switch are 20 million watches per year.

e. The watch firms and their workers in Norolex have gained. With the tariff, they produce more watches and receive a higher price. The Norolex government also has gained because it obtains revenue from the tariff, $300 million. (The tariff revenue equals the tariff, $15 per watch, multiplied by the number of watches imported, 20 million.) Consumers in Norolex and the Switch watch manufacturing firms and their workers have lost. Consumers have lost because they must pay a higher price for a watch ($35 with the tariff compared to $30 without the tariff) and so respond by purchasing fewer watches. Switch firms and workers have lost because the lower price they receive for a watch leads them to produce fewer watches for export (20 million with the tariff versus 30 million without).

■ You're the Teacher

1. "Look, you don't have the main idea here. Let's use some numbers because they should help you catch on. Suppose that American wages are 10 times higher than Mexican wages. Now, it's also a fact that American workers are more productive than Mexican workers. Let's take two industries. In the first, call it industry A, suppose that American workers are 2 times as productive as Mexican ones; in the second, say, industry B, American workers are 20 times as productive. In industry A, American firms won't be able to compete with Mexican firms. Sure, our workers are twice as productive, but they are paid ten times as much. Therefore American firms will lose out in this industry. But in industry B, American companies firms will drive Mexican ones out of business. Even though our workers are paid 10 times as much as Mexican workers are paid, they produce 20 times as much as Mexican workers produce. So the per unit cost of the good is less in the United States, so American firms are going to be able to compete and compete successfully.

"The United States won't be able to compete successfully with Mexico in producing every type of good or service but the reason is that the United States does not (and cannot) have a comparative advantage in all goods and services even though it might well have an absolute advantage. But in the industry with the comparative advantage — industry B in my example — the United States is going to be able to compete and to win the competition."

2. "Well, I'm glad you're catching onto some of the ideas of this chapter, but you're missing another key point. The chapter explains how trade allows all nation to consume more goods and services than it can produce. Remember the diagrams showing how a nation can consume more of everything if it trades? Obviously, this fact has to make nations engaged in international trade better off.

"But there's also another a way to tackle this point. I read somewhere that 'trade is not a zero-sum game.' Here's what that means: If you and I voluntarily agree to a trade, like I'll trade my economics notes for your chemistry notes, the trade has to make us both better off. After all, if the trade didn't make me better off, I wouldn't agree to it and if it didn't make you better off, you wouldn't agree to it. This type of trade will enable both of us to raise our grades: me in chemistry and you in economics.

"Well, it's the same idea with trading between nations. Suppose that we import a VCR from Mexico and the Mexicans use the money we sent them to buy 50 bushels of wheat from Kansas. Essentially, we've traded the 50 bushels of wheat for the VCR. If this trade didn't make us better off, we wouldn't do it. So, too, for the Mexicans involved: If they didn't want the wheat more than the VCR, they won't agree to the transaction. And, as the chapter explained, if we specialize in wheat and Mexico in VCRs, we both will be able to consume more wheat and more VCRs than if we produced VCRs and wheat and Mexico produced VCRs and wheat.

"Or think about this more generally. For two potential trading partners to be willing to trade, they must have different comparative advantages, that is, different opportunity costs. Then they will trade and *both* parties will gain. If the countries do not trade, each faces and must pay its own opportunity costs. The price at which trade takes place will be somewhere between the opportunity costs of the two nations. With trade, the country with the lower opportunity cost of the good in question gains because it receives a price above its opportunity cost. Similarly, the country with the higher opportunity cost gains because it pays a price below its opportunity cost.

"You know, I think this is really cool. What it shows is that just as trade between us makes both of us better off, trade between nations makes both nations better off."

Chapter Quiz

1. It is _____ to import a service and it is _____ to export a service.
   a. possible; possible
   b. possible; not possible
   c. not possible; possible
   d. not possible; not possible

2. The U.S. balance of trade is the value of _____ and has been _____ in recent years.
   a. imports minus the value of exports; positive
   b. exports minus the value of imports; positive
   c. imports minus the value of exports; negative
   d. exports minus the value of imports; negative

3. A *PPF* has corn on the vertical axis and computers on the horizontal axis. The opportunity cost of an additional computer is the magnitude of the
   a. slope of a ray from the origin to the *PPF*.
   b. inverse of the slope of a ray from the origin to the *PPF*.
   c. slope of the *PPF*.
   d. inverse of the slope of the *PPF*.

4. Between two nations, to determine whether a nation has a comparative advantage in a product, it is necessary to compare the
   a. total amount produced in each nation.
   b. opportunity costs in the nations.
   c. total demand for the products in each nation.
   d. None of the above.

5. If a nation does *not* trade with the rest of the world, its consumption possibility frontier
   a. is identical to its *PPF*.
   b. lies outside its *PPF*.
   c. lies inside its *PPF*.
   d. has no particular relationship to its *PPF*.

6. The direct effect of a tariff is to restrict _____ and benefit _____.
   a. exports; producers
   b. exports; consumers
   c. imports; producers
   d. imports; consumers

7. The United States today imposes an average tariff of approximately
   a. 4 percent on imports.
   b. 4 percent on exports.
   c. 40 percent on imports.
   d. 40 percent on exports.

8. When a quota is imposed, the difference between the domestic price and the world price is collected by
   a. the domestic government.
   b. the foreign government.
   c. domestic consumers.
   d. domestic importers of the good.

9. It is possible for expensive U.S. labor to compete successfully against less expensive foreign labor because U.S. labor
   a. pays taxes in the United States.
   b. can travel abroad to produce the goods in other nations.
   c. frequently belongs to powerful labor unions that protect their interest.
   d. is more productive.

10. If a poor nation exports a good to a rich nation, in the poor nation wages in the export sector _____ and employment _____.
    a. rise; increases
    b. rise; decreases
    c. fall; decreases
    d. fall; increases

The answers for this Chapter Quiz are on page 368

20 GLOBAL STOCK MARKETS*

■ Stock Market Basics

A **stock** is a tradable security that a firm issues to certify that the stock holder owns a share of the firm. The value of a firm's stock is called the firm's **equity capital.** Because stockholders are the firm's owners, they can receive a **dividend,** which is a share of the company's profit. People buy and sell shares of stock in an organized market called a **stock exchange.** A **stock's price** is the price at which one share of stock trades. The annual **return** on a stock consists of the stock's dividend plus its capital gain (or minus its capital loss) during the year.

♦ A stock's **capital gain** is the increase in its price and a stock's **capital loss** is the decrease in its price.

♦ A stock's **dividend yield** is its dividend expressed as a percentage of the stock's price. (So a stock with a price of $50 per share and which pays a $5 per share dividend has a dividend yield of ($5/$50) × 100 = 10 percent.)

The firm's accounting profit is called its **earnings.** Generally a firm will not pay out all of its earnings as dividends. The earnings not paid out are called retained earnings. The **price-earnings ratio** is the stock's price divided by the most recent year's earnings per share.

Stock price indexes are used to summarize the thousands of different stock prices. The three main U.S. stock price indexes are the S&P Composite Index (an average of the prices of 500 stocks), the Dow Jones

Industrial Average (the "Dow"), and the NASDAQ Index. Using the S&P Composite Index and after correcting for inflation, since 1871 the average annual increase in price has been 2.7 percent. However, the price rise is not smooth—during some years prices have jumped upward and during other years they have fallen dramatically. Earnings per share over this period of time have risen at an annual average rate of 2.0 percent. Because earnings have grown less than stock prices, the price-earnings ratio has risen.

■ How Are Stock Prices Determined?

According to the *market fundamentals* theory, stock prices are determined by the market fundamentals—the price people are willing to pay for the opportunity the stock provides to earn its dividend and a capital gain (or loss). Because the potential returns come later in time, they must be discounted; because the returns are uncertain, it is the expected returns that matter.

♦ The **discount factor** is the amount by which the *future* return is multiplied in order to express it in terms of *today's* worth.

♦ To forecast the expected returns, people form a **rational expectation,** a forecast that uses all the available information.

The market fundamentals conclusion is that the price of a share of stock today, P, depends on the expected value of its discount factor, b, its dividend, D, and its price next period, P_1 according to:

$$P = \text{Expected value of } [b(D + P_1)].$$

Because P_1 will depend on P_2, the market fundamentals theory concludes that the price of a share of stock today

---

*This is Chapter 34 in *Economics.*

depends on the expected value of the discounted dividends to be received throughout the future.

The speculative bubbles theory is an alternative view of how stock prices are determined. A **speculative bubble** is a price increase followed by a price plunge, both of which occur because people expect them to occur and act on that expectation. For instance, if people expect stock prices to rise significantly, they buy stocks and the increase in demand results in rising prices, in line with the expectation.

It is not clear if the booming stock market of the 1990s was the result of market fundamentals or was a speculative bubble.

■ Risk and Return

Stocks are risky because stock prices fluctuate unpredictably. Generally the greater the risk, the higher the expected return from the stock. The additional return earned for bearing the additional risk is call the **risk premium.** So, the riskiest stock has the highest expected return. Diversification, buying more than one stock, lowers risk. Diversification, however, also lowers the expected return. Most people prefer to diversify and tradeoff a lower expected return for less risk.

■ The Stock Market and the Economy

Effects from the rest of the economy affect the stock market.

♦ The expected growth rate of earnings affects stock prices. On the average, earnings have grown at 2 percent a year, but some years have higher growth and other years have lower growth. If the economy changes so that earnings grow more rapidly, then stock prices will rise.

♦ The Federal Reserve's monetary policy affects stock prices. If the Fed raises the interest rate, stock prices usually fall as people sell risky stocks to put their funds into now higher yielding bonds. If the Fed lowers the interest rate, stock prices usually rise. People try to anticipate the Fed's policy in order to profit from the rise or fall in stock prices.

♦ Taxes affect stock prices. A **realized capital gain** is a capital gain that is obtained when a stock is sold for a higher price than the price paid for it. People who realize a capital gain must pay a capital gains tax on it. The corporate profits tax affects firms' after-tax earnings and thereby affects stock prices. A

"Tobin" tax is a *proposed* tax on transactions in the stock market. This tax would raise revenue for the government but most likely would have little effect on speculation.

Effects from the stock market also affect the rest of the economy.

♦ The value of stocks affects people's **wealth,** the market value of assets. Wealth, then, affects consumption expenditure and saving through the **wealth effect.** The greater is wealth, the smaller is the **saving rate,** the percentage of disposable income that is saved. Since 1995, the measured saving rate that *excludes* capital gains plummeted and the measured saving rate that *includes* capital gains has risen.

♦ The value of stocks affects the distribution of wealth. Wealthier households tend to own stocks, so higher stock prices mean that the wealthier households gain more wealth.

Helpful Hints

1. **MARKET FUNDAMENTALS VERSUS SPECULATIVE BUBBLES :** The market fundamentals theory of stock prices argues that people care about the "real" economic factors (the so-called "fundamentals") that affect a company's profit, both today and in the future. If these fundamentals change so that the company's profitability changes, then the stock price will change. For instance, if people forecast that the demand for a company's good will increase, they expect the company's profit to increase and so they bid up the price of its stock.

The speculative bubbles theory of stock prices ignores the company's fundamentals. Instead it focuses more directly on the stock's price and people's expectations about this price. If people's expectations change so that they think the price will rise, then they buy today and so the price does, indeed, rise. The speculative bubbles theory looks at changes in stock prices as a self-fulfilling prophecy: If people think a stock's price will change, they take actions so that the stock price does change.

Which theory is correct? The answer is not clear-cut, though perhaps more economists favor the market fundamentals theory.

Questions

■ True/False and Explain

Stock Market Basics

1. If you own a share of stock in Microsoft, you are one of the owners of Microsoft.

2. Legally, firms must pay all of their earnings as dividends.

3. A stock's dividend yield and its rate of return are identical.

4. The S&P Composite Index is an average of the prices of 500 stocks.

5. On the average, after adjusting for inflation, stock prices have risen by 16 percent per year.

6. Currently the price-earnings ratio is above its average.

How Are Stock Prices Determined?

7. According to the market fundamentals approach, stock prices are determined by what people on the average are willing to pay for the opportunity to earn the stock's dividend and capital gain.

8. According to the market fundamentals approach, an increase in the dividend a company pays will increase the price of its stock.

9. The market fundamentals approach concludes that stock prices change because people expect them to change.

10. The booming stock market of the 1990s might have represented a speculative bubble.

Risk and Return

11. Stocks with greater risk have a higher expected return.

12. Diversification is an effort to increase the expected return.

The Stock Market and the Economy

13. Stock prices generally rise when the Federal Reserve raises the interest rate.

14. Lowering the capital gains tax raises stock prices.

15. The stock market boom in the 1990s increased the wealth of wealthier households.

■ Multiple Choice Questions

Stock Market Basics

1. Which of the following is correct?
   a. When a company fails, its stock holders must pay all of its debts.
   b. Whenever you buy a share of Microsoft stock, Microsoft receives the funds.
   c. Each company's stock price is set by the stock exchange upon which it is traded.
   d. If a stock increases in price after you buy it, you have a capital gain on the stock.

2. Suppose that a share of Merck stock has a price of $40. Merck pays a dividend of $2 and has earnings of $4. Merck's dividend yield equals
   a. $2.
   b. 10.
   c. 10 percent.
   d. 5 percent.

3. Suppose that a share of Merck stock has a price of $40. Merck pays a dividend of $2 and has earnings of $4. Merck's price-earnings ratio equals
   a. $2.
   b. 10.
   c. 10 percent.
   d. 5 percent.

4. The Dow Jones Industrial Average
   a. includes the prices of 30 stocks.
   b. includes the prices of 500 stocks.
   c. measures stock prices on the FTSE 100.
   d. includes only high-tech companies.

5. After adjusting for inflation, since 1871 stock prices have risen an average of _____ percent a year and earnings per share have risen an average of _____ percent a year.
   a. 2.7; 3.3
   b. 3.3; 2.7
   c. 4.1; 2.0
   d. 2.7; 2.0

6. Since 1871, the price-earnings ratio has
   a. averaged about 14.
   b. ranged between 2 and 4.
   c. never been lower than what it was in the 1990s.
   d. had a steep downward trend.

How Are Stock Prices Determined?

7. The two approaches to the determination of stock prices are the
   a. demand-only and supply-only approaches.
   b. market fundamentals and speculative bubbles approaches.
   c. trend reversion and trend dispersion approaches.
   d. capital market and profits approaches.

8. You are considering buying a share of stock. Your discount rate is 0.8, you expect a share of the stock to pay a dividend of $2 and you expect its price at the end of the year will be $48. The most you will pay for a share of this stock is
   a. $60.
   b. $50.
   c. $40.
   d. $2.

9. Suppose that IBM announces that in two years it will raise its dividend. According to the market fundamentals approach, this announcement will
   a. not raise the price of a share of IBM's stock today but will raise it in two years.
   b. raise the price of a share of IBM's stock today.
   c. lower the price of a share of IBM's stock today and raise it in two years.
   d. None of the above answers is correct.

10. According to the speculative bubbles approach to determining stock prices, if people expect the price of a stock to fall
   a. its price rises immediately.
   b. its price does not change.
   c. its price falls immediately.
   d. None of the above answers is correct.

Risk and Return

11. The riskier a stock, the _____ the risk premium and the _____ the expected return.
   a. larger; higher
   b. larger; lower
   c. smaller; higher
   d. smaller; lower.

12. Portfolio diversification generally _____ the expected return and _____ the risk.
   a. raises; raises
   b. raises; lowers
   c. lowers; raises
   d. lowers; lowers

The Stock Market and the Economy

13. Stock prices are affected by
   a. the expected growth rate of earnings.
   b. taxes.
   c. the Fed's monetary policy.
   d. All of the above answers are correct.

14. Data for the United States show that the stock price boom of the 1990s raised the wealth of
   a. poorer households proportionally more than wealthier households.
   b. poorer households proportionally by the same amount as wealthier households.
   c. wealthier households by more than poorer households.
   d. no group because for every dollar someone gains on the stock market someone else loses a dollar.

■ Short Answer Problems

1. How is a stock's rate of return calculated? Be sure to mention *both* potential sources of gain.

2. Suppose the price of a share of Pfizer stock is $40 and suppose Pfizer has earnings of $2 per share. What is Pfizer's price-earnings ratio? What is the earnings per dollar invested in Pfizer?

3. Since 1871, after adjusting for inflation what is the average percent change in stock prices per year? What is the average increase in earnings per year? The two averages are different; what does this difference mean for the price-earnings ratio?

4. Suppose Cynthia's discount rate is 0.9. She expects that a stock will pay $1.00 in dividends this year and that its price at the end of the year will be $49.00.
   a. What is the maximum she is willing to pay for this stock?
   b. Now suppose the company announces that it will pay $2.00 in dividends this year. If the price she expects at the end of the year remains $49.00, now what is the maximum Cynthia is willing to pay for this stock?

5. According to the market fundamentals approach to stock price determination, why are people willing to buy a stock (such as Microsoft) that currently does not pay a dividend?

6. Why do people buy more than one stock? Why don't they just buy the one stock with the highest expected return?

7. What happens when the Fed lowers the interest rate? Why might stock prices change *before* rather than after the Federal Reserve lowers the interest rate?

8. How has the personal saving rate changed in the United States since 1995?

■ You're the Teacher

1. "I don't understand the deal about why a stock with more risk has a higher expected rate of return. People don't like risk and so the riskier stock has a lower price, right? So why do we say it has a higher expected return?" Your friend is largely correct but is missing a point. Straighten out your friend by explaining how a riskier stock will have a higher expected return than a less risky stock.

Answers

■ True/False Answers

Stock Market Basics

1. **T** Stockholders are the owners of corporations.

2. **F** Each firm can decide how much of its earnings it will pay as a dividend.

3. **F** The dividend yield is one part of a stock's rate of return. The other part results from the stock's capital gain or capital loss.

4. **T** The S&P Composite Index includes stocks from companies spread throughout the economy.

5. **F** After adjusting for inflation, stock prices have risen 2.7 percent per year on average.

6. **T** Currently the price-earnings ratio is well above its average.

How Are Stock Prices Determined?

7. **T** The question presents the essential definition of the market fundamentals theory of stock price determination.

8. **T** The increase in dividend increases the amount people are willing to pay for the stock and so its price rises.

9. **F** The speculative bubbles approach concludes that stock prices change because people expect them to change.

10. **T** Some observers claim the prices represented a speculative bubble, while other analysts disagree.

Risk and Return

11. **T** There is a tradeoff between risk and expected return: stocks with greater risk have a higher expected return.

12. **F** Diversification lowers the risk and generally also lowers the expected return.

The Stock Market and the Economy

13. **F** Stock prices generally fall when the Federal Reserve raises the interest rate.

14. **T** Lowering the capital gains tax lowers the taxes that stockholders pay on capital gains and so increases the attractiveness of buying stock.

15. **T** The stock market boom made the distribution of wealth more unequal than was previously the case.

■ Multiple Choice Answers

Stock Market Basics

1. **d** A capital gain occurs when a stock's price rises after the stock is purchased. A capital loss occurs when the stock's price falls.

2. **d** The dividend yield is the dividend divided by the stock's price, then multiplied by 100 to create a percentage.

3. **b** The price-earnings ratio is the stock's price divided by its earnings for the latest year.

4. **a** The Dow Jones Industrial Average includes the prices of stocks of 30 large companies.

5. **d** Because stock prices have risen more than earnings, the price-earnings ratio has increased.

6. **a** The price-earnings ratio has fluctuated around its average and currently is well above the average.

How Are Stock Prices Determined?

7. **b** The market fundamentals approach and the speculative bubble approach present alternative theories of how stock prices are determined.

8. **c** You will pay $0.8 \times (\$2 + \$48) = \$40$ for this share of stock.

9. **b** The announcement of a dividend increase in two years means that the price in one year will be higher, which in turn increases the price people are willing to pay today.

10. **c** Because people expect its price to fall, they sell the stock, thereby driving its price down immediately.

Risk and Return

11. **a** The risk premium is larger the more risky the stock. And, the tradeoff between risk and expected return means that the riskier the stock, the higher the expected return.

12. **d** Diversification aims to lower the risk and by so doing generally also lowers the expected return.

The Stock Market and the Economy

13. **d** All of the listed factors feed back from the economy to stock prices.

14. **c** The stock market boom made already wealthy households even wealthier.

■ Answers to Short Answer Problems

1. A stock's rate of return is the sum of the dividend plus the capital gain, expressed as a percentage of the original price. So *both* the dividend (if any) and the capital gain (also, if any) figure into the stock's rate of return.

2. The price-earnings ratio equals the price of a stock divided by its earnings per share. With the data in the problem, Pfizer's price-earnings ratio equals ($40 per share)/($2 per share earnings) = 20. The earnings per dollar invested in a stock equals the earnings per share divided by the price per share, which is the number of dollars necessary to buy the earnings. In the case of Pfizer in the problem the earnings per dollar are ($2 per share earnings)/($40 per share) = 0.05 or 5 percent. As this example illustrates, the earnings per dollar invested is the inverse of the price-earnings ratio.

3. Since 1871, after inflation stock prices have increased 2.7 percent per year on the average. Over this same time period, earnings have increased 2.0 percent on the average. Because stock prices have increased more than have earnings, the price-earnings ratio has increased. Indeed, it has increased from around 15 in the 1870s to around 25 in recent years.

4. a. Cynthia will pay 0.9 × ($1.00 + $49.00) = $45.00 for a share of this stock.

   b. After the dividend hike, Cynthia will pay a maximum of 0.9 × ($2.00 + $49.00) = $45.90 for a share of this stock. So an increase in the dividend increases the price of the stock. Indeed, it generally increases it by more than the increase in dividend because the dividend also raises the price expected at the end of the year.

5. According to the market fundamentals approach to determining stock prices, people are willing to pay for the opportunity that the stock provides to earn a dividend and a capital gain. So, people buy Microsoft stock because they expect to earn a capital gain on the stock. But the reason for the expected capital gain is a bit more subtle. The market fundamentals are the expected dividends that will be earned though out *all* the future. People are willing to buy a stock that currently does not pay a dividend, such as Microsoft, because they expect that at some point in the future the company will start paying a dividend.

6. Buying more than one stock is called diversifying. People diversify because the expected return from a stock is risky. For instance, as the text points out, buyers of Enron stock in 2001 lost *all* of their funds. By buying more than one stock, people drastically reduce the risk of being wiped out. However, eliminating this risk is not free because diversification generally lowers the expected return.

7. When the Fed lowers the interest rate, the economy likely will expand and firms' profits will increase. The higher profits will increase stock prices. In addition, the lower interest rates make other assets, such as bonds, less attractive and so some bond holders will sell their bonds to buy stocks. The increased demand for stocks also will increase their prices. So, when the Fed lowers the interest rate, stock prices tend to rise. However, the prices might rise before the Fed lowers the interest rate. Why? There is a potentially large return to be made by buying stocks before they rise in price. So people try to determine the Fed's policy. As they become convinced that the Fed will lower the interest rate, people buy stocks to earn the high return when stock prices rise. As enough people become convinced that the Fed will lower the interest rate, the increase in demand for stocks means that stock prices will rise before rather than after the Fed's action.

8. The behavior of the personal saving rate after 1995 is unclear. If personal saving is measured without taking account of capital gains (that is, saving is measured as disposable income minus consumption expenditure) the saving rate has plummeted. However if the personal saving rate is measured taking account of capital gains (that is, saving is measured as wealth at the end of the year minus wealth at the beginning of the year) the saving rate has increased sharply. The truth of the matter likely lies between the two measures and so the behavior of the personal saving rate is, to a some extent, not known.

■ You're the Teacher

1. "You're exactly right that people don't like risk and so riskier stocks have lower prices. But it's this lower price that gives them the higher expected return. Let's use some numbers so that you can see this fact. Suppose we've got two stocks. We can keep it simple and suppose that neither is going to pay a dividend. OK, now say that you expect that at the end of the year each stock will have a price of $50. But,

the second stock is a lot riskier than the first. So, you might discount the expected price of the first stock using a discount factor of .8 while you discount the expected price of the risky second stock more, using a discount factor of .5. So, the price of the safe first stock is $40 and the price of the risky second stock is $25. Just as you said, the risky stock has a lower price. But what's the expected return?

The safe first stock is expected to climb from $40 to $50 for a gain of $10, which is a 25 percent expected rate of return. But the risky second stock is expected to climb from $25 to $50 for a gain of $25, which is a 100 percent expected rate of return! So, you see it's exactly the fact that the risky stock has a lower price that gives it the higher expected rate of return!

Chapter Quiz

1. Which stock index is an average of the prices of 500 stocks covering all parts of the U.S. economy?
   a. The S&P Composite Index
   b. The Dow Jones Industrial Average
   c. The NASDAQ Index
   d. The DAX

2. An increase in a stock's price after it is purchased creates a _____, while a decrease in the price creates a _____.
   a. price-earnings ratio loss; price-earnings ratio gain
   b. capital gain; capital loss
   c. higher dividend; lower dividend
   d. None of the above answers is correct.

3. Currently the price-earnings ratio is _____ average, which means that stock prices might _____ in the future.
   a. above; rise
   b. above; fall
   c. below; rise
   d. below; fall

4. John Maynard Keynes' idea that the stock market is like a beauty contest in which contestants must pick which person the other contestants will choose is most closely applicable to
   a. calculating a company's price-earnings ratio.
   b. the description of a speculative bubble.
   c. the market fundamentals approach to determining stock prices.
   d. None of the above.

5. There is a tradeoff between higher risk and
   a. higher speculation.
   b. higher expected return.
   c. higher dividend yield.
   d. lower price-earnings ratio.

6. You are considering two stocks: a safe one and a risky one. When would your portfolio have the highest expected rate of return?
   a. When you buy only the safe stock.
   b. When you buy only the risky stock.
   c. When you diversify your portfolio so 50 percent is in the risky stock and 50 percent is in the safe stock.
   d. All of the above answers are correct because the expected rate of return is equal for all the answers.

7. When will the price of a stock rise the most?
   a. When a company announces it will raise its dividend by $1 this year
   b. When a company announces it will raise its dividend by $1 next year
   c. When a company announces it will raise its dividend by $1 in two years
   d. The stock will rise by the same amount for each of the answers above.

8. If a company pays no dividend, then its
   a. price-earnings ratio is zero.
   b. price-earnings ratio is infinite.
   c. rate of return is zero.
   d. dividend yield is zero.

9. An increase in the capital gains tax will
   a. raise stock prices.
   b. not affect stock prices.
   c. lower stock prices.
   d. eliminate the effect of the "Tobin" tax.

10. Since 1995, the saving rate that includes capital gains has _____ and the savings rate that excludes capital gains has _____.
    a. risen; risen
    b. risen; fallen
    c. fallen; risen
    d. fallen; fallen

The answers for this Chapter Quiz are on page 368

Part Review 7 — THE GLOBAL ECONOMY

Reading Between the Lines

WTO OPENS WITH AGRICULTURE

On November 12, 2001 the World Trade Organization started a five day meeting in Qatar. The first topic on the agenda was agricultural subsidies. The European Union found itself defending its practice of subsidizing farmers and farm products. The European Union wants to continue its agriculture subsidies while nations such as New Zealand are calling for an end to the subsidies.

For details, go to The Economics Place web site, the Economics in the News archive, www.economicsplace.com/econ5e/einarchives.html

■ Analyze It

The European Union (EU) has given government subsidies to farmers for decades. Indeed, the EU's subsidies are probably the most generous of any major area in the world. These subsidies are the subject of a major dispute that also has raged for years. Most recently the World Trade Organization created a draft resolution that calls for reductions of agricultural subsidies with a movement toward completely phasing out all forms of farm subsidies.

1. Why does the EU support farm subsidies? Why is the World Trade Organization involved? Why wouldn't this issue be a purely European concern? In particular, why is New Zealand calling for an end to the subsidies?

2. How do these subsidies affect trade in agricultural products?

355

Mid-Term Examination

■ **Chapter 19**

1. If the United States has an excess of exports over imports, the United States has
   a. a negative net exports balance that is financed by U.S. lending to foreigners.
   b. a negative net exports balance that is financed by U.S. borrowing from foreigners.
   c. a positive net exports balance that is financed by U.S. lending to foreigners.
   d. a positive net exports balance that is financed by U.S. borrowing from foreigners.

2. If an efficient country trades with the rest of the world, it produces at a point that lies
   a. inside its production possibilities frontier.
   b. on its production possibilities frontier.
   c. outside its production possibilities frontier.
   d. either inside or outside its production possibilities frontier.

3. When the full effects are considered, a reduction in tariffs would
   a. decrease imports and increase exports.
   b. increase imports and decrease exports.
   c. increase imports and exports.
   d. decrease imports and exports.

4. Which of the following earns revenue for the domestic government?
   a. Tariffs.
   b. Quotas.
   c. Voluntary export restraints.
   d. Subsidies.

■ **Chapter 20**

5. A stock price index that includes the prices of stocks from 500 companies is the
   a. Stock 500 index.
   b. Dow Jones Industrial Average.
   c. the S&P Composite Index.
   d. NASDAQ Most Significant index.

6. If a company's stock price rises and nothing else changes, its price-earnings ratio
   a. increases.
   b. does not change.
   c. decreases.
   d. probably changes, but in an unpredictable direction.

7. According to the market fundamentals approach, if a company's earnings become less risky, its stock price will
   a. rise.
   b. not change.
   c. fall.
   d. probably change, but in an unpredictable direction.

8. If the interest rate rises, then stock prices generally
   a. rise.
   b. do not change.
   c. fall.
   d. change, but in an unpredictable direction.

Answers

■ Reading Between the Lines

1. The major reason the EU supports government farm subsidies is undoubtedly the lobbying done by European farmers. European farmers are amongst the most vocal of all lobbying groups in Europe. The World Trade Organization is involved because international trade in agricultural products is an important part of world trade. And, New Zealand is opposed to the subsidies because New Zealand believes that the subsidies decrease New Zealand's exports of agricultural commodities to Europe and other nations.

2. A subsidy is essentially a "reverse tariff." A tariff is a tax on an imported good or service that raises the price of the imported good or service. By raising the price of imports, tariffs help protect domestic producers. A subsidy is extra revenue given by the government to a domestic producer of a good or service. By increasing the revenue of domestic pro-

ducers, subsidies also help protect domestic producers. In both the case of a tariff and a subsidy, other members of the nation are harmed. The tariff harms domestic consumers of the good or service because they must pay a higher price for the good or service. A subsidy harms domestic taxpayers because they must pay increased taxes so that the government has the funds necessary so that can give the added revenue to the domestic producers. In addition, tariffs and subsidies both harm foreign producers. A tariff raises the price of imported goods or services while a subsidy lowers the price of domestic goods or services. So, a subsidy decreases the amount of a good or service imported into the nation and might actually allow the subsidizing nation to wind up *exporting* the subsidized good or service.

■ Mid-Term Exam Answers

1. c;   2. b;   3. c;   4. a;   5. c;   6. a;   7. a;   8. c.

Final Exams

Exam 1

1. A decrease in supply shifts the supply curve ____; a decrease in demand shifts the demand curve ____.
   a. rightward; rightward
   b. rightward; leftward
   c. leftward; rightward
   d. leftward; leftward

2. Which of the following can lead a perfectly competitive market to produce *less* than the efficient level of output?
   a. The market is a perfectly competitive industry producing a product with no externalities.
   b. The product being produced has an external benefit (for example, education).
   c. The product being produced has an external cost (for example, producing the product creates pollution).
   d. None of the answers offered above causes a perfectly competitive market to produce less than the efficient level of output.

3. New cars are a normal good and people's incomes rise. As a result of the increase in income, the equilibrium relative price of new cars ____ and the equilibrium quantity ____.
   a. rises; increases
   b. rises; decreases
   c. falls; decreases
   d. falls; increases

4. A natural monopoly has no deadweight loss when
   a. it is left unregulated.
   b. it is regulated so that it sets its price equal to its average total cost (that is, $P = ATC$).
   c. it is regulated so that it sets its price equal to its marginal cost (that is, $P = MC$).
   d. Both b and c are correct answers.

5. A lot of trade between nations involves trading similar goods (that is, the U.S. both imports and exports automobiles to Japan). Which of the following is <u>NOT</u> a reason for trade in similar goods?
   a. Diversified tastes.
   b. Absolute advantage.
   c. Economies of scale.
   d. None of the above because they are all reasons for why nations trade similar goods.

6. Which type of industry is characterized by having a few, mutually interdependent firms?
   a. Perfectly competitive.
   b. Monopolistically competitive.
   c. Oligopoly.
   d. Monopoly.

7. A 10 percent increase in the price of clothing results in a 2 percent decrease in the quantity demanded. Hence the price elasticity of demand equals
   a. 20.0.
   b. 5.0.
   c. 2.0.
   d. 0.2.

8. A feature of the labor supply curve is that, unlike most supply curves, it
   a. is always upward (positively) sloped.
   b. is always downward (negatively) sloped.
   c. might "bend backwards" so that at low wages it has a positive slope and at high wages it has a negative slope.
   d. None of the above.

9. Points outside the production possibilities frontier are
   a. efficient and attainable.
   b. inefficient and attainable.
   c. inefficient but not attainable.
   d. not attainable.

10. Between two countries, suppose that one nation has an absolute advantage in the production of all goods. Then
    a. international trade cannot occur.
    b. the nation with the absolute advantage will export all goods and import none.
    c. the nation with the absolute advantage will not gain from international trade.
    d. the nation with the absolute advantage will still import some goods from the other country.

11. Suppose the government taxes a product. The decrease in the quantity consumed is *smaller* when the elasticity of demand is _____.
    a. higher
    b. lower
    c. the premise of the question is wrong because the elasticity of demand has nothing to do with the reduction in the quantity demanded.
    d. the premise of the question is correct, but more information is needed to answer it.

12. Compared to an otherwise identical perfectly competitive industry, a monopoly firm will hire _____ workers.
    a. more
    b. the same number of
    c. fewer
    d. sometimes more and sometimes fewer workers, depending on whether the monopoly finds that MR exceeds or is less than P.

13. Which of the following does <u>NOT</u> shift the production possibilities frontier (PPF) rightward?
    a. An increase in the nation's capital stock.
    b. An increase in technology.
    c. A decrease in inefficiency (so that the nation moves from an inefficient production point to an efficient point).
    d. All of the above shift the production possibilities curve rightward.

14. Suppose that the cost of acquiring a skill rises. As a result of the increase in cost, the wage rate paid people with that skill will
    a. rise.
    b. not change.
    c. fall.
    d. probably change but in an ambiguous direction.

15. In the long run, firms in what type of industry structure can earn an economic profit?
    a. Perfectly competitive.
    b. Monopolistically competitive.
    c. Monopoly.
    d. Both monopolistically competitive and monopoly.

16. In a natural monopoly,
    a. the firm's MC remains above its ATC curve until the curves cross the demand curve.
    b. it is hard for a *small* second firm to compete with a *large* established firm because the second firm's ATC is higher than the first firm's ATC.
    c. society faces the problem of trying to insure that several firms compete and do not form a cartel.
    d. all of the above.

17. The closer a Lorenz curve for income is to the line of equality,
    a. the more competitive is the industry.
    b. the less competitive is the industry.
    c. the more equally is income distributed.
    d. the less equally is income distributed.

18. The following conditions characterize what type of firm? $P > MR$, $P > ATC$.
    a. Perfectly competitive in the short run.
    b. Perfectly competitive in the long run.
    c. Monopolistically competitive in the long run.
    d. Monopoly in the short run.

19. When MR exceeds MC by the greatest possible amount, the firm is
    a. maximizing its profit
    b. not maximizing its profit
    c. earning an economic profit if $P < ATC$
    d. both answers a and c are correct

20. When an increase in income shifts the demand curve for a good leftward, the good is _____.
    a. an inferior good
    b. a normal good
    c. a complementary good
    d. a substitute good

21. Which of the following influences does <u>NOT</u> directly shift the supply curve?
    a. An increase in income.
    b. Development of new technology.
    c. An increase in the cost of producing the product.
    d. A decrease in the number of sellers.

22. Which of the following is <u>NOT</u> an argument used by proponents of protection in favor of protectionist policies?
    a. The infant industry argument.
    b. The claim that protectionist policies saves American jobs.
    c. The rich nations exploit developing countries argument.
    d. The comparative advantage frequently switches argument.

23. The cost of wheat used to produce bread rises. As a result of the increase in cost, the equilibrium relative price of a loaf of bread _____ and the equilibrium quantity produced _____.
    a. rises; increases
    b. rises; decreases
    c. falls; increases
    d. falls; decreases

24. A nation can *produce* at a point outside its *PPF*
    a. when it trades with other nations.
    b. when it is producing products as efficiently as possible.
    c. when there is no unemployment.
    d. never.

25. A nation can *consume* at a point outside its *PPF*
    a. when it trades with other nations.
    b. when it is producing products as efficiently as possible.
    c. when there is no unemployment.
    d. never.

26. The government breaks up a monopoly so that the industry becomes perfectly competitive. As a result of the government action, the price of the product _____, the level of the industry's total output _____, and the deadweight loss _____.
    a. rises; increases; decreases
    b. falls; decreases; increases
    c. rises; decreases; decreases
    d. falls; increases; decreases

27. Suppose Microsoft will sell its Windows operating software to computer manufacturers only if the manufacturers buy Microsoft's Word software. If Microsoft's policy substantially lessens competition, it is
    a. illegal under the exclusive dealing clause of the Clayton Act.
    b. illegal under the tying contracts clause of the Clayton Act.
    c. legal.
    d. None of the above.

28. Due to a lot of workers taking early retirement, the supply of labor decreases. As a result, the equilibrium wage rate _____ and quantity of employment _____.
    a. rises; increases
    b. rises; decreases
    c. falls; increases
    d. falls; decreases

29. Suppose consumers become convinced that eating chicken is healthy while at the same time the price of chicken feed increases. Then, in the short run the equilibrium relative price of chicken will _____ and the equilibrium quantity will _____.
    a. rise; probably change, but in an ambiguous direction
    b. probably change, but in an ambiguous direction; decrease
    c. rise; increase
    d. not change; probably change, but in an ambiguous direction

30. The demanders pay all of a sales tax when the demand is
    a. perfectly elastic.
    b. more elastic than the supply.
    c. more inelastic than the supply.
    d. perfectly inelastic.

Exam 2

1. The price of meat used to produce tacos rises. As a result, the equilibrium relative price of a taco _____ and the equilibrium quantity _____.

    a. rises; increases
    b. rises; decreases
    c. falls; decreases
    d. falls; increases

2. The total cost of producing 6 pizzas is $24. The total cost of producing 7 pizzas is $35. The marginal cost of the 7th pizza is

    a. $4.00.
    b. $5.00.
    c. $11.00.
    d. None of the above.

3. Which form(s) of business organization have limited liability?

    a. Only sole proprietorship.
    b. Only partnership.
    c. Only corporation.
    d. Both sole proprietorships and partnerships.

4. A firm in what type of industry is necessarily characterized by the following conditions? $P = ATC$, and $P = MR$.

    a. Monopoly in the short run.
    b. Monopolistic competition in the long run.
    c. Perfect competition in the short run.
    d. Perfect competition in the long run.

5. For lunch you decide to eat either a slice of pizza or a taco; these are your only two alternatives. Last year, a slice of pizza cost $2 and a taco cost $2; this year, a slice of pizza cost $3 and a taco cost $3. The opportunity cost of a slice of pizza is

    a. highest last year.
    b. highest this year.
    c. the same in both years.
    d. None of the above.

6. A perfectly competitive firm

    a. produces a product identical to those of its competitors.
    b. has $P > MR$.
    c. can earn an economic profit in the long run.
    d. may incur an economic loss in the long run.

7. A good with perfectly elastic demand has a demand curve that is

    a. upward sloping, but not horizontal nor vertical.
    b. downward sloping, but not horizontal nor vertical.
    c. vertical.
    d. horizontal.

8. Because of technological advances, the price of a CD player falls. Simultaneously, technological advances take place in the production of CDs. As a result, the equilibrium relative price of a CD _____ and the equilibrium quantity _____.

    a. rises; increases.
    b. falls; increases.
    c. rises; probably changes, but in an ambiguous direction
    d. probably changes, but in an ambiguous direction; increases

9. The equilibrium level of output equals the efficient amount in a _____ industry producing a product with _____.

    a. perfectly competitive; no externalities
    b. perfectly competitive; an external cost
    c. perfectly competitive; a external benefit
    d. monopoly; no externalities

10. Of the following, which good would have the most elastic demand?

    a. Pepsi
    b. food
    c. insulin
    d. oil

11. Which of the following statements about the *PPF* is correct?

    a. Technological growth moves the economy to from producing at a point in the interior of the *PPF* to a point nearer the *PPF* itself, but does not change the *PPF* itself.
    b. The *PPF* shows that it is not possible for a nation to produce unlimited amounts of all products.
    c. The *PPF* shows that it is not possible for a nation to change the mixture of what it produces.
    d. The *PPF* shifts inward when the labor force grows because the unemployment rate rises.

12. If income is distributed so that everyone has exactly the same income, the Lorenz curve
   a. is horizontal.
   b. is vertical.
   c. lies on the line of equality.
   d. none of the above.

13. E-mail and regular mail are substitutes. Suppose that technological advances lowers the price of E-mail. As a result, the equilibrium relative price of regular mail _____ and the equilibrium quantity _____.
   a. rises; increases
   b. rises; decreases
   c. falls; increases
   d. falls; decreases

14. Leonardo's Pizza, a local restaurant selling pizza, discovers that a 10 percent increase in the price of their pizza decreases the quantity demanded 5 percent. As a result, the 10 percent increase in the price of pizza
   a. increases Leonardo's total revenue.
   b. does not change Leonardo's total revenue.
   c. decreases Leonardo's total revenue.
   d. increases Leonardo's average total costs

15. Present value implies that
   a. $100 to be received in one year is worth more than $100 received today.
   b. the farther in the future a sum of money will be received, the higher is its present value.
   c. the present value of money to be received in the future falls when the interest rate rises.
   d. None of the above because all of the statements are FALSE.

16. With the advent of AIDS, the demand for latex used to make gloves has increased. As a result, the equilibrium relative price of latex _____ and the quantity _____.
   a. rises; increases
   b. rises; decreases
   c. falls; increases
   d. falls; decreases

17. Which of the following directly shifts the supply curve?
   a. A rise in the wage rate paid workers.
   b. An increase in consumers' incomes.
   c. People deciding they want to buy more of the product.
   d. A decrease in the number of demanders.

FIGURE 1

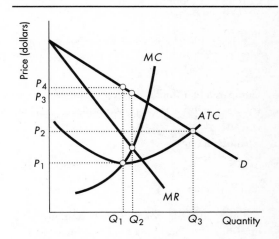

18. In the figure, a profit maximizing monopoly that does not price discriminate will set its price equal to
   a. P_1.
   b. P_2.
   c. P_3.
   d. P_4.

19. In the figure, a profit maximizing monopoly that does not price discriminate will produce how much output?
   a. Q_1.
   b. Q_2.
   c. Q_3.
   d. Q_4.

20. Suppose that the Board of Directors of Ford and General Motors are the same. This situation is
   a. legal.
   b. illegal under the Sherman Act.
   c. illegal under the Clayton Act.
   d. illegal under the Rule of Reason.

21. An increase in the minimum wage rate will
    a. increase employment.
    b. not change employment.
    c. decrease employment.
    d. increase employment only if the price of the product does not change.

22. Which of the following indicates that a company is earning an economic profit?
    a. $MR = MC$
    b. $MR > MC$
    c. $P = ATC$
    d. $P > ATC$

23. Compared to a similar perfectly competitive industry, a single-price monopoly produces _____ output and charges a _____ price.
    a. more; higher
    b. more; lower
    c. less; lower
    d. less; higher

24. A monopolistically competitive restaurant sells 3 meals for $5 a meal for a total revenue of $15. If it sells 4 meals, its marginal revenue from the 4th meal equals
    a. $20.
    b. $15.
    c. $5.
    d. some amount that cannot be calculated because not enough information is given

25. The difference between the maximum amount consumers are willing to pay and the amount they actually do pay for a given quantity of a good is called
    a. deadweight surplus.
    b. consumer surplus.
    c. producer surplus.
    d. total surplus.

26. Technological advances make labor more productive, that is, the marginal product of labor increases. As a result, the equilibrium wage rate _____ and level of employment _____.
    a. rises; increases
    b. rises; decreases
    c. falls; decreases
    d. falls; increases

27. Which of the following illustrates the concept of external cost?
    a. Bad weather decreases the size of the wheat crop.
    b. A reduction in the size of the wheat crop causes the income of wheat farmers to fall.
    c. Smoking harms the health of the smoker.
    d. Smoking harms the health of nearby non-smokers.

28. Suppose scientists perfect a bio-engineered tomato plant that is resistant to diseases and bears more tomatoes than before. As a result, the equilibrium relative price of a tomato would _____ and the quantity produced would _____.
    a. rise; increase
    b. rise; decrease
    c. fall; increase
    d. fall; decrease

29. The production possibilities frontier reveals that if less developed countries want to grow by producing more capital equipment, they must forego some consumption goods. But in the affluent countries of Europe and North America, the production possibilities frontier shows that this opportunity cost is not necessary.
    a. Both sentences are true.
    b. The first sentence is true and the second sentence is false.
    c. The first sentence is true and the second sentence is false.
    d. Both sentences are false.

30. International trade based on comparative advantage can allow each country to consume
    a. more of the goods it exports, but always less of the goods it imports.
    b. more of the goods it imports, but always less of the goods it exports.
    c. more of the goods it exports and imports.
    d. less of the goods it exports and imports

Answers

■ Final Exam 1 Answers

1. d;   2. b;   3. a;   4. c;   5. b;   6. c;   7. d;   8. c;   9. d; 10. d;
11. b; 12. c; 13. c; 14. a; 15. c; 16. b; 17. c; 18. d; 19. b; 20. a;
21. a; 22. d; 23. b; 24. d; 25. a; 26. d; 27. b; 28. b; 29. a; 30. d.

■ Final Exam 2 Answers

1. b;   2. c;   3. c;   4. d;   5. c;   6. a;   7. d;   8. d;   9. a; 10. a;
11. b; 12. c; 13. d; 14. a; 15. c; 16. a; 17. a; 18. c; 19. b; 20. c;
21. c; 22. d; 23. d; 24. d; 25. b; 26. a; 27. d; 28. c; 29. b; 30. c.

Answers to Quizzes

Answers

■ Chapter 1
1. c;   2. c;   3. c;   4. a;   5. d;   6. a;   7. c;   8. c;   9. d;   10. d.

■ Appendix 1
1. c;   2. c;   3. a;   4. c;   5. c;   6. c;   7. c;   8. d;   9. b;   10. b.

■ Chapter 2
1. b;   2. d;   3. b;   4. d;   5. a;   6. a;   7. d;   8. b;   9. c;   10. d.

■ Chapter 3
1. d;   2. d;   3. b;   4. b;   5. c;   6. b;   7. c;   8. a;   9. b;   10. b.

■ Chapter 4
1. d;   2. d;   3. c;   4. a;   5. a;   6. d;   7. c;   8. a;   9. d;   10. a.

■ Chapter 5
1. d;   2. c;   3. c;   4. b;   5. b;   6. b;   7. c;   8. c;   9. c;   10. b.

■ Chapter 6
1. c;   2. a;   3. a;   4. d;   5. c;   6. a;   7. d;   8. c;   9. d;   10. c.

■ Chapter 7
1. b;   2. d;   3. b;   4. c;   5. d;   6. b;   7. c;   8. b;   9. d;   10. c.

■ Chapter 8
1. c;   2. c;   3. c;   4. a;   5. d;   6. a;   7. c;   8. d;   9. a;   10. a.

■ Chapter 9
1. d;   2. a;   3. d;   4. c;   5. c;   6. b;   7. c;   8. d;   9. c;   10. c.

■ Chapter 10
1. a;   2. d;   3. c;   4. b;   5. b;   6. a;   7. b;   8. a;   9. b;   10. b.

■ **Chapter 11**
1. a;   2. c;   3. d;   4. c;   5. a;   6. d;   7. b;   8. a;   9. a;   10. b.

■ **Chapter 12**
1. c;   2. d;   3. c;   4. a;   5. c;   6. b;   7. b;   8. b;   9. d;   10. b.

■ **Chapter 13**
1. d;   2. a;   3. a;   4. d;   5. a;   6. b;   7. b;   8. c;   9. c;   10. a.

■ **Chapter 14**
1. d;   2. c;   3. c;   4. c;   5. a;   6. c;   7. a;   8. b;   9. c;   10. c.

■ **Appendix 14**
1. c;   2. a;   3. b;   4. b;   5. c;   6. c;   7. b;   8. d;   9. a;   10. d.

■ **Chapter 15**
1. c;   2. c;   3. c;   4. b;   5. a;   6. c;   7. a;   8. b;   9. c;   10. b.

■ **Chapter 16**
1. a;   2. c;   3. a;   4. b;   5. c;   6. c;   7. d;   8. b;   9. a;   10. a.

■ **Chapter 17**
1. d;   2. d;   3. c;   4. c;   5. d;   6. d;   7. b;   8. c;   9. b;   10. a.

■ **Chapter 18**
1. b;   2. c;   3. c;   4. b;   5. c;   6. b;   7. a;   8. b;   9. d;   10. d.

■ **Chapter 19**
1. a;   2. d;   3. b;   4. b;   5. c;   6. b;   7. d;   8. a;   9. a;   10. a.

■ **Chapter 20**
1. a;   2. b;   3. b;   4. b;   5. b;   6. b;   7. a;   8. d;   9. c;   10. b.

SHOULD YOU MAJOR IN ECONOMICS?*

Should You Take More Economic Courses?

Now that you have learned about supply and demand, utility and profit maximization, employment and unemployment, and good old Igor (at least in the Study Guide you learned about Igor!), it is time to look to the future.

- Should studying economics be part of your future?
- Should you take more classes or maybe even major in economics?
- What about graduate school in economics?

Economists generally assume that people make rational choices to maximize their own well-being. There is no reason to drop this assumption now. The purpose of this chapter is help you make that rational maximizing choice by providing low-cost information. Let us assess the benefits and see whether they outweigh the costs of studying economics.

Benefits from Studying Economics

■ Knowledge, Enlightenment, and Liberation

As John Maynard Keynes, a famous British economist, said, "The ideas of economists ... both when they are right and when they are wrong, are more powerful than is commonly understood. Indeed the world is ruled by little else. Practical men, who believe themselves to be quite exempt from any intellectual influences, are usually the slaves of some defunct economist." Studying economics is a liberating and enlightening experience. You don't want to be the slave of a defunct economist,

* This section was written by Robert Whaples of Wake Forest University.

do you? Liberate yourself. It's better to bring your ideas out in the open, to confront and understand them, rather than to leave them buried.

■ Knowledge, Understanding, and Satisfaction

Many of the most important problems in the world are economic. Studying economics gives you a practical set of tools to understand and solve them. Every day, on television and in the newspapers, we hear and read about big issues such as economic growth, inflation, unemployment, international trade relations, the latest moves by the Fed, the most recent tax or spending bill, the environment, and the future of Social Security. Your introduction to economics shows that learning economics will let you watch the news or pick up a newspaper and better understand these issues. As an added bonus, economics helps you understand smaller, more immediate concerns, such as: How much Spam should I buy? Is skipping class today a good idea? Should I put my retirement funds in government bonds or in the stock market? After all, as the famous author George Bernard Shaw put it, "Economy is the art of making the most of life." Mick Jagger, the lead singer of the "Rolling Stones" and who dropped out of the London School of Economics, complains that he "can't get no satisfaction." Maybe he should have studied more economics? The economic way of thinking will help you maximize your satisfaction.

■ Career Opportunities

All careers are not equal. While the wages in many occupations have not risen much lately, the wages of "symbolic analysts" who "solve, identify, and broker problems by manipulating symbols" are soaring.[1] These people "simplify reality into abstract images that can be rearranged, juggled, experimented with, communicated to other specialists, and then, eventually, transformed back into reality." Their wages have been rising as the globalization of the economy increases the demand for their insights and as technological developments (especially computers) have enhanced their productivity. Economists are the quintessential symbolic analysts as we manipulate ideas about abstractions such as supply and demand, cost and benefits, and equilibrium.

You can think of your training in economics as an exercise regimen, a workout for your brain. You will use many of the concepts you will learn in introductory economics during your career, but it is the practice in abstract thinking that will really pay off.

In fact, most economics majors do not go on to become economists. They enter fields that use their analytical abilities, including business, management, insurance, finance, real estate, marketing, law, education, policy analysis, consulting, government, planning, and even medicine, journalism, and the arts. A recent survey of 100 former economics majors at my university included all of these careers. If you want to verify that economics majors graduate to successful and rewarding careers, just ask your professors or watch what happens to economics majors from your school as they graduate.

Census statistics show that across the nation, economics majors earn more than most other majors. Table 1, from a 1998 study by the U.S. Bureau of Labor Statistics, shows that in 1993 (the most recent data available) middle-aged men with bachelor's degrees in economics earned more than those with all but a handful of other undergraduate degrees. Among women, economics was the *highest* earning major. (see Table 1)

That's the long-run picture. The short-run view looks much the same. In 2001 the average annual starting salary of economics and finance majors was $40,577. While this is lower than the salaries for those with degrees in computer science, engineering, and some other sciences, it is a couple of thousand dollars higher than salaries for those with degrees in business administration. Moreover, the entry-level salary of economics majors beats the entry-level salary of social science and humanities majors by a wide margin, as Table 2 shows. These numbers are updated annually, so feel free to look up the latest statistics. (In addition, the employment rate of economics majors is higher than that of many other majors, such as those in the humanities and other social sciences.)

The widening earnings gap between economics and similar majors helps explain why enrollments in economics are climbing. Since 1996 the number of

TABLE 1

Median Earnings by College Major Women and Men, Age 35-44 (1993)

	Women	Men
Accounting	$39,843	$49,502
Agriculture	28,752	36,758
Biological/Life Sciences	34,245	41,179
Business (except accounting)	34,638	44,867
Chemistry	37,501	44,994
Computer and information services	43,757	50,510
Economics	**49,175**	**49,378**
Education	27,988	34,470
Engineering	49,072	53,287
English language and literature	30,296	38,297
Health/medical technologies	35,526	36,269
History	30,553	38,095
Liberal arts/general studies	32,073	39,625
Pharmacy	48,428	50,480
Psychology	32,301	40,718
Sociology	29,532	37,250

Source: Daniel Hacker, "Earnings of College Graduates: Women Compared with Men," *Monthly Labor Review*, March 1998.
http://stats.bls.gov/opub/mlr/1998/03/art5full.pdf
Note: Figures are for those with a bachelor's degree.

TABLE 2

Average Annual Starting Salary Offers by College Major, 2001

Computer Science	$52,723
Engineering	51,910
Economics/Finance	**40,577**
Business	38,449
Political Science	32,774
English	31,501
History	30,375
Psychology	30,338
Sociology	28,812

Source: "New Salary Report Shows Many New College Graduates Continue to Command Top Dollar," National Association of Colleges and Employers, July 11, 2001. www.naceweb.org/press/.

economics degrees awarded in the United States has jumped about 14 percent, with similar trends in Canada and Australia.[2]

Even if you aren't planning on getting a job right out of college, economics can be a valuable major. Economics degrees are looked upon very favorably by MBA programs and law schools. Over one-third of economics graduates enter professional programs within two years of their undergraduate degree, divided equally between business and law. In fact, an analysis of Law School Admission Test (LSAT) scores from the 1990s showed that among the fourteen college majors with more than 2,000 students taking the exam, economics majors did the *best*. The average score of 155.3 topped second-place history (154.0), as well as English (153.7), Psychology (151.9), Political Science (151.6), Communications (150.7), Sociology (149.3), and Business Administration (148.6).[3]

A *Wall Street Journal* article announced that "Economics, Once a Perplexing Subject, Is Enjoying a Bull Run at Universities." Economics is not a vocational training program, preparing you for a single line of work. Instead, the career benefits of an economics major are so great because economics teaches you to *think* and thinking is what's ultimately rewarded in our dynamic economy.

The Costs of Studying Economics

Because the "direct" costs of studying economics (tuition, books, supplies) aren't generally any higher or lower than the direct costs of other courses, indirect costs will be the most important of the costs to studying economics.

◼ Forgone Knowledge

If you study economics, you can't study something else. This forgone knowledge could be very valuable.

◼ Disutility

If you dislike studying economics because you find it boring, tedious, or unenlightening in comparison to other subjects, then the opportunity cost is even higher because your overall level of satisfaction falls. (I know that this is rare, but it does occasionally happen).

◼ Time and Energy

Economics is a fairly demanding major. Although economics courses do not generally take as much time as courses in English and history (in which you have to read a lot of long books) or anatomy and physiology (in which you have to spend hours in the lab and hours memorizing things), they do take a decent amount of time. In addition, some people find the material "tougher" than most subjects because memorizing is not the key. In economics (like physics), analyzing and solving are the keys. The rigor of the major is an obstacle for many.

◼ Grades

As Table 3 shows, grades in introductory economics courses are usually a notch lower than grades in some other majors, including other social sciences and the humanities.[4] On the other hand, grades in economics are generally higher than grades in the sciences and math. Grades in introductory economics courses are generally a hair lower than grades in introductory courses to other majors, including other social sciences and the humanities.

TABLE **3**

Average Grades and Grade Distribution by College Major

Department	Mean Grade	% Above B+	% Below B−
Music	3.16	44	21
English	3.12	27	12
Psychology	3.02	28	23
Philosophy	2.99	29	21
Art	2.95	29	24
Political science	2.95	24	23
Economics	2.81	20	31
Chemistry	2.66	17	44
Math	2.53	22	46

Caveat Emptor (Buyer Beware): Interpreting Your Grades Is Not Straight Forward

High grades provide direct satisfaction to most students, but they also act as a signal about the student's ability to learn the subject material. Unfortunately, because the grade distribution is not uniform across departments, you might be confused and misled by your grades. You might think that you are exceptionally good at a subject because of a high grade, when in fact nearly everyone gets a high grade in that subject. The important point here is that you should be informed about your own school's grade distribution. Just because you got a B in economics and an A in history does not necessarily mean that your comparative advantage is in learning history rather than economics. Everyone — or virtually everyone — might receive an A in history. Earning a B or a C in economics could mean that it is the best major for you because high grades are much harder to earn in economics. It is fun to have a high GPA in college, but maximizing GPA should not be your goal. Maximizing your overall well-being is probably your goal, and this might be obtained by trading off a tenth or so of your GPA for a more rewarding major — perhaps economics.

In assessing the tradeoffs, you'll notice that mean departmental grades are higher where average earnings are lower. Employers know which departments grade harder. A recent article on grade patterns concluded that "those students who attend college primarily as a route to a better paying job should understand that 'easy' courses may be no bargain in the long run." [5]

Potential Side Effects from Studying Economics

Studying economics has some potential side effects. I'm not sure whether they are costs or benefits and will let you decide.

■ Changing Ideas about What Is Fair

A recently completed study compared students at the beginning and end of the semester in an introductory economics course.[6] It found that by the end of the semester, significantly more of the students thought that the functioning of the market is "fair." This was especially true for female students. The results were consistent across a range of professors who fell across the ideological spectrum.

For example, the proportion of students who regarded it as unfair to increase the price of flowers on a holiday fell almost in half. The proportion that favored government control over flower prices, rather than market determination, fell by over 60 percent. The study argues that these responses do not reflect changes in deep values, but instead represent the discovery of previous inconsistencies and their modification in the light of new information learned during the semester.

■ Changing Behavior

Many people believe that the study of economics changes students' values and behavior. Some observers think that it changes them for the worse. Others disagree. In particular, it is argued that economics students become more self-interested and less likely to cooperate, perhaps because they spend so much time studying economic models, which often assume that people are self-interested. For example, one study reports experimental evidence that economics students are more likely than nonmajors to behave self-interestedly in prisoners' dilemma games and ultimatum bargaining games.[7]

This need not mean that studying economics will change you, however. Another study compares beginning freshmen and senior economics students and concludes that economics students "are already different when they begin their study of economics."[8] In other words, students signing up for economics courses are already different; studying economics doesn't change them. However, there are reasons to question both of these conclusions, because it is not clear whether these laboratory experiments using economic games reflect reality. One experiment asked students whether they would return money that had been lost. It found that economics students were more likely than others to say that they would keep the cash.

However, what people say and what they do are sometimes at odds. In a follow-up experiment, this theory was tested by dropping stamped, addressed envelopes containing $10 in cash in different campus classrooms. To return the cash, the students had only to seal the envelopes and mail them. The results were that 56 percent of the envelopes dropped in economics classes were returned, while only 31 percent of the envelopes dropped in history, psychology and business classes were sent in.[9] Perhaps economics students are less selfish than others!

Obviously, no firm conclusions have been reached about whether or how studying economics changes students' behavior.

Costs versus Benefits

Suppose that you've weighed the costs and benefits of studying economics and you've decided that the benefits are greater than or equal to the costs. Obviously, then, you should continue to take economics courses. If you can't decide whether the benefits outweigh the costs, then you should probably collect more information — especially if it is good but inexpensive. In either case, read the rest of this section.

The Economics Major

The study of economics is like a tree. The introductory microeconomics and macroeconomics courses you begin with are the tree's roots. Most colleges and universities require that you master this material before you go on to any other courses. The way of thinking, the language, and the tools that you acquire in the introductory course are usually reinforced in intermediate microeconomics and macroeconomics courses before they are applied in more specialized courses that you take. The intermediate courses are the tree's trunk. Among the specialized courses that make up the branches of economics are econometrics (statistical economics), financial economics, labor economics, resource economics, international trade, industrial organization, public finance, public choice, economic history, the history of economic thought, mathematical economics, current economic issues, and urban economics. The branches of the tree vary from department to department, but these are common. It will pay to check your college bulletin and discuss these courses with professors and other students.

Graduate School in Economics

■ Preparing for Graduate School in Economics

You can prepare for graduate school in economics by taking several math classes. This would probably include at least two years of calculus plus a couple of courses in probability and statistics and linear/matrix algebra. Ask your advisor about the particular courses to take at your college. In addition, the mathematical economics and econometrics courses in the economics department are essential. (*Helpful hint*: Even if you aren't going to graduate school, these mathematical courses can be valuable to you, just as more economics courses can be valuable for nonmajors.)

If your school offers graduate level economics courses, you might want to sit in on a few to get accustomed to the flavor of graduate school.

Most graduate programs require strong grades in economics, a good score on the Graduate Record Examination (GRE), and solid letters of recommendation. It is a good idea to get to know a few professors very well and to go above and beyond what is expected so that they can write glowing letters about you.

■ Financing Graduate School

Unlike some other graduate and professional degree programs, you probably won't need to pile up a massive amount of debt while pursuing a Ph.D. in economics. Most Ph.D. programs hire their economics graduate students as teaching or research assistants. Teaching assistants begin by grading papers and running review sessions and can advance to teaching classes on their own. Research assistants generally do data collection, statistical work, and library research for professors and often jointly write papers with them. Most assistantships will pay for tuition and provide you with enough money to live on.

■ Where Should You Apply?

The best graduate school for you depends on a lot of things, especially your ability level, geographical location, areas of research interests, and, of course, financing. You should talk with your professors about ability level and areas of research. In addition, there are informative articles that give overall departmental rankings and rankings by subfield. See especially Richard Dusansky and Clayton J. Vernon, "Rankings of U.S. Economics Departments," *Journal of Economic Perspectives*, Vol. 12, no. 1, Winter 1998, pp. 157-170, Jerry G. Thursby, "What Do We Say about Ourselves and What Does It Mean? Yet Another Look at Economics Department Research," *Journal of Economic Literature*, Vol. 38, no. 2, June 2000, pp. 383-404, and John Tschirhart, "Ranking Economics Departments in Areas of Expertise," *Journal of Economic Education*, Vol. 20, no. 2, Spring 1989, pp. 199-222. There will probably be more up-to-date rankings by the time you apply. Ask a professor or reference librarian to help you track them down. For smaller specialties (e.g., economic history, urban economics) it is especially important to get up-to-date information on any particular program.

■ What You Will Do in Graduate School

Most graduate programs in economics begin with a year of theory courses in macroeconomics and micro-economics. After a year you will probably take a series of tests to show that you have mastered this core theory. If you pass these tests, in the second and third year of courses you will take more specialized subjects and per-haps take lengthy examinations in a couple of subfields. After this you will be required to write a dissertation — original research that will contribute new knowledge to one of the fields of economics. These stages are inter-twined with work as a teaching and/or research assis-tant, and the dissertation stage can be quite drawn out. In the social sciences the median time that it takes for a student to complete the Ph.D. degree is about 7.5 years.[10] Be aware that a high percentage (roughly 50 percent) of students do not complete their doctoral degree.

■ What Is Graduate School Like?

Graduate school in economics comes as a surprise to many students. The material and approach are dis-tinctly different from what you will learn as an under-graduate. The textbooks and journal articles you will read in graduate school are often very theoretical and abstract. A good source of information is sitting in on courses or reading the reflections of recent students. See especially *The Making of an Economist* by Arjo Klamer and David Colander (Boulder, Colo.: Westview Press, 1990).

The Committee on Graduate Education in Economics (COGEE) undertook an important review of graduate education in economics and reported its findings in the September 1991 issue of the *Journal of Economic Lit-erature*. COGEE asked faculty members, graduate stu-dents, and recent Ph.D.s to rank the most important skills needed to be successful in the study of graduate economics. At the top of the list were analytical skills and mathematics, followed by critical judgment, the

ability to apply theory, and computational skills. At the bottom of the list were creativity and the ability to communicate. If you are interested in economic issues but do not have the characteristics required by graduate economics departments, consider other economics-related fields, such as graduate school in public policy. Many economics majors go to business schools to ob-tain an MBA and are often better prepared than stu-dents who have undergraduate degrees in business.

Economics Reading

If decide to make studying economics part of your fu-ture, or if you're hungry for more economics, you should immediately begin reading the economic news and books by economists. Life is short. Why waste it watching TV?

The easiest way to get your daily recommended dose of economics is to keep up with current economic events. Here are a few sources to pick up at the newsstand, bookstore, or library over your summer or winter break.

■ The *Wall Street Journal*

Many undergraduates subscribe to the *Wall Street Jour-nal* (WSJ) at low student rates. Join them! Your profes-sor will probably have student subscription forms. Not only is the WSJ a well-written business newspaper, but it also has articles on domestic and international news, politics, the arts, travel, and sports, as well as a lively editorial page. Reading the WSJ is one of the best ways to tie the economics you are studying to the real world and to prepare for your career.

■ Magazines and Journals

The Economist, a weekly magazine published in Eng-land, is available at a student discount rate. Pick up a copy at your school library and you will be hooked by its informative, sharp writing. *Business Week* is also well worth the read.

Also recommended are *The American Enterprise, The Cato Journal, Challenge,* and *The Public Interest,* four quarterlies that discuss economic policy. Finally, there is the *Journal of Economics Perspectives*, which is pub-lished by the American Economic Association and written to be accessible to undergraduate economics students.

■ Books by Economists

I recently asked a group of economics professors from across the country (members of the Teach-Econ computer discussion list) the following question: "A bright, enthusiastic student who has just completed introductory economics comes up to you, the professor, and asks you to recommend an economics book for reading over the summer. What do you suggest?"

Here is what they suggested that you, the bright, enthusiastic student, should read:

■ Top Choices

Milton Friedman, *Capitalism and Freedom.*

Robert Heilbroner, *The Worldly Philosophers: The Lives, Times, and Ideas of the Great Economic Thinkers.*

Steve Landsburg, *The Armchair Economist: Economics and Everyday Life.*

■ Other Good Choices

Alan Blinder, *Hard Heads, Soft Hearts: Tough-Minded Economics for a Just Society.*

Hernando de Soto, *The Mystery of Capital: Why Capitalism Triumphed in the West and Failed Everywhere Else.*

Robert Frank, *Luxury Fever: Why Money Fails to Satisfy in an Era of Excess.*

David Friedman, *Hidden Order: The Economics of Everyday Life.*

Paul Krugman, *The Accidental Theorist and Other Dispatches from the Dismal Science.*

Susan Lee, *Hands Off: Why the Government Is a Menace to Economic Health.*

In addition, Adam Smith's *The Wealth of Nations* is a must read for every student of economics. Written in 1776, it is the most influential work of economics ever. Its insights are still valuable today.

■ Economic Fiction

For those with a taste for fiction, choices include:

Marshall Jevons, *Murder at the Margin, The Fatal Equilibrium,* and *A Deadly Indifference.* A trio of economics-based murder mysteries. Use your economic theory to solve the crime.

Russell Roberts, *The Invisible Heart.* An economics-based romance novel! "Can Laura love a man with an Adam Smith poster on his wall?"

Russell Roberts, *The Choice: A Parable of Free Trade and Protectionism.*

Jonathan Wight, *Saving Adam Smith: A Tale of Wealth, Transformation, and Virtue.*

Endnotes

1. This term is used by Robert Reich in *The Work of Nations.* The quote is from p. 178.

2. John J. Siegfried and David K. Round, "International Trends in Economics Degrees during the 1990s," *Journal of Economic Education,* Vol. 32, no. 3, Summer 2001, pp. 203-18.

3. Michael Nieswiadomy, "LSAT Scores of Economics Majors," *Journal of Economic Education,* Vol. 29, no. 4, Fall 1998, pp. 377-79.

4. Richard Sabot and John Wakeman-Linn, "Grade Inflation and Course Choice," *Journal of Economic Perspectives,* Vol. 5, no. 1, Winter 1991, pp. 159–170.

5. Donald G. Freeman, "Grade Divergence as a Market Outcome," *Journal of Economic Education,* Vol. 30, no. 4, Fall 1999, pp. 344-51.

6. Robert Whaples, "Changes in Attitudes about the Fairness of Free Markets among College Economics Students," *Journal of Economic Education,* Vol. 26, no. 4, Fall 1995.

7. Robert H. Frank, Thomas Gilovich, and Dennis T. Regan, "Does Studying Economics Inhibit Cooperation?" *Journal of Economic Perspectives,* Vol. 7, no. 2, Spring 1993, pp. 159–171.

8. John R. Carter and Michael D. Irons, "Are Economists Different, and If So, Why?" *Journal of Economic Perspectives,* Vol. 5, no. 2, Spring 1991, pp. 171–177.

9. "Economics Students Aren't Selfish, They're Just Not Entirely Honest," *Wall Street Journal,* January 18, 1995, B1.

10. See Ronald Ehrenberg, "The Flow of New Doctorates," *Journal of Economic Literature,* Vol. 30, June 1992, pp. 830–875. If breaks in school attendance are included, this climbs to 10.5 years. Of course, some students attend only part time, and most have some kind of employment while completing their degrees.